DAVID WILSON
AN UNLIKELY PHOTOGRAPHER

An Unlikely Photographer.
Published in Great Britain in 2025 by Graffeg Limited.
ISBN 9781913134815

Text by David Wilson copyright © 2025.
Designed and produced by Graffeg Limited copyright © 2025.

Graffeg Limited, 15 Neptune Court, Vanguard Way, Cardiff, CF24 5PJ,
Wales, UK. Tel: 01554 824000. croeso@graffeg.com. www.graffeg.com.

David Wilson is hereby identified as the author of this work in accordance
with section 77 of the Copyright, Designs and Patents Act 1988.

Printed by Bell & Bain Limited, UK.

A CIP Catalogue record for this book is available from the British Library.

This book is designed for general readers, printed with materials
and processes that are safe and meet all applicable European safety
requirements. The book does not contain elements that could pose
health or safety risks under normal and intended use.

We hereby declare that this product complies with all applicable
requirements of the General Product Safety Regulation (GPSR)
and any other relevant EU legislation.

Appointed EU Representative:
Easy Access System Europe Oü, 16879218
Mustamäe tee 50, 10621, Tallinn, Estonia
gpsr.requests@easproject.com

The publisher gratefully acknowledges the financial
support of this book by the Books Council of Wales.
www.gwales.com.

Cover photo: Ross Grieve.
Back cover photo: David Wilson.

1 2 3 4 5 6 7 8 9

DAVID WILSON

AN UNLIKELY PHOTOGRAPHER

For my beautiful Anna.

GRAFFEG

Chapter 1

I strolled out into the chill February air, put my helmet on, straddled my motorbike and kick-started the short journey that would change my life forever.

At the age of eighteen all roads led to the pub, to bask in the certainty of friendship over a warm pint of bitter. Drifting through the town, visor up, I gulped down the cold night, as the puny engine buzzed through the gears, belching out its aroma of spent two-stroke fuel. I was young, I had money in my pocket and I had a motorbike. Life felt good as I banked into a one-way street with two lanes that I'd ridden down countless times.

Memories of what happened are fragmented. A car moving from the adjacent lane across my path. A panicked swerve to avoid hitting it. Mounting the kerb at an inadvisable speed, the motorbike bucking like a rodeo ride on full tilt. My grip wrenched from the handlebars and being thrown off the rear of the bike. Then, a stolen breath, momentary weightlessness, and the back of my helmet hitting the pavement, followed by my body slapping down with blunt force on the concrete slabs.

Bludgeoned into semi-consciousness, a molten pain exploded in my neck, engulfing my torso and limbs, as if a million red-hot pins had punctured me. I gasped as waves surged through my body, each so agonising as to almost pass out. Or, die. Definitely, to die. I felt that I was slipping away, hovering between hellish survival and a willing acquiescence, an embrace of an end to the splintering pain. And it was there, waiting expectantly; death hung over me. It smiled, and beckoned, and I drifted to it. I yelped and screamed and convulsed, sucking in ignited roadside air, as I clung to the night's dim light, and fought off the pitch black of an ending. I wasn't ready.

On a damp pavement in a small town in west Wales, nothing of me moved. I *couldn't* move. I peered out from my helmet as a small crowd gathered. There were mumbled concerns, faces shimmering in a half-focused blur as the agony kept washing through me. A lady who lived across the road had come out of her house on hearing a crashing noise; having dumped me, the motorbike careered down the pavement, killing itself in some railings. She'd fetched a blanket to put over me.

'Has anyone called an ambulance?' someone asked.

'Yeah, shouldn't be long,' she said.

'What happened?'

'Don't know. Heard a noise...' said my Samaritan, '...and came out and found him lying here.'

The ambulance arrived and, observing procedures for suspected spinal injuries, the crew loaded me on-board and drove the mile to hospital; a fortunate proximity.

My recollections of A&E are more lucid. X-rays. Pain relief. Senior medical staff issuing instructions. Soothing words from nurses.

'Don't worry, sweetheart. We're doing all we can. Just stay with us.'

I recall a kaleidoscope of ceilings as I was trolleyed to one room, then another, beneath corridor strip lights. The x-rays revealed damage to two vertebrae in my neck; C5 and C6 in medical parlance. C5 had suffered a compression fracture, bursting into fragments, the result of the crushing pressure exerted when my head made contact with the pavement – anyone who's cracked walnuts at Christmas will be aware of the point at which the nut gives way. C6 had been dislocated, pushed out of alignment with the spinal column and was pressing against, or perhaps had severed, the spinal cord within. In layman's terms, then, it was all a bit of a mess.

It was imperative that I be kept immobile to avoid any, or as seemed more likely to those in attendance, further damage to my spinal cord. In this I was a very cooperative patient, as I couldn't move anyway.

My clothing, including my beloved Belstaff jacket – £2 a week for a year from Mum's Grattan catalogue – was cut away from my body to avoid the tugging and pulling of a conventional disrobing. In tandem with the shredding of my dignity, a nurse stuck a pin in my arms and legs to see whether I could feel it. I could, it was painful, and I let her know accordingly. I didn't realise the significance of this torture at the time but these pricks were defining moments; later in the drama, when presented with two options, the medical opinion went with the more optimistic choice, based in part on my reaction to the pin-pricking.

For an A&E department of a minor general hospital in western-most Wales, the unstable nature and graveness of the injury caused concern amongst the staff. I sensed apprehension as the consultant pondered how best to proceed. With a humility rare in any profession, he decided to phone a colleague in Cardiff who specialised in the treatment of such injuries. The seriousness of the situation was novel to me too; the only other time I'd attended A&E was when I bent my thumb back while competing in the shot put in a school athletics tournament.

News of the accident had somehow trickled down to the pub. No specifics, just that I'd come off. The gang convoyed their way to the hospital, beery and light-hearted, imagining a plaster-casted Dave waiting for a lift back to the hostelry where an assembled throng could be regaled with a tale of heroic derring-do. A puncturing reality settled over them when told of the true situation.

Mum was at home settling down to *Coronation Street* when a policeman knocked at the door. 'He's had an accident. Don't worry. Broken his leg, I think,' he said.

Dad had left the house just before me to walk to the club for a game of dominoes. I'd passed him on his way and we'd waved to one another. A couple of sips into his first pint, chatting with his mates, the barman leant over. 'Margaret's on the phone, Harry.'

Mum picked him up and drove to A&E, unprepared for the grim tableau that awaited. Dad told me months later how their evening unfolded.

They approached reception.

'We're here for my son. David Wilson?' said Dad. 'He's come off his motorbike. Broken his leg?'

I knew that bike would be trouble, he thought to himself. The receptionist disappeared, and on her return ushered them with sombre etiquette into an office.

'The consultant will be with you any moment,' she said, leaving the room.

Mum and Dad began to sense that it may be worse than they'd been led to believe. A bad leg break, perhaps. Mr Adams, the consultant in charge of my care, entered the room.

'Hello, Mr and Mrs Wilson,' he said, gesturing for them to sit.

'Where's David?' asked Mum.

'Please, Mrs Wilson. If you could just take a seat.'

'What's happened?' demanded Dad.

They were hit with a gut-wrenching certainty that something was very wrong, a broken limb being the least of it.

'What is it?' pressed Dad.

'Look, Mr and Mrs Wilson, there's no easy way to say this, but David has been very seriously injured.'

He described the extent of the injuries – damage to two vertebrae in the neck, resulting in paralysis from the level of the injury down, with just flickers of movement in the right hand. He was unable to indicate what if any damage had been done to my spinal cord but at that moment movement was almost non-existent. Dad professed many months later that he couldn't have felt more grief if he'd been told I was dead. He and Mum, standing in that office, collapsed into each other, hugged and wept. Two days before, on Valentine's Day 1984, Mum had celebrated her fortieth birthday. And just an hour earlier I'd headed merrily out of the house, strapping and capable, to go and meet my friends for a drink and a laugh. Now, all joy was extinguished.

I was parked awaiting the next stage of treatment when Mum and Dad appeared. Mum was weeping and incoherent. Dad was white and silent. She touched me. I yelped. My nervous system was in meltdown and physical contact was excruciating. They looked down at me with crucified eyes, unable to comprehend what'd happened. I looked blankly at the ceiling tiles, crying, scared, unable to speak. Traditionally, mums did the hands-on caring. Still do. Dads did the pep talks; the man stuff. But she couldn't touch me and he couldn't speak.

When I was about four years old, I had a tricycle. One day I was bombing down a path at quite a lick when the laws of physics intervened and I suffered a speed wobble. With no brakes, I grabbed at a wall to slow down. Not any old wall, mind, but a pebble-dashed wall. Anyway, I was thrown off. The only bit that hurt was my hand, and when I looked at it I could see why. A couple of finger-nails were missing – courtesy of the pebble-dashing – and another was hanging by a thread. I ran home crying.

Mum sprang into action, bathing the raw finger-tips as the crying escalated to screaming. She put plasters on, including one to reunite the dangling nail with its fleshy base so that it might reattach itself. I lay on the settee with my head on her lap that afternoon as she offered up rounds of sugar toast – literally toast with sugar sprinkled on – biscuits and beakers of squash in between stroking my head and soothing me with love and soft words. Hands-on care. The plasters were removed a week later and to our surprise, and disappointment, the dangling nail fell to the floor. Well, at least she tried.

The advice on the phone from Cardiff was to fit a contraption that would stabilise the trauma area, then to get me in an ambulance and on to the Royal Infirmary in Cardiff. The recommended device consisted of a pair of hinged stainless-steel callipers called a Raney-Crutchfield Skull Traction Tong; an ice bath of a product name. It was a medieval-looking implement, seemingly anomalous with modern medicine and surely hammered into shape in a blacksmith's shop. A doctor explained what was about to happen. Some of it registered.

A nurse approached with a set of clippers and shaved a patch of hair on either side of my head a little way back from the temples. A razor blade reduced the clearings to smooth skin and a local anaesthetic was administered. I must've looked like an extra from some dystopian B movie. Then the drilling began. Holes deep enough to receive the tapered ends of the two callipers were drilled into my skull. This demanded precise judgement on the part of the doctor cum DIY enthusiast; drill too hard and my evening would've gone from bad to worse, terminally.

The acrid smell of burning bone was a novel aroma and one which I've never since sought out. The tapered ends of the callipers were placed over the holes in my skull and a screw thread mechanism adjusted so that the ends docked into the holes, clamping the callipers to my head. Finally, weights were attached to the contraption and dangled off the back of the trolley. The theory behind this seemingly archaic approach was that the injury would be afforded a measure of stability and my spinal column stretched, so that the ruptured fragments of bone might with luck be coaxed back into shapes resembling vertebrae once again. There didn't appear to be much scientific veracity involved but it was the best course of action in the circumstances.

The alternative to Raney and Crutchfield's apparatus, I was to discover, would've been an operation on the trauma area to bind the fragments of vertebrae together with plates, hooks and screws, a sort of medical version of Meccano. The upside to such an intervention is that the broken bits are stabilised and you aren't laid up in bed for months. The downside is the possibility of further spinal cord damage due to the millimetre-accurate delicacy required in knitting the pieces of bone back together.

The earlier pin-pricking and my less than gallant response had persuaded the doctors to opt for the long-haul approach of steel callipers. Their reasoning was that I had sensation in my limbs so why risk a possible (though at that point unlikely) recovery by undertaking a hazardous op? It was to be steel callipers and, unbeknown to me, twelve weeks confined to bed. I was ready to be shipped onwards.

The ambulance covered the one hundred miles to Cardiff at a cautious pace, so as not to aggravate the injury. The driver's pothole avoidance technique was exemplary, while his circumnavigating of roundabouts was barely noticeable. It took nearly four hours to reach the Royal Infirmary, with my parents tailing the ambulance at its funereal pace in their car, their journey one of suffocating disbelief.

Generous doses of opiates had eased the pain flowing into every nook and cranny of my body. For the first time since meeting the pavement I was able to compute the ramifications of what'd happened – or at least attempt to; there was a lot to take in. Considering my predicament, I felt little sense of panic. I had sensation in my body from top to toe, give or take a few numb patches, which I figured must be a good sign – if I could feel, then surely I'd move again. That made sense. And, I was oblivious to the implications of breaking one's neck. Medically, I didn't appreciate what it meant, besides the infliction of passing-out pain. I'd never known or met anyone who'd injured their spine. I'd never encountered anyone in a wheelchair, aside from watching episodes of *Ironside*. It was all a foreign country to me. So, I lay in the ambulance convinced that the paralysis was a temporary state of affairs which'd gift me a few weeks off work; every cloud and all that. I did need some reassurance though.

'This not being able to move won't last long, will it?' I said to the on-board paramedic, fishing for confirmation of my unscientific prognosis. 'I mean, I can feel everything so I must be in some sort of… shock, is it?'

'Sorry, David, I can't say what'll happen,' he said. 'Best just to relax. We've got a long journey.'

He turned to check something or at least make a show of checking something. But I wasn't finished.

'Yeah, but surely feeling things is good? I mean, what are we looking at? A week… month, in hospital?'

He swivelled back to face me.

'Look, I'm not a doctor, so I just can't say. Sorry.'

His evasions did nothing to dampen my conviction that everything would be fine. It had to be fine. I mean, I couldn't simply go from being able to move to not being able to move, at all. It didn't make sense. It wasn't logical, for Christ's sake. Plus, it was my first proper crash; all of the previous incidents had been minor scrapes. I thought of Evel Knievel, the American stunt rider, who'd been smashing himself up for years and yet was still walking around. And, unlike him, I hadn't attempted to jump over twenty buses or a gaping canyon. All I'd been doing was going to the pub. So, it was settled. Whatever was causing the paralysis, it'd wear off.

Laying in the ambulance with no yearning to initiate a fresh topic of conversation with a cagey medic, my mind swam away to the previous day when I'd been consumed with more trifling matters: the soul-destroying emptiness of my job. I was a junior storeman in the Ministry of Defence (MoD), working at an armament depot in Trecwn, near Fishguard, storing bombs and sea mines for the Royal Navy. My grandfather had whiled away nigh on forty years in the depot as a senior storeman. It seemed that storing things, especially high explosives, ran in the family; my Aunty Linda worked there too. Gramps had retired the year before I started there and the higher-ups had deemed it appropriate that part of his reward for such sterling service was that the baton of life-long job security should be passed on to me, his grandson and heir.

'So, you're Charlie's grandson,' one of the interviewing panel said to me.

'Yeah, that's right,' I replied.

'Absolute legend,' his colleague contributed.

They dutifully went through the motions of a bona fide interview, but I knew the job was mine as I'd been told beforehand by Linda. It was all wrapped-up embarrassingly quickly and although they omitted to say so, I knew that I was starting two weeks later. I was assured by other lifers on the payroll that it was indeed a job for life, or perhaps they meant a life sentence. I didn't wish to test the theory but murdering a colleague was possibly the only way to get sacked.

Even then the union would've got involved and there'd have been an appeals process. I hated the place from day one. And I hated myself even more eighteen months down the line, in that ambulance, for not having had the motivation to get another job.

My first day in Trecwn had been inauspicious.

'Meet the bus by the Taj Mahal at seven,' I was told.

Eager, I turned up at ten to and joined a lengthening queue of likely looking fellow storemen with their blank expressions and accepting indifference at the uneventful day that lay ahead. Mum had bought me a Tupperware box for my sandwiches which I clutched under my arm. Looking around, I saw that my colleagues had sandwich boxes clutched under their arms too, cloudy with age, and some with lids held on by elastic bands. Perhaps many years earlier their mums had bought them a Tupperware box for their first day as well. A bus pulled up and they climbed aboard. I followed.

It soon became apparent that we weren't heading towards RNAD Trecwn, my new employer, but in the opposite direction. I should've spoken up but shyness and a conviction that it was simply a circuitous route silenced me. Thirty minutes later, having sat mute throughout the entire journey, the bus entered RAF Brawdy, ten crow miles from Trecwn, twenty by road. Still, alarm bells didn't ring. Just a drop-off, surely.

The bus came to a halt in the midst of a cluster of Nissen huts. The driver switched off the engine. People began to disembark as I sensed a ratcheting unease. 'How many more?' I thought. Soon the bus was empty. Still, I clung to the vain hope there might be a plausible explanation, though deep down I knew that there wasn't. I was on the wrong bus.

I walked down the aisle towards the driver, who'd already begun to digest that day's edition of *The Sun*. I hovered motionless over him, taking in his clumpy hair with its greasy sheen, his sweat glands having opened up bright and early. Born to sit, he turned with a start.

'Problem?' he asked.

I hesitated.

'We… we are heading to Trecwn, yeah?' I said, more now in prayer than expectation.

My question amused him.

'What d'you mean, heading to Trecwn?'

'I just thought, maybe you'd be carrying on,' I said.

His casual retort has stayed with me. 'Sorry, Tonto, this is the end of the line.'

He chuckled and carried on reading his paper. You see, the Taj Mahal straddled, and still does, a street corner. I'd joined the queue in Albert Street, whereas I should've joined the queue in Milford Road, around the corner. A queue that I didn't see.

I got off the bus and walked into one of the drab huts, seeking salvation. It was an office with half-a-dozen desks and numerous filing cabinets strewn along its windowless length. At the furthest desk a grey middle-aged man in a v-neck was regaling two young women with some animated tale at which they laughed without enthusiasm. At the desk nearest to me a tightly permed woman was lighting a cigarette – these were the days before health & safety frowned on workers inflicting lung cancer on non-smoking colleagues.

'Can I help you, love?' she said, belching smoke in my direction.

I leaned forward and, in a whisper, told her of the disaster that'd befallen my first day at work and asked if I could use her phone to summon Dad for a lift to where I should be. I expected a confidential nod and to be handed the receiver. But no, with a catarrh-infused cackle she informed her three colleagues at the other end of the room of my misadventure which proved to be much more hilarious than the limp story v-neck man had been spouting. When the laughter eventually died down, I phoned Dad.

'Can you pick me up. I've…'

'Pick you up? Christ, give it a chance. Only just bloody started,' he said.

Aware of the entertainment that my conversation was providing I cupped a hand over the receiver and said quietly, 'No, you don't understand. I got the wrong bus. I'm in… I'm in Brawdy.'

'What? Speak up.'

'I'm in Brawdy,' I barked.

To a chorus of sniggers, I explained what'd happened, then went outside to wait for a lift that I knew would be half an hour in arriving, preferring to stand in the cold.

Soon after starting in Trecwn – most likely on that first day – I began to contemplate other career options, inspired for the most part by television programmes. There was a series that persuaded me of the merits of joining the paratroop regiment. It all looked very thrilling and there were even regimental tattoos involved. Two fundamental problems presented themselves, though: I had a phobia of heights, so the prospect of edging towards an open door on a Hercules and chucking myself out wasn't very appealing, and secondly, I was a coward, so sticky situations with bullets whizzing past didn't grab me either. The paras idea was dropped.

Next, a series about the Metropolitan Police drew me in. Once more, it was the promise of excitement that snared me. Then again, any job outside of the depot possessed the rosy glow of adventure. Anything but the dreary life of a junior storeman. I made enquiries, and even got an application form, but it came to nothing on account of my not pursuing it with any vigour. Deep down, any career that threatened to tear me away from my mates and the pub had little credence.

Trecwn, then, was half-Butlins, half-open prison, with a freedom to roam within the confines of the valley and an expectation of occasional work-based activity, bookended by clocking in and out. When roaming it was advisable to carry something noticeable, such as a clipboard or a large tool, to ward off any suspicion of skiving.

The section I was attached to was based in a hut in a wooded area near to a narrow-gauge railway line that ran either side of the steep-sided valley. Inserted into the hillside at intervals along the length of the valley were twenty-foot-tall wrought iron doors behind which the narrow-gauge lines disappeared. Hauling those doors open revealed a curved blast-absorbing tunnel that led to the cathedral-like magazines where the bombs and sea-mines were stacked. It was civil engineering on a grand scale.

Six months before I started in Trecwn the 1982 Falklands war had brought a frenzy of activity, as this sleepy depot sprang into life. From dawn till dusk, the narrow-gauge engines clattered up and down the valley carrying tons of ordnance from the magazines to be loaded onto mainline trains for transportation to Royal Navy bases around the country. By the time I arrived the fighting was over – like me, the Argentinian conscript army had an aversion to bullets whizzing past and had run up the white flag. With no war to create demand, nothing much happened.

And so, to create the illusion of activity, bombs would be forklifted onto a carriage in one magazine and transported along the narrow-gauge railway to another magazine. A bit like musical chairs only with high-explosives. At the departure magazine triplicate paperwork would be generated and the same process repeated at the receiving magazine. All of this would be undertaken as a diesel loco ticked-over Treblinka-like, filling the magazine with a bluish haze. Whilst I bolted outside for fresh air the old hands were content to be gassed.

In the summer I climbed the zig-zag path to the top of the valley – shovel in hand, of course – and sunbathed, camouflaged in the long grass, daydreaming of not being there. Winter was spent hibernating in the hut's pitch-black drying room, catching up on my sleep on a canvas military stretcher I'd found in an abandoned hut down the line. The job had no challenge, day after day being swallowed up with a big fat nothing.

Infrequent sightings of a girl who worked in the main office at the bottom of the valley offered dreamy distraction. A few years older than me and undoubtedly experienced in ways that had as yet eluded me, I thought of her a lot and manufactured flimsy excuses to venture down the valley so that I might encounter her.

'I'll take it down the main office,' I said to my line manager one day, grabbing a memo.

'It's okay. I'll drop it off tonight on the way out of the gates,' he said.

'No, no, honestly, it's fine,' I insisted, bolting out of the door.

Riding the section bike down the valley, I was rehearsing a string of chat-up lines in my head when I saw her walking along the pavement in my direction. This was it. This was my chance. As I drew closer, I primed my brain to deliver some charming bon mot which'd make her laugh. Make her like me. But, before I had a chance to impress, I found myself lying in the road with the bike tangled on top of me. In my excitement I hadn't noticed the narrow-gauge railway line that crossed the road. On meeting the tarmac, the tracks became a pair of steel-encased grooves, and the front wheel of the bike had slotted into one of them and sent me flying. The pain of the fall was nothing compared to the pain of her not even noticing, as I looked up to see her disappear into a building.

The ambulance reached Cardiff and the Victorian edifice of the Royal Infirmary as dawn streaked the sky. The journey had felt like an eternity. Exhaustion and large doses of pain relief had numbed, though not eradicated, the severe discomfort radiating from the broken parts of my body. I was lifted from the ambulance and trolleyed into the hospital accompanied by Mum and Dad, who walked beside me in silence. A bomb had gone off – not in the depot, but inside my own body, with incalculable consequences. Perhaps waiting for the bus to Trecwn that morning wouldn't have been so bad after all.

Chapter 2

I began to stir from a nightmare of agony and near-death. It was time to get up, get dressed, make my sandwiches and set off for the bus to work, that joyless journey replete with the whiff of damp coats, Brylcreem and a whining gearbox. My eyes flickered, then opened, and as they did a surge of pain gripped me. And a room revealed itself. A large room. Not my bedroom. And still there was that pain, relentless, like a knife turning.

Then it hit me. It hadn't been a nightmare, at least not in the conventional sense. The panicked swerve. The momentary weightlessness. The popping and splintering of the bones in my neck. It'd all been real. It'd happened. And that maw of pain had me in its clutches – much like, I expect, decapitation, but with my head placed back on its plinth. Eyes wide open, I found myself staring at a new hospital ceiling.

I could hear muffled voices and a confusion of busy but quiet footsteps, but all I could see was the ceiling as I sensed a presence on the bed beside me. Unable to turn my head I screwed my eyes left and saw a dark shape brushing my arm. The shape bolted upright. It was Mum, who'd fallen asleep sitting at my side, her head resting on the bed.

'Oh, Dave... Dave, you're awake,' she exclaimed. An incredulous joy at my waking and the emotion of the night's events were palpable in her voice. 'How're you feeling?'

It wasn't so much a question as a plea. A hope that I'd miraculously raise an arm, touch her face and say, 'Fine, thanks.'

'Everything hurts,' I said.

When I'd been wheeled into the ward in the early hours of that morning then drifted off to sleep, I imagined that when I awoke all would, indeed, be fine. That the shock – or whatever it was I'd convinced myself was causing the paralysis – would've worn off. That I'd be able to move again.

'Why can't I move anything?'

She motioned to speak but her voice crumbled as tears rolled down her face. I too began to cry. She'd been there like a sentinel for hours, watching over her boy. What torments she must've endured looking at the wreckage that lay before her, tortured by the diagnosis of the previous night. Mr Adams, the consultant in A&E, had been gentle with her and Dad, but honest. Since arriving in Cardiff, though, she'd sat there with her naïve optimism, discounting the medical opinion. 'He'll be fine. He is fine, for God's sake.'

She'd prayed for me to wake, all the while steeling herself for the confrontation with reality. And the reality was, nothing moved, besides a slight curling of the fingers of my right hand. I had sensation from head to toe, with a few numb patches, but nothing moved. I was rendered still. A corpse. The physical David Wilson, junior storeman and motorcyclist of debatable skill – there'd been a number of warm-up crashes – had expired at approximately 20.00 hours on 16th February 1984 on a cold pavement in an unexceptional town in west Wales.

Mum stood and rushed off, returning a minute later with a doctor. A doctor, perhaps, that she imagined could make everything move again.

'Morning, David. How're you feeling?' he asked. I was already wishing people would stop asking me that.

'In a lot of pain. My shoulders. Neck. Everywhere,' I said, grimacing.

'I'll get some pain relief sorted. Back in a moment.'

Mum sat down, having barely collected herself, and began to say, with admirable optimism, that everything would be fine. Poor Mum; she had to say it if only to convince herself, in spite of what Mr Adams had presented her and Dad with the night before. She broke down again the moment she stopped talking. I couldn't move and she couldn't magic me to. How stark the situation was from a few nights previous when I'd given her a kiss and gone up to bed, falling asleep to the sound of Demis Roussos wafting up from the record player in the lounge – a large bearded Greek man in a kaftan, singing of 'sitting in the sun waiting for a senorita to come'. I never did work out why Demis did it for her.

The doctor returned with painkillers and Mum sensed it an opportune time to leave us. He sat and leant forward.

'So, David, I've got a few patients to discharge...'

Nice for them, I thought.

'But I'll come back in an hour or so and we can have a chat about what's happened. Is that okay with you?'

A politely presented *fait accompli*, to which I just mumbled in the affirmative. He didn't look much older than me with his shock of dark curly hair and the blight of once-rampant acne still discernible. With the vocational fervour of the recently graduated, he seemed to have hit the medical jackpot – a quadriplegic; paralysis in all four limbs. He patted my arm and strolled away.

Moments later, Mum returned.

'Where's Dad?' I asked.

'He went back home to talk to Andrew. Back as soon as he can,' she said, her voice fading as if falling down a well.

Andrew, my brother, was thirteen. His appreciation of the gravity of what'd happened would be as ignorant, if not more so, than my own initial grasp. That would change. My knowledge of spinal injuries and their consequences experienced a steep learning curve over the coming hours, days and weeks as the enormity of what I'd suffered was brought home to me both by the honesty of the medical staff and the refusal of my body to move – willing a foot to curl up or a hand to grip and getting no response is deflating to say the least.

At that moment, though, in the absence of an explanation of the medical situation from a doctor – I hadn't taken much in the previous night – I struggled to unearth any logic as to what'd happened. One moment I'd been able to move, the next I couldn't, accompanied by atomic levels of pain. It didn't make sense and I felt confused, but as the day began to pass, I also began to feel scared. What if it doesn't just wear off? I thought. I was able to bat the negativity away, though, as the only thing that made sense – the logical conclusion – was that the paralysis would wear off. I drifted off to sleep. Sleep meant not thinking about not moving.

When I woke, Mum was gone, which was a relief. I didn't have the capacity to absorb her grief and wanted to be left alone. I still couldn't move but kept reminding myself that I could feel everything, which helped alleviate the increasing sense of terror of not moving as the day went on. Not long now, surely, I thought.

Lying on my back without a pillow and unable to move my head sideways, my world had shrunk, tunnel-like, to the ceiling and whoever or whatever came within the periphery of my vision. I could hear the chatter and business of the ward but see nothing. Very quickly, my other senses became attuned to compensate for the visual deficit.

By early afternoon a dry antiseptic heat tinged with a profusion of odours, some bodily and not necessarily belonging to me, began to parch my throat. Saliva production seemed to have ceased and I began convulsing with fits of coughing. I coughed and coughed and retched until someone came and gave me a drink through a straw. That's how reliant I now was. The day before, in work, I'd hand-stacked a few dozen ammunition boxes, but now nothing happened without someone else's input. The only difference between me and the stiffs in the mortuary was that I could breathe and think.

The shiny young doctor returned and apologised for having been longer than he'd promised. Aside from a short sleep, I'd lain there waiting for the tide of movement to flow back into the muscular tributaries of my body. I had faith that I'd move again, very soon, but like religion, that faith was based on ignorance, a fragile creed to be easily dismembered.

For the doc I was his medical Ferrari, much more challenging, and rewarding, than the bland array of Ford Fiestas, Vauxhall Corsas and clapped-out Ladas of the general medical ward that I was on; ingrown toenails, mole removals, urinary tract infections and a tedious host of other ailments. I was a case he could get excited about, a proper medical catastrophe.

'So, how're you feeling now, David?' It was an introductory gambit that was to become the default amongst medical staff and I never did work out why anyone would ask that of a person who was so obviously fucked.

'In pain,' I said.

'Not surprising. You've had quite a bash.'

He pulled up a seat.

'Not sure what's happening,' I continued. 'I'm confused. I mean, I know not moving isn't good, but I can feel everything… pins stuck in me. When will I be able to move again?'

He glanced at my charts as if stalling, no doubt formulating as kindly as possible the prognosis he had to deliver. It was, after all, a learning curve for him too. Doctors, you see, don't deal in rosy scenarios, the sunny uplands of false hope. They tell it as it is, some better than others. He began to relay the medical situation to me, his bedside manner exemplary. He'd learned well at med school, or maybe he was just a nice person.

'You've suffered a serious trauma to your neck,' he said. 'Two of the bones – vertebrae – are damaged. X-rays show one is fragmented – sort of burst if you like – and the other's been… well, sort of pushed out of alignment. Dislocated. These vertebrae are called C5 and C6.'

He explained how the spinal column, a collection of these interlocking vertebrae, protects the spinal cord running within. The spinal cord is a complex bundle of nerve fibres, a bit like a telephone exchange – the medics' favoured comparison – that communicate instructions from the brain to the muscles in the body, the fibres radiating out of the spinal column at intervals. They couldn't be certain whether I'd damaged my spinal cord and if I had, to what extent. If the spinal cord is severed or partially severed the consequent loss of function is permanent. The picture in my case was confused. I could sense stimulation – pins prodded in me – but couldn't move.

'It could be that your spinal cord is bruised or swollen and that you might regain some or even all of the movement you had previously. Only time will tell,' he said.

That was the hoped-for sunny upland. I could live with that. Then I had to go and spoil it. 'What if that's not the case? That it's not just swollen?' I said, as if tiptoeing into a minefield. I should've taken note of the warning sign to keep out.

'Well, if the spinal cord has been damaged it could mean limited or...' he took a breath, '...perhaps no recovery of movement.'

It was possibly the hardest prognosis he'd had to deliver in his short medical career.

'But I've got sensation in my body,' I said, as prickles of panic bathed me. 'Get a pin. I'll show you. I can feel things. Honest... I can.'

'That's good, but... but it doesn't mean everything'll be okay.'

I wanted to grab him and shake him and tell him he was wrong, but, of course, I couldn't. Not the grabbing and shaking bit anyway.

He glanced down at the floor, and said in a near whisper, 'Sorry.' He waited for a response, but none was forthcoming. I had nothing to say. I couldn't speak. I was struck dumb.

He stood, imparted something caring that washed over me and left. I'd been stunned by a presentation of medical fact. Science had trumped faith. Having sensation, it seemed, didn't necessarily point to a recovery of movement.

The spinal cord, then. You could argue that it was a monumental design flaw to locate this spindly gossamer thread, this delicate elasticated strip of neuro-gristle, the body's vital blood-fed communications cable, within a stacked column of bones prone to destruction. In fact, there's no argument; it's a stupid design, full stop. I'd been undone, it seemed, by God's botched handiwork. Omnipotent and incompetent. Thank you, God.

The doc left me traumatised as my eyes filled, tears pooling and streaming down my face. The chemical miasma distilled within the brain, producing surges of excitement, anticipation, the promise of a bright future, had been snuffed out. Erased. The granite weight of his deliverance crushed me. George Orwell's novel *1984* is bleak and infused with a sense of hopelessness. My 1984 was turning out to be rather grim too. I closed my eyes and howled, no doubt to the irritation of patients recovering from an assortment of minor ops. I cried myself to sleep.

Mute was an unusual state of affairs for me, as I'd always been such a chatterbox. School days, in particular, had been filled with chat, during lessons, of course. Either chatting or staring out of the window wondering, especially during secondary school, what I was doing there. After a couple of warnings to pipe down, teachers who were squeamish about corporal punishment would send me out into the corridor till the next lesson, when the problem – me – could be shifted on.

There were some teachers, though, that embraced hard power: caning, slapping, punching, even kicking on occasion. I could never figure out whether their resorting to violence was borne of frustration, a predisposition to inflict hurt regardless, or dissatisfaction from having stumbled into the wrong job. There certainly didn't appear to be any hint of a vocational dynamism in most of them. Maybe they just weren't suited to other professions, in addition to not being very good at teaching.

One teacher had a novel approach to talking in class; he'd take aim with a wooden board eraser and propel it with unerring accuracy at the offender's head. Never the torso, always the head, wherever they might be in class. I can't tell you how much of a shock it is to be engaged in an important conversation with your mate and feel a piece of hardwood clattering the back of your head. As a deterrent, it did seem to work, though, as his classes were usually attentive.

I was seven years old and living in Bradford when I witnessed my first classroom assault. A boy – can't remember his name – was ordered to the front of the class for some misdemeanour.

'Hold your hand out,' she said. As he did so, she sharpened a pencil and then jabbed it into his palm. He squealed, returned to his seat and sobbed through to lunch. We kept our heads down, not wanting to catch her gaze. After lunch his father stormed into class and punched her, right in front of us. It was very exciting. We never saw that teacher again.

I was a pupil at Hilltop Primary School in Low Moor, Bradford. The school sat amongst rows of back-to-back Victorian houses, with many of them boarded up. It had the feel of an area on the cusp of being demolished. Clambering into the abandoned houses felt adventurous, and a touch dangerous; I remember a boy going upstairs and moments later coming through the ceiling, mostly unharmed.

It was Dad's hometown and we moved there when I was four after he left the Royal Navy. Bradford hadn't been kind to him as a child, making it all the more confusing as to why we moved there. His mum died the day after his eighth birthday, following his dad a couple of years earlier. I asked him once what they'd died of and he said with a thin smile, 'Being poor.' His abiding memory of childhood was hunger, supper often just a piece of bread and butter and an orange – at least he got his vitamin C.

A week after his seventeenth birthday he joined the Navy, escaping to brighter horizons, and food. The mess was a favourite place on board; he weighed nine stone on enlisting and three years later had padded out to a comfortable fourteen.

One of my happiest recollections of Bradford were the power cuts of the early seventies. The miners were on strike and each night the lights went out – the power stations having been ordered to conserve dwindling coal stocks. We'd sit in the lounge, candles at the ready, and the moment we were plunged into darkness, Dad would light them. It was exciting, and I've rarely felt safer, sitting between Mum and Dad as I stared at the wispy flame.

In the summer of '73 we moved back to Pembrokeshire and an identikit pebble-dashed bungalow in Haverfordwest, the town where I was born. A new school beckoned, down a high-hedged lane a few miles out of town. It was *Hammer House of Horror* eerie, surrounded by woods and cawing crows. There were just two classrooms and two teachers, one of them the headmaster, a man feared but respected, much like a banana-republic strongman, and who was arbitrary when it came to punishment.

Dinner was vanned in from a larger school, lukewarm and barely edible. One lunchtime I was contemplating cold mash, limp veg and a brownish-grey meat of dubious provenance when I was told that the head wanted to see me. I hadn't done anything wrong – to the best of my knowledge – so I strode to his classroom in expectation of some reward for having excelled; I was a studious little boy at the time.

'Ah, Wilson. Come in.'

He put his sandwich down.

'Put your hand out,' he said.

Mutely, I obeyed. Swish – one hand done.

'Other hand.'

With the deftness of a state executioner the other hand was done before I had time to draw breath. He placed the cane on his desk and continued eating his sandwich, the signal for me to leave. He didn't explain what I was supposed to have done and I reckoned it unwise to enquire.

Regardless of the season, he wore a faded olive-green mac and a Fedora, often taking the school bus home. His fondness for First World War marching songs made for a tuneful bus, as we belted out 'It's a Long Way to Tipperary' through a string of villages. In spite of the draconian discipline, he presided over a contented establishment, with a freedom that larger schools couldn't accommodate.

At Christmas the big house by the river donated a tree and two of the older boys would be dispatched with a saw to cut it down and drag it up the lane to school. We'd bring wellies and picnics in and trudge off on long, aimless marches through woods and by the river with the teacher, seemingly with no educational rationale except to wear us out and if we were lucky find a stick resembling a rifle with which we could run around shooting at one another.

Arguments in the playground, though, were subject to a unique form of dispute resolution; the head chucked the belligerents a pair of boxing gloves each and watched them slug it out. When he retired, the end of summary canings was welcomed by all.

The new head believed in encouragement and gentle persuasion as the way to model good behaviour and so an archaic collection of canes ordered by weight and length were disposed of. He also read to us and I have warm memories of *The Silver Sword* by Ian Serraillier.

The rattle of the tea trolley woke me. Mum was there, with Dad, hollow-eyed and spent having driven back to Cardiff after talking to my brother Andrew who'd gone to stay with my aunty. Dad stroked my arm.

'How're you feeling?'

I looked sullenly at the ceiling.

'Sorry, stupid thing to ask. I just... just... sorry,' he said.

Poor Dad, he didn't know what to say. But then, who did? What do you talk about with someone who appears to have lost everything? I could've made it easier for them, of course, but I reckoned that their suffering couldn't compete with mine and why the hell should I lift myself for them anyway. All I wanted to do was scream and bawl, and after the young doc's talk, die. They perched by my bedside like statues, paralysed – with grief – while trying not to show it. Every now and then, Mum would crack and start to cry, and then apologise.

The infirmary provided them with a room for a few nights – the city mini-break from hell – which was convenient for refuelling their continued agonies. They kept watch over me for days, sometimes together, more often in shifts. While one sat, the other left the ward and sometimes the building, a distraction from the vigil.

The infirmary was adjacent to Newport Road, one of the busiest in Cardiff. Mum would wander out of the main entrance like an automaton, unthinking yet prey to relentless thought. Leaving the ward didn't mean forgetting who was in it. She'd sit on a low wall at the side of the road, with the traffic drifting past, her face chiselled with anguish. Motorists would never have guessed what turmoil was enveloping the woman hunched yards away.

Mum and Dad are two of those anonymous heroes of society, raising themselves from humble beginnings through hard work and spotless honesty. Well, Dad's upbringing wasn't so much humble as dirt poor. They never asked for anything, which is just as well, as they were never given anything. They aspired to a better life, not just for them but for us, Andrew and I.

They found each other at the Drill Hall, Haverfordwest in November 1963 – the same month that Kennedy was shot. The Hall was Mum's release, where she could drink in huge gulps of abandonment away from the beige life of an end-of-the-line town. She liked to dance. And boy, could she dance. The jive, of course. She'd spin and juke and kick, with only the best partners as she was good, really good. With her beehive hair and fulsome skirts, she'd whirl like some West Walian Dervish. And one night in strolled Harry Wilson, the Navy boy out with his shipmates on the town.

If only: the two-word mantra that came to dominate my thoughts. If only I hadn't left the house when I did. Oh, and 'why me?', of course. Why did it have to happen to me? I mean, what proportion of the population ever suffers such an horrific injury? The odds must be extraordinary. I was in an elite club that's for sure. My mind churned over and over with the unfairness of it. What had I done to deserve it? How bad would a person have to be – how intrinsically evil – to be robbed of all movement; not forgetting the slight curl of the fingers of my right hand. But I wasn't bad – not too bad anyway – or evil. Just unlucky.

Thinking was now the enemy. I didn't want to think but couldn't stop. It's as automatic as breathing; something else that I wanted to stop. People often bemoan a lack of time to think, to zone out and contemplate bigger questions other than what's for tea, can I fit in a supermarket shop and all the other trifling shit that consumes a day. The long days of emptiness at Trecwn had gifted me so much time to think, to dream, to drift off. Lying on an army-issue stretcher in the coal blackness of the drying room, with the dehumidifier humming, I floated off to such splendid alternative lives, none of which would ever belong to me. Then I'd be roused by my watch alarm and head for the main gates and the bus home, refreshed and ready for a night in the pub.

Being hospitalised awards you endless thinking time in which to analyse one's predicament, and in my case, what'd been lost. And I'd lost everything. I rued the dashed imagined hopes and dreams for a future that would never have materialised anyway. Typical, really; I'd spent my late teenage years drifting along with no plan or aspiration. I hadn't been inquisitive about the world. There'd been no desire to travel as to travel requires a sense of the possible. Some bravery perhaps.

Nope, I was boring. A boring, predictable dolt. Yet, now that I couldn't move my body, I convinced myself that some great future had been snatched away. And the more I pondered the supposed theft of that imagined future the blacker my thoughts became.

I woke that morning in the infirmary convinced that the return of movement was a given. It made sense, as the alternative – ongoing paralysis – couldn't be allowed to make sense. I could feel therefore I'd move. The young doc had gently disabused me of that misguided faith. The evening was slipping away and I was still as still as I'd been at the beginning of the day. I sensed for the first time a darkness settling on me.

Mum had gone for a lie down in the room provided by the infirmary. Dad had picked up the baton and was sitting by me.

'What's the time?' I asked.

'Quarter to eight. Why?'

'Oh… nothing.'

Twenty-four hours earlier, almost to the minute, I'd been getting ready to go to the pub. What a difference a day had made.

Chapter 3

The days passed, motionless. Paralysed. And not just any old paralysis, but an almost complete absence of movement from my neck down. Yet, when not plunged into suicidal despair – a frustrating state of mind, as I had no physical means to bring about my end – there was a strangely reassuring unreality to my situation. Yes, the science had been explained and it didn't make for happy listening, but I didn't believe that I could be rendered a corpse from the neck down forever. It just didn't make sense. Maybe I should've paid more attention in biology at school. But I couldn't allow it to make sense, as to do so would've been to accept that perhaps I wouldn't move again, that the worst-case scenario could materialise. Anyway, the young doc, it'd seemed to me, had felt obliged to hit me with the worst possible outcome even though he didn't believe it'd come to that. He had to say it just in case, to cover all the bases, tick all the boxes.

Yet, a week in, I couldn't move a muscle, except for that weak curling of the fingers; not much to build a life around. They didn't even curl to the point where I could grip anything. In unguarded moments I contemplated a state of permanent paralysis, a dreadful possibility corroborated by the science, and the undeniable evidence that, at least for the time being, I was done for, and I'd sink into that black pit, bawling my eyes out. The young doc had said that I might not move again, and a week in nothing moved.

The year 1984 was a hot one. The sun came out with unusual vigour in February and was a near-constant presence till October. My bed was by a south-facing window, and my head and shoulders baked from the time I woke till late afternoon. The central heating seemed an unnecessary addition, so one morning I asked a nurse, 'Would it be possible to turn the heating off, please? So hot in here.'

She glanced at the radiator. 'Can't see a knob, but I'll ask.'

It stayed on; no doubt there were myriad levels of bureaucracy involved in isolating a single radiator. In this fan oven, time swam against a riptide of emptiness, the hours dragging, anchor-like. Days were the enemy, vast unwanted spaces filled with unwanted thoughts that I couldn't stop thinking. I longed for dusk, dark and sleep. Asleep, everything moved. Asleep, I ran.

In my inanimate state, I began to track particles of dust, floating above me, lit by the sun's rays, and suspended by the magnified heat of double glazing. Oh, and the central heating, of course. The specs took on an importance out of proportion to their actuality as I spied their trajectory and willed them to stay within my eye-line. I even gave them names. I personalised dust. I spent hours watching motes while the white noise of the ward continued around me. I thought of all the times I'd complained as a child of being bored. I now knew I'd never got close to boredom.

The days crawled, then, as my diaphragm expanded as if constrained by a large stone placed on my chest. I slept a lot, my preferred place to be. Awake, if I heard voices or footsteps approaching, I closed my eyes and feigned sleep, till I'd determined whether they were staff or visitors. The keeping still bit was easy. Well-meaning visitors whose breath I could feel would whisper, 'Oh, poor love's asleep. Best not disturb him,' and off they'd creep. I'd count to ten and open my eyes again.

A television was delivered by a porter – the institutional antidote to loneliness and a visual anaesthetic to nullify dark thoughts – a telly to numb the psychological pain. He placed it on a table at the foot of the bed.

'There we are, boy,' he said, as if bestowing some incredible gift. He plugged it in and turned it on. 'Right, what we got here then?'

'I'm on my back,' I said. 'Can't see it.'

'Yeah, sorry. You'll need some of those prism thingies. I'll ask a nurse.'

These 'thingies' were a pair of glasses with prisms instead of lenses – a periscope for telly on your back. Sorted. The telly benefitted the staff too; they could now pass my bed without having to enquire after me as I was being royally entertained through the empty desert of my waking hours. The young doc continued to stop by though, happy to sit and chat about anything and everything that didn't involve my situation, which suited us both.

Open University lectures on oxbow lakes, molecular biology and frequency modulation, presented by scruffily bearded men with leather elbow patches, were perfect for dozing off to. The post-lunch *Pebble Mill at One*, with its tired procession of book pluggers, killed-off soap stars and rehabbed end-of-the-pier comedians brought certainty to the day's middle.

Then there was *Emmerdale Farm*, with its escaped sheep and milk quota concerns, which in my little world assumed the stature of an Icelandic saga. This was prior to its rebrand as the cosmopolitan *Emmerdale*, with a shift in plotlines to include terrorist-downed Jumbos, kidnap and murder; from uneventful rural idyll to the crime capital of Yorkshire in the blink of a name change. Like some tramp rummaging through bins, I'd devour anything on the box if it averted the badlands of thought. Sleep and telly stopped me thinking.

For Christmas 1975 Mum and Dad gave me a portable television, a flickering box of black and white static for my bedroom. Twiddling the tuning dial while simultaneously adjusting the direction of the set-top aerial, I felt like a spy in enemy territory as I painstakingly sought a channel. Having achieved a stable picture, the moment I laid on my bed it'd break up again. It became apparent that I had to sit on the edge of my bed in close proximity to the aerial which, it seemed, required the dense mass of my head to deliver anything watchable.

There was one golden rule to abide by; no telly after nine on a school night or ten during holidays. This presented a dilemma when the 1976

Olympics were held in Montreal, Canada. Olympics events and finals are often held in the evenings, local time. The one hundred metres final, for example, would likely have been at eight o'clock Montreal time and broadcast live in the UK at one in the morning – Montreal's five hours behind Greenwich Mean Time. I'd go to bed with unusual willingness at the prescribed time, and set my alarm for midnight – seven in the evening in Montreal. I'd get up and sit on the edge of the bed a foot from the screen with the volume at its lowest audible setting; the bathroom was next to my room and it wasn't unknown for Mum or Dad to visit it during the night.

The subterfuge worked a treat, though after a few hours I'd slump forward, resting my elbows on my knees as exhaustion kicked in. Two or three nights – very early mornings – passed and my eyes began itching like crazy during the day. Another few days and they were streaming too as I took to almost permanently rubbing them. Then objects, newsprint, anything really, became blurred. Mum was concerned at my red running eyes and suggested a doctor's appointment. 'Could be hay fever,' she said. I resisted, knowing that the root of the problem lay in my sitting inches from a bright screen in a dark room in the early morning, every morning. But she persisted and dragged me to see Dr Barton, our family GP.

Dr Barton was ex-Navy and disinclined to pussy-foot about, especially when a young boy was hoodwinking his mother. He examined my eyes as Mum voiced concern that something might be terribly wrong – it had by now, in her estimation, ratcheted up from simple hay fever. He just gave a rueful smile and said, 'So, been watching the Olympics then?'

'A bit, perhaps,' I replied.

The game was up, as indeed my Olympic games were too. The telly was removed till it was over.

Back on the ward, I'd acquired a new skill; horizontal dining. I couldn't be propped upright, for meals, and so a nurse would sit beside me engaging in void-filling small talk while placing forkfuls into my mouth. The timing was rarely in sync. Often, I'd swallow and wait like a new-born chick, mouth agape, as my feeder stared into the middle distance.

'Ready,' I'd say.

'Sorry, love, miles away. Wondering what to make him for tea, I was.'

Or, there was the impatient feeder, anxious to get the ordeal over with regardless of my masticating tempo – overloaded fork ready to be shovelled in the moment I opened my mouth. Mealtimes were awkward mechanical operations reliant on the person in charge of the cutlery for any semblance of dignity. Choking was an institutional concern but they needn't have worried as I took to horizontal dining with aplomb.

Compacted food waste was a more unsavoury proposition. I suffered from constipation, a tendency unlikely to improve with a combination of immobility and an ambient heat that could desiccate a coconut. The solution were suppositories, with the ensuing evacuation being fast and fizzy. Waiting for a nurse to remove the offending mass – which could be a long wait – I was reminded that the accident hadn't affected my sense of smell.

A catheter was inserted down my penis into the bladder to take care of the waterworks. With no sensation of urinating, the bag self-replenished as if by magic. I couldn't eat, shit or piss without a helping hand, and these intimate invasions of privacy – desecrations, if you like – were hard to stomach, at least initially.

Every four hours my bodily position was adjusted to prevent bed sores, caused when unalleviated pressure from static body-weight forces bone mass to the surface, causing open wounds. They're painful and can lead to complications. 'Prevention's better than cure, David,' was one nurse's riposte when I groaned at being disturbed. There were three positions: tilted onto my left-hand side with pillows stuffed behind me to maintain position; ditto the right side; and flat on my back. Every four hours, twenty-four hours a day.

And so, a multitude of regimens had established themselves;

observations, pain relief, mealtimes, positional adjustment every four hours, waste disposal. The interventions dislocated the day and devoured time and I welcomed them. But, these tableaux of dependence were also coalescing into a gut-wrenching realisation that I was stuffed.

A week had passed since the accident. The intense throbbing throughout my body was easing, as I began to mend. Whether I could be mended back to normal was a different matter. I couldn't see my neck, shoulders or upper back, but that area, which'd been first to connect with the pavement, was still a deep ink black. Indeed, my left shoulder blade was the source of most discomfort and being turned onto that side was agony but they turned me all the same. My left elbow and hand were also very painful. The hand was swollen, and again heavily bruised.

One of my first visitors was Martin, the friend who'd introduced me to motorbikes; it would've been churlish to mention it to him. He was passing Cardiff, from Haverfordwest, on his way back to Norfolk, where he now lived. I'd first met him three years before when I enrolled on an engineering course at technical college. Why I opted for engineering, I don't know, since I had no aptitude or interest in things mechanical or electrical and precious little enthusiasm for getting oil or grease on my hands. Martin, though, was a born techy, forever tinkering with his motorbike, adjusting tolerances, lubricating cogs and sprockets, his head stuck in a Haynes manual, speaking a language I didn't understand and had no wish to learn. Lifts to college, though, as his pillion whetted my appetite for biking.

His dad's new RAF posting had dragged him away from our little gang of motorcyclists to Norfolk six months before my accident. I called to see him on the day of departure. Slumping around, he was badgered by his parents to help load the removal truck, with a look that suggested he'd been told to dig his own grave. The very last item to be put on board was his beloved Honda XL motorbike, which he solemnly wheeled up the ramp. And that was it. We said our goodbyes and he was driven away.

And now, he was sitting by my bed.

'You're here? Fuck me, I walked straight past,' he said, with strained jollity. 'Got to the other end of the ward and had to ask a nurse. Typical me, eh.'

I saw the shock as he took in the callipers clamped to my head.

'So, how's things?' he asked.

The question was redundant, and I could see that he knew it.

'Well, besides the fact I can't move a fucking thing, everything's just fucking great.'

He blushed.

'Yeah, sorry. Dumb question.'

I felt guilty at his discomfort, sitting there with his tangled nest of hair that defied all attempts at styling.

'Sorry, Mart.'

'It's okay. You've every right to be angry.'

There were heroic attempts at puerile banter and I tried to meet him halfway, the least I could do, but it was a doomed encounter. My heart wasn't in it. I'd forgotten how to laugh. I didn't want to laugh. A jovial soul, he rattled off the expected topics of conversation between two teenage boys in a hospital ward: what are the nurses like and is it true they're all gagging for it; is the food as shite as people say; and God, this is a cushy number, lying on your back all day watching the telly. I was ashamed at my relief when he made his excuses and left.

Having been Martin's pillion, in April of 1983 I rode a brand-new, gleaming black, bloody gorgeous Yamaha DT 125 away from Masons Motorcycles in Haverfordwest. Mr Mason was a bluff sixty-odd-year-old in faded blue overalls, with a collection of leaky pens and Allen keys lining his breast pocket. Carrying a faint whiff of pipe tobacco, his parting words were, 'Be careful with her, boy. She's a bit of a handful.'

With a derisive laugh I tore out of the showroom, barely in control, and onto the main road. I survived that first day, just. Like running with the bulls at Pamplona, it was exhilarating, but with the shadow of oblivion a whisker away. Mum hated the thing immediately, confiding later that she'd considered reversing the car 'accidentally' over it. Each time I walked out with my helmet she felt sick with worry, lying awake till she heard it being parked up. Dad wasn't keen either but didn't let on, as is the way with Yorkshiremen.

The bike gave me the freedom to explore my county, trundling down high-hedged lanes, traversing the Preseli Hills along rutted bridleways, getting deliciously half-lost, and falling off harmlessly. I saw places just miles from home I never knew existed. Family days out when I was young had revolved around a handful of beaches but now a whole new world opened up. To complement my exploring, I bought a camera and an Ordnance Survey map. The photographs I took lacked any merit but the click of the shutter enlivened me and something deep and permanent began.

The motorbike also bought acceptance into a new circle of friends – Martin's friends. I'd left school in '81 determined on a clean break with the boys I'd spent five inglorious, and often humiliating, years with. There's a scar on the back of my hand. It's not big, perhaps two centimetres long. One day I was filing a piece of metal clamped in a vice. My memories of metalwork at school all involve the filing of a piece of metal clamped in a vice. I looked up and he beckoned me. I was wary of him, and with good cause, but I went over and before I could say a word, I felt it; a searing pain. I looked down and saw a blister bubbling up on the back of my hand. He laughed, still holding the red-hot piece of metal he'd just placed on me. I rushed to the sink and ran my hand under the cold tap. The teacher passed and saw the blister.

'What's happened, Wilson?'

The brander was watching to see whether I'd snitch.

'Oh, nothing. Just a bit careless, sir.'

I walked to school each day with a knot in my stomach, wondering what they had lined up for me. Wondering whether it'd be physical or just aggravating – a torn shirt, my bag kicked down a corridor, or opening my lunchbox to find my sandwiches squished into doughy balls. And so, I came up with a survival strategy, a way of deflecting unwanted attention. I reinvented myself as the funny guy, the go-to idiot. I was rather good at it too, with the back-chat getting me chucked out of classes to a chorus of sniggering approval. Worse than bombing my education though, I conspired in the misery of others if it saved me.

There was an incident. Isn't there always? The brander and an accomplice decided it'd be fun to chase, with twigs, one of their regular victims out of school at the end of the day. I carried their bags as they whipped him and laughed. I reckoned it best to laugh too. The next day we were summoned to the head's office and caned – the boy's dad had complained. That night I made a pact with myself – no more cowardice. I attached myself to a couple of good boys outside of the hateful circle who had enough physical presence to be left alone and ticked off the terms to the end of an education that'd promised much in junior school but which suffered a slow death of increasing ignominy during the five years of secondary school.

During that post-school summer of '81, with no job falling as if by some miracle into my lap – perhaps applying for one would've helped – it was either college or sign-on for the dole. Dad wouldn't countenance me signing-on, so, in desperation, it was the engineering course and my first encounter with Martin. A well-crafted insolence was now ingrained and I was soon being ejected from lectures, once for throwing a lethal Chinese star into a blackboard as the lecturer walked in. Made from two triangular pieces of sharpened tin spot-welded together to form a six-pointed star, there were, it seemed, some elements of engineering that I excelled at.

Martin and I were in many ways opposites; for starters, he was hardworking and polite with an aversion to trouble. It didn't stop me eroding his scrupulous character, mind. There was a Kit-Kat vending machine in a corridor. We discovered that after putting money in and taking a Kit-Kat from the dispensing drawer, if you closed it very slowly, the next bar would drop before the drawer clicked shut. We emptied the machine and sold them to other students during the lunch break. The principal found out and summoned us.

'It's theft. No other word for it. Outright theft,' he bellowed. 'I've a good mind to call the police, and expel you both.'

Martin delivered a grovelling apology, quaking in his motorbike boots. I laughed. His pleading saved us though, just.

It was my new friends, then, that gathered around my bed. The friends acquired through Martin. I'd been worried that they wouldn't come. After all, I hadn't known them for very long and I feared they'd reckon that not visiting was somehow okay, perhaps convince themselves they had other more pressing things to occupy a Sunday than spending the day going to Cardiff to visit someone they didn't have sufficient emotional investment in. But they came, often, and said all the right things and laughed and joked while inwardly, no doubt, thinking I was done for. They were good at not showing it.

David – known as Mucky, on account of his surname McDonald – usually drove, as he liked to. And he drove as if delivering a freshly donated organ to a critically ill patient – very fast. Arriving in the ward, his passengers Simon, Stephen and Gary would be thankful for their survival, while knowing that a return journey awaited. Having been Mucky's passenger myself – the soundtrack to journeys often being AC/DC's *Highway to Hell* – I knew that sense of deliverance all too well. On their first visit, a few days after the awkwardness of Martin, there were the ritual topics to be dealt with.

'So...' said Stephen, leaning in, '...any smart nurses? Know what they say.'

'Yeah, lots of smart nurses, Steve.'

I'd been humoured by many kind people and now it was my turn.

'So, what's the food like then, Dai?' asked Simon, who'd studied catering at college.

'Not the best, Sime.'

That just left Gary to allude to my luxuriating in some kind of televisual heaven. Once they'd become used to the sight of me, they fell into the old comforting rhythms. Laughter is a great balm, a universal healer. It helped, as I too began to laugh again, though not perhaps with my usual gusto. I was fragile and scared but their regular visits helped loosen the steely grip of blackness, that treacly drowning in despair. I wanted to fight. I had to fight. It was bloody tough seeing them walk out when it was time for home though. Walking out to their mobile lives.

Mum was my most frequent visitor. Couldn't keep her away! Dad worked in a refinery and came whenever he wasn't on shift. She'd catch the train from Haverfordwest, arriving in Cardiff late morning. What must she have endured staring out of the window at Whitland passing, Carmarthen passing, Port Talbot passing; passing platform after platform towards the reckoning. In the corridor leading to the ward, she'd take a moment, put on her sunny face and sweep in, the cavalry rescuing me from my fears. She'd sit there for hours and not once did the mask slip, a feat of extraordinary maternal dedication.

She'd bring Red Cross parcels, an array of treats to compensate for the hospital swill – snacks, cakes and other confections laced with stratospheric levels of sugar. I developed an addiction for Mr Kipling Bakewell tarts. For the sake of variety, I'd also request apple sundaes – Mr Kipling's, of course. And, like a magician, she'd produce an anomalous cooked chicken breast from her bag and delicately pull it apart and feed it to me. I never did ask why.

She'd tell me the news from home, her soft tone infused with a sense of calm security. I'd drift off to sleep and when I woke, she'd be there looking at me, studying me. I had little to tell her, but words were unnecessary. She'd stroke my head or clasp my hand, the scent of her perfume heavy in the heat of a Med spring. Her love, and Dad's when he was able to come, enveloped and cocooned me, persuading me all would be fine even when the evidence suggested otherwise. And yet all the while behind those unconditional facades she and Dad were terribly fragile. We were all broken.

Chapter 4

In spite of the young doc's bombshell that first day in the infirmary, I'd woken each morning believing that the not being able to move stuff would somehow right itself. That the bruising or swelling or shock or whatever it was that was causing the paralysis would just go. Disappear. But ten days in, all I had to show for that faith – that conviction – was some recovered minor rotation in my shoulders and the ability to lift my arms weakly from the bed before they plonked back down, unable to compete with gravity.

That was the sum of my recovery, which felt like a paltry return for all my investment of hope. Any hint of waking optimism then, after ten days, now dissipated with the rapidity of an early morning mist as the realisation, perhaps even acceptance, began to take hold that I was indeed stuffed. That science had trumped faith. That my spinal cord was damaged.

During the previous few days, the doc and his colleagues had been discussing with me a transfer to a hospital in Cardiff that specialised in rehabilitating patients with spinal injuries, a place called Rookwood. It couldn't come soon enough. I'd languished in the infirmary for ten days, parked on a general medical ward. Ten days of lying in three positions. Ten days of having my urine bag emptied, intrusive bowel evacuations and food being shovelled into me. Ten days of watching telly and dust. Ten days of, for the most part, strained bonhomie with the poor buggers compelled to come and witness my destruction as they salved me with warm words. Ten days, at the end of which I hardly moved any more than when I'd arrived. I wasn't being treated. I was being stored, shelved, forgotten about. I was haemorrhaging hope.

On the morning of my eleventh day in medical purgatory, the doc appeared.

'Morning, David. How're you today?' he said, upbeat as ever. I didn't care for upbeat anymore.

'Great. Just wonderful,' I replied, my sarcastic streak, at least, intact.

'Ha, yeah, very good,' he said with a chuckle. 'Anyway. Good news. A bed's become available in Rookwood. We've spoken about Rookwood, remember?'

'Remember? Of course, I remember...' I replied, as my throat tightened, 'It's all I've been thinking about, lying here not fucking moving.'

I hadn't turned on him before. He looked wounded.

'Sorry. I know it's taken a while, but it'll happen today, honest. And, don't take this personally, but we'll be glad to see you go. You'll get proper care there.'

He flashed a disarming smile, pricking my anger. I liked him. I clung to him, not physically, of course. When he came to me, I did my best to keep him there. Junior doctors are busy, fire-fighting the whole shift long. But he'd sat with me so many times, doling out compassion and listening and just being a lovely person when I'm sure he should've been tending to others. But I was his Ferrari, of course.

'Sorry I swore. Just want to go home,' I said as the floodgates opened, the words pouring out like a torrent. 'I'm scared. Scared I won't move again. It's not fair. I mean, why me? Why fucking me?'

He touched my arm. 'I wish I could make it alright. But, just try and be positive. And, if it helps, we'll miss you. We really will.' He paused. 'Anyway, Mr Thomas is waiting to go home,' he said, pointing down the ward, 'and he can't go till I see him.'

He smiled and walked away. I never saw him again. If he continued his medical journey, which I trust he did, his future patients will have been very fortunate.

After a lunch I'd have happily foregone and with Mum and Dad in attendance, I was wheeled out of the ward without ceremony to an awaiting ambulance for the three-mile transfer to Rookwood Spinal Injuries Unit in Llandaff, a northern suburb of Cardiff, and something unexpected happened. Unexpected and welcome. It may've been the fillip of fresh air and the sun's rays falling on my face as I was trundled the few metres across the warm tarmac to the ambulance. Perhaps it was just not being in that bloody ward. But a door opened ever so slightly in my mind, allowing me to peer into a brighter space, as I became conscious of an emotion that'd been buried under a mudslide of coal-black misery; hope shimmered. Those al fresco seconds made me feel alive and positive. It was the tiniest of glimmers, a warm, fuzzy feeling, but it reminded me that perhaps all was not quite lost, at least not psychologically. I smiled.

Mum and Dad also allowed themselves the glint of a forgotten smile too, eyes half-lit for the first time since the accident. For them this was progress indeed, going to a place where the long haul of rebuilding could begin. For nearly two weeks I'd been subject to a holding operation, a source of intense frustration for them and me. But despite the harsh truths they'd been told, they believed that by just being in this other place it would make a difference. They'd been sold the dream of recovery. Having done a passable impersonation of a shop dummy for so long, I wasn't quite so evangelical. Spinal cord damage, if there was any, wouldn't just right itself because I was in this other place. But the broken person who watched those ambulance doors close was a little more positive than the one who'd left the ward minutes earlier.

The journey across Cardiff was short, the scale of the place being more big-town than city. Mum and Dad followed the ambulance in their car, once again, only this time in a more positive frame of mind. The sun shone like it was just for me, as I looked up and out of the windows at the city-centre buildings, the ambulance moving stop-start in traffic. After staring at polystyrene ceiling tiles for days on end this felt like something of an epiphany. Maybe this journey was indeed bigger than I'd imagined. Maybe this trumpeted special place could spark a response from my dead limbs. Those three miles felt transformative, almost Damascene. I'd been savaged by the black dogs and Rookwood had to be a turning point.

The ambulance slowed and negotiated a speed-hump, and then another, before it stopped. The engine was turned off and the back doors opened. I'd arrived at this supposed special place, this Lourdes. I was nervous. This was it. The months that lay ahead would determine what kind of life would stretch ahead of me.

The core of Rookwood was a large Victorian villa, bay-windowed and elegantly faded. Set in what were once expansive wooded and lawned grounds, it must've been an impressive residence in its day, perhaps home to a retired Major back from the Raj. But cruel necessity had transformed it into a tarmac-shod hotchpotch of car parks and ancillary buildings, with corridors sprouting like tentacles from the main house and terminating in numerous wards set in the once-open grounds.

The viewing arc as I was trolleyed through the main lobby to a ward in the outer reaches of the hospital didn't inspire confidence. It didn't feel specialist. The tired fabric and a sense of make-do-and-mend weren't what I'd anticipated on the journey from the infirmary. I'd dreamt state-of-the-art. There were surely Stalin-era sanatoriums on the Black Sea that were better appointed than Rookwood.

The ward that I arrived on was occupied by failed motorcycle stunt riders, toppled-off victims of garage roof repairs, bucking horses, collapsed scrums and misjudged holiday pool dives. Spinal injuries are inflicted in many ways, a split second of inattention or recklessness, or just plain bad luck, costing dearly. In most cases the consequences of that fateful second in time last forever. This was the 'if only' brigade writ large, the mantra for a ward full of wreckage.

I was transferred to a bed, a high-tech piece of kit that tilted electrically; no more being hauled onto my side and having pillows stuffed behind, which'd seemed a little agricultural considering the unstable nature of the injury. Mum and Dad unpacked my few belongings – consisting for the most part of a hoard of Bakewell tarts

– and blu-tacked family photos and well-wisher cards to the bedside cabinet, while I attempted to scan my new surroundings. Laid on my back I had no more success than when I'd been in the infirmary. The ward and its occupants were yet to reveal themselves.

No sooner was I settled in, than a nurse appeared.

'Hi David. Hope you're comfortable,' she said, nodding warmly to Mum and Dad as they stuck things up. 'I'm Julie. If you need anything, just call out.'

'Thanks.'

'No problem, lovey. And, lucky you… just time to get your order in for supper.'

She read the menu options and I plumped for corned beef and chips on account of its sounding the most edible. I'd been brought up with a blue-collar respect for the pink brick. Mum always kept a tin of Fray Bentos in the cupboard, with corned beef hash being a favourite.

Other members of staff stopped and introduced themselves, which hadn't happened in the infirmary, where I'd felt parked and forgotten. Rookwood, though, was long-term and the staff were eager to foster connections with the patients, radiating a vocational warmth. During months of intimate and emotional interaction, they truly got to know us, warts and all. I grew to love some of those people like family. When Mum and Dad weren't around, they *were* family.

My bed was parked parallel to a bank of windows. Tilted onto my right side I had a view of a lawn with mature native trees just beyond. It wasn't a scene that would've had the romantic poets swooning but it was a view, and it was my view. In the coming weeks I saw the trees bud and unfurl their leaves in the spring warmth. With the windows open I breathed in hot days and listened to birdsong. Complemented by blue skies and fluffy clouds, it was my very own Constable painting, nature's alternative to the telly, and it made me determined to get out there. It made me *believe* that I could get out there and was confirmation that I was indeed in the place where I needed to be. This was my best chance and I had to embrace it.

Tilted to my left I had a view of the ward and its patients. This was an altogether bleaker vista, ramming home the terrifying implications of a spinal injury. I watched as staff helped patients with simple tasks that the able-bodied do with ease. Then there was the stamina-sapping effort required to transfer the dead weight of immobile legs from a bed to a wheelchair or vice-versa; legs are bloody heavy when they don't help. Most poignant of all, there was the determined grimace of people getting used to a new normal. It quickly dawned on me that the reality of this place was redundant legs replaced by wheels. In the most unfortunate of cases, there were redundant arms too. It frightened me.

When tilted towards the ward, I determinedly watched the television, avoiding any temptation to glance at the patients. I didn't want to be them and I didn't want to see or hear them. Mum and Dad were also unnerved, made uncomfortable by the sudden profusion of the spinally injured. It takes time to acclimatise to such tragedy. In the infirmary I'd been the only one. Now we were surrounded.

During the coming days some patients dropped by, intrigued to find out who the new guy was. Affable and inquisitive, they wanted to know my story, compare the horror of what befell me with their own experience in a kind of benign spinal injuries one-upmanship. They carried their incidents with them like a cross, borne mostly with fortitude, but on occasion spilling out into dam-bursts of anger when grappling with tasks that would've been completed in a trice in their previous life.

To watch someone with impaired motor skills struggle is at once inspiring and deeply sad. What struck me as the days ticked into weeks was the unspoken ordinariness of the presence of, and need for, so many wheelchairs; it was a proper disabled car park.

The ward, then, bled with a resigned unity, and a bloody-mindedness infused with the darkest of humour. No one was spared the sledgehammer barbs and cutting ripostes that characterised a neurological Blitz spirit. Mentally I wasn't yet strong enough for these verbal sparring matches. I kept my distance and avoided eye contact, withdrawing into a televisual safety blanket.

It was a relief when I was on my back or, better still, facing the trees. I craved solitude, but whereas at the Royal Infirmary it'd been motivated by a sense of bleak finality, I now played the Greta Garbo as a way to fortify myself and prepare for the battle that lay ahead. I had to be strong in my head. I had to flush out all doubts, and seeing the other patients' struggles and hearing their outbursts was counterproductive. It felt shitty, but I blanked them out.

Supper arrived on the kitchen's heated wagon. A nurse collected my meal, brought it over and removed the plastic cover ready to feed me. She looked at the plate and frowned. The corned beef had evidently been a large pre-cut slab when it left the kitchen, about the size of a computer mouse mat. The chef – I learned to use the term loosely – had placed the slab over the chips, put the cover on, and placed it in the wagon. On its journey the corned beef had vanished, morphing into a pinkish, fatty sludge, as if a murder victim had been rendered in a bath of acid. Kitchen-wise then, nothing had changed from the infirmary. At least I still had the dependable Mr Kipling.

Chapter 5

It was morning and the ward was quiet, most of the patients having been wheeled off to physiotherapy or the gym. The cleaners had been and gone with their rhythmic swishing. The tea trolley had done its rattling round. The nurses were busy with the untold jobs that consumed their shift; it seemed they never stopped moving.

I felt safe at Rookwood. And hopeful. In the days since arriving, my mindset had experienced a tectonic shift, for the better. It was all so different. In the infirmary that flicker of partial movement in my right hand had mocked me; a burning reminder of all that I'd lost – everything. Death had mocked me too: 'Huh, so you escaped my clutches, for what?' And it had a point. Had I really clung to life lying on that pavement so that the fingers of one hand could move but not even make a gripping action?

Even when my shoulders had begun to rotate through excruciating pain – an undiagnosed broken shoulder blade was in the process of knitting itself back together – and I progressed to raising my arms a few inches into the air, was that it, I wondered? Would that be the extent of my recovery? And if that were my recovery then death would've been better, surely. After all, I was pretty much dead from the neck down, so why not from the neck up too?

As I lay there that morning though, my body with its broken bones was mending. The searing, wave-like surges of pain that'd radiated from the fractured pieces of me had eased to a bearable ache. The liquorice-black bruising that'd cloaked my neck, shoulders and upper back had faded to a blotchy purple. The core-rupturing shock of the accident had dissipated and I sensed an equilibrium of body and mind, a physiological coming to terms with and recovery from the violence of a near-death episode. I'd come through it. I'd survived.

The black dogs that'd run riot in the infirmary were padlocked in their kennel, for now. My private little wood with its chorus of bird and insect chatter contributed to a lighter mood. I breathed more deeply and thought brighter thoughts. I was building towards something momentous, something that I couldn't explain. It was a feeling unlike any I'd ever experienced. A sense of certainty filled me.

I was now able to ponder my lack of movement without sinking into troughs of despair as I'd done in the infirmary. It didn't panic me as it had. And yet I still couldn't move much, which just over two weeks on from the crash should've caused me great distress. But no, I was calm. Certainly, I was aware that it wouldn't be possible to build a future life around a flicker of partial movement in my right hand, restricted rotation of my shoulders and raising my arms up from the bed for a few seconds.

But whereas these pitiful remnants of a lost life had laughed at me in the infirmary, they were now divined as a positive sign. Rookwood made me positive. I believed it would happen, whatever 'it' was. Those billions of neurons, the building blocks of the nervous system, the connectors that crackle with instructions from the brain to the limbs were, I was convinced, waiting to be fired-up. The 'it', then, was recovery of movement.

Could faith alone make me move? No. There are no miracles, only verifiable scientific outcomes. Science and reason: it put an end to the burning of witches; Jesus didn't walk on water; Uri Geller couldn't will our broken timepieces to work again just by staring out of the television at us.

Limbs move when there is an uninterrupted neural connection between the brain and the extremity you wish to move. Simple. If a power cable is damaged or severed, things don't work. If the spinal cord is damaged or severed, things don't work. All the willpower in the world can't alter that. But that morning, and indeed all of the mornings since my arrival in Rookwood, there was a conviction that

I'd move, conveniently ignoring the fact I may have sustained damage to my spinal cord.

Part of the reason for this resurgent evangelism, of course, was my recognition of touch, the sensation of feeling. If I can feel I can move; that belief had been with me since the accident, though it'd been subsumed by despair during my time parked in the infirmary. It was a dangerous delusion, unscientific and without logic.

I'd learned in my chats with the young doc that sensory and motor nerves serve different masters. The former communicates touch, pain, extremes of temperature. They were functioning just fine, as witnessed by my voluble response to being pin-pricked. The motor nerves, on the other hand, move stuff. And I wasn't moving. Well, not much. It's possible to suffer a permanent state of paralysis yet sense you have cold feet. Feeling stuff doesn't necessarily mean moving stuff. It'd all been explained to me, yes, but I'd adopted a selective acceptance of facts, a kind of Stalinist sifting out of inconvenient truths; if it didn't fit my preferred narrative, it was erased from my consciousness.

It was a continuation of my mindset from school when I'd distrusted the certainty of scientific outcomes, much preferring history and English literature with its stories and characters and subjective interpretation. I was a dreamer. A fantastical dreamer too.

As a kid I possessed the power to move objects just by willing it to happen. At least, that's what I was convinced of. The absence of success in moving objects didn't deter me from honing my superpowers, although the powers, if they existed, didn't appear to be very super. Was I a weird child? Maybe, but surely part of the point of being a kid is to imagine the impossible and think it perfectly normal. Perfectly possible. So, I'd stare at Mum's ornaments – mementos of her and Dad's holidays to Spain – mentally charging like a dynamo to move a figurine along the mantelpiece. And I detected that same dormant gift as I lay there that morning, but rather than an inanimate figure of a shepherdess, it was my body I was determined to move. The time had come to reclaim 'it'.

I readied myself, disconnecting from the background hubbub, leaving the white noise of the ward behind. Nothing was to disturb me. Cleansing my mind, I fell into a trance-like state that we might call mindfulness these days. Slow, deep breathing. Focus. Emptiness. No thought, except to move. I sank deeper and deeper, visualising the neural pathway that connected my brain to the outer reaches of my body, sensing those extremities building a charge, awaiting an instruction to flex. To move. I was ready. Primed.

My brain fired off the instruction to the big toe of my left foot; as good a digit as any. The instruction, containing all my future Christmases in one, left my brain and crackled down the spinal cord like a burning fuse. The circuit was being tested. What would win? Science or faith, or perhaps both.

It fizzled along those charged neurons, down the communications cable that ran within my interlocking vertebrae, searching out the big toe of my left foot. I begged that toe to move. I needed that toe to move. Move, I said to myself. Just fucking move. I waited. Nothing happened. Was that it? It couldn't be. I'd invested too much mental capital to fail. And after all, I'd felt 'it'. Part of me didn't want to try again, terrified of repeating nothing. Try again later, I thought. Or tomorrow. But I was in too deep to postpone another attempt and so readied myself once again, willing that toe to move. *Move*, damn it.

And... it moved. It brushed against the sheet. I felt it. I felt the friction, thanks to those functioning sensory nerves. Flooded with adrenaline, I doubted what'd happened. Did it move? Well, yes, I felt resistance against the sheet. But, was it an involuntary muscle spasm? Or rather, was it bad luck, my body playing a cruel practical joke on me?

My faith-soaked certainty had much in common with voodoo, I expect. But I'd asked my toe to move and after a couple of goes it had. There was only one thing for it. I rebooted and fired off another impulse. It moved. The big toe of my left foot moved, again. Three times I'd asked it to and twice it'd obeyed. Twice! Scientifically, this experiment was achieving a measure of veracity. Maybe science wasn't so bad after all.

Again, I willed it. And again, it moved. Proven beyond doubt. I could move my left big toe on command. There was a connection. The pathway was intact. At least to the big toe of my left foot. Proportionally it was a miniscule part of my body but it was a beautiful development. And the toe felt big, enormous, as magnificent as Everest!

A prickly sweat cloaked me as I absorbed the fact that the furthest extremity of my body had responded to a neurological instruction to move. 'It' had happened. I bellowed a euphoric 'Yes!' and lay there bathed in an enormous smile. At last, we had a start, we had hope. I say 'we' as this was bigger than just me.

On hearing my exclamation, a nurse came to my bed.

'Everything okay, David?'

I asked her to lift the sheet to reveal my left foot. With a begrudging acquiescence – she had other more pressing matters to attend to – she did as I asked.

'Is that all?' she said, half turning away.

'No, wait… please. Just watch.'

'Watch what?' she said, folding her arms. 'I'm actually quite busy.'

'Sorry… yeah, I know. Just ask me to move the big toe of my left foot.'

She asked. It moved.

'Bloody hell! Do that again,' she said.

I did.

'Good God, you moved your toe. Brilliant.'

She couldn't have looked happier if she'd just been introduced to her first grandchild. After a celebratory fist pump – hers, not mine – she rushed off to inform some of her colleagues, returning with Julie, and a young nurse whose name I can't recall but who I fancied like mad. I dreaded this particular nurse giving me a bed bath and I don't need to explain why; remember, I could feel things.

'Go on then,' said Julie. 'Let's see.'

I moved it.

'Wow. That's cracking,' she said.

The young nurse smiled. 'Won't be long till you're on your feet,' she said. She reminded me of the girl from Trecwn and, as with the girl from Trecwn, I blushed whenever she was anywhere near me.

'Better go and give your mum and dad a call then,' said Julie.

They melted away to continue their labours, smiling at having witnessed a manifestation of hope, a rare nugget of good news on a ward littered with dying faith. It was a start, a tentative beginning to what promised to be a Herculean endeavour – to reclaim the physical me. A toe that moved was a prize indeed.

Mid-afternoon Mum and Dad cantered in, flushed and breathless, having driven up the motorway at perhaps a quicker pace than usual. They pulled up two chairs and sat either side of the bed radiating a Ready Brek glow of unbridled joy. They could hardly speak, such was their welling-up at the news of a miracle which indeed felt worthy of Lourdes; they hadn't bought into the science stuff either.

'Well, let's see it, then,' begged Mum.

The toe duly performed a star turn. She cried tears of relief, laughing as she dried them. Dad's eyes became a touch cloudy too.

They changed that day, as did I. In the realms of metaphor, it was but one very small step on what would be a long and emotional journey. But hope had sprung, offering a glimmer of a future that maybe hadn't figured in any prognoses to date. We had a start.

Chapter 6

Dusk encroached, wrapping up a hot day. Hot for March, at any rate. The window nearest my bed was open, with the air blood-thick, as a cacophony of birdsong bid farewell to the diminishing light. *Coronation Street* wasn't engaging me and I couldn't change channels as I couldn't hold the remote, let alone depress the buttons. And so, I shifted my gaze to the outside, and there, stepping softly, by the trees, was an angular reddish-brown shape; a fox.

A much-maligned creature, but so knowing and elegant. It stopped, raised its head and peered into the ward straight at me. For a few moments I felt connected to nature in a way that transcended any Attenborough documentary. This was real. This was there, right in front of me. I was enchanted.

Our respective situations couldn't have been starker: one creature with the freedom to roam staring at another manacled to a bed by his skull. I yearned to be that fox, to feel the swish of grass against my feet. It raised its nose, sniffed the air, then spun and disappeared into the trees – off to pad its suburban patch, to squeeze through fences and snuffle through suppertime bins.

I ached so much to be out there, to disappear amongst the trees and leave the place I was in, to head off on an adventure. It didn't matter where. I just wanted to go. When my body had worked, I hadn't acknowledged how incredible that bio-mechanism was and now that it didn't, I prayed for that ease of movement, the joy of being able.

Breakfast, the next morning, was concluded with no pining for an encore. The word breakfast, the mere ceremony of breakfast, conjures up heartening notions of a new day and its endless possibilities.

A Rookwood breakfast was borne with stoicism and, more often than not, cud-like chewing. I bolstered myself with a cherry bakewell, administered by an indulgent nurse, and awaited the shaming ritual of the bed-bath.

Julie arrived with a bowl of warm soapy water, a cloth and a towel. My bed doubled as a toilet cubicle, which, combined with the unseasonal heat, was proving to be a nasal challenge, both for me and anyone that came within the vicinity.

'Let's get you freshened up, lovey,' she said, beaming with a self-affirming joy that came from doing a job she loved.

'Yeah, getting a bit whiffy,' I replied, buoyed by her huge smile.

She pulled the curtains and went to work, starting at the top with the fresh soapy water and working her way down to the bottom half, where things got grubbier; a bit like washing a car. All the while she chatted away, which contributed to my brightening mood.

'Can't believe it's March,' she said. 'Derek and me went down Penarth last night. Lovely, it was. Walk along the front. Fish and chips on the way home. Cracking.'

For all her thunderous proportions she seemed to possess inexhaustible stamina, her work rate outstripping that of her younger, slenderer, colleagues.

'Julie.'

'Yes, lovey?'

'Who's that that shouts? Like they're in pain. Or angry?'

It'd bugged me since my arrival. The verbal torrents, the almost animal-like yelps, came from somewhere over my left shoulder, a way down the ward.

'That'll be Tom. Has no one told you about Tom?'

'No.'

She straightened from the task, chucking the flannel in the bowl.

'Tom's been with us… oh, let me think.' She put a forefinger to her temple, as if to extract the information. 'Yeah, must've been late sixties he had his accident…'

'What, his late sixties?'

'No, sorry. Late 1960s. About fifteen years ago. Remember him coming in,' she continued. 'And yep, he complains alright. Hates being turned over, that's his problem. Boy, he gives it to us.'

Tom was knocked off his moped on his way home from work one night in Cardiff and left in the gutter with neck injuries. He didn't recover any movement from the level of the injury down and when he was ready for discharge he had nowhere to go, as his parents couldn't cope with his care needs, so, he became resident in the ward, in a state of perpetual limbo. Fifteen years later Tom was still there and would be till the day he died.

'The physios will be here soon to stand him up for a while,' she said. 'Get his blood circulating. Won't like that, I can tell you!'

She wrung out the flannel and continued.

'Stand? But he can't move,' I said.

She chuckled, 'Sorry. Should've explained. They have this tilting board thingy, you see. They strap him onto it and tilt it upright. Hates it, he does, at first, then after a while he gets used to it and he's calm as anything.'

I was still trying to compute the time he'd served; most murderers got less.

'And he's been here, in this ward, for fifteen years?' I asked.

'Yep, poor bugger's known nothing else. But I have to say, besides the shouting he's happy as anything. Honest.'

To have learned of Tom's fate when I arrived from the infirmary weeks earlier would've been terrifying; the prospect that I too might've become a resident. But bits of me were beginning to move and I was confident of a full recovery. In fact, I contemplated nothing but a return to the old me.

'Right. Top half done. Now the crown jewels,' said Julie, with an off-duty wink.

This was the point where the bed bath unravelled, where having sensation, an acknowledgement of touch, was a curse. For an eighteen-year-old, having his penis vigorously buffed with a warm soapy flannel will invite a rush of blood south. She began and I stared at the ceiling, frantically trawling repellent mental imagery to staunch the migration of blood: hectoring speeches by Margaret Thatcher; the appalling ventriloquist Keith Harris and his Orville; the terrifying TV cook Fanny Craddock and her hapless Johnny. But it was all to no avail as the blood just kept gorging. Even Julie's aging, sagging appearance was no bar to its popping up. Every morning, I braced myself and every morning I glowed crimson with embarrassment, regardless of the one doing the buffing.

'Well, no need to ask whether that's working, eh!' she said, reprising her end-of-the-pier cackle.

Deep down there was a penile pride. It did indeed work. Lucky me. But I bemoaned my misfortune that my adolescent erectile adventures at the hands of a woman took place in a spinal injuries' unit in Cardiff. No sticky fumbling at a house party in Fishguard. No body-part-braille games at midnight in the back seat of a car down Broad Haven beach. And certainly not in my bedroom at home with my parents nudging up the volume on the telly to drown out any rhythmic creaking from above. No, my introduction to handjobs, albeit in a professional capacity, took place on a hospital ward, administered for the most part by post-menopausal or, worse, male nurses. No, even worse again, was the nurse I had the hots for, as she just giggled.

With the ward breakfasted and washed, the physiotherapists and their assistants came to spirit patients away. A convoy of wheelchairs exited, some under the steam of their occupants, others pushed. And amongst them was the walker. He said hello as he passed my bed but he'd never stopped to have a conversation. In fact, I never saw him in conversation with anyone. He was unfailingly polite and had the warmest smile but it was as if he were ploughing a lone furrow; a sense perhaps that he felt embarrassed by his good fortune, surrounded as he was by so many unresponsive limbs. It was strange to imagine that his recovery may've been a burden to him.

The ward's miracle, he was enveloped by a huge wheeled frame, seemingly designed by Brunel such was its robust engineering. And out he went, not so much walking as consciously placing one foot in front of the other at a pace which wouldn't have outrun a tortoise. I was mesmerised, as the physios shadowed his every painstaking, deliberate, brave step, ready to jump in if he stumbled, and beaming with pride at their walker. They were proud of all of the patients' bloody-minded determination to claw back as much functionality as possible, eke out every last muscle fibre of movement, but the walker represented the pinnacle of neurological redemption. It was as good as it got. And for him it would only get better.

I believed that I too would follow in his footsteps. The longed-for tide of movement was trickling back into those muscular tributaries that'd been arid for many weeks. Since the miracle of the big toe, more of my periphery had begun to wake. I had a range of movement in my left foot, drawing weak restricted circles under the sheets with the big toe as a pointer. The right foot was twitching into life too. My arms were rising higher from the bed and I could hold them in the air for what seemed ages – a few seconds – before they flopped down onto my chest.

I woke each morning as if it were Christmas, eager to discover what wondrous gift of partial recovery had been left in the night. Muscle groups would flex a little more than the previous day, while other groups that'd been dormant would come to life as if Arthur's knights were awakening from their slumber to rescue me. I still cried, but now the tears were for a rediscovered faith that all would be fine. I cried with relief.

My spinal cord was not severed. That didn't mean it wasn't damaged, though that consideration was purged from my mind. I told myself that when the traction came off in a few weeks, I'd alight from bed, phoenix-like, put my trainers on and go for a quick jog around the grounds before breakfast. My fox days were imminent.

I'd just endured another Michelin-starred supper: an anaemic salad of iceberg lettuce, cucumber and an unripe tomato, firm as a cricket ball. A stale bread roll accompanied this inglorious hint of summer and, to complete the palette of culinary indifference, a rubbery ingot of Cheddar remained inaccessible in its plastic packaging. It'd even defeated the nurse tasked with feeding me.

Then, my evening got better. Denis, my line manager from Trecwn – or, to give him his official designation, Stores Officer Grade D – appeared by the side of my bed.

'Hi boy. Don't mind me dropping by?' he said.

'Fuck me, Denis. This is a nice surprise.' And I meant it. I liked Denis. 'Don't mean to be rude, but what you doing here?'

'One of those bloody work courses. Staying at a B&B in Cathedral Road. Thought I'd take a stroll. Come and see you.'

His voice had a melodic cadence, like a finely tuned engine shifting effortlessly up and down the gears.

'Do us a favour, will you? Get that fucking cheese out,' I said, pointing at it with a floppy arm.

He laughed and tore the packaging open, and I instructed him to place it in my mouth. Each night of the week-long course he walked the four-mile round trek, arriving at seven o'clock and sitting for an hour. He wasn't a friend. He wasn't even a close work colleague on account of hierarchy. But he'd trudge there to keep me company, bearing gifts of grapes, Maltesers or some other offering. He'd bring a newspaper and, when conversation stalled, he'd flick through and divulge what was going on in the outside world. And he was there because I was there.

'So, just starting, *Top of the Pops*?' he said, scanning the TV schedule.

'Go on then.'

He reached over and put the telly on. Nena, a compact German lady with builders' armpits, was belting out some homage to ninety-nine red balloons. It was a terrible song, but I cherished those connections with life outside the ward, if only to remind me that I'd be released back into it at some point.

Denis glanced at the headline on the front page.

'Huh... Thatcher's bitten off more than she can chew with the miners,' he said. 'Scargill can smell blood... her blood.'

The National Union of Mineworkers were on strike and their leader, Arthur Scargill, seemed determined to bring down the Thatcher government. A miners' strike ten years earlier had been cause for excitement, with candles on the coffee table in Bradford during power cuts, sitting between Mum and Dad on the settee. This new strike brought with it the prospect of power cuts again, which, seeing as I was lying helpless and vulnerable in a hospital bed, didn't have quite the same appeal. It was to be a bitter dispute,at times more like a medieval feud as I watched TV coverage of the ferocious battles between the strikers and the police. It rumbled on for a year before the miners were finally routed.

Before his heroics of companionship on that ward Denis had stood out in Trecwn as being different to the other inmates, most of whom shuffled along with a lethargic gait as if debilitated by some radiation leak from a faulty reactor. Even opening their lunchboxes seemed an effort for some. Denis, though, had presence and charm. I've no idea whether he'd been in the forces, but he strode with a rod-straight back, his shoulders squared. He was also well-dressed, which was anathema to your traditional Trecwnite, often clad in what appeared to be demob clothing from the 1940s. Some, I suspect, were still dressed by their mothers.

I had run-ins with Denis, of course. My resentment at being in Trecwn manifested itself in wilful inactivity and skiving; he once found me asleep in the drying room. Sickies were another unofficial perquisite that I took full advantage of, until Denis deduced a pattern to my sick days. Afterwards, I was more randomly unwell. He tried to motivate me, but I was a lost cause. I often wondered what he was doing in Trecwn. Perhaps he did too. But there he was, sat by my bed. I missed him when his course ended.

Another visitor was a man that I idolised and who'd had a formative influence on my early adolescence. When I was twelve a new milkman began delivering to Masefield Drive, where I lived: John Roberts. We got chatting in the street one morning at the beginning of the school holidays and he asked if I'd like to help him on the round. A lazy kid, I surprised myself by saying yes. Those were the days when adults were viewed as benign mentors to the young unlike today's default where any interest in children must by definition involve questionable motives. Without any police checks I met him early one morning to become a 'junior' milkman. And his trust in me was demonstrated early on when he asked if I'd like to drive the float.

'Me, drive the float? Yes please,' I replied, wide-eyed.

The round was an adventure. I loved it so much that I'd even forgotten about my troubles at school. The other boys on the estate eyed me with envy, trying to elbow me aside and take my place but it was to no avail. John and I were solid. I'd be up before the rest of the house and out running to meet the float. We were two free spirits, renegades, cowboys. It was freedom. There'd be a bag of Chelsea buns from a bakery, as much milk as I could guzzle, and all rounded off with a bacon sarnie midday in a café before heading back to the depot to offload the empties. He'd drop me back home with another pound note to add to the pot I was accumulating from my labours.

We had a shared passion, too: boxing. I'd gone to the local club since I was eight and John had boxed in his youth. When there was a big fight looming – Sugar Ray Leonard, Roberto Duran, Thomas 'Hitman' Hearns – we'd weigh up their chances and the next time we were out there'd be the post-fight analysis. On the milk round there was a cul-de-sac of OAP's bungalows and we'd often entertain the residents with a sparring match on a patch of grass.

'Keep your guard up boy. And watch that left hook of his,' the old boys would bellow. The women squirmed and covered their eyes, begging him to take it easy on me.

'I'm training him up,' John would say, 'Boy's got potential.'

The old men nodded sagely in agreement as I was inflated with dreams of glory.

At fourteen, though, the novelty of rising early on a Saturday had waned, the round being no competition for the hormonal indolence of a teenager. I jacked it in and took a cushier number two evenings a week in a bakery where Mum worked part-time. Better money, as many cakes as I could eat, and a black-market trade in the contents of the confectionary cupboard; I was entrusted with the key to restock the shop. I'd wear flared jeans and knee-length socks into which I stuffed a dozen or so bars to hawk at school. What really quickened the pulse, though, were the inexpertly hidden top-shelf magazines. I curated a precious collection which I hid under a loose floorboard, under the carpet, beneath my bed; bit of a rigmarole to access when the fancy took me.

One Sunday I was laid on the living room floor watching James Bond on the telly. Mum was behind me on the settee knitting. Dad was in his armchair reading the paper. I heard Andrew come into the room.

'Look what I found in his bedroom,' he said, with smug authority.

I heard something, or some things, being chucked on the floor, and turned to see my prized collection of all my favourite women strewn across the carpet. Laziness had done for me; I'd taken to hiding them in my wardrobe instead – not very well, it seemed.

John, though, was the first adult male I became close to who wasn't related and he couldn't hide his heartbreak at seeing that contraption attached to my skull. I reassured him I'd be fine, with the performing left foot putting in a star turn amongst other body parts.

My brother Andrew wasn't neglected exactly, but he was certainly relegated in the pecking order. Everything was about me. In those first few weeks there was the suffocating disbelief at what'd happened and the grim prognosis of possible permanent paralysis. Then when I began to move, the talk – the obsession – revolved around miraculous recoveries or at least an acceptable level of recovery compared to the original doom-laden projection. I was inclined towards the miraculous end of the spectrum, of course – jogging before breakfast.

Andrew had just turned fourteen, a delicate age in any boy's life. Things happen at fourteen, things beyond your control. Those bubbling hormonal volcanoes can have a destabilising effect. Just when he needed the guidance and stability of the parental tiller, a rock to lash himself to, Mum and Dad were being tossed on their own stormy seas. In the early uncertain days after the accident Andrew was shunted off to relatives, often disappearing only to be found outside of our locked-up house.

His first visit to Rookwood was awkward. The enormity of what'd happened was perhaps on a scale he couldn't comprehend or perhaps didn't wish to think about. There was small talk, distracted glances out of the window and gentle coaxing from Mum and Dad. I felt sorry for him. He didn't know what to say. Why would he?

I remember the warm confusion of my first ever sight of him. Mum opted for a home birth, not unusual in the Bradford of 1970. Dad drove me across town to stay with my aunty Ruth, his sister, till the deed was done. On my return there was a carrycot in the living room. I was encouraged to go over and take a peek and there he was, a cherubic Andrew.

At eleven pounds there was a hint of gigantism and, indeed, Mum was worn out and battered by the ordeal. He was a big baby who grew into a huge kid. His angelic smile, golden locks and brown eyes like saucers belied a deep well of mischief which he plumbed on a regular basis. One peculiar trait was the cramming of earth into his mouth; it became imperative that we kept cats out of the borders. From toddling onwards, he was physically reckless, often tottering in from the garden, or further afield, bloodied. Injuries that would've brought hysterics from other children warranted little more than a momentary grimace from Andrew.

He appeared in the lounge one evening, blood streaming from his forehead, dripping from his chin onto a new carpet. There was a low stone wall separating our semi from next door. He'd run towards it, tripped just short and collided head-on. He was three years old, as he stared at us, not crying. Dad rushed him to hospital for stitches, which again, were administered with no tears.

We fought, of course. That's what brothers do. Or at least that's what you persuade yourself brothers do when you have dominance. Fighting's enjoyable when you know you can't lose. The misery of secondary school had fostered a meanness in me, as I gave no quarter.

But as Andrew hit his teens, the five years between us shrank in physical terms and in the period before my accident I'd begun to acknowledge a grudging respect for his strength and the increased frequency with which he was putting me in my place. As my dominance leached away the notion of truces became more appealing. Standing by my bed, we knew our battles were over. He may not have wanted it to end the way it had, but he'd won the war.

Chapter 7

Being aware of what day it is is of little consequence after a couple of months of lying in a hospital bed. The marking of time is an irrelevance as you drift from one day to the next. After all, it wasn't like I had any pressing commitments. I had no work to go to. No date with a girl. Nothing. But the telly was as good a marker as any and the opening credits to *Sportsnight* meant it was a Wednesday. Best of all, it was a fight night. And not any ordinary fight night. Barry McGuigan, featherweight champion of Europe, was taking on Jose Caba, a highly rated South American, in an eliminator for a crack at the world title. I'd been counting down the hours all day.

It was a huge fight for the Irishman: win and the world opened up with all the promise of a Knightsbridge safety deposit box; lose and he'd have to claw his way back to contention again. And so, *Sportsnight* and the clubbable Harry Carpenter – comfy as a worn Hush Puppy – transmitted the fight live from The Kings Hall, Belfast. For many weeks my life had been mote-watchingly dull but with the fight I had something to get excited about, aside from my feet, arms and legs moving a bit. Only a bit mind. Still, not an insignificant development, considering that initial prognosis. I was just waiting on the hands to start up now.

The master of ceremonies schmoozed through the preliminaries like a door-to-door salesman as I waited impatiently for the fight to start. I did clock that the referee was a certain James Brimmell from Cardiff, though, which felt immediate. The bell for the first round went and McGuigan bounded from his corner, a determined slab of white teak. A pattern of dominance soon emerged, and as the rounds progressed the Irishman's unremitting front-foot jab, jab, jab took its toll on Caba. In the fifth, McGuigan sensed an end and delivered the knockout.

Savouring the fight, memories of my own boxing club nights came flooding back. The wicker casket full of sparring gloves, clammy from a thousand sweaty palms and alive with the testosterone stench of decades of rounds. The dull thud of fists buried in punchbags and faces. Skipping ropes circumnavigating boys like blurred rotor blades and the loose-boarded ring clunking and flexing under dancing feet.

I was friends with a boy called Wayne and his dad Eddie ran the club – a large shed in a field – which I joined when I was eight. I fancied myself as a prospect to begin with but it became apparent that I was hamstrung by a fundamental flaw; when an opponent threw a punch, I closed my eyes. They were happy days, getting fit and getting punched.

At the age of fifteen, though, my boxing club nights came to an end. Sparring with one of the rougher kids, I took a punch to the mouth. My jaw jarred, I tasted blood, waved my arms in submission and climbed from the ring. I was busy checking how many teeth he'd loosened when he came over and whispered in my ear, 'We'll finish this in school.'

A cold fear speckled my neck – I didn't like fighting without rules. With his fellow delinquents he'd been having digs at me for months at the club. The odd push in the back, or a hissed 'fucking wanker' as he brushed past. As promised, he hunted me in school, aching for a rematch, and I kept slipping the net till one day he squared up in the corridor, surrounded by his braying associates. There was nowhere to go. 'I'm gonna fuckin' kill you,' he seethed. Not subtle, but at least I knew what was coming: a fight. Without rules.

He came at me fists flailing like some manic threshing machine while I put my guard up, opting for Ali's rope-a-dope strategy – let him punch himself out or, better still, cling on till a teacher could rescue me. Quickly. Hedgehog-like I curled into myself to deflect the attack, punches peppering my arms and the back of my head. I sensed a ratcheting humiliation, with the assembled throng lapping up the unrequited pummelling. He was in his element, dancing around hitting me at will, showboating to the only adulation he'd ever drink in.

Boredom must've been setting in, as he shouted, 'Fight back, you fuckin' shit.' There was only so much shame that even a coward like me could take, and at long last, something inside of me snapped. I clenched my fists as if to squeeze every last drop of blood from my palms, straightened and looked into those hateful glass-hard eyes. With volcanic anger I threw the punch, hard and direct, depressing the centre of his lean, pinched face. It was a beautiful connection. Before he could regain composure, I bolted forward, got him in a head-lock and constricted so hard I imagined his head might plop off. There were choking sounds which I found reassuring.

At that moment, a voice bellowed from along the corridor.

'Stop fighting. Stop right now.'

A teacher was metres away, pushing through the tight crowd. Our eyes met and he relaxed, convinced our mutual gaze comprised an understanding it was over. That I should disarm. But I hadn't exacted anywhere approaching my pound of flesh. I knew what was coming; a caning. So, as in the days of Georgian capital punishment, 'better to hang for a flock than a lamb', I thought. I drew my arm back and thrust one final piece of retribution into his clamped face.

'Wilson. I told you to stop,' the teacher said, shaking his head.

The caning was more savage than on previous occasions, my act of defiance contributing, no doubt. But I was gorged with pride. My tormentor, on the other hand, looked vulnerable with his artless crew cut, sallow expression and defeated eyes. After years of shit from various quarters, I'd done something. I'd stuck up for myself.

When word got around, I garnered a slither of respect for my feat of martial honour, my usual oppressors taking a step back, wary that maybe I wasn't the pushover they'd come to disdain. They dropped the physical stuff, opting for a verbal war of erosion instead. I could handle that.

John, the milkman, would've watched the McGuigan bout and it triggered in me a remembered joy of the milk round and our love of the big fights. On Saturday nights Mum and Dad headed to the club for their fix of the high life while I got a can of coke and box of Maltesers from the fridge and readied myself in front of the telly, the fights beamed in from America, usually Vegas. Pre-fight I'd shadow box around the lounge, with fancy footwork and blurred combinations, visualising my tormentors from school being pummelled, and getting my heart rate and endorphin levels to a crescendo in time for the first round. Between rounds I'd pump out sets of fifty press-ups with metronomic regularity and at great speed; I wasn't a physically imposing teenager but I excelled at the press-up. If it'd been a sport, I'd have been a name!

The boxer I most liked to imagine myself as was Thomas Hearns – 'The Hitman'. Overshadowed, perhaps, by his adversaries Sugar Ray Leonard and Marvin Hagler – all-time greats – Hearns, who fought out of the Kronk gym in Detroit, was a gangly and unorthodox fighter, seemingly ill-suited to the ring, yet when he unleashed combinations, his explosive power was utterly destructive – just walking onto a jab put opponents on the canvas. There was an insouciant swagger to him that I found mesmerising and he's the only boxer in history to have won world titles at five different weight categories, accruing fifty pounds of muscle mass during a very long career.

My parents would roll in, Dad tanked up with sweet Tetley breath, Mum with a radiant vodka and orange smile. Watching telly on the ward often kindled memories of the before me, which didn't necessarily make me happy. The recent past – my press-up past – was very touchable, and it hurt.

The ward was populated, for the most part, by young males; females could be thankful for the lack of equality. A momentary lapse of concentration, an ill-advised show of bravado, or just plain bad luck, was all it took to line up a lifetime of regret. I was aware that my apparent reprieve from the netherworld of paralysis was being noted by my fellow patients. Most bits of me moved. There was little strength and the movement was patchy, but I moved. How much more functionality I'd recover and how much stronger I'd become was an unknown.

On occasion I'd catch someone glancing my way, with a particular look in their eyes, a yearning that they too might experience some form of divine intervention. Hope: it hung in the air like a mirage. Others cruised by in their wheelchairs with a casual deliberation.

'Seen the legs going,' they'd say.

'Yeah, moving a bit,' I'd reply, trying to downplay my good fortune.

'That's great. Well done,' they'd say, in the same way you might congratulate a soon-to-be ex-work colleague on a huge lottery win. 'So, what did it feel like? You know, just before they started to move. Were there any signs?'

'Nah... just kind of happened.'

My prevarications couldn't douse their persistence, desperate as they were to correlate a shared feeling, some sensation, an inevitability of their own recovery. And why wouldn't they? If it could happen to me then surely it could happen to them. They were just as deserving. Deserving didn't come into it, though. It was high-stakes roulette, pure chance. I'd sustained dreadful damage to two vertebrae in my neck, yet it seemed I was being, if not spared exactly, then at least offered that precious glimmer of hope.

The medical opinion now deemed that my spinal cord was at worst partially damaged, although I believed it to be intact. Others on the ward who'd had their incidents earlier than me had, it seemed, sustained total or partial loss of the use of whole swathes of their bodies, for ever; legs and sometimes arms too. Imagine that: withered muscle and dense bone dangling from your torso, performing no function except to make your life so very much harder. Limbs are heavy when they don't help. They'd spend the rest of whatever life they had with an albatross of twenty or forty or more percent of dead body to lug around.

For their sakes, then, I exercised restraint, and reined in my exuberance. They had enough to contend with without witnessing me and my flashy limbs. I avoided moving when facing the ward, only releasing bursts of activity when the coast was clear or when I was turned towards the window. Towards the window was my private gym where I could smile and be thankful and move. I knew then why the walker kept to himself; he wanted to be invisible.

With the passage of time the faces of those I encountered, patients and staff, have faded like an old photograph. They're lost to me. But a tiny stellar cast remains as vivid as if it'd all happened yesterday; lucid and concrete. And of all the brave people I encountered, Dan is the one that burns most brightly. I close my eyes and he's there, forever young.

Like me, Dan was dealt his black hand through motorbikes, his accident occurring just before Christmas 1983. He was thrown from the bike, but such was his determination to remain with the machine he'd clung like hell to the handlebars with his right hand. He broke his back, but the grim resolve to hang on also shredded the nerves of his right arm from their juncture in the neck. The result was complete paralysis from the waist down and the loss of the use of his right arm.

His wheelchair had special gearing which enabled him to propel himself along using just his left arm while his right rested limp and Kaiser-like in his lap. He was a year or two older than me, and possessed of an ascetic saint-like drive. He'd stop for a chat, always measured and economical in his conversation, as if every impulse, every thought process was absorbed with some flinty resolve to eke out every last muscle fibre of power from that good arm. That arm was all he had to get him through the rest of his life. He was the most determined person I ever met.

April's fuse burnt itself out and my bed was turned to the more customary position, feet first into the central aisle of the ward. A new patient was due and they needed to create space. My dream of seeing the fox return, then, was over. As lunch approached the new addition to purgatory was delivered. Lying on my back I couldn't get a visual fix but went through the chirpy formalities of a threadbare welcome.

'Hi. My name's David.'

There was a pause as he no doubt tried to muster a reciprocal bonhomie, not easy when your life's been obliterated.

'I'm Jim.'

He groaned the groan of the defeated, my cue to leave him alone.

That afternoon, turned on to my left side, I got my first view of Jim. He was on his back, his profile confirming my earlier assumption of his age; languishing somewhere in his late fifties, grey and creased.

'Sorry about earlier,' he said. 'Wasn't in the mood.'

'It's okay, Jim. Don't worry.'

We talked, struggling to find a connection other than our mutual misfortune. The elephant in the room. He told me what happened.

'...so, I was leaving the party and fell down the bloody stairs. Can you believe that? Fell down the stairs. And here I am. Buggered.'

He bristled with anger and incredulity that he could've been so luckless. It gave him ward-wide novelty value, mind; there were no other stair fallers amongst us.

'You like boxing, David?'

The question came out of nowhere, direct and anomalous.

'Err, yeah, love it.'

'See Barry McGuigan couple of weeks back?'

'Yeah, what a fight. World title soon I think.'

'I was there. At the fight.'

'Really. Wow, lucky you.'

'Yeah, I was there alright. Refereed the damned thing.'

And so there he was: James – Jim – Brimmell, international boxing referee of repute. I never got a glimpse into the pre-trauma lives of the other patients. They came to me with varying degrees of paralysis, as if that's how they'd always been. But with Jim it was different. I'd witnessed him in his pomp, darting between McGuigan and Caba to break up clinches. And now he was lying feet away, incapacitated.

Chapter 8

'They're the vertebrae in your neck,' the radiographer said, pointing, while holding the x-ray up to a window. 'They're pretty well aligned. More importantly, they're stable. So, good news, traction's coming off.'

And that was it. The X-ray was conclusive. At last, after eleven weeks of lying on my back the traction was coming off. At times it'd felt more like eleven years. I was excited but also nervous at what lay ahead, as I'd find out what there was to reclaim from the wreckage. I was convinced I'd reclaim everything, of course, but I'd be lying if I said there weren't moments of uncertainty. Moments of doubt. Terror even. How else could it be when I was surrounded by so many incomplete recoveries.

Her assertion of the vertebrae in my neck being 'aligned' was putting a gloss on it, mind. From where I was lying, they resembled a stack of toddlers' building blocks placed haphazardly on top of one another. It wasn't pretty but it represented an acceptable resolution to two and a half months of having had Messrs Rainey & Crutchfield clamped to my skull.

The radiographer, almost as an aside, informed me of a broken shoulder blade that'd healed and damage to my lower spine suggestive of a break, which again had healed. These fractures were news to me, and indeed had been a bit of a surprise to the radiographer.

'You've knitted back pretty well, considering,' she said.

I'd been more smashed up then, than either myself or the medical staff had imagined. Already on this revised checklist of fractured bits was a damaged left elbow – not broken but rearranged – and two broken knuckles of my left hand, both injuries having been alluded to by a doctor at an earlier admission of medical oversight. I did wonder how so many broken bones could've been overlooked when I was admitted to A&E on the night of the smash, but they'd all fixed themselves as if by magic, so no need to complain.

I was computing the momentous event that was about to unfold – the removal of the callipers from my head – when the person appointed for the task appeared. Instantly, my blood ran cold. This supposed medical doctor stalked the ward like a spectre. To have called him a quack would've been an insult to quacks. Loathed and, even worse, feared by the patients, he lacked the fundamental qualities you might hope for in a doctor, that most noble of professions: empathy; a willingness to explain a procedure to a patient; and, above all, basic medical skill. 'Has he just walked in off the street and put a white coat on?' I often thought. Nurses whispered a litany of misdemeanours and complaints, none of which appeared to have impeded him. Even the first-day-at-med-school task of taking blood was a fraught exercise. In the weeks since arriving at Rookwood he'd jabbed syringes at my veins as if trying to harpoon a goldfish in a bucket, with a ferocity inappropriate to the delicate task in hand, and all executed with stony indifference.

He loomed over me and said, 'I'm taking the traction off.' And that was it, conversation over. He began to sigh as he fiddled with the screw-thread mechanism that released the two arms clamped into the holes drilled in my skull.

I felt vulnerable. For eleven weeks the staff had kept clear of the weights dangling over the end of the bed attached to the traction clamped to my head. The stretching action of the weights had, as hoped, coaxed the broken pieces of my neck into what were once again recognisable vertebrae.

There'd been just the one occasion, a week or two before, when a visitor to the patient next to me had managed to knock the weights, causing them to swing like a pendulum. It'd scared me, and angered me. I told them to 'be fucking careful', and they'd had the audacity to argue back and be affronted. So I told them to fuck off loud enough for a nurse to appear and ask what was wrong, at which point they skulked away. Now, though, I had Dr Death tinkering, which was far more terrifying.

He exerted force on the screw-thread mechanism. Nothing happened. He huffed and increased the force as my head began to rotate forwards, chin tilting towards my chest. I could hear his frustration at the mechanism's refusal to open as I sensed an increasing compression of my skull. It was apparent that instead of releasing the arms of the two callipers so that he could slide them clear of my head, he was tightening the mechanism, causing them to clamp even more.

'Whoa... whoa...' I yelped, with panic rising in my chest.

'What?' he barked.

'You're turning it the wrong way,' I shouted. 'It's anti-clockwise.'

I was frantic that he might undo eleven weeks of bone-knitting and in the process crush my skull.

With no glimmer of acknowledgement, he redirected his effort anti-clockwise and I felt the callipers release. With the contraption removed, he spun on his heels and was gone.

I was traumatised. It'd hurt. There was no saying it wouldn't have hurt with the attention of a sympathetic doctor but at least I'd have felt in safe hands. At least they'd have talked me through it. At least they'd have apologised for attempting to cause my skull to implode.

In his defence, though, he may have had other more pressing matters on his mind. Months after being discharged from Rookwood I was watching the Welsh evening news. And there striding out of the General Medical Council building in London, having been struck off for malpractice, was the vein-prodder cum skull-crusher-in-chief. The complaints had caught up with him. He may've lost his profession yet he still presented that same stony façade. Dispassionate to the last.

'Hi, David. I'm Sally, one of the physiotherapists. Come to see how you're doing.'

Her accent betrayed an upbringing down under, her pale, freckly skin doubtless relieved to have migrated to the northern hemisphere.

'Next couple of days, we'll be looking to get you sat up and then out of bed…'

'Sooner the better,' I said.

I ached to get my trainers on and get moving, walking, running.

'I like the enthusiasm, but you might feel a little woozy being sat up.'

'I'll be fine. Don't worry.'

It all sounded too incremental for my liking.

'Well, we'll see,' she said.

Sparky and assured, her tone made it clear I'd be going at her considered pace, not mine. 'Just going to tilt the bed up a bit… just a bit, mind… see how you feel.'

She grabbed the controls and began to tilt the bed upright. Having lain on my back for eleven weeks, my brain, internal mechanisms and blood circulation had got accustomed to horizontal rhythms. My world had been flat.

'How do you feel, David?'

I'd inclined about twenty, maybe thirty degrees. A whole new vista was revealing itself. It was exciting.

'Fine. Yeah, that's good,' I said, implying I could go much further.

Up I went.

'And now?'

My head began to swim, as a nauseous feeling welled up in the pit of my stomach.

'Good,' I said, with less conviction.

'You sure? Don't want to go too far.'

'It's fine. Go for it.' I wanted to get out of bed there and then, not a day or two later.

'Just a little more,' she said.

It was a tilt too far as my vision became shimmery and blurred, as if looking through a heat haze. I felt faint and about to vomit, then slid sideways. She caught me, preventing a fall out of bed.

'Too far. Sorry about that,' she said.

It was sweet of her to apologise for my stubborn pride. She lowered me back down.

'I can see you're itching to get going and that's great, but you'll have to be patient. You okay?'

'Yeah. Fine,' I said, demoralised by what felt like an immediate setback.

Then, like a wisp she was gone. I liked her. She was feisty and determined to help me on the most difficult journey of my life. I'd need people like her, people to push me, cajole me, not allow me to give up. Especially the giving up bit which'd always been a default position of mine.

The next day I was sat fully upright in bed, with pillows stuffed into my sides to provide support till my core strengthened – my midriff was a wobbly mush – and to prevent me from falling sideways. There was a bearable discomfort bordering on entry-level pain due to the fracture of my lower back, which'd healed after a fashion – two of the vertebrae had fused themselves together and so the bottom of my spine didn't appreciate being flexed into a sitting position. To support my neck, the muscles of which were weak, I wore a stiff collar. For all of the minor niggles it was great to be able to view the ward from a normal perspective.

This was when the hard graft began: nurses, physios, the whole gamut of the caring profession descended on me as if I were a special project. Like some benign mass mugging, a bombardment of exercises and tasks were thrown at me, anything to stimulate and fire up those muscles. There was to be no more reclining like some oriental potentate with every whim being catered for. The Sultan had work to do.

'Right, David, lunch'll be here soon. You're going to feed yourself today, okay?' instructed a nurse. It wasn't up for discussion.

I remember my first Action Man, when I was about six years old, with his moulded plastic hands. God, he was crap at holding stuff. Like him, the fingers of both my hands curled a little but I couldn't pick up or grip anything. So, how the hell was I going to hold a knife and fork, I thought. Lunch arrived. The holding-my-own-cutlery solution consisted of leather straps, one wrapped around each hand and fastened with Velcro, both with palm-side recesses into which a knife or fork could be slid.

The musculature and tendons of the human arm and hand are a marvel of evolutionary engineering. Electrical impulses and oxygenated tissue work in unison to perform tasks such as buttoning up a shirt, tying shoe laces, or operating the throttle, clutch and brake on a bloody motorbike. Or indeed, cutting up and forking food to your mouth. Then there's the opposing thumb and forefinger, an ingenious innovation which separates us from the apes. To pick up a grain of rice and in one sinuous action roll that grain around on to the nail of a forefinger and flick it away is incredible, the computing power required to replicate it inconceivable.

My computer, by the way, was functioning at optimum capacity; I hadn't sustained brain damage – thankfully. But what about the cabling – my nerves? The doctors were of the opinion that my spinal cord had, in all likelihood, been partially severed. Damaged. I was convinced otherwise. I was going to make a full recovery – of that I was certain. For the time being though, I had to have cutlery strapped to my useless hands.

Meals, then, were begun hot and finished cold. Ten minutes of corned beef and chips that'd once been forked in by a nurse now stretched to a frazzling half an hour by which time my arms hung by my sides, burning from the exertion. Cutting up food required levels of patience that'd always been elusive. Oh, and perseverance; I'd never persevered at anything either. The habitual laziness and lack of effort that'd been characteristic of my previous life had to change. I'd have to become the determined person I'd never been.

I took shortcuts when eating, stabbing huge lumps with the fork and shoehorning them into my mouth, like a python swallowing a goat. Once the big items were dispatched, I was left with those tantalising crumbs I used to finger-dab from around the plate after a meal at home. It was all too frustrating to even attempt.

Day by day the challenges ratcheted up at the spinal injuries boot-camp as I progressed to my trickiest food item to date: crisps. Julie opened a bag and spread them out on a table in front of me.

'Right, do your best, lovey!' She pinched a couple, of course.

Many of us may recall from our childhood the glass box in the amusement arcade with the grabbing steel claw, which always failed to lift and deposit some shitty faded toy down a chute. That's what my attempts at eating crisps resembled. Even when I managed to grip and raise a crisp, my wasted arm swung in mid-air like a crane in high winds, as I tried to direct the prize into my mouth. It took an hour of jaw-clenching determination and frequent rests to polish them off. But I did it. I was beginning to persevere.

'Well done,' said Julie, in the way you might offer encouragement to a spaniel at a dog agility class.

My life up until the evening of 16th February 1984 had lacked challenge. I'd been easy. Cosseted, even. What lay ahead, though, was daunting and not a little frightening.

Despite the gnawing frustration of every single damned thing being an effort, there was profound joy in partaking once again in the ritual of eating, to dictate my own rhythm, to pore over the selection and cutting and delivering of food to my mouth. I was beginning to feel a sense of normality return, to exist once again as a cog in the wider notion of society even if I was temporarily institutionalised. I was taking back control of my life.

There was a pressing hygiene issue that needed addressing: my long, matted hair, hadn't seen shampoo for eleven weeks. Eleven weeks of marinating in sweat. Eleven weeks of accumulated dead skin and coagulated blood from the holes in my skull. I imagined that I emitted a musky scent, an irresistible pheromone like some mythical beast from the deepest of Bavarian forests. In reality the stench was suggestive of five-day-old roadkill at the height of summer; putrid and retching. I stank. Even the flies seemed to be avoiding me.

The holes in my skull had scabbed over, and so I was plonked on a padded waterproof trolley and wheeled to the shower room for a shampooing as intense as any car wash. Doused by a delicious eternity of equatorial rain I was shampooed and rinsed, shampooed and rinsed, and shampooed and rinsed till the newly unscrewed bottle of Head & Shoulders was empty. The cleansing of grime and malodour was cathartic. I felt new and shiny, and able to face the world – or just the ward – without a miasma of rotting flesh circling my head.

I was transferred to a wheelchair for a more dignified, grand coiffed re-entry into the ward and on the way out of the bathroom came face to face with it; a mirror. And the mirror saw me, naked from the waist up. For a moment I was convinced that I must be studying someone else; a gaunt, pale, irregular stranger, bony and angular, their skin vacuumed to their ribcage. The apparition ran their fingers over the contours of those ribs and I saw that those fingers were mine. I saw that he was me and I broke inside. It shattered me. That torso, that other person, lacked symmetry. The left side was ravaged, with no chest muscle and a withered arm. The rest of him wasn't much better, stooped and bent like an old man. That was my body. It's what was left to me after eleven weeks of traction. Worst of all, I looked as you might imagine an irreparably damaged person would look like.

I could never claim to have been a sporty person – in that I hadn't excelled at a particular sport – but I'd had what could be considered a sporty physique. In truth, I'd been a bit of an exercise loner, going out to the garage on wet nights to lift and press and bench a bar of weights, with AC/DC blaring from a tape deck. There'd been a phase – if a few months could be described as such – of going for runs. And there'd always been a lord's prayer of fifty press-ups before bed. I'd kept fit for no other reason than fitness' sake and to look with pride in a mirror.

The summer before my accident, Martin and I had bombed down to the seaside resort of Tenby on our bikes. We sank a few ciders and strolled through the narrow bustling streets carrying our helmets, feeling golden. We arrived at South Beach.

'Let's go for a swim,' I said.

'We haven't got trunks,' said Martin.

'So what?'

We stripped down to our pants and ran into the sea.

'Race you out to the island,' I said.

St Catherine's Island, fifty metres out, looked Greek in that still blue sea. I got there first and clambered onto a rock. As I straightened, a girl, around my age, was standing nearby. She mapped me and smiled. She was cute and I smiled back. Just then, Martin emerged from the sea, muttering something about getting fitter. The girl smiled at me again, dived in, surfaced and glanced back before swimming slowly towards the shore. She liked me. I liked her. I should've dived in too and followed but I stayed with Martin; a dumb decision.

Looking in that mirror, the masculinity the girl had noted with approval was gone. And on the evidence, it wasn't coming back anytime soon.

Within days I'd regained enough strength in my arms to wheel myself to the bathroom in the mornings to wash and brush my teeth. Those tiny chores of daily life were necessary physical challenges. That mirror, though, was a cruel reflector of what I'd lost. I couldn't look at it and would stoop at the sink, determined not to catch a glimpse of myself, terrified of the misshapen ugliness that'd stare back. I had a long way to go.

Chapter 9

A physiotherapy assistant called Martin (there were a lot of Martins around in the '80s) appeared by my bed.

'Hi, David. Ready to go?'

'Yep, certainly am.'

I'd auditioned mentally for this moment for weeks, ever since the big toe of my left foot had moved. This was it. This was lift-off, the first instalment of Project Run. He transferred me to a wheelchair, gave it a brisk shove and we were off.

The tyres squealed along antiseptic-smelling corridors to the physiotherapy suite, arriving through double doors into a large, bright place, full of activity. I shifted my gaze left and right, glancing at the other patients, consumed with first-day-at-a-new-school nerves. I also felt conspicuous, as lots of me moved, though very weakly, and more was moving each day. Some halted their labours, giving me delving looks as if I'd entered some pub in a back-of-beyond village, while others flashed welcoming smiles and collegiate nods, confirmation that we were all in it together.

The room was dominated by two enormous, square, blue-padded platforms at seat height. Looking around, I noticed a set of parallel bars for those fortunate enough to have graduated to their feet. The 'walker' who I'd observed on the ward was striding purposefully back and forth along their length with just a brushing hand on the bars to steady himself. His recovery was going great guns and I was convinced I'd emulate him. Another patient was strapped upright in a wooden frame, designed to support paralysed patients in a standing position – good for the blood circulation, though his expression didn't belie any sense of beneficial joy. An array of exercise gizmos littered the floor, in a room kitted out for exertion and reeking of endeavour.

I recognised some faces from the ward. Dan nodded, busy fine-tuning one-armed transfers to and from his chair, a crucial skill if he were to have an independent future. Valleys' boy Terry, who'd cheered me when I'd been bedbound, was rolling sideways on one of the blue platforms, his dead legs twisting and flopping in his wake. Terry couldn't remember falling from the garage roof, only that he'd gone up to repair a leak. His wife visited most evenings, often bringing their two teenage kids. On discharge, weeks later, home for Terry would be a bungalow, not the terraced house the ambulance had been called to nearly a year earlier; he wouldn't be doing stairs any more. Then there was the well-to-do lady from mid-Wales who'd broken her neck falling from a horse. A physio was helping her to strengthen her right arm so that she could apply enough pressure to operate the joystick of her electric wheelchair. That was her goal. That, it seemed, would be her optimum outcome. There were patients from other wards that I didn't recognise, some of whom I'd come to know.

Spinal injuries constitute a communism of misfortune, with no discrimination between rich and poor; true inequality for all. Everyone in that room was consumed with their own private battle, desperate to extract every last drop of potential from their damaged bodies.

Martin wheeled me over to one of the padded platforms where my physio, Alan, awaited, kitted out in the department's uniform – a white polo shirt and blue tracksuit bottoms.

'So, how're you today, David?' he asked, with an evangelism that infused Rookwood.

'Bit nervous. Just want to start working on these,' I said, tapping my legs.

He beamed, 'Good, that's what we want to hear. First though, got to strengthen that core of yours. Sally says it's a bit weak.'

And so, it began. The odyssey. The struggle. That room and a separate gym I'd yet to be introduced to became my foundries of hope and despair. The person spat out the other end months later would be forged in those places. There were tears of relief when things went well and angered dejection when I hit a wall. Days when I felt biblically blessed, others cursed by demons of doubt and fear. But to start with I had to sit unsupported on a padded platform. Not walk or run or lift spleen-busting weights. No, I had to master sitting unaided like a six-month-old baby. It wasn't the auspicious beginning I'd dreamt of.

They lifted me from the wheelchair and swivelled me into a sitting position on the platform, holding me upright, with my knees bent, feet planted on the floor. I looked down at my legs which resembled sticks and swallowed hard at the realisation of what lay ahead.

'Right, David, Martin's going to let go and it'll be just me supporting you, okay?'

Alan stood square to me, his hands cupping my ribcage just below the armpits. 'I'm going to slowly move my hands away and see whether you can support yourself,' he said.

His Geordie accent was warm and reassuring, but I did wonder, impatiently, why all the fuss. Of course, I'd be able to sit unsupported. It'll take ages to get running at this rate, I thought. He removed his supportive embrace. I slumped sideways. He caught me.

'Don't worry, we'll soon get that sorted,' he said, looking at Martin and smiling.

So that was it. I couldn't even sit without support, never mind walk or run. There were more attempts at sitting unaided, with little success, then a demonstration of the restricted range of movement in my legs, and resistance exercises to determine how weak my arms were. They were very weak. I was wheeled back to the ward deflated.

That evening, I stabbed at my supper, imagining what dark disappointments may lay ahead. I'd gone to physio that morning floating on such bright hopes, ready to show off and exceed my wildest dreams, to become a star patient. From the moment the big toe of my left foot had moved, the projected narrative had been predicated on miracles and jogging before breakfast. After the morning I'd had, a jog might be a while in coming.

'Evening, lovey, how're you?'

'Hi, Julie.'

'Didn't fancy your supper then?' she said, glancing at the half-eaten meal.

'No.'

'What's wrong, lovey? Seem a bit flat.'

'Huh, went to physio this morning for the first time...'

'Great. How was it?'

'Not good.'

I wanted to tell her how terrified I was, since the physio session, of an incomplete recovery. But to have said it would've been to acknowledge it as a possibility. She pulled a chair up.

'Look, lovey,' she said, cupping my hand, 'it's going to be a long old haul. You're going to have to be patient.'

'I know. Doesn't make it any easier though.'

'Course it doesn't. But like I say, you have to be patient and hope for the best.'

'I know.'

'Anyway, you okay for me to have a look at that bladder of yours? Might as well sort it now, eh?'

'Oh, goody. That'll be fun.'

'That's better. That's the David I know. Back in a mo.'

I had to fight any negative tendencies, as there could be no regression to the bleakness of the infirmary. I had to believe. I had to be strong. It didn't stop me hearing those black dogs whining and scratching at the inside of the kennel door, though. As Julie had alluded to, and as I knew only too well, I had to recalibrate, adjust the pace of expectation. There wouldn't be a Christmas of huge leaps every day as I'd imagined. Indeed, it might be many weeks or even, God forbid, months before I ran again. I had to be patient. I also had to remember those on the ward who hadn't had the golden head-start that I had. She returned with the paraphernalia.

'Right, let's get this sorted then,' she said.

On the day the traction had been removed the catheter draining my bladder had been taken out. Having experienced no sensation of urinating and with no control over the discharge for eleven weeks, my bladder wasn't exactly watertight. Factor in possible nerve damage, and at the very least, initially, it was going to be a leaky ship; until I regained control of my sphincter, I'd piss myself.

The solution was an opaque plastic bag attached to my calf with a transparent hose leading from the bag and up the leg to my groin. A condom with the texture of a washing-up glove was rolled over my foreskin and secured to the shaft of my penis with an adhesive strip. An elongated cylindrical rubber chimney projected from the top of the condom into which the hose from the bag was inserted.

It wouldn't make for a good look in shorts but it allowed me the opportunity to discover whether my bladder responded to my neurological will without getting soaked. In other words, whether I had that necessary control. 'When you have an urge, hold it as long as you can. When you urinate, see if you can stop and start the flow,' I'd been told.

The concern was that my bladder may be spastic – a word I utterly loathed – meaning a lack of muscle tone, and hence control, due to nerve damage. Spastic bladders don't hold urine well or empty completely, tending to retain a residual puddle which risks infection; warm piss festers. And so, each night before winding down, a nurse catheterised me to drain any swamp-like residue and empty me properly. Patients whose bladders didn't empty to a sufficient degree, or at all, could remain permanently catheterised which in itself introduces a risk of infection from having the catheter changed on a regular basis; it's never a good idea to insert anything alien and potentially germ-laden into your body. I was concerned that my bladder may, in the long term, retain enough stale piss to warrant a permanent plastic tube stuck in me, or at the very least regular insertions to drain the swamp.

'Okay then, lovey, just injecting some lubricant. Sorry about this.'

A boy at school once confided in a friend that he'd experimented with inserting objects into his sphincter. His friend then informed the rest of the school, which was nice of him. I remember squirming so much on hearing this that I retched. How the hell could he? I thought.

Well, of late, I'd found out. With lubrication, the insertion of the catheter was bearable as Julie fed in the thin tube. I didn't look. When the tube reached the bottom of my penis, then proceeded to scrape through ninety degrees and up towards my bladder, I'd virtually jump off the bed. Just another procedure to tick off on my medical bucket-list of shit experiences. The tube was left in situ for a minute to drain the bladder then removed.

Julie said, 'That's not bad.' She showed me what she'd extracted.

'Not too much?' I asked.

'No. Bladder's emptying pretty much okay. Not completely, but plenty of time for it to improve.'

She bagged up the disposable gear and left me to the telly. Days later it was declared an unnecessary intrusion into my evenings. My bladder was emptying okay. Not perfect, but okay. There were to be no more inserted tubes.

Each morning, then, I was swooped upon and spirited away for physio and as the days progressed and I began to acknowledge improvements I looked forward to those sessions more and more. The usual group of patients would be spread around the room mining their recoveries, prospecting for that seam of gold, conscious of the hard-won progress of all, while single-mindedly focussing like hell on their goals. You've never seen such dogged determination. Bellowing anger and quiet satisfaction were the low and high marks of a session, as patients celebrated a tiny improvement or sensed – perhaps even began to accept – the inevitability of incompletion.

'Great, you're sitting really well. Strong,' Alan said to me.

He held his palms out to emphasise the point and Martin gave me an affirming smile. Daily life became a series of incremental victories, pushing, searching for that endpoint, the hoped-for return to normality; I wasn't prepared to settle for an acceptable level of sub-normality. I was in search of perfection, the old me. My midriff had tautened, got stronger, and I was now resisting little shoulder pushes as Alan tried to topple me. It'd taken a couple of sessions but I could sit unaided. On to the next challenge.

The gym, as opposed to the physio suite, was separate from the main building and redolent of a 1950s secondary school, with its scuffed parquet floor and wooden parallel wall bars. Getting there wasn't just a journey back in time either, as I was wheeled along corridors, through the cheerless entrance lobby, out of the main doors, down the driveway and, mindful of visiting traffic, across a car park. When the sun shone it was a bounding expedition. When it rained, I got wet. Whatever the weather it was invigorating to breathe in the outside, even if exhaust fumes from the catering truck delivering slabs of corned beef and hydrogenated soup, tainted the air.

The gym was an uninviting, echoing space with a mean huddle of dumbbells, loose weights, a bench, medicine balls and other yesteryear equipment, scattered in a corner, as if donated by a defunct weight-lifting club. Even in summer there was a musty chill which at least encouraged you to pump iron to keep warm. And that's what this arm of the Rookwood rehab regime was all about; building muscle and stamina, albeit primitively. It certainly didn't feel specialist, as once again comparisons with Stoke Mandeville were laid bare.

For all of the steely determination in that gym there was often laughter and games and a sense of the possible. We reclaimed bits of who we once were, or strengthened the bits we'd reclaimed already. Music often accompanied our labours, with tapes playing on a ghetto-blaster stored in a locked cupboard. I remember the theme tune to *Rocky* driving us all to raptures of exhaustion. With or without music, we pushed till there was nothing left to push against, all the while encouraging one another with mutual cajoling.

Over a period of weeks, Dan sculpted a vein-marbled, bulging left arm, pumping sets of bicep curls and triceps presses in his quest for a limb that could see him through the rest of his life. We watched and smiled and encouraged him. He'd heave and push set after set till he was rent doubled-up with lactic pain and spent lungs, returning to the ward with that arm hunked-up a fraction more.

Then there was Pete, the most audible patient on our ward. A native of Somerset, his voice a honey-coated burr, he was tough, tattooed and fond of a brawl in his previous life, his route to Rookwood also being by dint of the motorbike; how could it have been any other way? He was incendiary and opinionated – the physio would've done well to note his Motorhead and Iron Maiden tattoos before putting on Duran Duran one day. It wasn't on for long. Pete kept us on our mettle, his volcanic outbursts a release valve, venting a rage that his legs would never work again, often accompanied by something being chucked. We gave him lots of space. I admired him for the honesty of his anger. Thank God for Pete, inarticulate spokesman for our combined loss.

Chapter 10

I didn't know that she was standing nearby. Alan did, but said nothing.

'Nearly did it yesterday,' said Alan. 'Ready for another go?'

Yesterday had been a good day. Yesterday had been progress indeed. Now I had to build on that progress. Now I had to do what I hadn't quite done the day before.

I recited to myself what Alan had embedded in me, like some mantra: sit straight, lean forward, feel that core – those reawakened stomach muscles – and drive upwards. From the ward to the physio suite that morning I'd charged myself up mentally. I was convinced it'd happen. Sitting upright, I leant forward, tensed that core, and drove upwards through my legs with all of my might. I rose from the platform to a skiing position, feeling awesome. I was nearly there. I was going to make it. Then my thighs began to shake uncontrollably from the spasticity plaguing my muscles, I lost momentum and plonked back down. Just like the day before.

'Fuck it,' I shouted, borrowing Pete's verbal currency of despair.

'It's okay. You were nearly there,' said Alan.

He was a driver. He had to be. And because Alan believed, I believed.

I took a huge determined breath and said, 'Right. This time.'

I felt for that core again and pushed hard and up through my legs. Passing the point of my previous failures, I kept pushing and pushing till I was up. Unsteady, wobbling, disbelieving, I stood, legs straight, knees locked out. I was on my feet, and upright. And I'd got there without help. Perseverance; it was becoming ingrained. Summiting for a second or two, I collapsed back down onto the platform. But I'd done it. It was my very own Wright brothers moment, a first flight. The enormity of what I'd achieved hit me and I welled up. There was a cheer from the well-to-do lady from Mid Wales and Valleys boy Terry clapped, an incredible display of selflessness.

I still had no idea, though, that she was standing nearby.

'Guess who saw that?' beamed Alan.

I shrugged.

'Your mum. Just over there,' he said pointing, drinking in the satisfaction that came as a perk of the job.

I turned, but she was gone. When they took me back to the ward, Mum was sitting by my bed waiting for me. Her red eyes suggested there'd been tears. She'd seen me stand. A good day.

That evening, I was in a wheelchair on the grass by the trees, near to where I'd seen the fox. The fox which'd inspired me. It was early May, the sun refracting through the trees as it dipped west. Pete was within earshot, talking to another patient about his biking days. Anecdotes were all he had now. I was alone, it was warm and I was happy.

My recovery had leapt that day to a new and exciting dimension, and Mum had witnessed it, departing for the train lighter than I'd ever seen her, aching to get home and deliver the news. A nurse on the ward had made a fuss of me on my return from physio, which'd made me uncomfortable. I didn't want to be lauded for having stood when so many others couldn't, or wouldn't ever. But now, out on the grass, away from everyone, I closed my eyes and imagined the possibilities that my recovery would bestow. I couldn't think those thoughts when near to the other patients, as it felt like heresy, like they'd be able to read my mind.

By mid-summer I'd be home and back to my old self, I thought, or at least approaching it. I'd have the freedom to do what I wanted, go where I liked; Trecwn could wait, perhaps forever. The accident had been a wake-up call and I was determined there'd be adventures. I'd come close to losing my life and even my survival hadn't guaranteed me a life worth living. I'd been lucky.

In the months leading up to the accident I'd acknowledged that for all of my frustration at being a Trecwnite, it was, it seemed, my natural home. It spoke my language, a language of limited horizons. Well, no horizons really. No outlook. That pained acknowledgement was an admission of complicity in my own misery, a hostage as I was to inaction. Like a habitual offender stealing for a return to the comforting routine of prison – the security of not having to make decisions – I'd clambered aboard that bus every morning, persuading myself (rather too easily) that my life had meaning, as I had a job. And work was a good thing, wasn't it?

The bottom line, though, was I couldn't imagine my way out of Trecwn, as I had no imagination. Okay, that's not quite true; of course, I had an imagination – after all, I'd manufactured alternative lives in my head the whole day long – but what I lacked was the determination to enact what I imagined. To be brave. When I'd dared to envisage a way out – the Paras or the Met Police – I'd quickly snuffed the idea out.

When I made unconvincing noises about packing it in, Dad would remind me 'it's a steady job with a good pension'. He was right, of course, and his restating of this shibboleth was a convenient enough excuse for me to dispense with any fanciful notions of escape. It didn't take much to sway me. And who could blame Dad; with his impoverished childhood what he most cherished was financial security, and initially after he'd joined the Navy at seventeen, to eat. His mindset was forged by his childhood which hadn't been propitious. He was thankful for what he had, which just happened to be a well-paid job in a refinery that he enjoyed.

My inherited characteristics, it seemed – or maybe they'd been coded into me by example – shunned any notion of taking a chance. We were a good, safe family that took safe options. Riding my bike to parts of Pembrokeshire half an hour from home with my camera was as adventurous as it'd got. Twenty miles away could just as well have been the Amazon. Always a reluctance to venture too far. And when I had on occasion got lost, it was a planned and safe lost, close to signs pointing me home. All of that was going to change. When I got home my life would start again as someone more daring.

It was getting chilly, so I looked towards the ward, hoping to catch someone's eye to bring me in. Pete had already zipped past. I wasn't strong enough to propel the chair over grass, so I began to wave an arm with its floppy hand dangling at the wrist, a reminder of why I was in a wheelchair on a patch of grass in Cardiff and not in the pub with the boys. I'd regained some fine motor skills using my fingers – the occupational therapists seemed to derive a perverse pleasure from making me pick up and transfer tiny beads from a tray to a small box – but my wrists were still terribly weak. They'll get better, I told myself. I told myself that a lot.

When I saw who'd seen me waving, my heart raced as she came out and glided across the grass. I was prepared to overlook her giggling during my recurring bed-bath shames and after much deliberation – fixation more like – I'd decided she looked like Christie Brinkley, the American supermodel. She didn't really, but it cheered me to think it all the same.

'Ready to come in?' she said.

'Yeah. Getting chilly.'

She released the brakes and pushed.

'So, you stood in physio today.'

'Yeah. I'm very lucky.'

'Your mum saw it too, didn't she?'

'She did. It made her very happy.'

I felt my voice break as I said it.

'Well, keep it up and you never know what might happen,' she said, patting me gently on the shoulder.

You never know what might happen? Was she hinting at something? I certainly hoped she was.

Entering the ward, I shrank down in the chair, wishing to become invisible. I'd stood that day. It'd been talked about. I was embarrassed.

She wheeled me to my bed, put the brake on, pulled the curtains round, lifted the footplates, let me get to my feet – at which she smiled – and then she embraced and turned me through ninety degrees to sit me on the bed, before easing me down onto my back as I inhaled her.

There was a boyfriend, of course. From Cardiff, like her. They'd met on a blind date. They had a flat together. She spoke of him a lot, telling me what they'd been up to and the plans they had, usually because I probed so much. Never got the answers I wanted, though. The answers that would've confirmed my picture of him as some womanising, brawling drinker. Someone who treated her like dirt. Someone who'd push her into my arms. Not quite yet though, as my arms were weak.

He volunteered one night, with some others, to push a group of patients in wheelchairs around the local pubs. He was so damned personable. I liked him and hated that I liked him. After I'd sunk a couple of pints and filtered it through to the bag attached to my calf, he got down on a knee, emptied it into a plastic urine bottle and took it to the toilet to pour away. Fuck it, I thought, he isn't such a bad bloke.

It was torture being prepared for bed by a beautiful woman, knowing that I was damaged goods, that my masculinity was compromised. I'd watch and listen for any hint of pity in her smile or the way she spoke. I could take it from the other nurses, but not from her. I needn't have worried; the bed-bath giggles were her only transgressions.

She undressed me, which in another time and place in my head may've preceded something memorable; it simply allowed access to my plumbing. She removed the piss bag hose from the condom and replaced it with a longer hose from a night bag on a stand at the side of the bed. She put the telly on and switched it to the channel I requested, then tucked me in.

'Anything else, David?'

Plenty, I thought.

'No, that's great, thanks.'

Put to bed by Christie Brinkley. Lucky me.

Chapter 11

Nan, then Gramps, pecked me on the cheek.

'I got you these,' she said, placing a box of Bakewell tarts on my bedside cabinet as if it were an offering to a deity.

'Doing well, Dai,' declared Gramps, taking his cap off and unzipping his best coat. 'Said you'd be fine all along, haven't I, Nellie?'

Nan smiled indulgently. He'd prophesied it, and so it was coming to pass. Gramps was light on medical expertise but there was something of the voodoo seer behind those berry-brown features. The last of the small-town mystics, he brimmed with a host of superstitions, 'don't put vinegar on your food. It thins the blood' being one of the more memorable. He gave tomatoes a wide berth, as he'd heard of a peculiar case where the seeds had grown in a man's stomach. Earache? Easy; draw on a cigarette – in his case, a Woodbine – and blow hot smoke into the offending drum. Quite pleasant, as I recall. Superstition and faith trumping science. I wonder where I got it from?

I was the first-born grandchild and I imagined it gave me a privileged position in the pecking order over those that followed. One of my earliest memories, aside from a nightmare involving a flock of birds flying out of a wardrobe, was standing in the toy department of Woolworths holding Gramps' hand and pointing to a red double-decker bus that I coveted. I walked out with it, of course. Is there such a thing as a prodigal grandchild? Whatever my delusions, I felt special, much as I'm sure the others did, because that's what grandparents do. They make you feel you're number one.

Mum and Dad had brought them to Cardiff in their car, though having a lift with two non-smokers didn't mean abstention for the oldies. Dad despised smoking, insisting on winding the window all the way down, even on the motorway. Nan had asked him to close it as her own smoke was blowing back in her face. To avoid dirtying the ashtrays, Gramps flicked ash into the palm of his hand and chucked it out of the window, most of which, again, blew back in and onto the carpet. The journey for the quartet, of which there'd been many, was a tense affair.

Mum took a foil-wrapped lump the size of a piece of coal from her bag. 'Cooked it this morning,' she said.

Another sweaty chicken breast.

'Thanks, Ma. I'll have it later with my corned beef and chips.'

They'd arrived in time for my physio session, no doubt eager to marvel at my recent gains. A couple of weeks had passed since I first stood, with Mum watching, and the heady whirl of progress had felt near miraculous; the surge of rediscovered movement had a race to it like an incoming tide at Morecambe Bay.

I'd progressed to using Brunel's wheeled frame, bequeathed to me by the discharged walker. He'd bowed out of the ward for home as if in training for an Olympic walkathon, with a humble self-effacing nod, no hint of spinal cord damage and striding at a brisk pace as if to spare everyone the prolonged misery of witnessing his good fortune. I was inspired. His was the gold standard of recovery and I was going to join him on the rostrum.

However, I'd lost something precious in my recent wave of euphoria, something that the walker had demonstrated throughout his return to what appeared to be physical perfection: a shining humility and awareness of the plight of those on the ward who for all their bloody-minded determination wouldn't recover everything or, in some cases, anything. His physical quietness amidst all of those blighted lives had been noticeable and touching. He could've walked about incessantly – it's what I intended to do when I could, and go for those jogs – but instead he just sat and read or watched the telly as if determined to move around as little as possible.

When I first stood, I too had been conscious of the need to be unshowy, to spare those who weren't as fortunate, to remain below the other patients' radar. In my tunnel-like drive since though, I'd lost sight of the damage around me, obsessed as I was with Project Run. I was now able to manoeuvre myself from lying down into a sitting position on the side of the bed, with my feet on the floor. Holding onto the head of my bed I'd take a couple of careful steps to an armchair, but once sat, I was forever standing, squatting, stretching; anything to stimulate the regeneration of those muscles. Maybe not the most heinous of crimes but I'd do this even when the ward was busy, when I knew that other patients were looking or staring. Looking and yearning. The fact was, I no longer saw the other patients, only the finishing line of my complete recovery.

At eleven o'clock, on cue, Alan and Martin appeared.

'You've got an audience,' said Alan, as he took a moment to speak with my visitors. It was typical of his generosity but I just wanted to crack on. Talk of the incredible summer we were having was of little interest, seeing as I was spending just about all of it indoors.

Alan had brought the wheeled frame, Martin a wheelchair; he'd walk behind, ready to slip it under me if I looked like going down or needed to rest. Alan reversed the frame to the side of the bed where I was sitting. I grabbed the two moulded handles on the chest-high U-shaped bar. My hands could now form a gripping action, though any notion of a trapeze act was still a way off. With a heave I was up, feet planted and ready to trek the sixty, eighty or so metres to the physio suite. I didn't look at my four spectators, who'd yet to see me walk, but I guessed they were already bursting with expectation. I too was excited, and nervous, eager that I should perform well, and make them happy.

I ran the mechanics of the walk through in my head: lift one foot, place it forward and plant on the floor, lift the other foot, place it forward and plant. Repeat until I reached physio. Slow, methodical, deliberate steps. Don't give up. Never mind how fatigued I was, I mustn't give up. I'd failed the day before, failure perhaps a harsh assessment of what'd been a monumental effort, but on this day I was determined I'd get all the way there.

'In your own time, and don't rush,' cautioned Alan.

I plodded on, plotting my way through the ward as if operating some clunky Victorian steam-powered walking contraption. One foot forward. Stop. Other foot forward. Stop. Eventually, I exited the ward for what seemed like the endless tundra of the corridors. Halfway to physio, and I had a metronomic rhythm that seemed inexhaustible. I felt high, like I was on drugs. Past the secretary's office I went, on and on. In a trance-like focus, I heard nothing and saw nothing except the patch of floor immediately in front of me. Then, in the space of a few strides, I began to feel it, the burn, my legs morphing to jelly. I stopped, panting, and glanced at the wheelchair behind me.

'If you want to call it a day, that's fine,' said Alan. 'You're past where you were yesterday. Done well.'

He nodded at Martin, who was ready to push the chair under me.

'No,' I said. 'Just give me a few seconds.'

'Okay.'

The burn subsided and I set off again, my feet dragging now as if I were wearing deep-sea diving boots, legs trembling, the spasticity in the muscles struggling to cope with the demands I was placing on them. All the while, my cortege of four trailed quietly behind. In my pre-accident life, my ability to dig deep had been compromised by the pathetic mental trowel I was lumbered with. I'd never even scratched the surface of a problem or a challenge. Life had been easy. And if something wasn't easy, I gave up. In Rookwood though, my psyche had taken delivery of a massive spade with which I could shift shitloads of metaphorical earth when the situation demanded. And there were lots of situations that demanded it. I dug deeper than I could ever have imagined possible.

This walk, though, was tougher than anything thrown at me so far, and I desperately wanted to sit in that wheelchair but I could see the double-doors into physio ahead of me, and hear the hum of activity. I edged closer and closer, barely able to lift my feet, and with what felt like my last gasp I was in the room. I reached the closest platform and collapsed. I'd done it. Alan and Martin nodded their approval. Mum and Dad hugged me and cried. Nan and Gramps went out for a celebratory fag.

In the weeks that followed I retrod the route to physio, growing steadier and more fleet of foot. Well, my version of fleet, anyway. What'd been one-way walks became returns too as I dispensed with the necessity of Martin whizzing me back to my bed in a wheelchair. With the Nike trainers I'd had for my birthday to inspire me, I could taste the glory of that first run. But when?

I'd been on my feet for ages and yet I was still reliant on support when walking. Okay, I'd progressed to pushing a wheelchair instead of being cosseted in the supportive embrace of an enormous wheeled frame. My balance had improved so that I could employ micro-adjustments of my walking gait to maintain stability and control – empty wheelchairs have a habit of running away from you. All of these little fine-tunings and a gradual return of leg strength were contributing to a more normalised stride pattern. There were still asymmetric weaknesses, and anyone seeing me walk would've known that something unpleasant had happened, but all of that'd right itself soon enough, I was convinced of that. But when I thought of the discharged walker, I was sure that after an equivalent period of time on his feet he'd strode with such gusto around the hospital grounds with no support at all, then he was gone. He was probably running marathons already. I was becoming impatient with my recovery and resentful that it wasn't more miraculous. Like a spoilt child, I wanted more and more.

I'd just returned from physio quicker than ever and was sitting on my bed having a drink of squash.

'Alan, when will I be able to run?' I'd never asked before, as I feared the answer.

'That's a big question,' he said, shaking his head. 'Look, you're doing great. I mean, you walked back so well just then.'

Chapter II

'I know. But I just want to get back to normal.'

He put an arm around my shoulder.

'You're walking really well. Just build on that, and remember...' he said, lowering his voice, '...most of these guys will never stand again, let alone walk.'

'I don't care about the others,' I snapped.

He bridled. 'Look, I know it's hard, but as I say, just look around. You're lucky.'

His tone had hardened, and it unsettled me. I only ever wanted to please him, to be the star pupil.

'Sorry, that was a bit harsh,' he said. 'But, even if today is it, you're way ahead of these guys.' He grinned and jabbed a soft fist into my shoulder. 'Just keep trying, and see where it leads you.'

He stood to leave.

'Anyway, Sally'll be taking over from me tomorrow. Remember, just keep trying your best.'

He smiled and walked off. The baton was being passed on, which was okay, as I liked Sally.

The conversation with Alan was the most defining of my time in Rookwood. Those around me had experienced varying degrees of recovery, or a permanent loss of function below the level of their injury. Permanent. For ever. No reset button.

I, on the other hand, woke each day anticipating an improvement on the day before. Everything that dangled from my torso moved. Okay, the range of movement was weak and incomplete, but I believed I'd achieve a full recovery. There was no doubt about it.

After supper, when I'd turned in for the night, I looked into myself and didn't like what I saw. How had I become so oblivious to those around me? It all came back to the walker, of course, who'd gone about his business with a respectful deference. And now he shamed me in his absence. Sure, I had to continue pushing, searching out those parameters of recovery, hoping to claw back every last bit of normality. You see, I dreaded the plateau, the incomplete point where recovered function ceased, a point short of how I used to be. But I was surrounded by recoveries that'd petered out or had never even begun. Lying there, I knew what I had to do, and I'd do it the next morning.

Tom, the ward's fifteen-year resident, wasn't expecting me. Why would he? I'd never gone to him before. Every day I'd heard him bawling at the staff like some cornered animal with a thorn stuck in its paw, and in my imagination I'd built him up into this terrible ogre, a crazed spectacle I was too cowardly to confront. Now I went to him to face up to my fears and try and reclaim some emotional generosity.

He'd been breakfasted and washed, and lying on his bed presented as a pitiful vision. In the fifteen years since the accident his tendons and muscles had contracted and shrunk, twisting his limbs into macabre, contorted sticks. His hands were closed tight as a clam, his fingers hooked into his palms. He sensed my presence, muttering something indecipherable. Julie walked past and gave me an encouraging wink as if to say, 'Don't worry, he won't bite.'

'Hi, Tom, my name's David. I'm in a bed just down the ward.'

His rheumy eyes swam with a trapped energy, a frustration that would never, could never, leave him in peace. He saw everything, heard everything, but could do nothing. Then, to my astonishment, he spoke; quietly, each word punctuated with a pause, as if he were playing Scrabble in his mind, grabbing each letter in real time to form the next word.

'Hello. David. Seen. You. About.'

This man, whom I'd dismissed as a noisy crank, who I'd built into a terrifying spectre, transcended all of us. He didn't say much – speaking for Tom was exhausting – and I didn't know what to say besides commenting on the weather and asking if he'd enjoyed breakfast. He'd growl at passing members of staff but they'd just laugh. I suppose that's all he had left, the power to be obstinate. Tom cursed as that was his thing, the trait that gave him a sense of uniqueness. Otherwise, he'd have disappeared off the radar, a crumpled collection of bones lying in the corner.

I went to Tom's bed regularly after that, if only to sit there and look at him and see in his fate a lesson to each and every one of us: to be thankful for whatever we got back. He was a totem, a reminder of how bad it could be. And because of him, because of the hand he'd been dealt, I rediscovered an empathy that'd deserted me.

Chapter 12

I'd just finished lunch at the communal dining table in the centre of the ward when Dan wheeled himself over.

'Guess what?' he said.

I shrugged.

'I'm going Friday.'

'What? Discharged?'

'Yep. I'm done. Can't do any more for me,' he said, flexing his bulky left bicep. 'The big wide world awaits!'

I was envious. He was going home. Out of there.

'Wow, that's brilliant,' I said.

Behind that weak grin there was a nervousness to his bravado. With his raven-black swept-back hair, angular features and penetrating eyes, he'd always seemed so determined, so certain that the accident wasn't going to change his life, dictate the narrative, even with just one workable arm. But, like the rest of us, he was putting on a front. Dan's smiles had often been like half-finished paintings, as if he begrudged any reward of mirth. Arm first, fun later. Now that the rehab comfort blanket was to be taken away, he seemed unsure of himself, as if he hadn't contemplated the actual leaving bit.

A herd psychology pervaded the ward, a reassuring familiarity in belonging to a group of like-damaged people, the normalisation of a host of abnormal experiences binding us together, yet at the same time hating being part of that group and perhaps even persuading yourself that you weren't one of them. On the outside though – discharged – we'd be alone and exposed to scrutiny and pity, our physical shortcomings visible for all to see. On the inside, no one gave a shit.

'So, your parents ready? Probably got your favourite posters up already, eh!'

'Sorry, I'm not with you,' he said.

'Well, it'll be strange for a while. Moving back in with them.'

His face darkened. 'You think I'm going back to my parents?'

'Well, yeah. Aren't you?' I said, realising I'd wandered into a minefield.

'Why the fuck would I do that? Jesus, is that what you think? Dan's got one arm so Dan's going back to mummy and daddy.'

He clenched the armrest of the wheelchair, dissipating his distress like a conductor channelling lightning to the ground. He was angry, as much with his life-changing limitations as my crass assumption.

'Sorry, Dan. Really sorry. I shouldn't have assumed.'

He released his grip and shook his head. 'It's okay. I mean, look at me. One fucking arm. They're booting me out with one fucking arm. Not going back to my parents though.'

'You don't say!'

He laughed. A proper full-faced laugh. It was nice. I'd watched Dan in the gym day after day, pumping that arm for all it was worth; the strength of two arms in one. There'd been little laughter, just a saint-like drive. Building muscle is a serious business, especially when any hope of an independent life is reliant on it. Having one arm with which to live that life would be a challenge. His was going to be a smaller, more constricted existence, which he knew only too well.

Over the months I felt that I'd come to know his parents without ever having spoken to them. They were so unassuming, ghosting into the ward with an apologetic slipper-stealth and departing without ceremony. I suppose, they weren't that different from the other parents who had to visit their children. A child, your child, is a beautiful gift. They are you, your essence, part of a generational relay race, continuing after your time. Parents tell their children they can achieve anything, and to grab the world and its possibilities; well, maybe I hadn't had that conversation myself. Then they get a motorbike or collapse in a scrum or dive in the shallow end of a pool and end up in Rookwood.

And the parents steel themselves and walk in with a sunshine face, each visit killing them just a bit more.

Dan's parents, I guessed, were in their fifties, though as an eighteen-year-old anyone over thirty looked ancient, and guessing their age was a haphazard affair. His dad was, and indeed looked, the quintessential country vet in brogues and tweed, all worn-in, high-end tailoring, straight off the set of *All Creatures Great and Small*. His mum, surely a stalwart of her local WI, was turned out just so. They were respectable middle-England people and just wanted him back home safe in the family nest. Dan had other ideas. He was a computer programmer, and this at a time when any association with computing bestowed an aura of genius, guardians of an as yet untouchable future for the rest of us.

'So, what's the plan?' I asked.

'Simple. Got a ground floor flat sorted and someone coming in mornings and evenings to help with stuff. And I'm going back to work.'

He said it as if he were contemplating a change of T-shirt, which in itself would've been an arduous enough task. His independence, his hopes and constrained dreams, would be reliant on a carer helping 'with stuff'. Reliance would be the new thread woven into every aspect of his life. But his attitude ensured he'd rely as little as possible. He'd been robbed of three of the four extremities of his body, and that good arm would have to push, pull, haul and heave that carcass around like some stone-dense curse. Over the months I'd witnessed many patients being discharged and I imagined it felt as terrifying as a first parachute jump, or worse,and looking at Dan in his chair it was as if he were being pushed towards the door of the plane without even a parachute.

Friday arrived and Dan departed without fanfare, his parents following a few paces behind with his belongings. We shook hands and I wished him well. He didn't say much but then he never had. Perhaps the magnitude of what lay ahead was weighing heavy. Pete patted him on the back and said something Pete-like about being lucky to escape and to be sure to have a skinful on our behalf. He then propelled himself out of the ward and I watched as he turned the corner at the bottom of the corridor and he was gone.

Dan became my barometer by which to compare all others' woes and physical travails, not just in Rookwood, and in the decades that've passed I haven't encountered anyone so bereft as he was of the physical tools required to get through a day. He'd live his life in the muscle-deprived borderlands, every action an effort, every task a toil. He'll forever sit at the top, the very apex, of human endeavour. The bravest person I ever met.

Pete followed a week later, as if there was a sudden fire sale of damaged people. His was a more vocal departure as befitting a vocal man. There was jocularity and mention of a slate of celebratory ciders on getting home. But again, for all the bravado I detected the same trepidation that'd emanated from Dan, a gallows humour masking a fear of the unknown. Or maybe it was the known that scared them.

'Well, Davy boy, that's me done. Keep up the hard work and don't let the bastards grind you down!' he said, in his delicious west-country burr.

With that he gave a determined push down on his wheels, shooting off along the length of the ward shouting jovial 'byes' to everyone he passed. And he too was gone, to embrace whatever his altered life had to throw at him.

With the time-servers departing, seniority amongst the patients shifted and it was clear that I was being pushed up the pecking order, my own release date edging closer. Jim was out of bed and progressing, though not with the rapidity he'd have liked. Nothing came quickly for him, each day a dogged battle to regain some precious ground before that dreaded plateau; the grimmest of attrition warfare. Not only had Jim refereed the big fights, the biggest of which he himself was now embroiled in, but he'd judged them too from ringside, none more epic than Sugar Ray Leonard versus Roberto Duran back in '80. They were two fighters that John and I discussed on the milk round and it was a bout I'll have watched at home with chilled Maltesers and coke.

I felt cast adrift without Dan and Pete though, my affinity with the others less solid. Into the fag end of rehab, I too yearned for the exit, or at least I thought I did.

'Right, David, we've had a meeting,' said Sally. 'You're coming on really well and we think you're ready to go home. Be discharged.'

The cell door was to be flung open and I suddenly felt vulnerable.

'Right, okay, that's err… good. When?'

'Next Monday.'

A week? Really?

'Okay. Next Monday it is then. Great,' I said.

After six months of a parallel existence with the outside world, in seven days I'd be expected to drive my own recovery, albeit with regular sessions in physio outpatients at my local hospital. Like Dan and Pete, I was brimming with uncertainty. I'd be leaving that place to go home. Rookwood had been my surrogate home but now the real thing was closing in. I felt happy. I felt confused. I felt scared. What would people out there think when they saw me? I was imperfect, with a long way to go to get back to the person I'd been. Had Sally made a mistake? Maybe, I thought, I should ask if I could stay a bit longer, to claw back more recovery before presenting myself to the world.

My last day on the ward was a maelstrom, charged with excitement at the prospect of going home but with sadness too for the people I'd be leaving behind. That jog before breakfast hadn't happened and the faint prospect of incompletion was beginning to dog me.

Triceps are the muscles at the back of the upper arm. They enable you, for example, to push a heavy bag up and into an overhead locker, like on a plane. They're also crucial for doing press-ups. I'd been pretty bloody brilliant at pumping out press ups. My triceps were gone, though. Disappeared. Also disappeared was the left side of my chest. It was as if it'd been surgically removed. Nothing but skin and ribs where my pectoral muscle once sat proudly. The calf muscle of my right leg was wasted when compared to the left, though my preference for attaching the piss bag to it helped bulk it out! My bladder was nowhere near secure enough yet.

I had a pronounced limp, due in part to my right leg being weaker than the left but also because the vertebrae that'd been broken in my lower back had healed, producing a curvature of the spine that had the effect of tilting my pelvis, thereby raising my right hip while dropping the left; when I lay down and put my legs together it appeared that my left leg was appreciably longer than the other, when in fact they were the same length. Walking the parallel bars in physio, without the support of a wheelchair, my stride pattern was irregular and stumbling, presenting exactly as someone who'd sustained a spinal cord injury, which was not supposed to have been my departing performance. The walker strode out of the ward to freedom with aplomb. I would at best shuffle out. If they'd offered to put me up for another month, I'd have taken it. Anything to avoid having to depart incomplete.

Yet for all of the creeping doubt I was still buoyed by the epiphany on the lawn that evening months before. I'd promised myself adventure, a rebirth, to take on the world. And when I recovered fully – which I surely would – there'd be expedition plans aplenty. So, uncertain as I may have been, it was time to go. I decided that I was excited.

I went to see Tom. He beamed when I said it was my last day, that I was going home, a conversation he'd never had. Hundreds of patients had passed through over the years, leaving him behind.

'Good. Luck. Boy,' he whispered, his eyes glinting with an invested hope in me, in my future happiness. He'd never leave that place but was elevated nevertheless by those who trickled out.

With a core-tautened heave, I stood, squeezed his bony shoulder, gave him a wink, turned and plotted a path back to my bed, leaning – more lightly now – on the handles of a wheelchair. Sally had been encouraging me to walk short distances around the ward without support but I was concerned that a possible fall could delay my parole so I opted for the added piece of mind of the wheelchair. There'd be plenty of time for audacity when I got home.

Mum and Dad had packed my belongings, including a couple of unopened boxes of Bakewell tarts, into some plastic bags. They'd unstuck the blu-tacked family photos and well-wishers' cards from the wall, all evidence of my tenure erased. I took one final look at that space – bed, locker, table, window. A blank canvas ready for the next victim on a conveyor belt that never stopped.

And that was it. I was done. A farewell posse approached. My throat tightened, eyes filling ready to pour out months of suppressed emotion. Months of blocking out unwanted thoughts.

'Well, lovey, this is it. We'll miss you,' said Julie. 'Remember us, and call in if you're passing.'

It was sweet of her but the likelihood of me passing was slim, and calling in even slimmer. Once out of there I had no intention of returning. She engulfed me in a huge embrace, and as I eased away I saw there were tears. We'd become close. We'd shared highs and lows, all mine, of course. She'd been my go-to counsellor, confidante, confessor. She'd been my hands before mine came back to life. Washed me, fed me, evacuated me. Doesn't get much more personal than that; not forgetting the inadvertent handjobs as well, of course.

I looked at Dad and beckoned him close, wanting to go before I dissolved. 'Can you support my arm? On the way out,' I whispered. He smiled proudly and cupped my forearm and hand. I'd hoped to see Alan, Sally and Martin but they were busy; their focus was on others now. Christie Brinkley was there though. She gave me a hug, which threatened to cause all manner of internal eruptions, and wished me well. I took a deep breath, thanked the staff for the umpteenth time, wished the gathered patients the very best and began the long plod from the ward, lapping up the byes and smiles.

Dad applied the lightest of supporting touches, determined I should own the weight of my forward motion, correct any stumbles and sways, allowing me to drink in the satisfaction of an upright exit. I was leaving on my feet and was thankful for that. Down the corridor, past the slops room, then the shower room and out of the side door to the car, Mum following with the bags. It wasn't the longest walk I'd undertaken but it was the biggest; it was my walk to the outside, the other side, to my rebooted life.

Dad opened the car door ready to help me in. I took one final glance at the ward, that unassuming bolted-on building that contained so many hoped-for recoveries, and cried. Not some torrential outpouring but a quiet private tear. Aside from the good fortune of the walker and other rare examples over many decades, the overwhelming majority departed as physically lesser individuals than they'd been in their previous lives. So it was with me, for the time being. Dad helped me into the front passenger seat, pulled the seatbelt across and clicked it in. Mum stroked my shoulder from the back seat as Dad got behind the wheel.

'Ready?' he said.

'Yeah, let's go.'

As he started the car, Sally came running out. She opened the door.

'Christ, nearly missed you,' she said.

'It's okay,' I said, elated at her late showing.

'Just wanted to say, good luck. Keep plugging away and remember what we said.' She leant in through the door and kissed me on the cheek. I started to cry, again. She ruffled my hair. 'Just keep trying.'

With that she closed the door, stood back from the car and waved as we pulled out onto the main road. In two hours, I'd be home.

Chapter 13

There was an overwhelming sense of relief but also fragility as we pulled up. I was home, and not in hospital, but so much had changed since I'd straddled that bike on the driveway six months earlier. Snapshots of that last ride came to mind: the pleasant chill of that night; putting my helmet on and kick-starting the bike; waving to Dad as I passed him walking to the club; the sudden outline of a car moving across my path. Then, pain. I'd only been going to the pub; huh, I'd been gone a long time. I'd dreamt of home from the first day in the infirmary and now that I was back, I was nervous. I was supposed to have returned complete. I wasn't, and that lack of completion was beginning to haunt me.

'Can I just have a couple of minutes in the car… alone,' I said. 'Lots to take in.'

'Of course,' said Mum. 'I'll go and put the kettle on.'

Mum went indoors, and Dad stood by the car while I remained belted-in looking out at the estate. The man at number eleven, who I'd had run-ins with when I was younger, was mowing his lawn. Mrs Thomas two doors down was cleaning windows. A neighbour's kid was going down the hill on his bike. I was re-immersed into a world of a million acts of nothing. Normality. It felt weird.

We moved to number four Masefield Drive in November 1974, a neat cul-de-sac of a dozen or so new builds in various stages of construction running down a hill. Our house was the only one that'd been finished, and so, as the sole occupiers on a building site, I was presented with the most exciting playground in the world. I'd enact war games in the evenings and at weekends when the builders weren't around jumping into muddy trenches, climbing scaffolding and building bunkers out of breeze blocks. It was fun and dangerous and I loved it.

Then one morning a removals lorry appeared outside a newly completed house and with it came a boy called Aled. By the end of that day, we were best estate friends, which considering the absence of other candidates had an inevitability to it. Our friendship blossomed though, even when challenged by subsequent newcomers. We were an entrepreneurial pairing. In the run-up to Christmas, we went carol singing, divvying-up our takings under the streetlight by my house. It was a profitable gig, making sure to target old people who were more generous, and appreciative, often inviting us in for a private performance, especially if they had visitors to entertain. Belting out *Silent Night* to a bunch of nodding geriatrics was strangely satisfying.

Aled collided with the kerb halfway down Masefield Drive on a skateboard once, coming off and breaking a wrist. Dad had made the skateboard from a piece of plywood and a dismantled roller-skate. Evidence of his woodworking skills was at best patchy. He'd built some bookshelves in my bedroom from scaffolding planks he'd filched from the site late at night.

There was an industrial simplicity to them, though without a sander to smooth the rough wood they were soon removed after I got umpteen splinters in my hands. So, when he suggested a skateboard, I frowned. 'It'll be easy,' he said, reminding me of his being apprenticed as a cabinet maker when he left school at fourteen. It was all the assurance I needed, in spite of the fact he only completed a few months of the apprenticeship.

The roller-skate wheels that he nailed to the front and rear of the rectangular piece of plywood weren't aligned properly and so the skateboard pulled to the right in a gradual arc. Aled had picked up quite a lick by the time of his meeting with the kerb. There was no Aled on my return home though; he and his family had moved away a few years before my motorbike accident.

I gave Dad the nod. He opened the car door, unbuckled the seatbelt and helped me out. I was relieved that the street was quiet. I'd dreaded some well-meaning welcoming committee. Neighbours assessing my physical deficiencies – 'Well, better than I thought he'd be,' or 'Christ, he's got a way to go.'

Dad held me steady as I dragged my feet up over the threshold into the kitchen and went through to the lounge. It was as if I'd never been away; the busy wallpaper, plumped cushions, the catwalk of dust-free ornaments. We all sat and had a cuppa and cried, the dam bursting after months of resolution. It felt cathartic, cleansing, a necessary storm. I decided there and then though, that I'd had enough of crying. It was time to stiffen one's resolve for the upcoming battle, or as seemed more likely, battles.

After swigging my last mouthful of coffee, I said, 'I'd like to see my room.'

The council had installed modifications, including double handrails on the stairs. With Mum in front and Dad behind we ascended slowly, as if tied together on the north face of the Eiger. Climbing stairs represented a major victory, as wheelchairs and Daleks don't do stairs. Those thirteen steps were the most I'd scaled in one go since I was last in the house. It was a good start.

The bedroom was tiny and accommodating three people was a squeeze, but more presciently they sensed that I might want a bit of time to myself. Mum said, 'We'll go and get supper on. Gammon and chips?'

'That'll be lovely. I'll call when I want to come down.'

The last time I'd been in the room I'd put my prized Belstaff jacket on – subsequently shredded in A&E – grabbed some money from the drawer, picked up my helmet and galloped down the stairs and out to the bike, with Mum calling after me to be careful. Now I was back, a different person, depleted and damaged, both physically and psychologically.

The familiarity of the room, though, made me smile as I took in the headache-inducing curtains throbbing in the window above the single bed and the walls boasting an eclectic array of posters: Debbie

Harry cavorting beneath a glitter ball, positioned so that she was the last thing I saw as I fell asleep; Lemmy from Motorhead, mean and warty; and my favourite band, The Specials, looking disconsolate on some post-industrial waste ground. A wood-effect unit from MFI made up of wardrobe, drawers and bookshelf overawed the room. If the fitted carpet had been cut around it, it would've slashed half the square meterage off the price. And there, taking pride of place on that MFI unit, was my radio cassette player. I thought of all those Sunday evenings sat poised with a blank cassette on pause, ready to hit the record button, as I listened to Radio One's Top 40, one of an army of teenagers up and down the country making compilations of the latest hits.

I sat on the bed. My bed. For the first time in months, I was alone. Not just with my thoughts but alone physically. In Rookwood there'd always been someone in close proximity. There are those that are unnerved by their own company but I embraced it. Always had. Not the desperate loneliness of exclusion but a loneliness of choice, a detachment from the human sphere knowing I could re-engage at will. I liked to think, muse, and dream, you see. I was always mulling, but sadly, never doing. But now that there were grand plans to make, adventures to contemplate, once the old me was back, of course. I'd need lots of thinking time.

I'd been discharged from hospital but was still hostage to certain medical interventions. Bladder control was weak, with the time between the urge and discharge short. Not pissing yourself is one of those norms of self-respect, contributing to a basic quality of life, so away from the house I continued to wear a bag. With the fine finger skills of a shop mannequin, I needed assistance with the installation of my personal plumbing. Dad would do it. When he was in work, Mum would do it. Something to bring us all closer together! Dignity, then, in addition to that first run, would have to be put on hold. After a couple of weeks, I reclaimed sufficient manual dexterity so that I could just about manage it, accompanied by some ferocious outbursts.

If only I'd been rolling a condom on for a more pleasurable reason. For the time being though, girls were off the menu, as stripping off to reveal a bag full of urine strapped to your calf would be a guaranteed passion-killer.

My friends were magnificent, heroes to a man, and the odd woman; attentive, indulgent, patient. Part mates, part carers, they treaded carefully, mindful of my fragile mental state and tailoring outings to accommodate my restricted physical abilities. Everything had to be exact. When I began venturing to the pub – where else? – they'd sweep in ahead of me like secret service agents sussing out the joint, ensuring the path to our table was clear and forming a human shield as I walked falteringly amongst the patrons. I'd drink two pints with Viking enthusiasm, heady and happy, acquiring a warm calf as the bag filled. Never more than two, for the time being, as my legs couldn't take my desired quota. They'd escort me back to the car, perhaps with a little more support than when we'd arrived, and taxi me home to Mum and Dad, who'd trot out to meet me with relaxed concern, relieved I was back safely but determined not to show it. It was like I was five again, being taken out by family friends who could be entrusted with my well-being.

Mucky was jobless and so he became the most attentive. That's not to suggest he felt duty-bound. He called most days, as he was a kind person and he was my friend. Mum welcomed him with a warm but nervy smile. She adored Mucky but was wary of his speedy alter ego, and what seemed like stunt-driving auditions for a sequel to *Bullitt*. He drove fast, the long drag between zero and flat out an inconvenience. When travelling – with anyone, but especially with Mucky – I wore a rigid collar round my neck for added support till my muscles strengthened. He'd belt me in, then, with business-like determination, roll up the sleeves of his checked shirt, the sign for take-off.

'Fancy an ice cream down the beach?'

'Aye, go on then.'

We got there, rapidly, and sat in the car with our cones, windows down, staring out to sea like a couple of OAPs. With some of the other boys prolonged silences were uncomfortable, feeling the need to puncture a hush that got heavier and heavier. With Mucky it was different, more relaxed. It was okay to sit mute for five or ten minutes, just absorbing the sounds and smells of being by the beach on a summer's day.

'So, work. When you going back?' he asked, after a lengthy bout of licking.

I'd promised myself I wouldn't return to Trecwn. But then again, ex-cons often swear they'll never go back inside.

'Dunno. Get fit then think about it perhaps.'

'Perhaps? Don't sound so sure.'

I wanted to shout, 'No fucking way I'm going back.'

'Don't know whether I've gone through all this... this fucking nightmare, to go back there,' I said. 'Must be more to life.'

He didn't have a job and wanted one. I had a job that I didn't want.

'Any luck with you, then? Jobs?' I asked.

'Nah, nothing.'

Waves crashed against the shore, the tinkling of pebbles dragged by the ebbing water sounding like a discordant xylophone. With the sun beating down on my face, the tang of salty air on my lips, I closed my eyes and drank in the freedom, my senses reawakening.

Making our way back from the coast we came up behind a spud lorry trundling along a dusty lane.

Mucky sighed the sigh of the rudely delayed. 'Come on, for Christ sakes,' he snarled.

The road was little wider than the lorry as he began veering from side to side hoping to glimpse a gap. I may've been damaged and weak but I realised the wisdom of bracing myself best I could for the impending manoeuvre.

'Hold on,' he said.

With my Action Man hands – the moulded plastic ones of my early days in Rookwood had been superseded by the more functional, yet still weak, grippy rubber hands of the later Action Man – I grabbed the door handle and stiffened my stick-like legs against the footwell for all I was worth. He knocked it down a gear, floored it, and pulled out, hugging the outside of the lorry like a mountaineer clinging to a precipitous ledge. The wheels on my side were running on tarmac while his side was rutted in a shallow ditch. As we juddered by, I peered out of the window to see the underside of the lorry overlapping the roofline of the car; we were technically under it. Then we were past.

'Sorry about that. Bit tighter than I thought,' he said.

It was strangely reassuring that he'd overlooked my recent travails and treated me as he'd have done pre-accident – with disregard. But I'd known the deal before I got in the car. He'd drive fast and overtake anything that deigned to place itself in front of him. It was the compact by which all of the boys entered the vehicle.

Mucky and I had come a long way since our first encounter. After leaving college in '82 with a borderline pass in engineering – and a less than borderline intention of pursuing it as a career – I endured a friendless summer, aside from the hope I invested in Martin, who I'd met on the course. He had an established circle of friends, which included Mucky, so pursuing our potential wasn't an imperative for him. It was for me, though. Martin was it and I clung to him like a drowning man to a piece of driftwood. He was indulgent and polite in entertaining my suggestions for meeting up, and gradually my tenacity bore fruit as he began to view me as more than just an eager irritant on the other end of the phone.

'I'm meeting up with the boys' tomorrow night. Fancy coming along?' he said.

He'd regaled me with tales of the gang. Their exploits, scrapes, perhaps even the semi-mythical standing attached to some. And now Martin deemed it safe to introduce me, as if he'd been appraising my potential, weighing me up to see whether I might fit in.

He picked me up on his bike and we drifted out of town along lanes to the Olde Inn, a pub situated nowhere in particular in the countryside. The car park was full, as the drink flowed with blanket levels of intoxication. An illogical calculation deemed driving home along quiet lanes tanked-up as acceptable. Who could you possibly collide with except a drunk driver heading home from another pub?

I was apprehensive, as if auditioning for the most important role of my life, a part in the ongoing soap opera 'Martin and his friends'. He introduced me with a salesman-like eagerness, conscious that his reputation was on the line. If I bombed, it wouldn't reflect well on him. They smiled and nodded without conviction, perhaps unsure as to whether they needed a new addition. The Olde Inn was their den and I was treading on hallowed turf.

Simon, Stephen, Gary and his girlfriend Heidi, and Mucky, and the notorious Julian were all sitting huddled around a small table. They budged up, making just enough space for one more stool; Martin's stool. I sat at an adjoining table on my own, an inconsequential moon orbiting the planet I wanted to be on. It wasn't going well. I made attempts to break into the conversation from outside of the circle but lukewarm sideways glances suggested a lack of success. Martin tried valiantly to involve me, but they weren't buying it. I prayed for a hole to open up and swallow me.

Then, Mucky got up to get a refill. Five minutes later his stool was still vacant as he was deep in conversation by the bar. I was desperate to make inroads and saw my chance. I sat on his stool and began a charm offensive with the remaining throng, who suddenly seemed attentive now that I was on the same table. Mucky returned.

'You're in my seat.' Delivered with stony determination, he was confident his alpha-male posturing would shift me, and if necessary humiliate me.

I half stood and glanced behind. 'Funny, can't see your name on it,' I replied, playing it for laughs, of which there weren't any, as the others began to fidget and look away. Mucky couldn't back down at such a challenge and they knew it.

'You're in my seat. Move.'

He was a principled man. Principled and, when it suited, bloody belligerent.

'Look,' I said, pointing to the empty table I'd escaped from. 'Plenty more seats.'

He glared at me with a visceral and intense dislike and took a step closer, to within range. If I continued to resist, a fight was on the cards, so I moved back to the orbiting table, defeated. An inauspicious beginning to our friendship.

Simon, Stephen and Gary were surfers. Well, when I say surfers, what I mean is they owned surfboards. I came to realise that ownership of a board didn't necessarily mean being able to surf. Gary was the best – it was marginal – as he could actually stand for a few seconds. After I came home from Rookwood, Simon would pick me up in his British racing green Morris Marina, a four-door version of Mucky's British racing green Morris Marina. Simon's driving didn't unnerve Mum, his style more excitable vicar than Mucky's adrenalised Steve McQueen. Gary also owned a British racing green Morris Marina. It was the car to have; British, green, but not that racy.

On arrival at the beach the three wise augurs would study the waves for an age to determine whether the lines were right or if it was a little mushy or some other vague surf-speak. Eventually, they'd commit and canter in, full of brio, sitting out on their boards, waiting, waiting, waiting to catch a wave and falling off the moment they attempted to stand. They'd haul themselves back on and paddle out again to wait, wait, wait for another wave and the whole process would repeat itself like some groundhog afternoon. As hypothermia began to set in, much like the contestants in a Japanese endurance game show of the '80s, each was determined to be the last to head to shore, regardless. I concluded that when I recovered, I wouldn't be getting into surfing.

Mum had a full-length mirror in her bedroom and one morning after showering I decided to confront it, imagining, praying, that somehow, all of the emaciated muscular imbalances would've corrected themselves and that I'd see symmetry. See perfection. See bulk. I didn't. Deep down I'd known that I wouldn't. I may have avoided mirrors after that first encounter in Rookwood, but I'd still been able to feel the wasted left side of my chest, the empty space where my triceps should've been, the bony forearms and, of course, those spindly legs. Like a community returning to its bombed-out village after a war, I couldn't even begin to imagine how I'd ever rebuild what I saw was still missing. It was too much, surely, the destruction having a totality – even a finality – to it. Had I been fooling myself with all of the messianic certainty of a complete recovery? I was beginning to ask that question more and more. But the moment I wavered, I regathered myself and reaffirmed my conviction that, in time, I'd return to who I once was physically. The faith remained. It had to, as the alternative was terrifying. As the weeks since discharge were beginning to cluster into a month and more though, I was wavering more often as the pace of recovery was falling behind the graph of expectation in my head.

All of that pre-accident exercise pride, those press-ups, the boxing club, pumping iron in the garage, going for runs, was gone. I couldn't pretend I'd ever been a serious contender, or shown promise in any sport, but there'd always been a discipline of fitness, a willingness to jog, cycle to the beach, anything that pushed me. I'd been fit, taking vain pleasure in feats of strength and endurance, like the time I pumped out a set of fifty press-ups for a lunchtime audience in Trecwn with ease while my challenger struggled to do thirty.

When I was fourteen, I joined the tennis club, a five-minute run from the house. I liked tennis and the sense of achievement from hitting a ball, a game that bestows an immediate delusion of competence. This is easy, I thought. My technique, if that's how it could've been described, manifested itself in hitting the ball very hard, so that it rarely landed on the playing surface. But boy, when the ball did land in the court, it was unplayable. There weren't enough unplayable shots to win many matches though.

Tennis, I came to realise, is a game of precision – and yes, power – dependent on footwork, racquet head alignment, regularity of stroke and an almost balletic poise. I displayed flashes of those individual elements allied to a lack of synchronicity; the good bits never came together at the same time. Frustrated, I went through a number of racquets, pinging them at the floor or hurling them against the practice wall at the back of the court.

'What do you want for Christmas?' asked Dad one summer. He liked to plan ahead.

'A Dunlop Max-ply Fort please.'

'What?'

'It's a tennis racquet. Really good one. God, if I had one of those,' I said.

John McEnroe used one, and perhaps I felt an affinity with his temper tantrums.

'Okay. Fine,' said Dad. He smiled the smile of paternal beneficence fused with relief that he'd parked that particular festive headache.

A couple of days later I was playing a heated match with my mate Paul, all of the heat coming from my side of the net. Paul was one of the few trusted boys that I limped through school with. He drank in life with gleeful headiness, always smiling, always positive, always the generous spirited one. There was no side to Paul. And he had enough physical deterrence to ward off any unpleasant attention. I envied him. And Paul was a calm tennis player as Paul had a smattering of talent. He was better than me and I knew it and I hated it.

It was a baking hot day as I wilted on the dusty clay surface. With each winning shot that flew past me and my own inept returns slamming into the boundary fence without deigning to kiss the court's surface I became more agitated. To the surprise of neither of us, I threw my racquet against the practice wall. There was a sharp crack, like a rifle shot, and I dragged my feet over to pluck a broken racquet from the floor. As I swore and ached to rewind just half a minute, Paul came over and whispered, 'Don't look, but your dad's watching.'

Sick with embarrassment, I sneaked a furtive glance and saw the back of him as he walked away. I put off going home for as long as I could, as I knew the aching, quiet disappointment that'd greet me. If only he'd shout and get it over with, I thought. I crept in, praying he'd be at the club playing dominoes; he liked that. But no, he was in the kitchen with his back to me, washing up. Without turning he said, 'Broken?'

'Yeah,' I mumbled and went upstairs. I was assured there'd be no Dunlop Max-ply Fort that Christmas. With the money I'd earned on the milk round I bought a replacement racquet, being more inclined to control my temper from then on.

School rugby was another arena of sporting mediocrity. Initially I'd shown promise, a standout player on the seconds pitch, jinking and side-stepping and executing technically incorrect tackles on a host of fat kids. Then, one day the hoped-for call came.

'Hey, Wilson, fancy a go with the firsts?' said the games teacher.

With the humble nod of the rightfully anointed I trotted across to where the action was hotter, more intense and more brutal.

The moment I arrived on the pitch, a player with a number of Welsh youth caps plotted a path my way. Tackle him, this particular beast, and my place in the Sir Thomas Picton hall of sporting fame would be guaranteed. Muscular and bull-like, dripping with malevolent levels of testosterone, away from the rugby pitch he was feared county-wide for his fighting prowess. He'd even taken on teachers, and won. I positioned myself for the tackle and crouched, ready to nail him.

I don't remember the collision, only that he ran over me, wiping his feet on my chest and strolling over for a try.

'You getting up then, Wilson?' asked the games teacher with scant sympathy. I got to my feet. The concussion check consisted of being asked what day it was. With just seven to choose from, it didn't take too long. He offered me an escape back to the safety of the fat kids. I took it.

When not doing twelve-hour shifts at the refinery, I often remember Dad dozing in the chair with an exhaustion not unlike jet lag. It was hard on him, but he never complained, about anything, ever. Even years later, when he underwent a quadruple heart bypass in his early fifties, he returned to work before he was expected to. He just got on with things. As I morphed into a teenager, which in my case took the form of an anti-social disease, I became wilful and surly, a symptom perhaps of my unhappiness at school; watching your back every day gets you down. There was a period of possibly six months when I didn't speak to my parents – as in initiate a conversation – furnishing them with just clipped responses. Dad's awkward attempts at fostering a deeper connection were spitefully rebuffed, like I was testing his mettle, seeing how much he really wanted it. Without memories of his own father there was no dad manual to refer to. But he kept trying, somehow suppressing the urge to throttle me.

He played cricket for the refinery team. I liked cricket and had been selected as twelfth man for the school team. Twelfth man is like being invited to the coolest house party in town, only to be told you have to witness it from out in the street; you can see and hear the action but aren't a part of it – a sub that never gets to play.

'Playing St Ishmaels tonight. Fancy coming down? Might get a game if we're short,' said Dad.

He was inviting me to join the men, his mates, and I felt an inflation of masculinity.

'Yeah, okay,' I said, being careful not to sound too enthused.

They were indeed a player short, and I was in. I didn't disgrace myself, cutting off a couple of boundaries, batting at the end of the innings and edging a couple of fluky singles. In the club afterwards I stood with the men at the bar as they quaffed pints, listening with rapt attention as they laughed and joked and swore with regal authority. Some of them even spoke to me. What a night. And others followed.

During his time in the Royal Navy, Dad had served on the aircraft carrier HMS *Ark Royal*. In the mid-seventies, a decade after he'd left the service, a documentary about life on board the carrier – aptly called *Sailor* – was aired. The throaty vocals of Rod Stewart's 'Sailing' accompanied the opening credits as we'd settle down to watch. The footage and narration brought it all back to him and he became animated, telling me about working on deck, launching jets using a steam-powered catapult.

'Bloody dangerous. I remember we lost a young pilot over the side. Landing a jet on deck when it's pitching and rolling is a bugger,' he said.

'Pitching and rolling?'

'The ship... going up and down and side to side at the same time. Poor sod misjudged and went over the edge...into the sea. We ran over and saw him in the cockpit. Couldn't get out. Went down with him in it.'

He looked away, no doubt taking a moment to think of him, whoever he had been.

'Another bloke walked behind a jet on full throttle... ready for take-off. Blew him in the air and over the side. Never found him.'

And this at a time when the navy issued a daily quart of rum to each of the crew. 'If I was on duty I'd give mine away. Others didn't,' he said.

Dad and I now had a joint endeavour into which we could pour our energies: getting me fit. Getting me back to normal. He revealed a hitherto camouflaged love, manifested in little acts of selfless dedication. He didn't always know what to say when I broke down and wept and cursed and blamed everything on anything or anyone other than myself. But I could see in his face that he was with me even if he couldn't articulate it.

I needed to walk to build strength so that I could walk like everyone else; the kind of virtuous circle I liked the sound of. The easiest and most convenient option would've been to walk around the wider estate, of which Masefield Drive was a small part, a flat, even surface, the ideal strolling-for-beginners terrain. But my irregular stride pattern and need for a supporting arm made me achingly self-conscious. I dreaded the thought of twitching curtains and pitying glances, craving privacy instead, a secret programme out of view so that I could focus on the task at hand. And so, we drove to a spot a mile from the house in a quiet lane, parking at the bottom of a hill. I got to know that hill well, its gradient, its camber, the foot-catching grittiness of the tarmac. Asleep, I dreamt that hill and woke knowing that it was waiting for me, like a training partner, drawing me to it. At the beginning Dad would cup my arm and gently clasp my hand.

'You ready?'

'Yeah, let's go,' I'd say.

And off we'd stride, me faltering, out of sync at first but increasingly in tune, like a couple of soldiers marching in step as the weeks went by. Up the hill, round the bend and onwards to a tumbledown manor that I'd played on as a kid with my estate friend Aled, we'd then turn and retrace our steps back to the car. The same walk, day after day – I liked the measurability of it. It was tough in the beginning, with halts from exhaustion, legs shaking spastically, lungs rasping. Dad would hold me firm while I recuperated and we'd carry on.

I was in an exclusive club that I hadn't asked to join, much like the other members. Certainly, a lesser injury and the forgoing of membership would've been welcome: a broken leg or a ruptured spleen perhaps, the humdrum knockabout of gone-wrong motorcycling. But no, I went for the platinum level injury, the show-stopper, the tragically wounded hero. Indeed, all of the attention I'd basked in on coming home had invested me with delusions of heroism. It soon waned though, as reality bit. Struggling up that hill didn't feel heroic, just bloody hard. But it worked. Each week I walked further and faster and soon I was walking without support. That run was coming, I was certain of that.

The summer of 1984 was a good time for any recently discharged spinal injuries patients in search of motivation on their road to recovery – the Los Angeles Olympics were on. I'm not saying that it was a good year per se to mangle your spine, as to suffer a spinal injury would be an *annus horribilis* regardless, but the sight of Steve Redgrave winning his first rowing gold was certainly inspiring, at least for me. In his honour, and in my own quest for gold, I ordered a rowing machine, from Mum's Grattan catalogue, of course. A huge box arrived, I unpacked it and got stuck in. However, stroking across the surface of a glassy lake in California with the scent of gold in your nostrils is a world away from the static exhaustion of a paisley-patterned living room in west Wales. I soon discovered that strenuous, often painful exertion merely to produce motionless motion made for a soul-destroying oxymoron. My enthusiasm waned. Cheap and clunky, it was a contraption that provided little joy, and it soon began to gather dust. Having gathered a decent layer, it then went to live in a cupboard.

Maybe, I thought, an exercise bike might be more enjoyable; I'd always liked cycling. Another huge box arrived from Grattan and in my head I began to compete in stages of the Tour de France. Alas, it wasn't long before the problem-solving skills of a Krypton Factor contestant were required to work out how to jam the bike into the same cupboard as the rowing machine.

As an arena of physical expression, the swimming pool retained my affections a lot longer than my rowing or cycling aspirations.

Initially, Dad or, when he was working, Mum, would come with me, standing in the shallow end and watching as I cautiously descended the ladder. On breaking the surface, the coldness of the water would trigger riotous spasms in that leg, as if electrodes had been attached and the dial whacked right up. Gripping the ladder tight, I'd wait for the twitching and jumping to ease, then drop the other leg in and go through the whole process again. At last, though, I'd be in, laying back in the water and spreading my arms as I pushed away from the side and glided out into the middle of the pool.

The sensation of buoyancy was freeing, the swimming pool coming close to delivering that illusion of physical normality. Running, jumping, pirouetting like a ballet dancer; I could do it all – in water. In the pool I was the same as everyone around me, and I craved swimming more than anything else, the activity that most kept alive that belief in a return to the old me. Plus, if I went at lunch times there was always a chance of seeing a particular young blonde lady in a leopard-print swimsuit doing breast-stroke lengths. She didn't notice me, of course, but her indifference didn't make the vision of her gliding by any less gratifying.

An incremental clawing back of confidence meant that it wasn't long before I went to the pool alone. By this point I'd taken to diving in untidily off the side rather than using the ladder. The overwhelming shock of my entire body being submerged instantaneously seemed to negate the spasm issues. In the pool, then, everything seemed possible. Guaranteed even.

There were days when I was physically spent from overexertion the previous day; when I exercised, I tended to overdo it, convinced that the more I pushed the quicker I'd recover everything. And so, on these dead muscle days, I'd settle down to do Airfix models. I remember painting a Panzer MK IV in the desert colours of the Afrika Korps. It was to share a shelf with a Stuka dive bomber and a Messerschmitt Bf 109. Aside from the British Spitfire and Mosquito aeroplanes, the Germans had built the best-looking kit during the war, just not enough of it to win, thankfully.

It was often an infuriating exercise, with the occasional model destroyed before it had even come off the production line; my temper was hotter than ever, with a hare trigger that was perhaps unsuitable to the task in hand, literally. But, with a number of models built, I managed to reclaim a fine-ish manual dexterity, or at least an acceptable level of motor function. The smaller the scale, the bigger the challenge.

Walking up and down 'the hill' was all well and good but I craved variety and so began going to the beach in the early evening when the holidaying hoards had packed up and gone. The sands were too public compared to the private hill that Dad and I had walked, so we probed the headland paths away from the beach below. One evening, at sunset, I thought, 'I should bring my camera.' Languishing in a cupboard at home, it was associated with treks into the hills on my bike. And any association with the bike was a reminder. A reminder of loss.

I dug it out, though, and it helped, providing a psychological cloak to hide behind, and a mechanism to distract me from the anguish of my ugly walking. With the camera I discovered a renewed sense of purpose, taking forgettable photographs, but wanting to take more. It felt productive. And it gave me another reason, besides getting fit, to venture into open spaces. The camera was back in my life.

By the end of the summer of '84 I was still determining improvements in my physical abilities, but there was no doubt that the pace had slackened. I seemed to be running out of momentum but remained convinced that I'd avoid the feared plateau; that petering-out of recovered function short of normality. It was taking longer than I'd hoped, but the old me – the boy on the rock in Tenby – was surely within my grasp.

Chapter 14

It sang to me, and I coveted it as I ran a hand along its sleek lines.

'This is the one. Definitely,' I said.

'You sure? What about the one yesterday?' asked Dad.

'No, I like this one more.'

I turned to the salesman perched at my shoulder. He'd given me the one lady owner from new, fully serviced, not a mark on her spiel and was hovering in expectation.

'Yeah, I'll take it,' I said.

'Great. Won't go wrong with this one, sir. Best example around. Absolute beaut,' he wittered, with practised enthusiasm.

In the wake of his professional smile, I followed him into a faggy Portakabin, being treated like his latest best mate on account of my desire for a car on his forecourt. He went through the documentation with slavering efficiency and it was mine.

The next day, in early January '85, my new 'best mate' delivered a red Ford Escort XR3 to our house. Mum insisted on offering him a cup of tea and, much to my annoyance, he insisted on accepting. I just wanted him to leave so that I could go out and coo over my car.

He made himself at home in the lounge, reeling off a string of supposed adventures in various exotic parts of the world before washing up in Haverfordwest – and why not? – ate the best part of a fruit cake, washed down with two cuppas, then left. Finally, I was able to go out and marvel.

I'd attended a medical the month before to determine whether I should be allowed back on the road in control of a vehicle. The prospect of independence had been dangled before me and I'd been nervous, concerned that I might be deemed physically incapable. I was also fed up by this time of being taxied around by my parents and friends.

Sitting in the doctor's waiting room I'd dreamt of a return to two wheels, while knowing deep down it wasn't going to happen. Knowing that ten months on from the accident I hadn't returned to how I once was and that the leaps of recovered function that'd been apparent after coming home from Rookwood had become snail-paced, or even undetectable. Operating the brake and clutch levers on a bike, then, was a fanciful notion, let alone swinging my leg over to get on the bloody thing. Had I arrived on the dreaded plateau, short of the glittering peak of a complete recovery? The evidence suggested I may have, though I still had faith that I'd get everything back. That faith, though, was beginning to weaken.

The medical consisted of tests of balance, strength, coordination and especially hand grip. I focused and tried harder than in any test or exam or assessment ever in my life; my school days would certainly have benefitted from an equivalent effort. Even so, there were gaps, blank physical spaces, glaring inabilities – disabilities; a catchall that I despised but which seemed to be cropping up more and more in conversations with the caring and medical professions. They were mistaken, of course.

The doctor conducted the examination with cheerless indifference, issuing instructions, ticking boxes and writing notes. I wanted him to put an arm around me and say, 'You're okay to get back on a bike. And don't worry, you'll make a full recovery.' He said nothing. Or at least nothing that I wanted to hear.

His subsequent report stated that I was physically competent to drive a car, without adaptations – which was a relief – but not to ride a motorbike. Mum and Dad were quietly ecstatic. I was downcast. The withholding of my bike licence was confirmation that I was indeed compromised. But then I knew that already. Reflecting on what an accident-prone biker I'd been – there'd been many warm-up collisions before the main event – the doctor was, if nothing else, saving me from myself. But, a bit of who I'd been was gone and that made me sad.

Riding a motorbike, you see, is to straddle a line – in my case a very fine line – between preservation and oblivion. It's exciting, hanging out there on the edge, keeping just enough back to ride another day. In the end, I wasn't very good at keeping just enough back. Did I have a death wish? Well, no, but I certainly rode like I might have.

After the accident, A&E had bagged up my helmet, boots and cut-off clothing; the loss of the Belstaff still rankled with me. My identity in a plastic bag. Dad took it straight to the tip, not wanting it in the house. There'd been another bike too – a Honda 250cc Superdream – in the garage. I'd bought it as a project to do up for when I passed my bike test. When I came home from Rookwood, it was gone. A workmate of Dad's had bought it. A motorcyclist himself, he didn't want it but knew Mum and Dad couldn't cope with it being around, so he made it disappear. The bike I'd crashed on the night was already scrapped, after killing itself in some railings. With all physical evidence expunged, it was like I'd never been a motorcyclist.

I passed my driving test in May '83, days before my eighteenth birthday. A few weeks previous to passing my driving test I'd ridden the gleaming black Yamaha out of Mason's Motorcycles in Haverfordwest; Martin had sold me on the biking life in spite of the driving lessons I'd been taking. I just couldn't resist the lure of the two-wheeled horse. If a four-wheeled metal box had been wrapped around me on the evening of 16th February 1984, at most I'd have sustained bruising and would, no doubt, have had a temper tantrum due to a dented motor. Car: bruised ego. Bike: catastrophic injury. If I'd passed my driving test earlier, things may have been very different. As Mark Twain said, 'Life's like rowing down a river: you don't know what's coming till it passes you by.' Or something like that.

If only – yes, another 'if only' – I'd left the house that night a minute later, or earlier even, the accident wouldn't have happened. It couldn't have happened as I'd have missed the slot allotted for my demise. But – call it fate if you like – a day of little acts and occurrences and decisions and indecisions had coalesced to cause me to leave the house when I did. But who knows, if I'd left home that minute earlier or later, I might've been squished by a lorry a bit further along the same road; different timeline, different ending. Or, perhaps, I'd have made it to the pub; the more probable outcome.

Bad stuff happens. It's a part of life. Perhaps not a road traffic accident resulting in near total paralysis but bad stuff all the same. And good stuff, of course. The highs and lows of living. You don't know what awaits, good or bad, till it hits you. Twain's rowing boat.

I like to think of life as a cricket innings. As analogies go, it's good. It fits. You head out to bat with the possibilities of your span stretching ahead. Stroke-making though, the actual act of living, is a risky business and close calls occur; dropped catches, failed LBW appeals, near run-outs. Life's little scrapes: falling from rope swings; coming off your bicycle; plunging out of trees. Aled and his broken wrist. Having my fingernails torn off on a pebble-dashed wall. Heart in the mouth moments.

All innings are terminated, but in the mean-time you just keep flashing that bat, plugging away, hoping to rack up a decent score, a fifty, a century even. Having nudged my way without major incident to eighteen – not a broken bone to my name – I skied a catch to the wicket keeper. My innings, it seemed, was over.

Doubtless there'd been previous fateful incidents lined up for me that I managed to avoid, being that minute early or late. Goodness knows how many appointments with oblivion Mucky had avoided in his Morris Marina. I do recall a carful of us bouncing off a hedge once, though, when he was at the wheel; a weak LBW appeal, perhaps.

But, at 20.30 hrs on 16th February 1984, I was bang on time for the rendezvous. Bugger. With the arrangements made, the meet set in motion, he donned his black shroud, sharpened his scythe and waited for me on the pavement opposite Jubilee Gardens at the bottom of Barn Street, Haverfordwest, Pembrokeshire, Wales, the world. He had business to conduct, and I was that business.

The end of my innings was nigh. With beautiful clarity he witnessed the tragic tableau unfold: the car descending the one-way road in one lane, me bearing down in the other. Closer, closer, yet closer still, his calculations were exemplary as the car drifted across, I swerved, hit the kerb, trampolined in the air and landed right at his feet. Inch perfect.

'Good evening, David. Been expecting you,' he said, glancing down, ready to harvest me. But the wicketkeeper went and dropped it. I was unreaped and still out in the field, just.

A year before landing on the pavement I had my first driving lesson. At that point there were no motorbiking aspirations as such, being undecided as to whether I'd opt for two or four wheels. Mr Smithies, the instructor, picked me up in a pale blue Ford Escort then drove to a layby on the edge of town where we swapped seats. It was the first time I'd sat behind the wheel of a car with intent.

'So, just touch the accelerator pedal with your foot,' he said.

I placed my right foot on the accelerator. Then he instructed me to touch the clutch pedal.

He sighed. 'No, the clutch is the left-hand pedal. That's the brake.'

I had a mechanical understanding of how a car achieved forward momentum courtesy of my wasted year on an engineering course. Converting that theory into practice would be the challenge, a challenge that promised to be insurmountable, seeing as I couldn't even locate the clutch.

After a tetchy lecture, Mr Smithies instructed me to start the engine, dip the clutch, engage first gear, and let the clutch out slowly while releasing the handbrake. I stalled. I continued to stall, and the more I stalled the more likely it was I'd stall again, a vicious circle of self-fulfilling idiocy. He lit a cigarette and glanced out of the window, drawing heavily and no doubt wishing he were somewhere else. Decades of first lessons seemed to have sapped any distant recollection of satisfaction the job may once have held. We got going, eventually, the stench of burnt clutch nullifying the reek of his stubbed-out fag.

Nudging retirement, he had the crumpled midriff of one who'd spent an inordinate proportion of their life sitting down.

His vocabulary soon revealed itself to be quite naval, more suited to the lower decks than the pinched confines of a Ford Escort. I warmed to his gruffness and blaspheming, though. I liked him. After six lessons he suggested without enthusiasm that I should put in for my test.

'Be a couple of months down the line if we apply now. May as well give it a go. Good experience if nothing else,' he said.

Not the most sweeping endorsement of my driving prowess, but I went with his advice and signed the form. And as the weeks wore on, test experience was seemingly all I'd get out of it. Lessons were a litany of repeated errors and each time I got into the car I wondered what would go wrong and how he'd react; tact wasn't one of his strong points. As the hour-long lessons progressed, I'd begin to get a feel for driving once again, sense the clutch's resistance, begin to own the road and judge the car's tempo. Slot into the groove if you like. Then it'd be over for another week, seven days in which to lose all that I'd assimilated during the latter part of the lesson.

On the day of my presumed test failure, I had a half-hour warm-up lesson. Driving instructors are creatures of habit, prone like murderers to return to particular spots. Three-point turns were conducted on a road near to his bungalow, handy for nipping in when he'd forgotten his fags. Hill starts were performed close to the bakery I'd worked in as a kid. Reversing round a corner was my most error-strewn debacle, his favoured location running adjacent to a privet hedge with no pavement to separate the hedge from the road. And, as usual, I reversed into the hedge.

'Jesus Christ, boy. Why do I bloody bother?'

I put it in first gear and disentangled the car. He lit up and we made our way to the test centre.

'Give it your best shot. Never know, you might pass,' he said, with all of the conviction of Charles Manson's defence team.

Mr Smithies got out of the car and leant back in. 'I've got a form ready to reapply,' he said, then after a long pause, added, 'If you need it, that is.'

The examiner appeared, took his place in the passenger seat, went through some formalities, then instructed me to depart from the test centre. Mr Smithies was reconciled to failure and I was inclined to agree. It'd be good experience though. Yeah, definitely good experience.

The first obstacle loomed – a roundabout, my stalling *Top of the Pops*. But, with no traffic to give way to, I sailed onto it imperiously and onwards. The next ambush was the emergency stop; I didn't skid or stall the engine. The motoring gods were with me. The three-point turn was performed on a wider road than usual. Faultless. Just the reversing round a corner to go. There was no privet hedge to embed the car in and I completed it without scuffing the kerb. Perfect. A warm realisation began to well up; keep it together for the Highway Code at the end of the test and I was in with a shot. For weeks in Trecwn I'd foregone my afternoon nap to bone up on the laws, rules and regs of the road and knew every braking distance, street sign and road marking he could possibly throw at me.

After a number of questions, he said, 'Congratulations, you've passed your driving test.' He handed me a pass notice, declining to shake my outstretched hand as he got out of the car. I was dumbstruck as I too got out. Mr Smithies walked towards me.

'I've filled the form in. Just need to sign it,' he said.

I held up the pass notice.

His jaw dropped. 'You passed? Bloody hell.'

'Surprised you ever doubted it,' I said.

We laughed furiously, which was nice, as during my twelve lessons with him there hadn't been much cause for laughter. I couldn't safely drive a car, yet was legally entitled to, having completed a fault-free run. A first. He offered me a lift home. I lived five minutes away, so said I'd walk. Still shaking his head, he wished me all the best, no doubt deliberating over whether I should be allowed onto the public highway. Had he created an imminent pile-up?

I strolled home in the May sunshine, eager to get out on my bike, which I'd had for just a few weeks, and was the mode of transport I felt most affinity with. Cars could wait. Twelve lessons, though. That's all it'd taken. There were countless disgruntled yet eminently more competent learner drivers who'd failed their tests. But it was me that had the official piece of paper stating I was qualified to drive a car... alone. I may've stolen someone else's dream, but I had no intention of living it. The Holy Grail, for me, would be the motorbike test I was yet to take. Pass that and I'd progress to bigger beasts, a Kawasaki GPZ 1100 perhaps, replete with a woman of lax morality perched on the back. The girl from the office in Trecwn perhaps. That was my dream; big bike and loose girl.

A few months later I took the bike test, with promotion to deadlier machines tantalisingly close. I failed it. My motoring paradox was laid bare that day: according to the examiner, I lacked the basic skills to be a full-fat motorcyclist, yet was deemed competent to drive a car. I could legally drive what I didn't want but couldn't ride what I desired the most. Events yet to unfold would crystallise that paradox.

And so, in January '85, nearly two years after passing my driving test, during which time I hadn't driven a car, and with my licence reissued after the medical – minus permission to ride a bike – I contacted Mr Smithies for refresher lessons to prepare me for the freedom of a car, the consolation prize I'd previously shunned. The red Escort XR3 would have to suffice. There was a perverse pleasure in being smoked over once again, his irascible honesty as heartening as ever.

Having reacquainted myself with the synergy of driving, I became a taxi service for the lads. It was nice to return the favours. But there was no Mucky to pick up. He'd struggled to find a job in the area commensurate with his high expectations and so had joined the MoD police. The new career meant a new country: England. He moved away to build a life and have an adventure, returning occasionally, but as time rolled on it became ever more occasional and then he was permanently gone. I was glad for him that he'd found the job he deserved. Didn't stop me missing him though.

Chapter 15

'Been nice seeing you progress. All the best,' she said, motioning to leave and reaching for the door handle. But I couldn't let her go without asking.

'Can I ask something?'

'Of course. What is it?' she said.

It was a big question. Enormous, in fact. And being a district nurse, it made sense that I should ask her. She had to give me the right answer, though.

'When will I... well, get back to normal? What I mean is, when will I be like I was? Before the accident?'

She'd been professional and polite in her dealings with me, an insecure nineteen-year-old with a spinal injury, but there'd been little warmth or rapport between us, despite my efforts. During the months she'd been calling, I'd never managed to get beneath that matronly façade.

'So, you had your accident...'

'Last February,' I said.

'Right. Just over a year ago.'

I looked at her still mouth, waiting for her to continue. The pause made me uneasy.

'Well, look, David, you've come a long way in the time I've known you...' There was a 'but' coming. '...but I think you've gone as far as you can recovery-wise. What you have now is probably it.'

The words thudded into me with the power of a Frank Bruno jab.

'No, that... that can't be right. I mean, surely if I keep trying it'll come back,' I implored.

I stared at her with pleading desperation, as if my life were on the line.

'Sorry, David. You've done well. But this…' she said, gesturing with a hand from my head to my feet, '…is it. Considering how you were after the accident, you should be pleased.'

I fell back against the wall as my insides folded and began to howl tears of despair. Tears of anger. Tears for a decreed loss that I couldn't accept. And anyway, who the hell was she to tell me that I 'should be pleased'?

Perhaps discomfited at witnessing this unexpected outpouring of emotion, she hunkered down into nurse mode, explaining how nerves regenerate at a particular rate and that after a certain period of time they stop regenerating. Fucking science, again. But how could I disagree? She had qualifications, pieces of paper demonstrating her authority to pronounce my death of hope. She glanced at her watch.

'Sorry, but I really do have to go. Running late for my next patient.'

There were awkward disentangling niceties, a watery smile, and then she was gone. I slid down the wall onto the floor and curled up, her words still hanging in the air, settling on me like a pall.

She'd been assigned to me when I came home from Rookwood, calling once a week and then monthly to chart my progress and provide a conduit with other health professionals. Now, her tenure was up. Her job was done. She'd ticked all the boxes, except for the one marked empathy. I had, according to her, achieved my optimum outcome. And that parting shot, her candid neurological assessment, penetrated like a crossbow bolt. I went to my room and broke something. I was to break a lot of things.

As those first sun-shiny weeks of unbridled optimism after discharge from Rookwood had turned into months, the nagging doubts had begun to solidify into a dark certainty as the torrent of improvement dried to a trickle. When I'd asked her the question, I knew what the answer would be. I just had to hear it, I suppose, to confirm a self-evident truth while not wanting to be told. And the truth was that I was incomplete and time had run out.

In the weeks preceding her declaration of what felt like a life sentence, I'd acknowledged the missing of one physical aspiration after another. Why couldn't I run? Why were muscle groups wasted after so much effort to build them up? Why was I hamstrung by debilitating spasticity, locking my body into stone-like cramps? Why was my hand grip weak and why were my wrists so fucking floppy? Why, why, why? Of course, I knew why; my spinal cord was damaged. Months of outpatient physiotherapy, swimming, walking, exercise machines, hope, determination; it'd all been a mirage, a trick, a cruel hoax.

Possessed of some masochistic Tourette's, each morning I'd punished myself, standing in front of that full-length mirror imagining that I could optically distort perception and add bulk to my left arm and chest, add bulk to my right calf, add bulk to my thighs and sketch in that missing symmetry. The apparition I saw reflected back, though, was ugly, a Picasso disfigurement.

There was no NHS letter confirming the nurse's bombshell. No appointment with a doctor to add medical weight to her on-the-hoof verdict. But I didn't need official confirmation; she was right. I'd arrived on the dreaded plateau, short of the summit. Short of perfection. Looking up, I could still make out the vague outline of the 'walker', but rather than beckoning me on with that ever-giving smile he'd turned his back. I wouldn't be joining him. Instead of ascending a mountain and planting my own flag of complete recovery, I was faced with a flat, endless desert, an infinite horizon of despair.

I parked and walked over to the entrance gates, taking time to glance at the red-brick office buildings and warehouses stretching up the valley. I'd been away for just over a year and had been determined never to return. During that time, I'd experienced the deepest troughs of anguish, followed by periods of glittery hope and an absolute faith in a return to physical normality. Of late, the glittery hope and faith had been less apparent. Extinguished, actually.

My GP had been very accommodating, writing one extension to my sick leave after another, each one kicking the can of reckoning down the road. But the bureaucratic drag net had caught me and

Trecwn had requested my attendance at the depot for their own determining medical. They'd doled out a year's sick pay and wished to see whether they'd been investing in an irreparably damaged employee. I approached the gatehouse and tapped the sliding window. A policeman I recognised opened it.

'Bloody hell, good to see you. How you doing?'

'Yeah, okay. Here for a medical,' I said, pointing to the surgery next door.

'You're coming back, then?'

'Well, we'll see.'

I walked through the gate and along the pavement, hoping to catch a glimpse of the girl from the office. She'd surely take an interest in me now after all I'd been through. I loitered for a minute but there was no sign of her so I went in.

The surgery was a single room with a smattering of entry-level medical fixtures and equipment: a wrought-iron weighing machine with sliding counterweights, which'd surely been cast in a nineteenth-century foundry; an upholstered examination bench; a host of obtrusive spotlights seemingly nicked from a minor league football ground; a trolley displaying a collection of stainless-steel instruments. It looked like a museum to medicine, everything neat and untouched. So long as no one from the valley presented with anything other than a cut or sprain, it sufficed.

'David, lovely to see you. Take a seat. We'll get started soon as the doctor arrives,' said the nurse, who'd worked there since the time of my Grandad. She fussed with some items on the trolley while asking how I was. Creating an impression of activity was an art form in which everyone was well versed.

The doctor arrived. The nurse clucked attentively. I waited for it to begin. For the driving licence medical I'd put on the performance of my life. I wanted – no, needed – to drive. For a medical to gauge whether I should return to the open prison I was less inclined to put on a show. He began the examination.

'Raise and hold your arms out straight in front of you at shoulder height,' he ordered. 'Now, I want you to twist from the hips as far as you can to your right. Don't push it. Only what feels comfortable.'

I began to twist, suddenly buoyed with a yearning to exceed my earlier disinclination to do well in the medical. I couldn't help but show off, wanting him to be impressed and say, 'Great. That looks normal.' I'd turned about sixty of the desired ninety degrees when I sensed a wooziness of imbalance flooding me and took a step to the side to correct a fall.

'Okay, if you can twist to your left now,' he said, as he wrote on a sheet attached to a clipboard. 'Remember, just what's comfortable.'

Like a toddler eager to please, I overdid it and lost my balance, again. A rash of other tests followed, all completed with sub-normal outcomes: gripping his fingers as hard as I could, but not very hard at all; bending from a standing position to pick an item up from the floor, which remained on the floor; standing on one leg, which required an urgent replanting of the other leg to stop myself from falling over. And on it went, like some unintended humiliation.

To perform the duties of a junior storeman, never an onerous burden, required occasional physical exertion such as the lifting and stacking of ammunition boxes and the carrying of tools and equipment; also, the ability to traverse railway lines safely or hop up onto pallets of ordnance, amongst other basic physical competences. At the end of the medical it was apparent that even though I'd tried my best, it seemed likely that I hadn't achieved the required level of physical ability to be able to fulfil my job. His mollifying grin and the nurse's saccharine tone said one thing and one thing only – 'Disabled.' That bloody tag again.

The doctor thanked me for attending and departed, while the nurse insisted on making me a cup of coffee.

'If I'm not mistaken, there might be some chocolate digestives in here,' she said with a mischievous grin, opening a desk drawer. I suspected she'd opened the drawer a lot, as there weren't many to offer.

She was telling me about some comical incident from years gone by involving Gramps, when the door to the surgery opened and in she came, the girl from the office. I emitted a weird half-strangulated noise as the blood rushed to my cheeks. She was within touching distance, the closest I'd ever been.

'Just come for the post,' she said to the nurse, smiling at me with a trace of recognition as she strode across the room. I breathed her in as she passed, my heart racing. She picked up the internal mail pouch, turned and said, 'You're the boy that had the motorbike accident?'

Boy? Not a good start. 'Yes, thanks,' I said.

My incontinent reply drew a quizzical look. 'Right, well, nice to see you… er, doing so well.'

And then she was gone. All the times I'd run the script through in my head of how I was going to captivate her with some witty aside. She must've imagined I'd received a bloody brain injury. Deflated, I stood and turned towards the door. 'I'll be on my way now,' I said.

'Well, really good to see you back on your feet. Hopefully see you back here soon.' Even as she said it, I think she realised the redundancy of that last bit.

'Yeah, hopefully.'

A short self-conscious stroll outside of the main gates was the depot's social club. At lunchtimes the place filled for forty minutes of drinking before a return to weak labours. It was just after midday, so I walked up to the club to await the influx. It was affirming to see the joy on the faces of people I'd once worked with when they came in and saw me sitting by the bar. I'd rarely felt so central to the attentions of such a large group, all asking when I was coming back, all fed the same disingenuous evasion, 'Oh, sometime soon.'

'Your stretcher's still in the drying room waiting for you,' Bryn said, laughing.

'Please, feel free to use it,' I replied.

'Don't worry. We have!'

Bryn had intrigued me prior to my first encounter with him a couple of years earlier. One afternoon in the shift room it was announced that a Bryn was joining the section, which engendered great excitement.

'So, what's the big deal with this Bryn, then?' I asked.

'You'll see,' smirked a colleague.

At mid-morning break the next day we heard a loco clattering down the line and went out to meet him. The train came to a halt and out jumped a tall, well-presented man with neat, scraped-back hair and a perfectly clipped moustache. This Bryn has presence, I thought.

'Bryn, good to see you,' said one of the welcoming party.

'Good to be here,' he replied.

He had the confident ease of a man who knew he was wanted. He glanced at me.

'Hey, boy, give me a hand with this.'

He dragged an ammunition box from inside the loco. I grabbed the other rope handle, we carried it into the shift room and placed it down on the table, dense and heavy. The contents of the box were evidently of great interest, as the boys gathered around. Bryn took a chain from around his neck with a key on it, unlocked the padlock and lifted the lid.

'Just a couple of rules,' he said. 'Make sure you put them back when you finish... in proper fucking order. And in the same condition,' he added, with particular emphasis.

The mystery of Bryn was revealed: a collection of dozens of glossy magazines, curated from his various stints on Royal Naval supply vessels around the globe. A world of out-of-reach women in a box. Whenever Bryn was back on dry land, he was deemed an asset to any section. And we'd been gifted him, and his mags.

It was comforting to see and hear the old rhythms that day in the club. Trecwn, you see, wasn't a place of work in a conventional sense, more an institution, affording a community of like-minded individuals an opportunity to while away a day in pleasant company. And to top it all it paid a wage. Meagre, but a wage. A little bit of Soviet Russia transplanted to British soil, efficiency and productivity were anathema to the regime. They clocked in, spent the day creating an illusion of activity interspersed with rest breaks, the breaks often consuming more of the day than the illusion, and then they clocked out.

The lunchtime drink, or drinks, was part of the fabric of Trecwn, a time-honoured ritual heralding an afternoon of faulty decision-making and sleep. All of this in the midst of high explosives could've been a deadly cocktail. Indeed, there'd been a threatened clamp-down on the boozing at one time.

A forklift driver who was a bit too smiley on his return to the depot misjudged the placing of a sea mine onto a flatbed narrow-gauge rail truck in one of the magazines, dropping it from an inadvisable height and obliterating the truck. Fortunately, fuses were kept separate from stacked ordnance, so at least it didn't go bang. There was an investigation, some sucking of lemons and a scratched brow or two. A report was produced. Finally, a meek reprimand was issued: the driver was advised – only advised, mind – to cut down on the lunchtime ciders. Plenty of fudge to go round and no harm done.

The hierarchy, you see, was made up of men who'd climbed up to their pedestal from boys and were loath to come down hard. They were us, only better paid and with their own office. A lunchbox democracy, never mind how far you ascended the pyramid, you brought your sandwiches in with you in the morning.

The only conspicuous nod to seniority was the navy-blue Vauxhall Cavalier that chauffeured the top brass around the valley. Two ladies shared the driving, not always amicably, both resplendent in official green uniforms. Driving the Cavalier brought kudos and a sense of superiority compared to the pool drivers shuttling the plebs up and down the valley in minibuses. It was an important car, as witnessed by the official pennants fluttering on tiny poles either side of the bonnet when it swished past. A Vauxhall with pennants; says it all.

And yet, at lunchtime all of the ranks would be in the club supping together. When I left the club that day, convinced I wouldn't see any of them again, it saddened me.

At Rookwood I'd been determined to change my life, reset the parameters of expectation and have an adventure. Of course, all of that'd been predicated on a full recovery, a rebirth of the running man. As I walked from the club back to the car, that version of David Wilson didn't, and it seemed wouldn't, ever exist again.

The driving licence medical and its denial of a resumption of biking had been a huge jolt. It was the first time since leaving hospital that the doubts began to give way to a certainty of incompletion. Then came the district nurse's lacerating prognosis, which drove a stake into me.

In that golden and boundless period in the summer of '84 after being discharged from Rookwood, and yet later still, I saw a return to the perfect me with absolute clarity. Now, the vision of that perfect me had slipped away.

A week later I received a letter terminating my employment with the Ministry of Defence on medical grounds. I was, as I'd wished to be, free of Trecwn. But free to do what?

Chapter 16

'So, fancy it then, Dai?'

Of course, I fancied it. I was heady with the thought of it.

'Nah, it's okay, Sime. Maybe next year.'

Two weeks in Tenerife with Simon and Stephen was too big a leap. In fact, as leaps go it was immeasurable. Beyond contemplation. A moonshot of a leap. On the day of their departure, in July '86, I stood in the garden looking up at the sky, imagining them sipping their in-flight G&Ts. I should've said yes. It would've been an adventure, the first since my determination in that wheelchair on the grass at Rookwood two years earlier. But I'd said no. And it wasn't a no to be mulled over and shaped into a yes. As no's go it was as definite as it could be.

Tenerife aside, there was a despairing realisation that I had to do something, anything, to throw off the blanket of negativity I'd wrapped myself in since the departure of the district nurse. Over a year had passed and I couldn't shake what she'd said, as if the words had been branded into me. She'd only confirmed what I'd suspected, but it was the way she told me, like it was nothing. Like I should be thankful for my recovery. Well, I wasn't.

My life was small and afraid... and angry. There was so much anger. Not a great line-up of emotions then. Most people, I expect, struggle to comprehend the mental torture of being wrongly convicted of a crime and spending decades in prison – the gut-gnawing bitterness of it. I remember the Birmingham Six walking out of the Court of Appeal after having their convictions quashed for planting bombs in two pubs in 1974 which killed twenty-one people. They smiled but were broken, drained by their seventeen-year incarceration, as if the colour had leached from them. Well, I felt wrongly imprisoned – in my own body. I hadn't deserved it, but it was a life sentence all the same. And, unlike a wrongful conviction, there was no appeals process.

In fairness to that nurse, if she hadn't told me, someone else would've. I'd have asked another medical professional and been told. Just happened to be her that did the telling. And it wasn't her fault that over a year on I was, well, I suppose you'd call it, depressed. Depressed, not caring to live and saying no to just about everything, including Tenerife. Being alive was a bad start to a day. I opened my eyes thinking bad thoughts – doing myself in bad thoughts, as in what'd be the most painless way – and went to bed thinking bad thoughts.

That run – the jog before breakfast – hadn't come. It wouldn't ever come. That'd been the headline aspiration, to be able to run again. Not that I'd ever been a runner in a competitive sense. Not that I'd been anything in a competitive sense. To be competitive you have to be motivated and disciplined. But the freedom to accelerate from a stroll to a jog to a sprint had seemed magical. To feel the air rush over your face. To experience those endorphins coursing. To be free. But the run hadn't come and it never would.

Diego Maradona's 'hand of God' took Argentina past England in a 1986 World Cup quarter final in Mexico, on their way to winning the tournament. Being Welsh I accepted Diego's explanation of his handball as being divine intervention. England had lost because God had decreed it. Simple. But where was my hand of God? I could walk, and yes, maybe I should indeed have been thankful for that. But I wasn't. I could walk, but it wasn't a beautiful walk. It was a stuttering, unsure walk. A self-conscious walk. Always a short walk. And on bad days a stumbling shuffle. On very bad days a catching-my-foot-and-falling shuffle. I felt no joy then from walking which considering all of the wheelchair bound patients I'd left behind in Rookwood showed incredible self-absorption. Everything was focussed through the prism of me and my loss.

You see, two years on from the accident I could still visualise that pre-accident me with painful lucidity. It was easy to compare the damaged me with the old me. The press-up kid who now couldn't even pump out one. The boy who'd benched a hundred kilos but would now just about be able to push an empty bar into the air, thanks to those withered triceps. No strength. No stamina. Plagued by spasticity and cramping muscles. Every facet of the physical person I'd once been, blighted. Damaged.

It was a book from the library, though, that led to a plan. A long-overdue plan. The library was one of a handful of places where I felt invisible, with not too many people to avoid as I hobbled around. The library, the pub, my grandparents' house, quiet spots in the countryside with my camera; all safe spaces away from prying eyes – except for the pub, perhaps, but the alcohol helped mask my insecurities. Away from the house I was hyper-alert, stopping dead still if anyone approached or if I heard footsteps behind, and making a show of checking my watch or pretending to root around for something in an inside pocket. Once they'd passed, I'd carry on. It was an exhausting and frustrating strategy in busy places.

But I saw it in a book from the library – an aerial photograph of Avebury in Wiltshire. A large, circular ditch with a raised perimeter mound, containing prehistoric standing stones and a straggle of cottages clustered around a dogleg crossroads. I was fascinated and decided I wanted to see it. I wanted to go to Avebury. My preferred choice had been Tuscany.

Again, it was a book from the library chucking fuel on my dreams. Florence, Siena, the leaning tower of Pisa. Cypress trees snaking through a crumpled landscape. Drinking wine while reclining in the arms of olive-skinned women (this last bit wasn't in the book). One day, perhaps. One day, when the mental brakes were off. For now, it was to be Avebury, a warm-up act. A toe in the water, as it were.

'I'll be fine. Don't worry,' I said.

Mum was clucking and fussing, like mums do. Well, maybe not around a twenty-one-year-old. But we'd been through a lot and she was just being protective. Dad was airy and outwardly unconcerned, as dads often are.

'So, where you going first?' pressed Mum.

'Don't know really. See when I get there.'

'You must have an idea.'

'Mum, just relax. I'll be fine.'

Her concern was understandable. For a year I'd hung around the house like some biblical plague since the district nurse's departure. Mum had taken a lot of shit, bobbing back off the ropes with a smile on her face regardless of the verbal pummelling I dished out. Now she had to let go, and it wasn't easy.

'Look, if there's a problem, I'll phone. Honest,' I said.

'Make sure you do. You got plenty of change for the phone?'

'Yeah, yeah, don't worry.'

I'd packed the car with great care, as if I were venturing off on an epic journey. Duvet and pillow. AA map book of Britain. Camera and tripod. Music cassettes, the greatest hits of The Cure and Echo & the Bunnymen – I craved feel-good tunes as the soundtrack to my adventure, not album-fillers. And a Tupperware box of ham sarnies, enough to start a catering round on a building site.

The two-door Ford Escort XR3 wasn't designed with mobile living in mind. It had though, seemingly, been designed as a mobile water feature; the sunroof was ill-fitting and the passenger footwell often sloshed with a pool of rainwater which'd tsunami back and forth with the car's momentum. Thankfully, it was July, so it'd dried out. In spite of the cramped living arrangements, I had a romanticised itinerant life all sorted in my head. I'd gather small branches to make campfires and wash my clothes in streams. Foraging for food was unrealistic, but there'd be plenty of garage shops and chippies.

I hugged Mum, gave Dad a warmish nod and got in the car.

'Look after yourself and drive carefully,' she said.

'Yeah, okay, Ma, don't worry.'

'Don't fuss, Margaret. He'll be back tomorrow,' said Dad drily.

'Yeah, yeah, very funny. See you in a week or so,' I said.

Hurtling out of town with the windows down and the Bunnymen on full blast, I could sense the constrictions of a safety-first life loosening.

Bath would be the first destination, as I'd seen it in so many period dramas on the telly. Twenty-one and a fan of historical dramas! Said it all, really. At school, history had been the only subject that managed to capture my imagination, in spite of the teacher's best efforts to strip any semblance of passion from it. A barrel of a man, he was awarded the less-than-flattering epithet of Jelly Belly. Perched on a chair behind his desk, like a sumo on a milk stool, he'd parrot forty minutes of unrelenting, wrist-aching dictation: the American War of Independence; the accession of the house of Hanover in 1714; Arkwright's spinning frame; the three-field system – the touchstones of British history teaching delivered as a tired recording.

As a child, I'd pored over the thin collection of artefacts in the town's museum with Gramps and his brother Ernie. Ernie, the family's very own hermit and tramp-like shuffler, lived in a tiny cottage outside the castle gates, near to the museum. Generations had filled the house with curios, junk, the accumulated ephemera of a hundred years of the Jones clan. The house was more interesting than the museum. Gramps and Ernie fired my addiction to history with embroidered tales of a bygone Haverfordwest and its characters, even the medieval tunnels under the town. Walking by the river at low tide, I scoured the mud for swords, helmets or just old bottles, but all I ever saw was the odd shopping trolley.

I was a history boy, then, and Bath, Avebury, maybe Stonehenge and all points in between beckoned. The boys were in Tenerife, lapping up whatever it deigned to offer, which apart from sunburn, hangovers and the odd snoggy fumble wouldn't be much, while I'd be trundling around Wiltshire admiring neoclassical architecture and prehistoric stone circles. I reckoned I had the better deal.

I lived, now, with the certainty of spinal cord damage. The faith of Rookwood and the immediate months after discharge that a full recovery was assured lay heavy on me, as I grieved for the loss of who I once was. A sense of nihilism gripped me, inclined towards death, with my car seeming to offer the easiest way out. I drove recklessly. I drove without a seatbelt. The fact that I might take others with me didn't register.

But on the road to Bath, I found that I wasn't being so brutal with the accelerator, as if the potential of the journey had infused me with a brighter outlook. I didn't want to crash. I had a seatbelt on. With satisfaction, I passed the sign for Cardiff, the furthest I'd ever driven, and on the approach to the Severn Bridge I switched cassettes, with The Cure taking me into England, another country.

The leg bag had by this time been discarded and my bladder was behaving as yet, with no panicked swerves off the motorway to look for a quiet spot required. Or, more usually, it was a blind spot; I'd become very adept at pissing while hidden in plain sight – visible to all yet noticed by no one. A weak bladder lends any journey an anxious logistical bent. Control, or at least the comforting notion of it, depended on taking bird-like sips of water often rather than gulps. In the latter part of the day, I'd sense a hint of dehydration setting in, with a dull thud in the back of my head.

I turned off the M4 for Bath. I'd seen it all before, of course, on the telly, what felt like a couple of hundred years ago. Parking at various points of interest around the city, I only ventured a small distance from the car. The whistle-stop tour took in exterior views of the Assembly Rooms and Roman Baths, then a ham sandwich overlooking Pulteney Bridge, and to accompany the grandeur of the Royal Crescent I spied an ice-cream kiosk. After deliberating over the menu prices, which seemed to have been lifted from a kiosk in Monaco, I treated myself to a 99. A 99 that I made sure to savour.

Avebury, though, was the goal. And so, nudging teatime, I departed for the main event. The A4 took me past signs to hamlets and villages with names that gurgled warmly in the throat like your favourite childhood medicine: Monkton Farleigh; Compton Bassett; Honey Street; Lower Shockerwick; and the winner, Tiddlywink.

I pulled into a layby for another ham sandwich – curling and sweaty by this time – and the tepid dregs of a flask of coffee. Standing on the baked concrete earth, the parched grass looking like strewn tobacco, I peered into the dun-coloured hills folding into the distance and promised myself that this was the first of many adventures. It was the start of something; I wasn't quite sure what, but definitely something. I'd even stopped checking my watch, that ticking constraint that dictated everything. I felt proud, a feeling I'd seldom experienced. There'd been little in my life to be proud of. Munching on curly ham sandwiches by the side of the A4 in the evening sun was happiness indeed.

I arrived in Avebury an hour before sunset. The photograph in the book hadn't prepared me for the wonderment of happening upon this place. When the ancients decided on this mad civil engineering project five thousand years ago, there were no mini-diggers, just rudimentary tools. A huge circular ditch was dug and the displaced earth formed a perimeter mound. Irregular standing stones, some weighing tens of tons, were placed within the circle.

Archaeologists have speculated on the reasons for such superhuman endeavour: ritual, the position of the sun, or doing it simply because they had time on their hands. You don't need to know the reasoning, though, to be overawed. Many of the original stones are gone, broken up to build some of the cottages lining the crossroads within the circle.

I found a small car park, perfect for later sleeping arrangements, and walked through a gate and out across the grass to touch a stone. In the fading light, they looked like gigantic sentinels standing guard over the village. A visit to Avebury might entail a mile-long stroll around the site's circumference, an opportunity to immerse oneself in the enormity of what those people achieved. For me that wasn't possible, so touching a stone would have to do. And I found a beaut. The height of a telephone kiosk and twice the girth, I leant with my back to the sunny side and felt the stored warmth. I was there. I was in the circle. It felt magical. I was happy.

The sun was kissing the low hills, so I headed for the pub, the Red Lion, a large thatched building beside the crossroads. The interior was a dark, uninviting version of every Tudor-period ye olde England hostelry of imagined folklore, the distractingly busy carpet negating any possibility of the local migraine support group meeting there. The barman was hanging up a strip of nuts, half-turning as I approached the counter.

'What can I get you?' he said with cheerless indifference.

'Bitter top, please.' I looked around for an empty table. There were plenty to choose from. 'What a lovely day it's been,' I continued, wishing to converse after a day of talking to myself.

'Has it? Been stuck in here.' He finished pouring the pint and placed it on the bar without meeting my eye.

'One pound ten. Please.'

I wanted conversation. He wanted to go home. Perhaps hospitality was an inappropriate sector for him. I opted for a table in a corner with a view of the bar and entrance, perfect for people-watching. If anyone came in, that is.

Somewhere in the building a deep fat fryer was putting in a heavy shift, soaking the bar with the odour of plunged frozen chips. At a table near to me, an elderly couple sat in silence, stabbing without enthusiasm at two artlessly assembled meals. Dressed by the small ads at the back of the *Daily Express*, they seemed to have gone past the companionship bit of marriage and entered the realms of barely disguised mutual repulsion. Meals half-finished, they stood without speaking and shuffled out one behind the other.

I gulped then sipped at my beer and recapped my day, thirsty and exhausted and elated. I'd done it. I'd gone on an adventure and knew that my life could be different from what I'd allowed it to be.

A woman entered. I guessed in her early thirties, with a hunch of tiredness, the white blouse and plain skirt tending towards utility – a long day at the office, perhaps. With her hair scraped back and a shoulder bag bulging and spilling, beneath that shroud of tiny neglects was an attractive lady. The barman certainly thought so, dumping the corporate gurn I'd endured for a cheeky glint. She didn't engage, but picked up her drink and sat at a table. She looked at her watch as I sipped my pint and thought of where I'd been that day. A couple of minutes passed and she checked her watch again, as she began to finger drum the table.

A man came in, glanced over and nodded discreetly to her. With his sober tie and grey suit – a bit shiny, like he resented the investment of a back-up suit – he looked much younger. He got a pint and sat beside her, their shoulders brushing, almost conspiratorial in the way they lent in to one another. Her right hand was placed flat on the table. He gently cupped his left hand over it and squeezed. Boyfriend and girlfriend? Maybe. Office romance? I liked the idea of that. She was his line manager. He was an admin assistant.

I became conscious of my unusual – okay, unhealthy – interest in them, and so looked away. What about tomorrow? I thought. Where should I go? My ad hoc itinerary kept throwing up Stonehenge. Why not? It wasn't far away. The thud of dehydration in the back of my head was easing, and I began to think about parking up for the night. I continued to make plans, occasionally glancing over to the office romance.

Suddenly, she stood, tapping her watch as if late for something she hadn't wanted to be on time for. She kissed him on the cheek, picked up her bag and departed. He slumped forward on his stool as if some air had been let out of him and continued with his pint. Catching my eye, he gave me a rueful smile, swigged a last mouthful, got to his feet and left. I wondered where they were going, sensing it wouldn't be the same destination.

I finished my pint and departed too, driving to the car park I'd earmarked earlier, and pulling up adjacent to a fence with a view out to the stones. It was ten o'clock, and midsummer dark with a half-light. There were no walkers now, just the stones, a full moon bathing them bluish. I got the pillow and duvet from the boot and reclined the driver's seat. I thought calm thoughts as I waited for sleep.

I was woken by a noise near to the car. Not a startling noise, more a snuffling, animal-like noise. I looked out but couldn't see anything. Then I looked at my watch. Half five. I'd slept fitfully and was exhausted; the car hadn't quite lived up to my mobile home pretensions. Peering out at half silhouetted cottages, as my eyes acclimatized to the dim light I picked out the stones and the encircling mound. A mist was forming, and looking east the horizon was beginning to warm, with weak incremental smears of orange and yellow brushing the sky. I hadn't witnessed a sunrise since my Trecwn days. It was exciting.

Something bobbed up on the brow of the mound – small, delicate, prowling. It dropped down into the ditch, then up into the field just past the farthest stone from me. Too big for a cat. Not a badger either. It moved in my direction and gradually I made it out: a fox. It halted near to the stone I'd leant against the previous evening. I thought of getting out and edging closer, but stayed put; it would've bolted with my clumsy approach. Two years before, I'd been inspired to dream big by a fox, and once more I felt its power. Its insouciance. Then it was gone.

Dawn was now colouring the skyline deeply as the mist thickened. I decided to get out of the car to experience this special morning; my morning. I opened the door and lifted my right leg out of the footwell, placing my foot on the tarmac, and sensed the charge building like a dynamo. I swung my other leg out and perched on the side of the seat with both feet on the tarmac. I could feel that charge cranking to trigger point as I leant forward and grabbed the top of the door.

Heaving myself up and off the seat, my legs straightened to an upright position, then it kicked in – the most diabolical muscle spasm. My body jerked in a violent folding motion, like a flick knife in reverse, almost collapsing to the floor, desperately gripping the top of the door to keep me upright while fighting the contraction. My calves cramped to granite, wracked with dog-bite pain, so I set to loosening them, banging my feet on the ground, trying to coax the spasm out; straightening, stretching, swearing. I felt it ease and fall away as the last vestiges of clenched muscle fibre relaxed. First obstacle overcome.

Now I had to take those first tentative steps, aware that I might stumble and fall. I focussed on the stone I wanted to get to and staggered towards it. After a dozen or so strides I could sense myself unwinding, beginning to stroll with fluidity. Or at least, my version of fluid.

I reached the stone and looked around, hoping to see the fox. It was gone. It was the stone I'd reclined against when I arrived in Avebury and now I leant against the other side to face the sun as it rose. I inhaled the stone which smelt of damp cottage, a metallic tang of ores, and the whole time of the world. The first rays streaked over the fields like lasers, hitting my face. I closed my eyes. It was first light, I'd hardly slept, I was knackered, but in ecstasy. I'd never greeted the sun in such a personal way. Ceremonial almost.

That fit boy with the bike could never have stood where I was. He would never have thought himself capable of such an adventure. I looked at my legs and felt like it didn't matter that I'd stumbled out from the car just about on my feet. I was in a field leaning against a stone with the sun coming up and it trumped my issues, at least momentarily. It was an exceptional moment, but it was just that, an exception. The dark side would still blight me, but at least I could hope for more bright moments, more exceptions.

I stood for an age before realising how tired I was. I ached. My body throbbed with exhaustion. I had to get back to the car. I had to eat. I needed water. I had to take the Baclofen tablet that would ease the spasticity in my body, relax my muscle tone and give me a fighting chance of a day; in my excitement at the sight of the fox I'd forgotten to take it before I set off. I pushed away from the stone and headed back, stumbling again, struggling to control the placing of my feet, with muscles as responsive as teak. Nearing the gate to the car park, I caught my foot on a dense clump of grass and fell to the floor.

I swore and punched the ground then crawled on my hands and knees to the gate, using it to pull myself up, before staggering to the car. Falling was part of the new me, so no sooner had the anger risen than it dissipated. I was used to it. I took the Baclofen, guzzled half a bottle of water and inspected the ham sandwiches. They whiffed of a porcine clamminess, but I was hungry. Accompanied by ready salted crisps and a banana, that was breakfast sorted. It was nearing seven o'clock, and I wanted to sleep. I reclined the seat, again, and closed my eyes.

I woke and looked at my watch; nine o'clock. I was still exhausted. I ate the umpteenth ham sandwich, which I decided was rank, earmarking the last half dozen for a bin. A hint of survival desperation was beginning to taint the day already. My remaining supplies of crisps and an assortment of chocolate bars weren't going to sustain me. I had to get some proper food or at least something that wasn't a ham sandwich.

I studied the map and located Stonehenge, about twenty-five miles away. First, though, I had to find a spot in Avebury where I could get to the top of the mound, to alter the topography of viewing and see the village and stones from a higher elevation. I drove out of the circle in the direction of Swindon and there at the side of the road was a gate that led to a gently sloping section of the outer mound.

Leaning into the slope, I attacked it with all the forward momentum I could muster and pushed and pushed till I reached the top. I was up, and the view was thrilling: the prehistoric landscape and the footprint of the medieval village. I took some photos, more as mementos than with any pretension to artistry – proof that I was there.

It was time for Stonehenge, the big boy down the road. I descended the slope gingerly and returned to the car, feeling more depleted by the moment. With a broken night's sleep, and the prospect of a second day fuelled by crisps and Mars bars, I didn't feel confident in the continuation of my trip. The wheels were coming off.

I set off for Stonehenge more in hope than expectation then. The first test of my determination came not far on the road out of Avebury – the fuel warning light. A few miles further on I pulled into a garage, filled up, and went in to pay, my feet scuffing along the forecourt, the tiredness in my leg muscles causing me to stagger and sway more than usual. On entering the shop, I tripped over the threshold and nearly fell. I glanced around for witnesses. There was just one; a short middle-aged man standing behind the counter. I nodded and smiled. He turned away without acknowledgement. What's your problem, I thought.

Hunting for food, his reaction began to bug me. It was the disdain as he'd turned away. Actually, disdain is the wrong word; he'd made a judgement. And it'd happened before.

After being discharged from Rookwood two years earlier, my friends picked me up one day to go to Tenby. We were walking at my pace – slowly – down a pedestrianised street towards the harbour.

Coming towards us was a couple, perhaps in their sixties, chatting and laughing. As we got closer, the woman glared at me. What's your problem? I thought. Passing them, I heard her snipe, 'That boy's drunk.' Aside from her misconception, what really hurt was that a year before I'd walked down that same street with Martin, helmets in our hands with our cider smiles as we headed to the beach and the swim out to the island. What a difference a year had made.

In the garage shop, my darkening mood lifted on spotting the chilled cabinet. Pasties. Pies. Culinary redemption. I grabbed some pastry products and dumped them on the counter. So, a pisshead on his way home after an all-nighter eh, I imagined him thinking.

'Nice day,' I said over-brightly, goading him to react.

There was no reply as he rang up the items on the till. A dead ringer for Bobby Charlton, he sported an equally ludicrous combover. I forced a smile and paid.

'Well, thank you so much,' I said, leaning into his personal space, if only so that he could detect my booze-free breath. Again, no response. I spun and began to walk out but halfway to the door turned round.

'You think I'm drunk, don't you?'

'Well, aren't you?' It wasn't so much a question as confirmation of his conviction that I was.

'No, not drunk,' I said.

I took a minute to explain and he came from behind the counter and apologised. And, I think he meant it. Of course, he meant it; he was Bobby Charlton, after all.

I found a lay-by in which to gorge on a pasty. Savoury, dense, a little chewy in parts, but a breakfast saviour all the same. I contemplated my options. I was about ten miles from Stonehenge and desperately wanted to continue. I could've struggled on, but walking round the site would've been impossible. The prospect of viewing one of the iconic historical sites in Britain from the driver's seat of a Ford Escort saddened me. I couldn't face the angered reckoning it'd bring.

So, for the sake of my fragile mental state, it was better to abandon the adventure and pretend I'd never been fussed about Stonehenge anyway – just a disparate pile of stones after all. So, I finished the pasty and turned for home. I was beaten. Beaten by my damaged body. Beaten by lack of sleep. Beaten by a diet of empty carbs. But in spite of the defeat, I'd won. I'd had an adventure. One thing irked me, though: Dad was right, 'He'll be back tomorrow.'

Chapter 17

Wiltshire and Avebury changed me. Just two days and one night. Though not the epic I'd imagined, the trip was a catharsis of the nurse's words all the same. For over a year I'd sat in the lounge staring at patterned wallpaper, asking, 'Why me?' Why the fuck had it happened to me? After Wiltshire I began to emerge from that small dark space with more confidence and the awakening of what felt like self-belief; it's amazing what standing with your back to an enormous stone in a field at sunrise can do!

I was still wary of change, and inclined to the familiar, but now I was prepared to embrace new experiences and opportunities, rather than discounting everything outright as I'd done before. I'd broken the cycle of desperation and bitterness, the clock-watching, day-filling routines. I'd become, perhaps, just a little braver.

Mum had most to celebrate from my renewal, having felt much of my anger at close quarters; Dad could escape to work. She wasn't a psychologist, and hadn't read any quick fixes on coaxing out a recluse, but she was a mother with an instinct for what to do. And she'd employed certain ruses to winkle me out. Or at least try to.

'We're out of bread. Can you nip to Tesco and get some?' she'd say.

I remember the panic that'd grip me.

'No.'

She'd persevere, prodding gently. 'Look, I haven't got time. Just jump in the car and get some, will you?'

The prospect of walking into that vast space with people coming at me from all directions terrified me. She may as well have asked me to walk out onto the pitch at Wembley in front of a capacity crowd.

'If you need bread, you go,' I'd bellow, stomping off to shout some more and break something. The next day, she'd try again with another suggestion.

After many months of taking on little challenges to my routine, since Wiltshire, in the spring of '87 I made a decision, my boldest yet, which wasn't hard, as truly bold decisions had been a little thin on the ground. The gym was in the sports hall of my old school, an airy, high-ceilinged '70s space with stained carpet tiles, a rickety multi-gym and an array of loose weights. I sat in the car outside, shaking. I felt sick. The shrunken person in my head told me to postpone it, go back another day, or better still, just forget it. But I was there and I couldn't unthink it. I was committed.

I visualised the interior from memory, that vital strategy of knowing the terrain in advance, rehearsing my passage through the slow return doors and past the hot sweatiness of the changing rooms. I was as ready as I'd ever be, though nowhere near as ready as I'd have liked. I walked towards the entrance, muttering to myself to drown out the voice in my head. The voice that was shouting, 'Abort. Abort.'

There was a small glass-fronted office just inside the building. A paunchy man in a white polo shirt and tracksuit bottoms was sitting with his feet on a desk watching telly. I stepped into the office. He removed his feet.

'Hi. Want to use the gym, please,' I said.

He flashed a faint smile. 'No problem. That'll be a pound. First time?'

'Yeah.'

'Good. Well, gym's through there...' he said, pointing.

'Yeah, I know. Thanks.'

'If you want me to run through anything, multi-gym, weights or whatever. Just give me a shout. Be no trouble.'

'Thanks. I'll be alright.'

This was Phil. Phil ran the sports hall after the school day and during the holidays. He'd been a handy weightlifter in his time but that time had evidently passed, and he now sat in the office with his feet up, collecting money. Occasionally, for the sake of variety, he'd alight from his seat and conduct a cursory tour of the sports hall to ensure everything was running smoothly and to chat with the punters. Phil knew everyone and everyone knew Phil. And not only did everyone know Phil but they had great affection for him. In time, I too viewed him as a warm and encouraging man, counting it as one of life's happy accidents that I got to know him.

I looked into the gym through the glazed double doors. There were half a dozen individuals pushing, pulling, lifting and sweating. A CD was playing *Now 10* or *11* or something. I wanted to turn around and leave, but I couldn't. I was there. I could see it.

'You going in?'

A voice from behind startled me and I turned to see a middle-aged man angling to get past. Smiley, chest out and in a tracksuit with an official-looking badge, he wafted his hand towards the door. And so, I was swept in by Lynne Roach, an ex-weightlifter who'd represented Wales, who ran the weightlifting club that met there.

'Haven't seen you before,' he said.

'No. First time.'

I glanced around. It was a large room but I felt like it was closing in on me. I was anxious and struggling for breath, eyeing the exit, desperate to get out.

'If you need any help, just call me over. Be no trouble,' said Lynne.

He smiled with such a depth of beneficence that it lifted me, and at that moment I realised I was in safe hands. The room stopped closing in. I began to relax. I'd made the right decision, arriving at the most opportune moment.

The initial sessions were nervy, and I willed it to be quiet so that I could feel my way into the rhythm and tenor of the place, get to know what weights to select and how the machines worked, their quirks and foibles. I wanted the chance to make mistakes without an audience. That shrunken person in my head continued to hang around, and there were occasions in the carpark when I almost capitulated and turned for home. But somehow, from somewhere, I found the resolve to keep walking into that gym even when it was a struggle and my legs were all over the place. I soon became comfortable with the biomechanics of using the cable-operated system and felt that I belonged there, had blended in and become unnoticeable.

I'd often watch the weightlifters, embroiled in a brutal, visceral poetry of motion. The technique of heaving granite-dense weight. The clean and jerk. The snatch. Squatting to the floor and back up with a bar on their shoulders that would've caused most people to collapse in a heap. All executed with the sweetest of timing.

Their discipline and mutual encouragement reminded me of Rookwood; steely endeavour channelled towards a specific improvement. A goal. They were searching for their own pinnacle and their physical aura carried me with them, letting me imagine, again, that there was still a summit to be reached, a place where perhaps I could reclaim that elusive running man. Maybe it wasn't over. Surely, if I worked much harder than I ever had, the dream of physical completion could be rekindled – a bit of the faith still flickered.

Two, three, four nights a week, I went in search of that El Dorado, convinced that discipline and hard graft would reap the rewards. My rehabilitation regime on leaving Rookwood three years earlier hadn't, in hindsight, been as intense as it could've been. Yes, there'd been the rowing machine, walking up that hill and swimming. But I hadn't been determined enough, having conspired with the comforting assumption that a return to the old me was a given. When it didn't happen, I gave up.

This time, in the gym, it was for real, as I sensed myself climbing off that plateau of incomplete recovery that I'd been wandering about on. Each week I added more weight and repetitions to the punishing circuits of set after set of what was the most extraordinary pain and endorphin-driven ecstasy. I was intoxicated by the potential. The rowing machine, that hill and the swimming pool hadn't come close.

As the weeks turned to months, though, the leaps of physical progress became less perceptible, less obvious, and eventually non-existent. I couldn't add any more weight or repetitions and going to the gym became the means by which I maintained my new level of reclaimed functionality rather than retrieving yet more of what I'd lost. I'd arrived on another – higher – plateau, but not at the peak of perfection I aspired to. Some muscle groups remained withered, an asymmetric oddity, and I still limped like a bloody pirate. The spasticity, that muscular handbrake, had not been wholly released, though it was improved. I couldn't lift the weights that those around me could. I couldn't run. It'd been a last hurrah, and I knew then with absolute certainty that my spinal cord had been damaged. The nurse had been right. Well, sort of; I was past the point where she'd declared my recovery to be at an end, edging closer to the person I'd been before the accident. I was stronger, more muscular and had greater stamina. I was also happier and, perhaps, learning to accept and move on.

It was ironic that at my moment of absolute acceptance that my spinal cord had been compromised – that I would never get back to being that boy on the rock in Tenby – the place where I felt safest, the place where I felt most uplifted, was in the gym surrounded by the undamaged. I was aware of the higher, inaccessible peaks all around me, of course, but my loss didn't hurt as it'd once done, as I felt a part of something fraternal, something that was bigger than me and my hang ups.

The '88 Olympics were held in Seoul, South Korea. I was in the office one evening with Phil, having just paid for a session. He had his feet up, telly on.

'When's the hundred metres final, Phil?'

'Now, boy, in a few minutes.'

'Great. I'll watch it with you.'

The race was billed as an epic clash between the impenetrable Canadian Ben Johnson and the US showboater Carl Lewis, plus some inconsequential others. The starting pistol fired and 9.79 seconds later

Johnson bulleted over the finishing line, leaving Lewis floundering in his magnificent wake and setting a world record.

'Fuck me, he left them for dead,' said Phil.

Phil's vocabulary was deliciously Anglo-Saxon and, as with Mr Smithies, my driving instructor, I admired him for the honesty of his language. In today's world of easy offence, he'd no doubt be shunted to a back-office role. The race was a kind of 'where were you when Kennedy was shot?' moment, the nature of the victory beyond emphatic, bordering on the super-human. I trained that night with more vigour than usual.

The next evening, I was back in the gym. Phil sauntered in on his rounds.

'Fuck me, you heard about Ben Johnson?'

'No. What's happened?' replied Lynne.

'Failed a drugs test. On steroids. Mind, I knew there was something dodgy about him.'

Lynne nodded sagely. 'Yeah, he certainly bulked up quickly, that's for sure. Didn't look like protein shakes to me.'

Everyone laughed as Phil posited a strident theory on the demise of integrity in top-level sport before continuing on his way.

It was heartening to watch Lynne circulate amongst his lifters. Always encouraging. Always suggesting tweaks to their technique that might be beneficial without it sounding like some diktat. And at the core of his labour of love were his two teenage boys, Mark and Simon, shifting hernia-inducing weight above their heads. His pride in them and all of the lifters, was affirming.

Julian, one of the gang, bought a terraced house in Haverfordwest. Weekdays, he was a sober and diligent Jekyll, balancing figures in his dad's accountancy firm. Come Friday nights though, he became Hyde the entertainer. Presenting as a gangly collection of elongated limbs and levers, he exerted a magnetic pull, drawing us minor moons into his comical orbit with his antics and feats of absurd derring-do; a stuntman masquerading as an accountant, at closing time one night he swam home upriver in the dark, somehow avoiding a minefield of submerged shopping trolleys and snagging weeds. His little house – or clubhouse as we came to view it – sat on a heavy metal San Andreas Fault, with the stones and mortar shaking to Guns N' Roses and Whitesnake.

Residentially, we were all still suckling from the parental teat and so to have a place that belonged to a very generous-spirited friend who was partial to a bit of high jinks was a real boon. Weekends began there and mornings were blearily welcomed in, though his neighbours never seemed to be in the party mood.

Leather trousers were Julian's signature garment and I emulated him by acquiring a pair from Mum's Grattan catalogue. To accompany my foray into the sartorial badlands I had my ears pierced, each sporting a gold hoop you could hang a towel over. With a concurrent increase in alcohol consumption, I felt rock 'n' roll. I discovered that I liked drink, floating off to extraordinary and happy places where I could forget my limitations. Drink, it seemed, liked me too, as I didn't suffer hangovers. Mind, my limited capacity was at odds with the likes of Simon and Gary. They could, if the fancy took them – and it did, often – drink as if the Guinness book of records was in town. Sundays were payback though, with the boys presenting as varying shades of suicidal grey. I called to see Simon one Sunday lunchtime, still ensconced in the parental bosom.

'Okay, Sime?'

He squinted and shook his head, looking brittle and pallid.

'Coffee, Dai?'

'Aye, go on then.'

His mum popped her head into the kitchen. 'Simon, have you done the pheasant yet?'

'Yeah, yeah. I'll do it soon.'

'Well, it'd be nice to have lunch before supper time, if you don't mind.'

He drank his tea then went to fetch the bird from the garage where it'd been hanging a few days – the thing to do, apparently.

'Jesus, Sime, that thing stinks,' I said.

Simon was a chef and part of his keep was to do chef-like things. He held the bird by its neck over the sink and began to yank its feathers out. As he pulled, the bird evacuated its innards out of its back end into the sink.

'Oh, fuck...' he said, as his legs buckled.

Dropping the bird, he ran for the bathroom, emerging a few minutes later a greenish hue. I reckoned it best to leave him to his rotting cadaver and departed.

And so, with a gym habit paying dividends and the alcohol training, I ticked the prime performance indicators for a Tenerife fortnight. If the Wiltshire adventure had been a Snowdon climb, these two weeks promised to be an Everest of endurance. I'd never wanted anything so much in my life but it also scared the hell out of me, conscious that I was straying far from my comfort zone, relinquishing control over the ebb and flow of days.

A magnificent six congregated in Cardiff airport and decamped to the bar, the boys swigging numerous settlers for the flight while I sipped an orange juice, ever wary of bladder control. My coping mechanisms and practised camouflage techniques for avoiding public scrutiny had been cast away and I was psychologically naked.

The recently disbanded pop duo Wham would've been proud of me as I boarded the plane resplendent in leather trousers and huge gold earrings, though I did get some uncertain looks from a bunch of rugby boys jetting off on a stag do. On arrival in Playa de las Americas we dumped our bags in the apartment and headed into town. Compared to my tour of classically proportioned Bath, civic planning in Playa was a little wild west, with ugly utilitarian architecture, billboard signage the size of a tennis court and countless half-built apartments; it was a cement dealer's heaven. The tacky roads shone under a punishing sun, and the air was sub-Saharan and dense. Like Blackpool without rain, every nasty theme pub and Union Jack caff had been transplanted, the town's ecosystem servicing a tawdry Bacchanalian nightmare tailored to rowdy foreigners who fought in the streets, threw up in the streets and pissed in the streets. Britain had exported its grotty, drink-fuelled subculture, and we were only too happy to sign up.

The author Laurie Lee walked through Spain in the mid-thirties and found a proud country mired in poverty, but with a spirit, an identity, and a fierce culture baked hard by an equally fierce sun. What would he have written now? I tried to imagine what it'd be like if the situation were reversed. If the predominant tongue in Pembrokeshire was Spanish. If our high streets were clogged with tapas bars. If the visiting hordes treated us with ignorance and disdain. The boys didn't appear to be hamstrung by such sensibilities.

'Good to be back,' sighed Simon. 'What do you think, boys? Is this the life or what?' We all agreed that it was.

They adjusted their walking pace to suit mine without any grumbles, and if they inadvertently went on ahead one would drop back to accompany me and call them into line. They looked after me. We ducked into a backstreet supermarket to stock up on essentials: beer, spirits and even some food, but not so much as to displace alcohol on the Sherpa trck back to thc apartmcnt. We put some beers in the fridge and headed down to the pool. That was where I felt most on show, stripped down to my trunks, my bodily imbalances exposed.

Wc bought a bottle of tanning agent; watery creosote with no UV protection, it was guaranteed to give a superfast tan and a delightful array of melanomas years down the line. Then the chilled beers appeared. Suddenly, this was indeed the life, reclining on a deck bed in the setting sun, sipping San Miguel. Maybe Laurie Lee's Spain had had its day.

We showered, changed and ventured out. Having done the groundwork the previous year, Simon and Stephen were our scouts. A stream of bars funnelled us along the seafront like a series of beacons towards the mecca, a three-storey concrete block next to the beach crammed full of clubs and pubs, mostly British themed with British owners, possibly on the run from serious offences back in Blighty.

And the epicentre of this tottering pile was Mrs T's, the number one nightspot in town.

Lardy blokes in pseudo-police uniforms with guns provided security on the doors. Bouncers with firearms? What a fantastic idea! Months before, a Brit had been shot in the head while allegedly playing Russian roulette with a doorman. It was a murky incident shrouded in competing interpretations, but it was widely believed he'd been the victim of a less than professional ejection from a club. The police were little better, rounding up overenthusiastic party animals, stripping them to their pants and driving them out to the desert for a sobering walk back to town – if they were lucky.

It being the late eighties, we all conspired in a de facto mullet dictatorship, preening and fighting over the hairdryer before going out clubbing. Like an extra in a touring country and western show, Stephen fancied dungarees were the way to impress the ladies. With his beaming smile and forearms like marrows he looked like a hick labourer on the pull. Simon imagined himself as alternative and edgy: he'd been into Joy Division before they sold out as the poppy New Order.

He professed, without prompting, an encyclopaedic knowledge of every number one single from years gone by and when it charted. Like a stage psychic he'd hear a song, ponder a second, and then decree with absolute certainty, 'Number one, March 1978.' None of us were knowledgeable enough to challenge his pronouncements; I was never wholly convinced of his alleged powers of recall.

Gary preferred to absorb rather than provide mirth. He'd sit back, quietly quaffing pints, and breaking into uproarious laughter at our capers. Steven number two was the volatile element. Four seasons in a day, he veered between unalloyed joy and mute darkness, the unpredictability of which added a frisson of tension on occasion. But, in his defence, when he was on form, he was achingly funny. Then there was John, my cousin, the tanning king. No matter how much creosote we slathered on he'd be a few shades ahead.

We were six young men thrown together on foreign shores and

it worked, aside from the odd incident when Steven (number two) careered over to the dark side. Simon produced the odd chef-like trick of culinary redemption to ensure we ate just well enough and we were a sensible bunch that mostly knew our limits. Mostly.

As the full-on days and nights passed, I sensed an improvement in my stamina levels, with all of the walking into town to restock on beverages, walking to the aqua park, and the long hike to the clubs at night. There were periods away from the apartment under that fierce sun during the day when I didn't drink enough, that obsession with bladder control, but I compensated by overhydrating by the pool and, of course glugging the nights away. I'd found a way to make it work and I was happy that holidays abroad with the lads were a goer. Another insecurity banished.

I met her in Mrs T's. She just came up to me and started talking. It was ear-bleedingly noisy, with revellers packed on the dance floor, swaying in unison to the music like pine trees in a storm. I couldn't hear her nor her me, so we headed outside to the beach front and sat on a bench. We met up over a few nights. Her two friends, forever cavorting drunkenly with inadvisable looking blokes in the club, thought Tenerife might help her get over a long-term boyfriend who'd dumped her.

'We were in Paris this time last year,' she said wistfully. 'Bit diffcrcnt.'

She didn't want to be there, and I felt sorry for her. She told me about her life.

'A lab technician? Wow, that sounds interesting,' I said.

'It's not that interesting. Trust me.'

At least she worked. The idea of employment hadn't appeared on my radar.

'So, what do you do for a living?' she asked.

Truth or myth?

'I'm a photographer.'

'God, how exciting. What kind of photography?'

'Oh, all sorts really. Landscape. Bit of portraiture. Quite varied, really.'

There were admiring glances as I warmed to the deceit. If ever I imagined a dream job it was always to be a photographer. That's holidays; you can be whoever you want to be and I wanted to appear a bit glamorous and she fell for it. We sat and talked and it was innocent and lovely, neither of us inclined to head down to the beach to trip over and join the drunken humpers in the dark.

'So, what happened to you?' she asked.

It was the last night, and the question caught me off guard with its directness. Naively, I'd hoped she hadn't noticed, as if she saw me in the same way as she saw everyone else.

'Sorry, you don't have to tell me if you don't want to.'

'No, it's okay,' I said.

I told her and she listened and said, 'If it's any consolation, I saw past that and just saw you. It was you that made me come over that first night.'

I'd spent over three years since the accident imagining that any girl who showed an interest, pitied me. She made me realise, believe, that it wasn't a defining issue. She was interested in me in spite of it. And, like me, she just wanted to be held tight without feeling obliged to do anything else. We were therapy for one another.

On the fourteenth morning the taxis arrived for the airport and I was glad of it. I'd survived my sternest test, but my body was stripped bare. I was exhausted from bad sleep, and cup-a-soups and white bread, and standing in grim clubs making inaudible conversation with Dawn from Wolverhampton or Tracy from Bristol or whoever from wherever. The highlight had been meeting the lab technician, a girl who helped me to believe in myself. Just wish I could remember her name. On the flight home, drifting off, there was a sense of pride at what I'd endured, but more importantly, what I'd achieved. Physically and mentally, I was a notch up on the person who'd flown the other way two weeks earlier.

Chapter 18

When I woke in the morning, I'd lie on my back, dead still. Literally, as if I were dead, as the slightest movement or attempt to slip out from under the duvet triggered a kind of rigor mortis, my torso and limbs stiffening like planks, locked by the muscular spasticity of nerve damage. So, I'd lie and wait for five minutes, perhaps ten, before gradually moving an arm or a leg, ready to play dead again if I felt it coming on. On bad mornings it could be half an hour before I was on my feet. Bad mornings were a bad start to what would be a bad day.

On this particular morning, though, my limbs were more cooperative than usual and I was off the mattress before the cramps got me; a welcome exception. It was early, at least for me, and the day seemed to hold a promise that I couldn't quite picture. I felt physically capable. I felt positive. Something was definitely in the offing. I just had to decide what it was. After showering, I stretched my hamstrings at the bottom of the stairs, trying to flush out a residual morning resistance in my muscles. Confident and adequately limber, I made a decision, and after breakfast I was gone.

I'd begun to explore further afield with my camera, discovering that Wales didn't end at the Pembrokeshire border, and having told the lab technician in Tenerife that I was a photographer I'd taken to impersonating one on a more regular basis. Taking photographs, albeit not very good ones, gifted me self-esteem. I enjoyed clicking the shutter. I enjoyed the illusion of creativity, and, trust me, it was indeed an illusion on seeing the resultant prints! But, in spite of the mediocrity of my compositions, photography made me happy. It got me out of the house. My ad-hoc destination on this day was to be Cwmystwyth in Ceredigion, a few miles inland from Aberystwyth on the coast.

It was a reasonable expectation of society that I should be working four years on from my accident. After all, I could walk, hold a pen, lift and carry light items a short distance. I was a regular at the gym for Christ's sake. So, I could function productively, if you like. Well, when I say productively, as an ex-Trecwnite I wasn't destined to score at the upper end of any measurement of output. The type of work that I could undertake would be limited, but I could've done something. Dan from Rookwood, with his one arm, was in all likelihood working at that time. I too could've held down a job.

But I existed in a parallel sphere, from where I looked upon the workers with a sense of detachment, and I suppose entitlement, convincing myself that I had better things to do than work. I had, after all, tried employment and never really taken to it, convinced that it'd been an affront to my freedom and dignity. Viewing the world of work through the distorted prism of Trecwn, though, was an unreliable barometer. I was oblivious that there may well have been a great job out there with my name on it, if only my outlook hadn't been tainted by my experience of Trecwn, which'd persuaded me that work was dull and soul-destroying. An ingrained laziness didn't help either – lazy at school. Lazy in college. Lazy in Trecwn (though it went unnoticed there).

The core truth of my reluctance to be employed, though, was fear, the fear of being exposed in an environment I couldn't control. A workplace, after all, isn't home. I had, of late, made great strides in normalising my life, but for the time being I rationalised that work could wait. After all, I had crap photographs to take.

Having been inducted into the motoring hall of shame by Mucky, I too drove like a special delivery service for donated organs, racing up the coast road and arriving in the Ystwyth Valley, seventy miles from home, before I should have. If the Job Centre had ever advertised for getaway drivers, I'd have been a shoo-in.

These new landscapes excited me, making me feel like a pioneer venturing into uncharted territory. Yet, there was a drive-through familiarity to those hills. When I was a kid, Dad would drive via Aberystwyth on our tortuous returns up north, to the places of his youth. They were yearly pilgrimages, and without exception we'd stop for lunch in the Milk Bar in Newtown; sausage, beans and chips every time. I remember the succulent pleasure of that sausage up to the point when I chewed on the first marble of gristle.

Each year dished up that helter skelter of gastronomic anticipation and subsequent nausea. The landscape we travelled through left no lasting impression on the boy in the back of an Austin Allegro, engrossed in a book of word searches, the silence broken by Dad's withering complaints of being stuck behind lorries on the twisting roads or, even worse, tractors. I grew up imagining that farmers were deliberately bringing the country to a halt.

Blackpool and Bradford were our destinations, the former cheerfully grim, the latter bleakly so. Blackpool meant a visit to Aunty Lois, the elder sister who'd taken Dad in after his parents died, and her husband, Uncle Norman. Norman had been an accomplished saxophonist, a regular big band performer on the radio in years gone by, but a diagnosis of Parkinson's as a young man put paid to that. Lois was barrel-shaped and smiley, a confusion of maternal affection and sisterly love. She and the town were dear to Dad for having held out their hands at his moment of deepest emotional peril. After losing his parents as a young boy he'd had to start again, accumulating a new bank of happy memories, most of which starred affectionate Lois, the bright lights, eating chips while strolling home along wet pavements and big acts at the Tower Ballroom. He loved Blackpool, and it loved him back. He'd felt safe.

Another of our Blackpool rituals was the unending seafront stroll – or as I preferred to think of it, death march – terminating at the Pleasure Beach, an award-winning misnomer. It was loud, lurid and populated by tough kids with home-made tattoos, the air a competing miasma of candy floss, dodgy meat and diesel. I couldn't wait to leave, a yearning repeated on arrival in the brown splodge of Bradford.

We stayed with another of Dad's sisters, Ruth, as we always had.

Cousin Tony would vacate his room for Andrew and me, his spirit living on in the odour of sweaty feet in the carpet. There'd be rounds of relatives to visit, making it not so much a holiday as a series of familial chores.

On this day, though, in the Ystwyth Valley, I took in hills that soared with a weather-blasted beauty, the gorges scoured by rain and boulders. I was speechless. The landscape threatened and flexed and enlivened. It had an edge, a crushing splendour. I drove through one-blink Cwmystwyth, stopping by an abandoned lead mine to refuel – ham sandwich, crisps and a Mars Bar, the brunch of champions. I set the tripod up for a selfie, proof of having been there, and eyed up the derelict mine buildings which were ripe for exploration.

The land was vast and empty, a scaling up of Pembrokeshire. I realised that morning how much more there was to this country, this Wales. Sitting on a low stone wall, I imagined the unexplored vistas that awaited, not just that day but in the years to come, and it thrilled me. Having languished for so long, I was looking out at last, and a world was presenting itself to me, inviting me in.

Compositionally my capturing of all this newly discovered landscape was hit and miss. Awed by my subject, I gave little thought as to what I was photographing, the images being just snaps, mementos of burgeoning horizons. The camera, you see, justified my wanderings, providing the excuse around which to build a day. But something in those hills spoke to me. Something was awakening, stirring inside. With my camera and maps I was beginning an emotional journey around Wales. Perhaps the lie I'd told the lab technician could become the truth after all. Perhaps I could become a photographer.

Chapter 19

Life in late '80s Haverfordwest was not what you might call fast-moving. My own improving steps – mostly getting-my-head-sorted steps – were small ones but there seemed to be little magic around during the years of limbo when I was sometimes accepting, occasionally optimistic, but all too often raging against the real and perceived restrictions of my life. The injustices that I felt had been heaped on me. The town, then, offered scant romance or stimulation for a young, unemployed – possibly unemployable – man. I was aware of a sense of confinement, not to mention boredom, and could scarcely remember how the streets had once appeared so exciting to me.

I have fond memories of walking with Gramps through the town as a child on winter nights, the cold, smoggy air wrapping itself around us like blankets, keeping out the world. Enveloped in cigarette smoke he'd recall the town of his youth as I hung on his every word. Great-uncle Ernie's cottage by the castle gates would be our destination – two cramped rooms and a lean-to kitchen downstairs.

We'd give a knock on the stunted front door, its layers of lead paint hard as steel, before strolling in. A dark corridor led past the parlour, the door of which was always shut, and onto the backroom where Ernie sat, lit dimly yellow by a nicotine-coated bulb hanging by thirties wiring. The walls were brown and tacky from decades of tobacco smoke and the spluttering cast-iron range and through the haze I'd make out the shape of Ernie in his chair.

Straight away, they'd light up.

'Does the boy want one, Charl?' Ernie would ask.

I was always 'the boy', even when I became a man.

'Told you before, Ern. Doesn't smoke.'

This ritual had played itself out since I was about ten, around the age at which Gramps had sworn allegiance to the mighty Woodbine.

'Charl, have a look at these, will you?'

Ernie would bung him official-looking letters; notices from the council, benefit forms, anything in a brown envelope. He wasn't good at that stuff.

'Does the boy want to see the stamps? Coins?'

It was as if I spoke another language, as Ernie diverted conversation through Gramps. Slowly, though, he'd warm to his regular guest and address me directly, getting the stamp books and coins from the cupboard and coming alive, bristling with knowledge.

'Know what that is? Penny Black,' he'd say, as if it were the most precious object in the world, conscious of his role in preserving those little bits of gummed paper.

Ernie was the family's dark secret: a reclusive welcomer of stray cats and the odd rat: a work-shy, bardic storyteller. Mum begged me not to tell my friends he was my uncle if I saw him shuffling around town. But I told them. I was weirdly proud of him, thinking it cool to be the only one with a tramp-like relative. Water came from a tap in the yard but he hadn't washed in years, grime-layered,with blackheads like grit. Coming at you out of the gloom he was the bogey man, with bulging rheumy eyes and a meagre assortment of blackish-brown teeth; a Tolkien character, seemingly of the earth.

Having studied the stamps and held and rubbed some coins, I'd ask if I could root around and look and touch and marvel. A brown-painted dresser groaned under lifetimes of accumulation. Ornaments, coronation mugs, cigarette cards of thirties movie stars, curling family photographs and all manner of ephemera preserved under a filmic coating of soot. It was like an archaeological dig but with the treasure above ground. My favourite piece was a painted stoneware cottage – Gramps would place a cigarette through the front door and smoke rose out of the chimney. I'd emerge from the house with stinging eyes and tracks of flea bites, brimming with tales and sagas and endless imaginings.

My last visit to Ernie's was in July '88, declining the customary offer of a Woodbine. He was quiet and grumbly. Gramps asked if he was okay.

'It's my guts, Charl. Sore, they are. Can't keep anything down.'

'I'll make an appointment Monday,' said Gramps.

'Don't fuss. It'll be nothing.'

He didn't make conversation except to state, without malice, his oft-repeated belief that I'd be 'no good for the army now' on account of my accident. You might've imagined that the army had made him, but he'd never worked. There was talk in the family of a funny turn when he was in his teens. After that, whenever the subject of work arose, it brought on another turn.

His mood was dark that day, the air thicker than I could ever recall; it may've been summer but the range was always kept in. We left him sitting in the haze, layered-up for winter in July. A week later, he dropped dead in the street. The death certificate pointed to a heart attack. Perhaps strolling down town in the August sunshine buttoned-up in the heavy woollen overcoat he always wore had caused his ticker to fail. If his heart hadn't given in, the post-mortem discovered that his oesophagus would've finished him off in any case – the fags and decades of sitting in what was in effect a herring smokery, thanks to the leaky cast-iron range, had done for his throat.

The house was listed to go to auction and we set about clearing it. Standing outside the back door, I'd always imagined that the property ended at the ten-foot-high wall of brambles hemming the yard in. Over a period of a week, like intrepid Amazonian explorers we hacked the thicket back to expose a garden a hundred feet long. Gramps seemed happy to have rediscovered it and perhaps some childhood memories.

I opened the door to the parlour. Gladys, my great-grandmother, had died in 1972 and the door had been closed, as if on a sealed capsule. I have vague recollections of Gladdie, a bird-like woman in a pinny with a cigarette stuck to her lower lip. A layer of dust snowed the room. There were two deco-style armchairs and a glass-fronted display cabinet. A calendar hung on the wall, from '72. There were items of clothing: a mac, a cardigan, a scarf.

I picked up a large bible, the pages stiff and brown. An inscription recorded it as having been bought in London in 1765. One page had a hand-written recipe for pease pudding, dated to the late eighteenth century. Another page entranced and saddened me: a list of births in the 1880s and 90s, a record of Gladys and her siblings. There were seven names. One had died as a baby, another didn't reach three. It was a sobering read. On other bits of loose, yellowing paper were hymns, childish doodles and even a shopping list.

Upstairs in Gladdie's bedroom – another capsule – neatly folded clothing, laundered sixteen years earlier, sat in drawers lined with even older newspaper: a man sentenced to six months' hard labour for theft; a photo of the winner of the 1953 open at the golf club and a home furnishings store advertising their new range of three-piece suites – perhaps the armchairs in the parlour had come from there. There was a Lipton's tea caddy stuffed with handwritten receipts from a local shop that no longer existed. Vegetables, packets of tea, cigarettes; all dated around the turn of the century and accounted for in scrupulous copperplate writing.

The house sold and the new owners gutted the interior, stripping it back to its four outer walls, the ceilings and stairs removed. A shell. The front door and sash windows – painted shut – were replaced with plastic. About a year later I spoke to a friend of the new owners, who'd also known and visited Ernie. He shook his head as he described the new open-plan living space, the fireplace blocked up and skimmed-over, an exorcism of character. It was as if the house in my head had never existed.

When I think of Nan and Gramps during my childhood, I'm reminded of Sundays. Sunday often meant putting my trainers on after lunch and running the mile and a half to their two-bedroomed council house. Likening myself to Seb Coe, I floated through town, each stride spring-loaded. I just ran and ran and ran, stumbling into their kitchen panting madly. Nan would be sat in the lounge, often glued to a black and white western, fag in hand.

She was an accomplished smoker, lighting one after the other as if single-handedly rescuing her preferred brand from bankruptcy. A cup of Mellow Birds – a fine brown powder purporting to be coffee – and a biscuit or three was the only surefire way to break the Embassy chain. As for Gramps, he lit up less often, accumulating a pyre of butts before winkling out the pinches of tobacco, with which he'd roll a bonus smoke.

Nan would stir mid-afternoon to make custard, never with any success; it was always the texture of whale blubber with a spoon-resistant skin. Paired with a tin of fruit cocktail, it constituted the Sunday teatime treat. I'd race through mine perched on the edge of the settee, as the moment she'd dispatched her last mouthful she'd light up again. I hated eating with that grey wisp snaking round me.

Every couple of years, Mum would say, 'If you get some paint, Harry will come up and do the lounge.'

Dad would roller-out the room, covering up the previous few grands' worth of nicotine staining.

'He said make sure you buy the decent stuff, mind – Dulux or Crown, so he can put it on thick,' she'd beg, knowing his dread of the five-coat curse.

Oblivious, Nan would buy discounted trade paints from somewhere – we never knew where – which guaranteed two-coat coverage.

'Where did she get that bloody paint from?' was Dad's perennial cry after the first day of what would be the dreaded five-coater. As he painted, they lit up, browning the new white before it'd even dried.

Nan was Glaswegian and vehemently tribal about it, her reddish, tightly permed hair and fireiness testimony to her roots. Gramps had been posted to Glasgow with the army at the start of the Second World War. They met, married and after the war she moved to her new life in west Wales, never reconciled and always aching to return.

Her Presbyterian obsession with cleanliness manifested itself in wiping down kitchen surfaces with diluted bleach; I never took to the chemical toast she made for me afterwards. Tartan-themed kitsch displayed in a glass cabinet offered pyrrhic comfort, more a reminder of loss than any clan-like belonging. Once a year she'd catch the train to Glasgow and her beloved neighbourhood of Maryhill to stay with her widowed mother, a cold lady who'd shown her little affection.

Top of Nan's familial pecking order was her older brother, Gilbert. She adored him. A physically imposing man, his broad chest sported a huge tattoo of the protestant William of Orange on horseback. Gilbert followed Rangers' Football Club and took pleasure in baring his chest to incensed Celtic fans – with their catholic leanings – on the terraces. He led a comfortable existence, the funding of which was a mystery but which involved wearing snappy suits and going out a lot at night; he drove a Jaguar at a time when they were the preserve of shadowy figures or the police that chased them.

Nan, then, would return from Glasgow with another bagpipe-playing doll to add to her collection, a suitcase full of shortbread and a stronger accent than when she'd left. She shone with rejuvenated zeal, reconnected to her home patch, but as the weeks passed she'd regress once again into misty-eyed reminiscence, weighed down by the heavy heart of the internal exile.

After the war, Gramps got a job as a storeman at RNAD Trecwn, my future employer. Thirty-six years later, he retired, having ascended to the position of senior storeman, a notch above where he'd started – allegiance to the boys took precedence over promotion. He adored the depot so much that he insisted on working his allotted annual leave. Like a bigamist, his loyalties were torn between two families – home and work – and retirement, when it came, was a blow from which he never really recovered.

His sustaining passion were the lovebirds he kept in a shed out in the yard. I'd watch him pluck them ever so gently from their perch and caress them, stroking their tiny heads and whispering sweet nothings. He pottered out there, whiling away time, munching on cheese sandwiches, and sipping tea with the odd smoke.

There'd been a dog at one time; Kim the Alsatian. It'd been Mum's dog, which became theirs when she got married and had me; an Alsatian and a baby were deemed an inadvisable mix. As a toddler I remember cowering by Mum's side as she shielded me from Kim's suspicious welcome, her hot barked breath blasting my face as we scurried across the yard to the back door.

After Kim died, Nan fancied a cat, of the Siamese variety. Tiddles would lie on her lap regarding all comers with malicious contempt. It tore strips from Gramps's arms, with scram and teeth marks that would've impressed the most determined self-harmer. I dreaded that cat springing on to the sofa to settle on my lap.

'She really likes you,' Nan would say proprietorially. Tiddles would let me pet her till she'd had her fill, then plunge her claws into my thigh as I'd chuck her onto the floor.

'She's only playing with you,' Nan would protest.

Tiddles enjoyed a surprisingly long life, considering, and then another Tiddles was sought. I went with aunty Linda and Nan to collect it. A large woman in a nylon tabard welcomed us into her house which doubled as a litter-tray; it was full of cats. She invited us to sit. I insisted on standing and mouth-breathed while she engaged with Linda and Nan.

'I've put her in here for the journey home,' she said, handing Linda a cardboard box with the lid taped shut. Didn't seem like standard procedure to me: a cat in a box?

'Best not open it till you get home,' the woman said.

I sat in the back with the box on my lap. Nan sat in the passenger seat and Linda drove. Curiosity killed the cat, apparently, and I too was curious. Surely, I thought, this new Tiddles couldn't be as vicious as its predecessor. Maybe if I took it out and placed it on my lap and stroked it and reassured it during the journey, it might look favourably upon me.

I peeled the tape back, opened the lid of the box, and out of the darkness it sprang, lodging its claws in my chest. Nan and Linda were busy chatting and didn't hear the commotion. I yanked the cat out of my chest and set about shoe-horning it back into the box; a box it was unwilling to be returned to. It scrammed and clawed and bit with all the ferocity it could muster, a worthy successor to the old Tiddles.

'Everything okay back there?' enquired Nan, half-turning.

'Yeah, no problem,' I replied, wincing.

I jammed it in, extricated my torn hands, pushed the lid down and held it in place till we got back to the house. Tiddles Mk II and I didn't get on after that.

Gramps taught me manly skills such as chopping sticks for the fire. A couple of nicks of the finger with an axe soon concentrated my aim. There was a white Ford Fiesta which seemed forever parked up. He spent so much time checking 'her' levels and tyre pressures. 'Took her out last night for a spin just to charge the battery. Goes like a bomb,' he'd say. He hadn't taken her out; driving at night with oncoming headlights caused his eyes to stream like a waterfall – his words, not mine. He kept it so we could 'borrow her whenever,' and to have something to tinker with. A stroll down a leafy lane and across a meadow to the river bank was the more likely outing, when the weather obliged, to go fishing together.

Best of all, were the stories, an inexhaustible stockpile of fantastic tales that even Roald Dahl would've envied. It seemed an injustice that he never received a Victoria Cross for his wartime exploits. He and his mate Nobby marched ten thousand Italian prisoners-of-war into Tripoli. Just the two of them. Mind, the Italians didn't have a great war, so perhaps it wasn't that far-fetched. High command transferred them to Burma where they inflicted similar single-handed damage to the Japanese cause – 'A cruel race, Dai,' he'd say.

And then there were the visitors.

'Never guess what I saw last night, getting logs in from the yard. Tell him, Nellie.'

Nan would break off momentarily from whatever was engrossing her on the telly and roll her eyes. She'd played the game forever.

'UFO, on the shed roof. Bold as you like. Wasn't it, Nellie?'

'Aye, a UFO. On the shed,' she'd say dryly.

Saturday afternoons he'd be gripped by televised wrestling mania. I knew it to be a choreographed spectacle whereas he believed it was a fight to the death. Big Daddy and Giant Hay Stacks were colliding with perfect timing one day when I decided to drift off and rifle through some drawers. The treasure hunter in me always lived in hope of the glittering find, the curio, some fragment of the past.

I saw it half-hidden amongst an assortment of old letters in the back of a drawer, fished it out and held it, confused and uncertain. It felt real; cold and heavy in my hand. But it couldn't be, surely.

'Gramps.'

Haystacks had Daddy in a half-nelson.

'Gramps,' I repeated.

'Yeah,' he replied, without turning.

'Is this real?'

'What?'

'This.'

He spun round in his seat.

'Yep,' he said, and turned back to the action.

I suddenly felt nervous.

'Right. So, where did you get it?'

'India. In the war.'

I had to ask, even though I knew the answer would be no.

'Can I have it?'

There was a pause.

'Yes,' he said, much louder than was necessary.

'What? Really?'

It couldn't be that easy, surely.

'Yes. YES! Counted out. Knew he'd win,' he said, turning to me, 'Sorry, what did you say?'

'Oh, nothing.'

He said that I could have it – sort of – and though it seemed crazy

I was now the owner of a revolver. A Smith & Wesson. No bullets, though. Recently, a boy had brought a baby adder into school in a hessian sack. He'd found it in some gorse bushes. At break he put on a pair of welding gloves and goaded the snake into biting his thumb, with twin dots of venom wetting the leather. The assembled throng were spellbound and I imagined that a gun could elicit even more acclamation. It turned out I was right, though how I got through the day without word of my show-and-tell leaking to the staff I don't know.

At home, I wrapped it in a cloth and hid it under the rafters in the garage, reckoning Mum and Dad wouldn't be too happy at me being in possession of a firearm. My yearning to garner respect, though, made me less than discreet as I showed it to all manner of friends and neighbourhood boys. Not surprisingly, it was stolen. I found out who'd taken it – the same boy had nicked an Airfix model of a Japanese Mitsubishi Zero I'd made. I went to his house and challenged him but he denied taking either, of course, before instructing his mum to shoo me from their drive. We stopped hanging around after that.

I'd like to remember Nan and Gramps as having been fit as fiddles to their dying day, but that's not how it was. Cigarette companies, you see, push the ultimate Ponzi scheme, with a twist: invest for decades and when the plan reaches maturity you're rewarded with a pitiful demise. From the glossy catalogue of ailments, Nan's annuity comprised an initial stroke, from which she made a fantastic recovery. It was truly beautiful to behold. She came home from hospital, lit up, threw up and never touched another fag. But the damage was done.

The second stroke was catastrophic and not long in the offing, leaving her speechless and barely able to move. A residential home welcomed her into its financially driven grasp, a world of budget care and easy-wipe furniture. It was horrid, a waiting room for damaged people praying for a swift end to their indignity. Hers was neither swift in arriving nor rapid when it did.

Gramps insisted he'd die at home, even before death's shadow cantered over the horizon; he was a man racked with premonition. 'Whatever happens, I'm not going into hospital,' he'd declare. His was a peculiarly dark and conscious spiralling. It began with complaints of what felt like indigestion and discomfort when eating. The mild facial contortions ratcheted over the weeks into excruciating masks of pain. We took to cooking him sausages and cutting them into tiny pieces, but when he swallowed they were retched straight back up. His doctor called, examined him and said that time was short. The mighty Woodbine had got its man.

When he finally let go, in his own bed, I went to his room, sat by his side and caressed and kissed his cooling forehead. He'd got what he wanted; no hospital for Charlie. There was a peacefulness to his still features, his face shedding twenty years. Even the burst blood vessels seemed to have been Photoshopped out.

Wiping away tears, I glanced over at the spare single bed separated from his by a small cabinet. Myself and my cousins would sleep in it when we stayed over, not all at once, of course. I recalled lying there watching him go through his bedtime routines as he folded his trousers and lifted the mattress to place them under to press overnight.

That little house had been a constant nearly all my life. Big Daddy Saturday afternoons. Chopping stick in the yard. The tall tales. Nan's determined Scottishness. Even the rubbery custard and scrammy cats were fondly remembered. The house was sold and became someone else's home.

Chapter 20

By my mid-twenties I'd fallen into a pattern of daily living based on a lie. The lie that I was content. The lie that my life had meaning, even that I was a busy man. It was a flimsy delusion with which I was only too happy to conspire if it meant I didn't have to face up to the truth. And the truth was, I was hiding.

My parents took the *Daily Express*, not a newspaper destined to detain anyone for long. Yet I managed to eke out its woeful content to fill a day, eager, it seemed, to read all about the latest Aspirin scare in the elderly, how Britain was in for the coldest winter on record, or that drinking a glass of red wine a day warded off Alzheimer's. It wasn't so much a newspaper as a series of scare stories and alleged wonder cures. Not even the *Express*, though, could ignore the first Gulf War, which began in January '91, its readers foregoing their usual front-page diet of pre-Internet click-bait stories for coverage of the conflict. In spite of Saddam Hussein's threat to inflict untold slaughter on the invading infidels, the war lasted just a matter of weeks, as the Iraqi forces crumbled in the face of terrifying force – it was as if the allies' equipment was on a month-long lease and they were mindful of having to return it. It was to be another six years till the death of Princess Diana, the ramifications of which would furnish the *Express* with its front page – seemingly every day – for more than a decade afterwards.

Lunch would be taken early because I was bored rather than hungry, eating as a way to kill time. Then there was the daytime television schedule, with *Murder She Wrote* or *Quincy* to be circled in biro; anything to punch holes in the day. And not forgetting *Pebble Mill at One*, of course. When the tedium became too oppressive and my anger began to rise, I'd break out and do a few circuits of the town in my car, with the stereo turned up to max.

If the weather was amenable, I might venture off around the county for a few hours with my camera, taking snaps that wouldn't even have made it into print as a postcard. When my muscle tone allowed, I'd travel further afield for a day's photography, returning home for supper, of course, at five on the dot. Sending the films off for developing, I'd wait with a sense of anticipation for the prints to come back, but when they did, after one dispiriting flick through, they'd be consigned to the drawer. I liked playing the part of a photographer but lacked the discipline to compose and execute images with any artistry. The camera was a displacement activity, allowing me to pretend that I was fulfilled while killing a day.

I still had the gym, which lent my life a veneer of accomplishment and which I enjoyed. There were once-a-year blasts to Tenerife with the lads, though after the third ground-hog fortnight the sheen had worn off. There'd been no more encounters with lab technicians, just a weary re-run of the previous re-run. Jolly minibus ventures up to London to see the likes of INXS – I imagined myself as West Wales's answer to their frontman, Michael Hutchence – and The Who at Wembley Arena felt faintly rebellious. Being from Haverfordwest, though, just having your ears pierced was deemed a potentially seditious act.

The British Grand Prix at Silverstone fermented great excitement the first time I went; the white-hot scream of oiled metal on metal, the dizzying smell of burnt fuel, the thrum of an engine in your chest as the cars passed and passed, again and again, lap after lap, a gradual processional boredom setting in, with only the occasional crash reigniting my waning interest.

One year, after the race had finished, four of us found ourselves on the circuit crammed into a Vauxhall Astra-max van; an open gate had been just too inviting. We set quite a pace, only stopping on the pit straight to pick up a clutch of Fosters' hospitality girls. On our third lap the organisers had managed to block the track and directed us off the circuit amid threats of arrest.

All of these distractions, then, weren't much to build a life around but just enough to persuade me that all was fine. As when I'd leaned against that stone at Avebury watching the sun rise, they were exceptions that threatened to spark something meaningful but never did. The moment the euphoria died down, I'd shrink again.

Mid-week would be an impatient waiting game for Friday and Saturday night, when alcohol would salve any nagging reproaches and reaffirm the conviction that life was good. Sitting beered-up under the stars after throwing-out time, I'd imagine the adventures that lay ahead once I was ready to embark. Such embroidered narratives were spun in my head involving travel and, of course, great acclaim. I craved recognition for something. Anything.

My most common flight of fancy was to become a professional photographer. I had it all laid out in my head. When the time would come to depart for these hopeful horizons I didn't quite know, only that it'd happen soon enough. I was, as always, preparing myself for something while doing nothing. Then I'd hail a taxi for home and wake the next morning to reality, to stasis.

Meanwhile, my brother Andrew worked in a DIY store. He'd worked from the day he left school at the age of sixteen. In fact, he started work weeks before school officially ended. He just wanted to get on with life and school to him was a handbrake. So, while his friends were kicking their heels in class, counting down the days, he was earning. I was both proud and envious of him.

'How was work today?' Dad habitually enquired at the supper table.

'Good. Yeah, really good...' Andrew would reply, going on to regale us with snippets of his day in between shovelling in groaning forkfuls; he ate as if his plate might be snatched away at any moment. The mealtime debriefs were an unwelcome reminder of my continued hiding. Mum and Dad sensed my unease but were determined to expose me to convention; people worked, and when they sat together to eat, they talked about their day. Tough love. Andrew was oblivious to their manoeuvres while I ate in silence and left the table the moment I finished.

Each week Dad read the *Western Telegraph* jobs section, not because he wanted a job – he had a well-paid one in the refinery – no, he read it so that he could dangle opportunities before me like an angler trying to hook a particularly elusive fish.

'That looks good. Trainee accountant?'

He paused, waiting for a response. It would've been a long wait and he knew it.

'What do you think? Fancy applying?'

I was obliged to answer, as to feign deafness twice would've been insulting.

'Yeah, maybe.'

'Good starting wage. Deadline's two weeks.' He peered over the top of the paper.

'Okay. I'll get an application form.'

And I did. I filled it out and even made a show of addressing the envelope and putting a stamp on it. They witnessed me leaving the house to post it. I drove to a car park, tore it up and chucked it in a bin. Time and again I went through the charade, feeling guilty at their hopeful smiles as I left the house and even more ashamed when they berated the company for not having had the decency to inform me that I hadn't made it through to the interview stage. But those suppertime chats and Mum and Dad's drip-drip of encouragement forced me to confront the demons. I couldn't hide any longer. It was a classic pincer-movement worthy of any Prussian general, a coming together of dual prongs of attack. The other prong was the welfare state. It came calling with its glossy suggestions and one-on-one case workers, applying gentle then less-gentle shoves towards employment. My resistance weakened as my shame increased.

I knocked on the door.

'Enter,' boomed a commanding voice.

I walked into the room. A man was sitting behind a large grey desk and I recognised him immediately; Mr Kelleher. He considered me for a few seconds.

'Do I recognise you? Sir Thomas Picton?' he asked.

'Yes, that's right, sir…'

'Please, I'm not a teacher anymore. We can drop the sir.'

He motioned for me to sit.

'When did you leave?'

'Nearly ten years ago.'

'And…' He paused. 'You had a younger brother? Andrew?'

'Yeah, that's right.'

As if recalling a traumatic period in his teaching career, he said, 'Yes, I remember Andrew well. Very well.'

Mr Kelleher was now tasked with finding work for the unemployable, and I was his latest challenge.

In his previous incarnation as deputy head, he'd oozed authority. He rounded up my mate Paul and I once during lesson time. It was too sunny to be stuck in class, so we decided to take some time out – get a bag of chips and head to his place to watch the first day of Wimbledon. Within sight of Paul's house, a car screeched to a halt and out he jumped.

'Where on earth are you going at half two in the afternoon?'

Like Dickie Attenborough in *The Great Escape* we'd almost made it, our plan foiled within sight of sanctuary. He taxied us back to school for a stern talk and, of course, a caning. Beneath that crocodile exterior though was a man determined to extract the best from all of us, a trait lacking in many of his colleagues, who went through the motions of teaching without any conviction. Some didn't even bother with the motions. There was a deadness in their eyes, pension age the only glimmer on the distant (or in most cases not-so distant) horizon.

The worst offender in this pantheon of indifference was a religious education teacher. A small, wiry man, lessons followed a predictable pattern: he put the telly on and played a video. We'd watch in silence while he sat at his desk reading a newspaper. The programme would be a random offering. I recall, for example, a short film about a gamekeeper with a graphic scene in which a rabbit had its neck wrung. Perhaps there was a subliminal pastoral message about God and the natural order of things which I failed to detect. Every so often he'd peer hawk-like over the top of his paper to ensure adequate crowd control, sometimes catching the eye of one of the boys to run an errand to the shop. A pouch of Golden Virginia, Rizla papers and a packet of Polos was the order I was once given. I got the wrong papers, so he sent me back to exchange them. On my return my lesson had finished and another class was in situ watching the same film in equal silence. I crept in, grabbed my bag and raced off to the next lesson, arriving ten minutes late.

'Where've you been, Wilson?' barked the teacher.

'Sorry, sir, I had to go to the shop for Mr Jenkins.'

'Oh, right. Well, sit down and turn to page twenty-three,' he said, turning an institutional blind eye to the inclusion of errand-running on the syllabus.

A handful of teachers were the exception to the general malaise, their shining example shaming their colleagues – not that their colleagues would necessarily have felt any shame; they seemed oblivious to the damage they were inflicting on so many youthful hopes.

I'm lifted when I think of the good ones. Mrs Getvoldsen taught English, and not only taught the subject but lived and breathed the beauty of the language. When I wrote an essay or story, I wrote to please her. I wrote to impress her. Mrs Blacker taught art. I painted and drew more intently for her than any other art teacher. The good ones got the best from you. The good ones made you care. There just weren't enough good ones.

In addition to being deputy head, Mr Kelleher doubled as the careers' teacher, a thankless task.

'So, David, any ideas about what you want to do when you leave school?'

'Not really.'

Undeterred by my lack-lustre response, he pressed me.

'I suggest you start giving it some serious thought, boy. Can't just drift through life.'

I shrugged.

'Look, David, I think you're a bright boy, contrary to the evidence. You need to get some focus or you'll regret it, trust me.'

The hectoring prized out a half-hearted show of positivity. 'Well, maybe a policeman or something. Dunno, really. Or maybe the Navy. Yeah, my dad was in the Navy,' I said, without conviction.

And so, there we were – me and Mr Kelleher – nearly a decade later, reprising that conversation. He flagged up a number of training schemes and placements, which were met with quiet apathy. Finally, though, he pulled something out of the bag that elicited a flicker of enthusiasm.

Quayline Reprographics was a graphic design house supplying content to local newspapers and other publications. What now takes minutes to produce on Photoshop took Quayline hours of fine scalpel work and photographic layering. Rick was the entrepreneur behind this cutting-edge, Thatcherite enterprise.

'Davey-boy, been expecting you.' We shook hands. 'Welcome to my little empire,' he said, before introducing me to Trevor and Andrew, the graphic designers.

Rick was a piece of wide-boy estuary-English transplanted to west Wales, and he didn't lack confidence. With a gaudy assemblage of tattoos, he lived in short sleeves, better to show off his artwork and what he imagined to be Schwarzenegger arms. He worked out, which we were reminded of most days, but not enough to warrant the delusion.

Mine wasn't a job in the traditional sense as I wasn't technically employed. It was a work placement. Rick paid the government a pittance each week for the pleasure of allowing me to make tea, pick up lunchtime takeaways from the Chinese over the road, execute mundane tasks and laugh at his jokes. In return, the government paid me a marginally less insulting pittance in the expectation that I would turn up for forty hours a week. Rick got a gopher and the government massaged the unemployment stats.

His ambition, though, couldn't be faulted. The digital scanner he had installed was huge, resembling the jet-powered car Richard Noble piloted for his land speed world record attempt. A wall had to be removed to accommodate the beast, as it straddled two rooms. Buried in the centre of its enormous casing was a small Perspex tube that spun at incredible speed; the bit that did the scanning. The technology was pioneering, Rick's very own pre-Hadron Collider.

One day, a salesman named Pete called, all smiles and professional friendliness, one of the boys, if it helped seal the deal. After a meeting, Rick brought him out to show him the scanner – everyone was introduced to the scanner. Pete was impressed. Before he left, he asked if he could use the toilet and disappeared.

'Quick, pass me the mags,' said Rick.

He'd accumulated a collection of hardcore euro publications, and donating them for general office perusal confirmed his status as one of the lads. He grabbed a pair of scissors and cut out some images.

'Right, just slip these in here,' he smirked, interspersing them amongst the pages of a product catalogue in Pete's briefcase. Pete returned, picked up the briefcase and left.

Later that afternoon, Rick came out of his office in convulsions.

'What's so funny?' asked Trevor.

Rick could barely speak. 'Just had... Pete... on the phone.'

'And?'

'He only went and gave the catalogue to someone at a meeting. And they opened it. Fucking fuming, he is.'

We never saw Pete again.

Rick's financial acumen, though, was no match for his ambition: there were liquidity issues, and on the principle of last in, first out, I was gone. Rick could be brash and conceited, and on occasion very funny, but he'd given me a chance and helped me banish that tiny person in my head, just a little. I'd surrendered the micro-management of Mondays to Fridays, my life becoming more normalised, and for that I am forever indebted to him, and his tattoos.

Mum and Dad were emboldened by my short-lived career as an assistant graphic designer, and once again the trusty *Western Telegraph* provided them with an avenue of attack.

'See the College's got an open day next week.'

Dad dripped it in innocuously, as if asking me to draw the curtains, but I could hear the hope in his casual pronouncement.

I stood by my car eyeing up the long walk to the entrance. The college was new, big and daunting. Individuals and small groups were heading in, coming out, standing and chatting. There was no cover, just a seemingly unending walk, demanding a very public performance. I felt the anxiety of the maiden gym session all over again, only worse. This was nightmare territory.

Whenever I walk in a public place with potential spectators around, the mantra of 'pick your feet up' plays on a loop in my head. Walking, you see, is a fraught exercise, a Russian roulette of risk and reward. I've caught a foot and fallen many times, the mental scars taking longer to heal than a bruise or graze. Mind, I did tear a large patch of skin off the palm of my hand once when breaking a fall, which became infected, suppurating and weeping pus for weeks. Indeed, some of my falls have achieved the status of anecdote, such as the time I was walking home from the pub alongside the river in Haverfordwest. I tripped on a broken paving slab and was heading into the rushing waters when a trailing arm hooked itself around a horizontal railing and saved me. At the college, though, I got to the entrance intact.

The atrium was an open multi-storey space of glass and steel and just inside its main doors a table groaned under stacks of prospectuses. A young man handed me one and asked if I needed any advice which I declined. He invited me to stroll around and browse the various pitches manned by staff from different departments. I thanked him, spun and walked out. I'd done what was required of me. My conscience was clear. Mum and Dad would be oblivious to my hasty retreat, and given fresh, though illusory, hope.

When I got home, I browsed the prospectus with them, making suitably positive noises, which made them happy, while feeling like a fraud, once again. And that should've been it. Duty discharged. But in the weeks that followed I surprised myself by returning to the prospectus and beginning to imagine the possibilities, the notion that maybe I could actually sign up for a course.

As if the contemplation of enrolment in college wouldn't be a big enough upheaval to my managed existence, I'd recently welcomed a huge recalibration of my routine: I had a girlfriend. For the average twenty-five-year-old man that might be deemed a run-of-the-mill occurrence, the latest squeeze in a succession of romantic interludes stretching back to their teens. Some of my friends were serial offenders in the relationship stakes, and in between girlfriends they searched out transient encounters to keep their hand in. They had form. But aside from a number of dalliances in the depths of RJ's nightclub in Haverfordwest, amongst other insalubrious settings, this was my very first proper relationship.

She was studying for a teaching degree in Cardiff, returning to Pembrokeshire and home in the holidays. During term time I'd drive to Cardiff to stay with her. It was serious and liberating. The lab technician in Tenerife made me realise that my issues were only an issue when viewed through the prism of my insecurity. But she'd been a holiday encounter and on my return I'd soon regressed.

A relationship, though, has a comforting permanence, and the constancy of my girlfriend's unspoken reassurance sparked a conviction that the sum of my parts was indeed greater than any physical limitations. There was more to me than the damage.

We were a couple and it felt great, a bit of me basking in a glow of societal normality, like I was accumulating the trappings of a fuller life. She had to be patient, mind, as years of daily routine, deciding what and what not to do in advance, had made me less than receptive to ad hoc suggestions. I was inflexible and bloody infuriating. It was a revelatory period though, as an emotional intelligence blossomed within me, experiencing feelings that'd been suppressed for too long. She was good for me.

Chapter 21

Seven and a half years had passed since the accident – not that I was counting! They'd been tough years, dogged by self-loathing and hate, with just the occasional glittering exception. It was a hatred of the permanence of my physical situation that the gym gains couldn't compensate for any longer; hatred of those I deemed too bloody fortunate, but mostly hatred of myself, and in particular my inability to break the cycle of despair.

Conjuring all of my resolve, then, in September '91 I embarked on my bravest course of action yet. Stood by my car, I readied myself to join the busy scrum of students getting off buses or walking from their vehicles into the college. I too was one of those students, enrolled on a BTEC National Diploma in Business and Finance. I set off with a gut full of butterflies and that mantra repeating in my head – pick your feet up – as I made my way towards the entrance.

During my brief tenure at Quayline Reprographics, I'd drive around the streets near to the building before work, hoping to park close to shorten the walk in, but whatever the distance I had to cover I'd be filled with anxiety. If I heard footsteps behind or saw someone coming towards me, I'd do my usual thing and stop. Dead still. Glancing at my watch or rooting around in an inside pocket in search of some imaginary object, I'd wait till the coast was clear, then continue.

If I'd employed the same tactic walking into college, I'd never have covered the hundred metres in time for the first lecture, maybe missing the one after that too. So, I had to grit my teeth and go for it, focusing like mad on my stride pattern, hoping I didn't fall, and pretending there was no one in the vicinity. Pretending I was the only person on earth. Another mental obstacle, if not exactly banished, at least challenged.

The class of new students glanced nervously around, with some, including myself, initiating small talk. Then, a man swept in, and stood in front of the whiteboard.

'Good morning, everyone. Welcome to Pembrokeshire College. My name's Tony Davies and I'm your form tutor,' he said cheerily. 'I'll also be taking you for the accounting module, so you'll be seeing a lot of me.'

Tony sported a fulsome and scruffy beard allied with a beery conviviality, and I liked him immediately. At the age of twenty-six I was one of the older students on the course, my previous experience of education having instilled in me a disparagement of the teaching profession. At school there'd been that tiny stellar cast of teachers who'd shone with vocational fervour, while most of their colleagues gave the impression of being tired journeymen, or women, who'd stumbled into the profession with little enthusiasm, or perhaps by accident. Some of them, I'm sure, were shocked to discover after teacher training that they'd be spending their working day in the company of children, such was their apparent loathing of little people.

So, it was heartening to be lectured for two years by a cadre of college tutors who seemed almost evangelical. They wanted to be there and they wanted to educate us. I also discovered that I'd grown up, no longer the class joker, consuming knowledge with a voracious appetite, and determined to excel. It'd taken far too many years, but I felt as if I was starting out at last on my future.

As those initial weeks turned to months, I gradually shed the self-conscious ache of the damaged person, aided in my rehabilitation by an inspiring young man on the course called William. I needed individuals like him to admire, to pull me up. Years before, it'd been the walker at Rookwood, and I still thought of one-armed Dan, of course. With William, though, I sensed a parity, an equivalence of physical misfortune. Like me, he walked with an irregular gait and stood out as being different. I never asked him why because perhaps, like me, he dreaded the question and believed there was more to him than that. He was bright and smiley, drinking in each day with the most extraordinary positivity, a state of mind I'd striven for so long to achieve, without any noticeable success.

With the physical demands of college life and regular trips to Cardiff to stay with my girlfriend, I felt, at last, that I was becoming indistinguishable from the masses, at least in my head, as I embraced a more normalised existence. I worked hard, graduated with a distinction and relished my newfound habit of looking forward.

Days before the end of the course, I encountered Tony in a corridor.

'So, David. What now?'

'Look for a job, I suppose.'

I never imagined I'd hear myself say that.

'Any ideas?'

'Nah, not really. Something will turn up though.'

'Hope so. But listen, don't forget the university option.'

'University? Really?'

It hadn't seemed relevant to me. None of my family or friends had been to university. It was for others.

'Yeah. You could do uni. No problem.'

I beamed at his belief in me. Why hadn't there been a bunch of Tony's at school?

Andrew, my brother, had bought a terraced house which he was doing up while my future promised a continuation of living with my parents. He had plans, and soon he'd be gone. I didn't want to be the elder sibling left behind so I made the decision to flee too.

The Crows' Nest was a renovated farmhouse on an island of greenery on the outskirts of Haverfordwest, its once rolling fields given over to an industrial estate and hemmed in on all sides by new roads. A friend, Nick, and my cousin John were resident, there were empty bedrooms and they needed the rent as much as I needed the independence. I also needed a job, now that college was over; I was now the one searching the situations vacant section of the *Western Telegraph*. Times had changed. I'd changed.

The social scaffolding that'd sustained me was being dismantled, the ties of friendship weakened as marriage claimed members of the gang. Gary had led the way, with Simon and Stephen following – not to each other – and then it'd been Mucky's turn. He'd cantered off to England eight years earlier to join the MoD police, his returns becoming less frequent as time passed. We gathered in Bristol to see him off with Karon to start married life and a family near Swindon.

Martin joined us at the wedding too. Following his exile to Norfolk in '83 he'd joined the RAF as a technician, indulging his passion for soldering circuit boards, adjusting tolerances, and oiling things. And like Mucky, his returns to west Wales had become rare.

It was as if a Sunday league football team, after many happy beer-fuelled seasons, was haemorrhaging players to bigger, more serious clubs. I was being left behind and began to sense an imperative to build my own life, a life that wasn't reliant on 'the lads'. A life where I'd have to take more risks away from the safety of them.

The Nest, then, felt like the beginning of a new chapter; three blokes and a rudimentary cleaning rota, which was soon discarded, with dust allowed to settle as if bestowing some magical aura. An industrially robust deep-fat fryer, donated by Nick's parents, who ran a guest house, took pride of place in the kitchen as I discovered the menu freedoms that come with independent living. Those nutritious parental meals that'd engendered little gastronomic enthusiasm were dumped in favour of a star-studded cast of high-carb, high-saturated-fat indulgences. This eagerly adopted though repetitious new diet was soon noticed by Nick's mum, Pat, who'd breeze in occasionally.

'See you've gone for the full English again then, Dai,' she'd say with a smile, polite enough not to mention it being two in the afternoon. To accompany chip suppers in front of the telly, Nick and I quaffed park-bench measures of cheap sherry. A full-sized table tennis table was accommodated in the vast kitchen, hosting a tournament most nights and a pool table wended its way from a pub to a downstairs room.

To complete this Las Vegas of leisure there was Nintendo's *Super Mario* interspersed with *Streetfighter* when our testosterone levels needed dowsing. Initially, I watched with disdain as Nick played a steady stream of callers, determined that I shouldn't stoop to such puerile pleasures. Curiosity weakened me though and I became just as hooked, if not more so, seeing as my hunt for employment had drawn a blank and I didn't have to get up for work.

John decided to move on and we needed a replacement to financially sustain our palace of frivolity. Dan, a young student, auditioned for a room. Hailing from Devon, he was affable but dishevelled and we took pity on him. John's vacated bedroom had no furniture, but we found an old mattress to chuck down on the floorboards, and Dan arrived with all of his possessions crammed into a large rucksack, emptying its contents onto the floor as if a clothes grenade had gone off. 'I can get up in the morning and scan my wardrobe in seconds,' he said with satisfaction. Dan was attuned to The Nest's prevailing culture, the regularity with which he rolled relaxing cigarettes being an added bonus.

The remaining spare bedroom was rented to Chris, whom we vaguely knew from the local pub scene. He arrived with a saga-like collection of tales – mostly involving alleged sexual conquests – and a saxophone. Local bands had been badgering him to join, apparently, and we looked forward to many sherry-fuelled musical evenings.

After numerous requests for him to perform, inspired by his self-professed brilliance, he brought the instrument down from his room and, striking an insouciant pose against the frame of the open back door, he rifled through some warm-up notes. He then repeated them. And he continued to repeat them till one of us asked for a tune we might recognise, at which point he confessed to not being able to play the thing.

We laughed a lot when Chris was around, though not always with him, as sifting fact from volumes of fiction was a challenge. Had he really been injured as a battlefield stretcher bearer? Did he really have a priceless collection of classic cars stowed away in garages up north? And if he did, why was he always broke and asking us for a sub?

A string of job interviews came my way, none of them successful.

I became disheartened, especially when one interviewer was less than tactful.

'So, David. You've seen the warehouse and the office and you can see how busy it is. Big place too. Lots of ground to cover.'

'Yeah, bit of a trek,' I said.

'Can be pretty hectic. Full on.'

'That's fine. Makes the day fly.'

He smiled, though not with the eyes.

'Look, don't get me wrong. Your qualifications are good,' he said, glancing down at my CV.

'Thanks.'

'But you didn't mention on the application form any... well, you know... problems.'

'Problems?'

'What I mean is, I couldn't help noticing you having a little difficulty keeping up on the walkabout.'

'Just office work, isn't it? Not like you're expecting me to dig graves or anything,' I said, noticing his unease.

'No, no, of course not,' he replied, with a hollow laugh. 'But maybe you should've mentioned any physical problems on the application form.'

'Why? So, you could chuck it in the bin?'

He straightened in his seat.

'We'd never do that,' he protested.

'Really?'

He leant forward, resting his elbows on the desk.

'Look, being honest with you, I don't think a disabled person would keep up with all the getting around.'

He'd uttered the one word that was prohibited in my vocabulary.

'Don't call me disabled, okay? Less able, yes. Bit slow perhaps. But not fucking disabled.'

'No need to swear. Just saying, that's all.'

'Tell you what. Why don't you stick your job where the sun don't shine?'

He shot to his feet.

'Right, that's it. Out,' he said, pointing to the door. 'I don't come to work to be spoken to like that.'

'No? Where do you normally go?'

I stood, took a few seconds to iron the spasticity from my legs, walked to the door, turned and said, 'Fucking shit place anyway,' and left.

I returned to The Nest churned up with anger and decided there and then that Tony had been right: I should go to university. Months of applying for jobs had got me nowhere and the novelty of deep-fried sausages, cheap sherry, table tennis and *Super Mario* had worn thin. Too much freedom isn't always a good thing. After the sense of achievement of my BTEC qualification I'd allowed myself to regress, to lose sight of the horizons that the course had seemed to promise. Tony was convinced I had what it took to go to university, so that's what I'd do.

The summer holidays arrived and Dan packed his rucksack to head home to Devon. Chris left as well, continuing a nomadic existence, as if staying a step ahead of something – or perhaps someone. And after twelve months both Nick and I decided it was time to rejoin the real world.

'Germany. Wow, that'll be good,' I said.

'Yeah, time to move on,' said Nick.

He was heading to the continent to work. I'd applied to Cardiff University to study law and been accepted. I looked around the sparsely furnished lounge that'd witnessed many parties, and concluded that it'd 'been a very good year'.

I'd paddled down the brook and out of Rookwood ten years earlier with the safety of the banks in touching distance. The trip to Wiltshire and joining the gym had flushed me out into the stream but still there was that sense of security. That sense that I was in control. Enrolling in college had dumped me out into the river, a faster-flowing, more white-knuckle ride, but still within my contemplation. Still within the bounds of what I perceived as achievable. But now I was to be washed out into the ocean that was Cardiff and a law course. There would be no sign of land, cast adrift and vulnerable, the bravest decision yet.

Mum was very excited at the prospect, if not a little proud, and yes, a bit boastful too. 'David's off to study law in Cardiff,' she'd purr to anyone who'd listen.

Dad felt the same too, I think. I was the first of our family on either side to go to university and I felt the glow of expectation, the kudos of such vaunted heights. I was proud of where I'd got to. Law had been my favourite module in college and I'd chosen a law degree on that basis. I visualised myself as a solicitor, back in Haverfordwest, of course, and I rather liked it.

My girlfriend and I would be changing places, though – she'd graduated and was back home from Cardiff, teaching in Pembrokeshire, while I'd be heading the other way. I was nervous. In fact, nervousness doesn't come close to encapsulating the terror that I felt. And what of my motives for going? Was I going for me or was I going because I felt I had to do something that was a step up, in the eyes of those closest to me, from Pembrokeshire college? I certainly felt that after a year of living it up at The Nest and a string of unsuccessful job applications, Cardiff was the only game in town.

The flat in the halls of residence was made up of four pinched bedrooms like cabins on a cross-channel ferry, each with integral furniture and an enclosed shower and toilet cubicle. An uninviting communal kitchen and eating area smelled of transient occupation and cold corners. With no lounge in which to congregate, Mark, Rob, Mikey and I led solitary lives in our rooms, only encountering one another at the cooker. Mark's waking hours throbbed to the metronomic beat of house music and whether we liked it or not we throbbed along too. I imagined that once lectures started it'd die down, but I was mistaken. Mark's course accommodated a lot of stereo time and I seemed to be forever knocking on his door.

'Hi, Mark. Hope you don't mind, but could you turn it down a bit?'

'Oh, sorry. Is it too loud? Yeah. Sure. I'll turn it down. Sorry. So sorry.'

He always spoke with a hand cupped to his mouth as if his words were a deadly contagion, but he was a sweet boy who was always mortified at having disturbed me. It'd return to ear-bleeding levels soon enough, though, as if he were bemused as to who or what had turned it down – a groundhog that blighted the flat.

Rob was pale and sallow, rarely emerging from his room. If I met Mark in the corridor he'd nod towards Rob's door and shrug his shoulders, as if there was some doubt as to whether he was even still alive. I'd hear his door open late at night as he scurried to the cooker to rustle up beans on toast to eat back in his room. Always beans on toast, as evidenced by the empty tins that never made it to the bin.

Mark was lovable but oblivious then, and Rob all but invisible, whereas Mikey was just plain annoying. Twentyish, moustachioed and from Merthyr, he was a Valleys Magnum P.I., with what seemed like a market-stall supply of palm-festooned Hawaiian shirts. He survived on dubious takeaways, Coke and little sleep. Frenetically chirpy and with a bunch of keys worthy of a prison warder attached to a belt loop, his jangling return in the early hours couldn't be missed. He'd crash into his room, adjacent to mine, with just a thin partition wall separating us, and chuck his fist of keys onto a Formica table top inches from my head. Awake, I'd listen to his telly blaring all the way through to my alarm.

'Late in last night, Mikey,' I said one afternoon as he emerged bleary-eyed from his room.

'Yeah, what a night. Must've been about two when I got in.'

'Nearer three, actually. Do me a favour...'

'Yeah, what?'

'Could you avoid chucking your keys on that table when you get in...' I said, glancing at the offending bunch, '...and keep the telly down.'

He looked confused.

'The telly?'

'Yes. The telly,' I said.

'Oh, you mean the volume?'

I nodded.

'Huh, funny thing is, I don't watch it,' he said, laughing. 'I only put it on to help me get to sleep.'

'Sorry?'

'Can't get off without it, see, ever since I was a kid. But, five minutes with it on and I'm gone.'

Lights out at The Nest had been the prelude to a countryside sleep. Lights out in Cardiff was a continuation of an ongoing racket that crushed all hope of restful slumber. He never did turn the telly down.

My flatmates, it seemed, had chosen courses that weren't academically onerous, allowing them to indulge in a kaleidoscope of social distractions whilst surviving on stroke-inducing levels of sleep, confident they could limp out the other end with a passable 2:2. Law, on the other hand, was destined to lash me to an unrelenting yoke of study with its dense programme of lectures, tutorials, library research and evenings poring over dry statutes. I realised I'd made a mistake both in my choice of course and accommodation. I was beginning to feel that perhaps heading out to sea had been a mistake.

The months dragged on to Christmas, when I decided I'd complete the first year and bail out. I should've finished there and then. I began to develop an unhealthy fixation with the myriad ways I could do away with key-jangling Mikey. A hacksaw and disposal of his body parts down the toilet seemed the most attractive option, but then I remembered Dennis Nielsen had tried that method without success.

On the rare occasions when peace descended – an edgy calm – the tiniest puncturing was like a rifle shot, ratcheting up my anxiety. I sensed myself unravelling and took to returning from the supermarket with more sherry than food, slumping into detached hazes. Unable to beat them, I too cranked my stereo up in a volume war, deriving great pleasure from having Mikey bang on my door to turn it down. Cheeky bastard.

By the spring I questioned whether there was any point in attending lectures and tutorials, so I didn't. The days were spent sleeping while my flatmates attended the few lectures demanded of them, and on their return the sherry would be poured. My mood darkened and I became unpleasant to be around. And, having tired of visiting her moody, monosyllabic boyfriend, I was dumped. Cardiff, in so many ways, had turned out to be a disaster.

But, something in me dictated that I went out with a bang. I was determined that I'd sit the end-of-year exams and do well in them. I trudged into the hall for the first paper, one amongst a couple of hundred wannabe lawyers. Sitting dead centre, I looked around at the eager faces, ready to unleash all that they'd learnt.

When instructed, I turned the paper over and read the questions. Then I read them again, as if repeating the exercise might somehow aid me in retrieving some knowledge. It didn't. I hadn't a clue what was being demanded of me, which wasn't surprising, seeing as I hadn't set foot in the law school for months and had done little revision in between emptying bottles of medium dry.

Ten minutes into the exam, I decided to leave, but not before I'd written a pathetic half-page apology for having wasted the university's time. I stood and walked out of the hall, the odd head bobbing up as I passed between the rows of desks, cleared my room and headed for home.

Chapter 22

I parked in a bay far from the busy road, not wishing to be seen near the building, let alone entering it. The concrete sprawl of Withybush General Hospital with its hordes going in and out was on the other side of the road, but this was a quieter department and I was glad of the sparse footfall. I looked at the appointment letter, a reminder of why I was there. A reminder of the shame that I felt.

I'd returned from Cardiff two months before, an ignominious end to my legal aspirations. Haverfordwest's answer to *Kavanagh QC* I wasn't to be. The law degree had promised the fulfilment of a longed-for dream, a dream of being just like everyone else. To be seen as normal; not physically, of course, but in the way that I went about my daily life. To have a job – a profession even – and to not feel like an anomaly.

Like some Vegas high-roller, then, I'd staked everything on that new life and lost. The old insecurities – the old hang-ups – had done for me. I just couldn't shake my history, clinging to me, as it did, like napalm. Mind, choosing the wrong course hadn't helped. And to cap it all, I'd shared a flat with people who had no off switch. But at the root of my failure was fragility.

Driving home along the M4, having cleared the halls of residence, the tears had flowed. Mentally brittle, I snapped, as the tenuous thread which'd held me together for eleven years let go. Eleven years of teetering over the abyss. Eleven years of extinguishing those tiny fires in my head, knowing that if they got out of control, they could destroy me. Well, a fire had well and truly taken hold and there seemed little chance of me putting it out.

Adding fuel to the flames, I'd been ditched by my girlfriend, a determined young woman, who aspired to a future which her self-absorbed boyfriend didn't seem able to give her. I'd taken her for granted, assuming with blithe arrogance that she'd stick with me and my darkening mood. I'd been wrong, and the shock of her dumping me was seismic.

And the final blow of the triple whammy that pushed me over the edge: I'd just turned thirty. Thirty was big. Thirty was old. My friends, of course, were thirty, but they were married or in relationships, had their own place, and worked, weaving together the strands that build a life. My thirty wasn't theirs: physically damaged, mentally broken, living with my parents once again, jobless and girl-less. Whereas my friends had a sense of purpose, humming with plans, hopes and dreams, I was empty. The contemplation of a better tomorrow is what separates us from other species. I had no yearning to see tomorrow.

It was Mum who found me lying on my bedroom floor, face down in the carpet, willing the day to come to an end. Willing myself to come to an end. She lay down by my side and wrapped her arms around me.

'You can't keep on like this,' she said. 'Me and your dad are worried.'

Her voice was strained. She and Dad had been emotionally chained to me for eleven years, hoping and praying I'd make a life. Get over it. Get on with it.

Dad came in and sat on the bed as I continued to breathe in carpet.

'This isn't good?' he said, with typical Yorkshire understatement.

I didn't reply.

'Your mum and me have been talking.' He paused. 'We think you need to see someone. Get help.'

It was hard for him, the emotional stuff. He'd grown up without parents to show him how it's done. In moments when I wasn't so self-absorbed – rare interludes – I admired him for his efforts.

I sat in the doctor's consulting room and blurted everything out. The black thoughts, the suffocating emptiness, not eating, not sleeping, the self-hatred and the wish for an end. A tsunami of deep, visceral pain. He listened patiently, allowing me to unburden myself. He wrote a prescription. He arranged an appointment.

I looked at my watch. It was time. I got out of the car and walked towards the entrance of the mental health unit, ducking so that passing motorists on that busy road wouldn't see me. I approached the automatic doors. They opened. I wasn't ready, so I stepped back and they closed again. I didn't want to go in. I didn't want to be seen going in. But I had that letter in my hand and I knew that I was sunk and this was the only option, so I stepped forward and went in.

I sat in the waiting area, head down, avoiding eye contact. My name was called – too loudly for my liking – and I walked down the corridor to the room. Depictions of psychologists on television often portray middle-aged men swivelling on Swedish-designed chairs, surrounded by shelved books and potted ferns. On entering the room, I was disappointed at how young she was, as if youth suggested a lack of expertise. A lack of wisdom. I wanted the person tasked with sorting my head out to be older than me. Much older.

I was invited to sit as she scanned the letter she'd received from my doctor. The room was sparsely furnished, with no ornamentation or personal effects, as if it weren't anybody's room in particular. I glanced at the door, wondering whether I should get up and leave before I couldn't. She was just too young, I thought, and she didn't even have a swivel chair. But as with other pivotal moments in my life I knew there was no chance of leaving that room. I was there and, more importantly, I needed to be there. I'd kicked the can down the road for years. I'd run out of road.

She finished reading the letter, turned to me, pulled her seat a little closer and smiled. There were introductory pleasantries, then she relayed the letter's contents and my doctor's concerns for my mental health. I was, it seemed, mad. Or at least mad enough to be referred to her.

'In your own time, just tell me how you've been feeling. And don't worry, everything you tell me in this room is confidential. It's just you and me.'

And so I began, conscious of the sentences I formulated in my head and the words I spoke, editing out the painful truths. I was embarrassed by my situation and wary of opening up. Wary of admitting what a failure I was. Wary, perhaps, of confronting the demons. Nan had suffered mental health issues. As a kid I'd witnessed her having a breakdown. It'd scared me and repulsed me. I didn't want to be like her. The psychologist sensed my reticence.

'I know this must be hard, but if it's any help, the mind, like the body, gets ill sometimes,' she said. 'Treating mental health issues isn't really any different to treating other illnesses. So try not to think too much. Just let it out.'

I gradually loosened, and after a couple of sessions trusted her, as I began to sing like a canary, the internal censor discarded, with a stream of consciousness pouring forth. And it was a beautiful emancipation. It's incredible how you can blurt out your deepest despairing thoughts to a stranger more freely than those closest to you.

Unaffected by the accident, my jaw muscles performed admirably, as if I were speaking to a warm and receptive human Dictaphone. I just talked and talked and talked, cleansing myself as if my life depended on it. Perhaps it did. Not once did I sense her judging me or pitying me as she absorbed the bloody lot. To her I was just another messed-up individual in need of help.

As the weeks rolled by, I hungered for each session, aching to empty myself of yet more bile, so that when I emerged from the final session I did so with a sense of incredible hope. I'd confessed. I'd cried. I'd bellowed like a mad man. We'd laughed, in the later sessions. And at the end was a cleaning, an expunging of years of bottled-up anguish. She knew me better than I did, arming me with the mechanisms to begin again, reboot, reset the programme. It wasn't complicated; small daily goals, nothing too ambitious, just a series of tiny victories and the nurturing of self-esteem.

The first job was to round up those black dogs. Rather than shooing them back into their kennel as I'd done countless times, I shot the bastards. I walked out of there that last time feeling sad that I wouldn't see her again, as if we'd forged such a deep emotional bond that somehow it constituted the beginning of a friendship, or perhaps more. I suppose that's a testament to just how good she was. But, of course, it'd all been one-way traffic and she had other troubled people to rescue now that I was safe.

That summer of '95 witnessed the birth of the person who would take me through the rest of my life. The blighted David Wilson who'd clung on doggedly since 16th February 1984 had been put out of his misery along with those damned dogs. I became another person, a composite of positive attributes, someone with a bright future and not my tortured past. It was as if I were a method actor immersing myself in a role. I still lived in that imperfect body but I possessed the psyche of a stronger, reinvented character.

The most important change of outlook was that I thought only of what was possible, not what I'd lost or couldn't physically do. I'd finally, properly, come to terms with my loss, and I knew full well that I had, as I didn't see or think of that loss any more. I stopped comparing my deficits to other people, seeing myself as being the same, only with certain physical quirks.

Everyone has perceived or actual weaknesses, and mine just happened to be physical issues which were no longer going to blight my life. They were a part of me. A part of who I was. Those sessions with her saved my life, and, crucially, gave me a life worth living.

Andrew sensed my yearning for a fresh start and asked if I'd like to move in with him in the terraced house he'd renovated, demonstrating yet again that he was a bigger man than me – I think the rent helped, too. With the coping mechanisms that therapy had given me and the continuing medication, moving in with Andrew felt like another large piece of the happy jigsaw had fallen into place.

There were days on the river on his speedboat as I discovered an aptitude for being dragged at inappropriate speeds in an inflatable ring, relishing the physical challenge but also the danger that many of the other boys shunned; an Isle of Man TT on water. I'd always embraced reckless behaviour, confident that I could push it all the way to 99.9% in any given situation while retaining just enough slack and composure to avoid disaster. I felt no fear. Being thrown out of that ring at over forty miles per hour and cartwheeling across the water was perhaps riding my luck. But I'd rarely felt so alive.

The speedboat escapades were nothing when compared to some of the performances of my youth. In the year leading up to the bike accident, coming home from the Old Inn with Martin driving his mum's Mini, I took to opening the passenger door, climbing out of the seat and standing on the door sill with my torso outside of the car above the roofline, clinging to an inside strap with one hand and waving to the boys in the car following with the other.

I was that show-off from school, desperate to entertain what were a fledgling circle of friends. I was an idiot. But I also felt in control, like nothing could go wrong, seeing everything in slow-motion and reasoning that I could make any necessary adjustments to avoid oblivion, so long as I remained calm. Nothing panicked me.

After acquiring a motorbike, that conviction in my indestructibility began to prove itself misplaced as the incidents racked up. One Saturday afternoon I was beetling out to the Old Inn with Martin on the back – he'd crashed his bike the week before. Exiting a corner, I was confronted by a stationery milk tanker. I braked hard, but still connected with its rear light cluster. Martin and I lay on the floor with my bike on us as the tanker drove off, the driver oblivious. With minor grazing, we got back on and continued to the pub.

The next day, there was a glancing collision with a car, at low speed, again with Martin on the back. Not surprisingly, he declined offers of a lift after that, insisting on using the Mini till his bike was back on the road. I was, it seemed, predisposed to coming off, and you can only ride your luck for so long before you come off hard. If only I'd recognised the pattern that was forming.

Those days being dragged on the river, with endless sunshine, endorphins galore and lunches at riverside pubs, made me believe in myself as I never had. I laughed a lot. The physicality of it, the adrenaline rushes and the joyous exhaustion helped to turn me round. At the summer's end there was a sense of wonderment at the person I'd become, forgetting that the old me had ever existed, as the happy pills were chucked in the bin. Bodily, nothing had changed, but mentally everything had. Therapy and a summer on the river saved me.

Putting the disappointment of law school behind me, I enrolled on a business degree. For the first two years I studied at the college in Haverfordwest that I'd attended previously, all the while living with Andrew. That first day I sat in a classroom with a brand-new bunch of potential friends and who should walk in but Tony and his beard. It all felt right.

Reflecting on the many false dawns over the years, I knew for certain, now, that I'd arrived at a resolution. A point where I felt at ease with myself. Confident in my skin. The trip to Avebury, going to the gym, working at Quayline Reprographics and college the first time round had all felt huge.

All had persuaded me, at the time, that I'd solved the puzzle. That I was over it. And yes, they'd all been important steps in my rehabilitation, but at no point had I resolved the fundamental hang-up. I still bristled with resentment and compared myself to others. I was still angered by all of the physical possibilities denied to me. Now though, all of that was finished.

Living with Andrew, I acknowledged through him what it is to aspire in life and have pride in going out each morning to work. Andrew worked hard. He always had. He had his house and I saw that there were rewards to this work thingy. Sure, his life was conventional, but what's wrong with that? He was happy.

I'd looked upon convention from a distance for years, shunning it, disdaining it, but most of all being afraid of it. The new me craved it.

And the most wonderful thing about us living together is that I truly got to know him and found that I admired him. The five-year gap between us as kids had seemed an unbridgeable gulf, but as adults it was inconsequential.

There were bones of contention, of course, such as my insistence on burning four gas rings to yield supper for one – that one being me – which was unlikely to be appreciated by the bill payer. And he was house-proud – well, it was his home, after all – whilst I left a trail of drunk coffee cups, licked plates and discarded clothing in my wake.

When I got up from the settee, he'd swoop. 'Bloody hell, Dai. Sort the cushions when you get up,' he'd say, as his plumping OCD kicked in. I became convinced there was a tidying fairy hiding somewhere in my room, as I often turned in at night to find my duvet neatly spread. His house. His standards.

There was just one occasion when we almost came to blows. Mind, when I say we, the notion that I could've held my own against a six foot two, eighteen stone mass was laughable; when I came off that motorbike my physical domination came to an end. There was a storm one night, and I was woken by what sounded like Andrew's car alarm in the street. The power had tripped, so I edged my way to his room along the walls in the dark, arriving by his bed with a clattering of shins against the wooden frame. As I leant over to rouse him, a flash of lightning illuminated the room and a clap of thunder shook the house; it was right over us.

To be wrenched from deep sleep by a loud bang that felt as if it'd taken the roof off is unsettling enough. Factor in the vision of a blue-lit naked man reaching towards you and it's no wonder he took a swing. Thankfully, he missed. Watching the horror film *Shallow Grave* before going to bed hadn't helped either.

'Your car alarm's going off,' I shouted, before he could throw another.

He calmed down and went out to sort the alarm, returning a minute later. 'It's the fucking Post Office over the road, you twat,' he said, and went back to bed.

The final year of my business degree was based at the University of Glamorgan in Pontypridd, where I shared a three-storey terraced house with five others. The property had been bought as a cash cow at auction that summer by a Greek lady who lived in London, and any notion of a refurbishment budget had evidently been ditched; it was tired and grotty. How many backsides had sat on that bog? I wondered as I mastered the art of the hover. It was a house of multiple occupation that had been occupied multiple times over many years.

I was throwing myself back into the fray and there was more than a tinge of trepidation, concerned that I might be holed up with another noisy bunch as I'd been in Cardiff. But I needn't have worried; my housemates were animated and good company but valued outbreaks of quiet as much as me. I had a large room with views over the rooftops to the hills and, in spite of the shabbiness, felt at ease.

The owner would swoop unannounced from London to conduct inspections of the premises along with other local properties that she owned. I was never sure as to how she could determine whether any damage had been done; further damage, that is. Wrapped in a heavy shawl, her complexion suggested a long-standing love affair with the sun, her presence accompanied by the faint whiff of a cigarette-filled car journey. During one spot-check I happened to be home alone and had just boiled the kettle as she entered the kitchen.

'Hi, fancy a cuppa?' I asked.

She turned and considered me in a curious, detached manner, much like a minor royal encountering an inmate on a tour of an open prison.

'No,' she said. Then, as if recalling a childhood lecture on manners, she added an unconvincing, 'Thanks.'

She looked around, ticked a sheet attached to a clipboard, then left the room while I made a coffee and watched the lunchtime news. The advantage of being alone was that I could sit on the bit of the settee that wasn't stained.

Unlike when I'd been cast adrift in Cardiff, Pontypridd was a calmer sea, with reassuring views of the coast. I felt safe and in control. On days when my muscle tone was golden, I'd stroll from the carpark up to the campus with a sense of purpose.

On stiff, wooden days, I went more slowly, with rests, but without the negative self-image of old as the bad days were literally taken in my stuttering stride. The months dissolved and I found myself walking across a stage to receive my degree, with Mum and Dad in the audience. At thirty-three, I was ready to take on the world, at last.

Chapter 23

I got out of the taxi and leant back in. 'I'll give you a bell in the week,' I said.

'That'd be nice,' she replied.

I closed the door and smiled at her as the car pulled away.

I was an inveterate promiser of getting in touch, but rarely did so. I could persuade myself out of it, rationalising that perhaps now wasn't the right time or some other cop out. The king of emotional displacement, I was wary of commitment.

The weekend after, I bumped into her in a pub in town. She was stony-faced, reminding me of my broken promise. I repeated the promise but she didn't seem convinced. This time, though, I did phone and we arranged to go out on a date.

Anna possessed an incredible vitality allied to an innate kindness and generosity of spirit; there was no malice. I'd never met anyone like her. She was also spontaneous and daring, traits that I lacked. Sure, I'd gone to Pontypridd to complete my business degree and was proud of what I'd achieved. Not that I'd been enthused with the course – should've studied history – but I was proud all the same.

The moment the course ended, though, I jumped in the car and headed west, moving back in with my parents – for the time being. Or at least that's what I told myself. I may've had a degree, but there was no yearning for some imagined glittering career if it meant not being in Pembrokeshire. And there weren't many glittering careers to be had in Pembrokeshire. But I knew that.

Anna had studied French and Spanish at university and had worked in France and Spain, which made sense. She'd also travelled round Europe by train on her own, carrying a rucksack the size of a small wardrobe. She was gutsy, determined and, it seemed, afraid of nothing. That, and the fact she resembled a young Jenny Agutter snared me. I wanted to be around this woman who radiated boundless possibility. She wanted to go places, to see things. And I wanted to go with her.

There was a knock at the door and Anna walked in.

'Oh. Hi,' I said, glancing back at the cooker. 'I was... err... just about to have lunch.'

As a welcome it lacked enthusiasm, distracted as I was by a pan of Scotch broth simmering. Not much came between me and a tin of Scotch broth.

'Sorry. I'll call back later?' she said, looking unsure.

'Err... no. Just give me ten minutes?'

I poured the soup into a bowl. It was midday. I always had lunch at midday, a routine person, the son of routine parents.

'Okay if I make a cup of tea?' she asked, wondering whether self-service was permissible.

'Yeah. Sure. Help yourself.'

I turned away and cringed. For Christ's sake, loosen up, I thought.

And in the months that followed I did loosen up. She'd call unannounced and whisk me off for a walk up the Preseli Hills or chips at the beach or the cinema or whatever, wherever. Mum and Dad were bemused by my sudden spontaneity as I embraced it. My days, particularly those involving Anna, became less planned and structured. More fun. More exciting. Her vibrancy and unpredictability were among the many traits that caused me to fall in love.

I soon learned, though, that her ad hoc embrace of life was allied to a casual disregard for timekeeping, which for someone brought up on Dad's naval punctuality was frustrating. Did she own a watch, and if so, why did she adhere to some vague Aboriginal instinct for an approximation of what the time might be, give or take an hour? So, in the interests of maintaining a harmonious relationship, I became less anal and Anna a touch Teutonic and timely. We met in the middle and settled on turning up just a little late for things.

I'd enjoyed – and on occasion endured – a number of culturally barren foreign jaunts with the lads. Three trips to Tenerife had provided irrefutable confirmation that it was a seedy dump. There was a stag do in Ibiza, the perennial British excuse to trample over accepted norms of behaviour like a bunch of beer-mongering Anglo-Saxons. By the time the Greek islands beckoned, however, in the late '90s, the boys had mellowed and grown up, but not so much that our days weren't still filled with puerile antics. Very funny puerile antics, as it happens.

But, like footballers in their mid-thirties, our youthful stamina – especially when putting in the night shifts – had waned, with just a good first half in us before retirement to bed. We happened to be on Crete at the time of Princess Di's funeral in '97. Nudging a hundred, a gaggle of Brits wilted in a windowless room watching the cortege on a flickering telly as we toasted her from the bar by the pool. A year later, I sat pillion on the rear of a moped on the island of Zakynthos, banking into corners and drawing in deep breaths of freedom. There were some very memorable moments.

By the time I met Anna, though, I'd tired of that formula, wanting more from my holidays than just drink, pranks, innuendo and lack of sleep. For our first adventure together we flew to Bilbao, a rusting hulk of a port city on the north coast of Spain, picked up a hire car and drove out of the airport armed with a map, heading inland to the town of Logroño, in the heart of Rioja country. Anna had taught English as a foreign language there and yearned for a return. Using a *Rough Guide*, we stumbled across a gem of a room near the old quarter, chucked our gear in and freshened up.

'Come with me,' beamed Anna. 'Just up the street. You'll love it.'

Calle Laurel was the old Spain of promenading families and blood-deep custom, an alley, two body-lengths wide, lined with tapas bars. We entered the first establishment, loud and smoky, and eased our way to the bar for blue cheese and chicken with a tumbler of thick red.

Next door served up sizzling lamb chops brought out on huge metal platters, the staff navigating through a sea of people, all chatting and laughing and embracing one another. Another thick red washed the fatty treat down and then it was onwards to garlic mushrooms the size of cocktail umbrellas with, you've guessed it, another thick red. There were lots of reds.

By the time we reached the other end of the alley, our hunger was sated and our eyesight a bit squishy. It was like nothing I'd ever experienced, and I wanted to experience so much more.

The next day, we met Anna's friend Jenny – from her Logroño days – and her boyfriend Juan outside the Café Mercato in the square opposite the cathedral. Jenny, who'd travelled with Juan from their home in León a couple of hours away, was a vibrant bundle of opinions and conversation. Juan, I soon deduced, was a socialist firebrand, radiating a Castro-like intensity; he dismissed Logroño as petit bourgeois and provincial. As the day progressed, though, and after he'd sunk a few reds, a hint of joy cracked forth, albeit with a droll Jack Dee humour, Latin style. We got on well.

Anna had once worked in the ski resort of Chamonix in the French Alps. On her days off she packed a rucksack and headed up into the mountains to explore the glaciers and peaks. She loved walking. Now she was in a relationship with someone possessing that oft-used euphemism of the social care profession, 'limited mobility'. If she was frustrated at my restrictions, my constricted range, she didn't show it, easing her pace and expectations while I drove myself beyond my usual parameters, drawing on depths of stamina I didn't realise I possessed. I didn't want her to think she'd been lumbered with a dud, and so half-killed myself to keep up.

Logroño was the Spain of warm, verdant air, old chatting men leaning on sticks, the aroma of rich coffee, the fatalistic exuberance of dark-eyed young men and the strutting certainty of proud *señoritas.* It was intoxicating.

After a couple of days, we departed for the Pyrenees, driving by instinct across the plains and into the foothills, the peaks beckoning us on. We didn't know where we were going, only that we were going somewhere.

That evening, we booked into a hotel in Valcarlos, a drive-through village in a mountain pass high up on the Spanish side. Supper was served in an empty mahogany-lined dining room by an over-thankful waitress. Devoid of guests, it felt as if we were in a sequel to *The Shining* and couldn't wait to leave the next morning, pootling down into France and St Jean de Luz, a genteel yesteryear resort on the Atlantic Coast.

Our schedule was unrelenting and I loved it but after three days of physical Armageddon, my body ran up the white flag, waking in St Jean the next day to an empty tank.

'Have a lie-in. I'll head out shopping for a couple of hours,' she said, breezing out of the room. We were learning how to make us work.

St Jean was a charming '*belle epoque*' stop over, giving me an opportunity to recuperate for the onward journey along the coast road and back into Spain. Near the border, we stopped at a fishing village for coffee and cake by the harbour.

Anna fixed me with an inquisitive look. 'This is quite tough for you, isn't it?' she said.

'Tough?'

'Yeah. The walking. Constant pushing.'

'Suppose it is. But, I could be with someone whose ideal holiday is basting by a pool all day sipping gin. I want to see things. Like you do.'

We carried on over the border and onto the grandeur of San Sebastian. Our determination – okay, Anna's determination – to hoard any uneaten picnic food for the next day was dispensed with on opening the boot one lunchtime to the odour of bubbling brie. Fortunately, there was a bin close by.

On the verge of exhausting our *Rough Guide's* recommendations, which in itself had exhausted us, and more particularly me, we finally found a vacant room above the narrow streets of San Sebastian's old quarter. Offloading our rucksacks, we grabbed a pizza and a beer in a nearby bar then hit the sack. It'd been a tiring day and I looked forward to a dreamy sleep.

Spain is a country steeped in the custom of fiesta. Imagine my joy, then, on being woken in the early hours by what sounded like a fiesta of metal dustbin lid rolling in the street below. I looked over to Anna in the half-light, sunk in sleep and oblivious, as I rued having the nocturnal alertness of a Vietnam vet. The rolling celebration lasted, intermittently, most of the night, and I managed a couple of hours' sleep before the lady who owned the apartment tapped our door – the signal to pack and leave. Give me bullfighting or that other fiesta where crowds chuck overripe tomatoes at one another any day.

Guarding our rucksacks, I was sitting outside a shop watching Anna browse postcards inside. In war, it's said there's a bullet with your name on it. Well, in life I believe there's a woman with your name on them, or a man if you're a woman, or a whole range of options if your leanings dictate otherwise. Whatever, there's a person out there who's your fit, and I was looking at mine, and she was beautiful, and an explorer to boot.

I was shedding my straight-jacketed inhibitions and going with the flow, freeing my mind to embrace new experiences and, best of all, I was doing it with this woman. We returned to Bilbao and the architectural splendour of the Guggenheim Museum, and then our flight home. Our first holiday had passed muster.

In March of 2000 Anna and I moved in together in a converted outbuilding near the coast. Down a bumpy lane, Lower Honey Hook Farm lived up to its idyllic name. It was as if we'd been dropped into an episode of *The Darling Buds of May*, though one thing unnerved Anna: the spiders. It was crawling with them.

We'd spy them emerging from gaps between the floorboards and the rough-hewn walls. They skulked in cupboards awaiting a hand to make a grab for a tin of beans. I welcomed the opportunity to play the Sir Galahad, having been desensitised to arachnids in Trecwn, and removed a lot of them at Honey Hook. The Trecwn variant, though, had been much more unsettling; big, glossy, Amazonian-like creatures with bodies the size of a duchess's brooch. It often felt like I was working in an exotic petting zoo; I encountered a huge coiled adder on the path to the top of the valley once – no sunbathing for me that day.

As autumn drew in, it dawned on us that surviving the winter in an open-plan stone outbuilding with Economy 7 heating would be a challenge. It was toasty warm as we left for work in the morning and a walk-in fridge on our return. We got the local paper to look for a suitable bolthole.

'This could be okay. In Llangwm? Cottage with central heating,' said Anna.

The first time I ever went to Llangwm was with Graham, a school friend, who lived in a towering Georgian terraced house in Haverfordwest. The attic space had been converted into his bedroom, a vast boys' zone of scattered magazines, dirty clothes, bits of machinery and, best of all, an air rifle with telescopic sights. It was his own personal fiefdom, an autonomous republic, with parental control ending at the top step. I was jealous as hell.

In the summer we'd climb out of a Velux window onto a roof gulley and listen to *Regatta de Blanc* by The Police on a cassette player, while drinking Coke floats and becoming bloated to the spot. When the nights darkened, we sniped with his air rifle at the drunks tumbling out of the pub opposite.

We decided to show two girls we fancied a good time with a walk from Haverfordwest to Llangwm – six miles of futile adolescent chatting-up hiking along a busy road on a baking hot day. About halfway we began to bicker as to whose idea it'd been as the girls became surly. In desperation, we stuck our thumbs out and a flatbed pickup stopped: the Llangwm milkman. The girls got in the front with the driver while Graham and I clambered into the open rear and clung on for dear life as our spinal columns bounced the few miles into the village.

Unsure as to why we'd gone there, we ambled into The Cottage Inn to discuss our next move. It was empty. The girls took a seat while we girded ourselves to get a round in. Graham was confident that his spiky Sting-inspired hairstyle – self-inflicted with a razor comb he'd ordered from a magazine – would project an air of legality. It was an irregular cut with the odd nick of the scalp, resembling a mangy dog.

I was sixteen years old, facially fourteen and bodily twelve, but I beat Graham to the bar and deepened my voice to order four lager and limes, sounding like a choir boy with a cold. With a knowing smirk, the barman poured the pints and we swaggered over to the table. The girls were impressed. We gulped our beer and discussed options, the most popular being to call it a day. I got a Swiss roll from the shop and Graham phoned his mum to come and collect us. The girls were busy the next time we suggested an outing.

My next venture into the heady uplands of romance, just weeks later in June '81, proved more successful, at least initially. I'd just sat my 'O' Levels – without any expectation of glowing results – and with my school days drifting to an end, I attended a house party. The boy's parents had absented themselves, perhaps confident in their son's assurance he'd be sensible and look after the place; I'm glad I wasn't there when they returned the next day. The party was memorable on two counts: my antagonists from school weren't there, but better than that, there was a girl. After mutual staring smiles across the lounge, she came and sat by me, clutching two cans of Skol.

'Fancy one?' she said, pushing a can my way.

'Tidy. Thanks.'

The host was into Adam and the Ants and there were only so many repeats of 'Stand and Deliver' we could take, so we decamped to the kitchen. Things were proceeding well, with no need for me to resort to rash displays of bravado, but the showman in me couldn't resist indulging in a random act of idiocy – I downed a bottle of Martini. She seemed impressed, or maybe I just thought she ought to be. The kitchen began to swim around me as she grabbed my hand and pulled me into the hallway and upstairs. Our host's policing of his parents' bedroom was less than vigilant as we discovered two couples busying themselves on the double bed. To a chorus of begrudging moans, we wedged ourselves between the twosomes.

Laid on my back, with the girl astride, we were engaged in an exploratory frenzy when my stomach brought home the folly of glugging a bottle of Martini. With a yelled, 'Shit,' I pushed her away as up went a geyser of vomit. The laws of physics passed me by in school but there'll be a scientific formulation, no doubt, explaining why liquid when it's forced upwards into the air fans outwards on its descent.

The girls on either side screamed and jumped off the bed while their recently acquired love interests began punching me with impressive ferocity. As they continued to punch, I continued to vomit, the correlation seemingly lost on them. Realising they had no intention of stopping till an ambulance was required I squirmed and wriggled my way off the bed and bolted downstairs out to the garden.

I took my puke-soaked T-shirt off and threw it in a bush then sat on the grass with my back against a cool wall. I slumped and slept, only waking to throw up some more. Dawn was coming as I finally summoned the wherewithal to stand and contemplate the walk home. I skulked through the house, which looked as though it'd been vigorously burgled, not wishing to bump into my victims, and shut the front door behind me as I departed. Weeks later, I saw the girl in the street and called to her, but after a cursory glance my way, it was apparent that she didn't know me.

Llangwm, then, is a village at the end of a minor road, huddled around an inlet of the Cleddau Estuary. You don't go there to get anywhere else, lending it a majestic sense of isolation. Its people once survived on fishing and going down local mines, and it had been a deeply tribal community with a penchant for stoning strangers. Thankfully, there was no stone-throwing rabble to welcome us when we viewed the cottage – a cottage with central heating! Afterwards, we went for a deciding wander around the village before informing the owner that we'd like to rent it. In October 2000, Llangwm became our home.

Relationships form and often founder as pairings discover their partners foibles, that mish-mash of characteristics and habits, some endearing, others annoying, or even distasteful. But, after a year of our cohabiting test drive, nothing deal-breaking had emerged, at least not from my perspective. I even laughed off Anna's propensity for mislaying car keys – usually mine (I found them in the waste bin under the sink once, eventually) – and thought myself a lucky man. It was working.

Not long after moving in, we decided to look for a place to buy, viewing a number of houses in the village. We even looked further afield but weren't propelled into making any offers for those properties, mainly because they weren't in Llangwm, the place we'd grown to love. A national property boom was nudging prices ever higher and a hint of panic was setting in.

Then, one Saturday afternoon, Anna came rushing in. 'Oh my God. Number eleven. It's for sale. They've got a sign up,' she said.

We were renting number one in a row of late Victorian cottages and we'd always coveted number eleven. To us it was the most beautiful house in the village. We rang the agent and arranged a viewing for an hour later, after which we offered the owner the asking price, there and then, which was accepted. We then had to wait for two months for the house to become ours, all the while dreading some hiccup that'd scupper the deal.

In July 2001, we got the key to number eleven. We still have the key to number eleven. We probably always will. There was a vigorous decorating scheme to cover up and a new kitchen and bathroom to install. Our dads painted and did jobs as dads do. We bought and begged furniture and began to build our first home together.

It'd been fifteen years since I'd got the book about Tuscany from the library, the book that'd made me dream of far-off travels. I'd decided, of course, that it was just too adventurous, opting instead for Avebury and Wiltshire.

Now, though, it was time. Anna and I landed in Bologna, collected a hire car and consulted the map: ninety miles to Lucca and our first accommodation. If we imagined that having driven on motorways in Spain and France we were somehow prepared for the Italian variant, we were soon disabused. This was a whole new level of terror, immersed in what seemed like a real-life video game. Tailgating seemed to be the national sport, with juggernauts in particular hugging our bumper as if connected by a short tow rope. Seeing a huge radiator grill fill the rear-view mirror brought to mind the 1971 cult classic film *Duel*, where a demon truck followed and terrorised Dennis Weaver across the Mojave Desert in California. Unnerved, we stopped halfway at a service station to discuss our options; in reality, there was only one, and after a fortifying coffee we continued, reaching Lucca mentally frayed but glad to be alive.

The city's enclosed by a circuit of Renaissance walls almost three miles in circumference. Arriving on the outer ring road, I marvelled at such an incredible feat. After a few circuits trying to find the correct gate to take us into the city, I marvelled less. Frustration was setting in when divine intervention smiled on us: we spotted a priest mounting a moped and begged him to guide us in. Our shepherd led the way, his weaving path suggesting he'd been at the communion wine as we followed him through a gate into the medieval city. With a vague Latin flourish, he directed us to the street where our accommodation was, hugged us in an over-familiar fashion and rode off.

I'd employed a novel approach to chatting Anna up in the depths of RJ's nightclub, Haverfordwest's premier entertainment venue. I'd bumped into her a few times in between her scooting back and forth to the Continent, even forming a loose pact to go off in a camper van together. On one particular night I felt emboldened – and drunk.

Peering at her in the murk, I said, 'I want to see Tuscany. Go to Florence. See frescoes. Nobody in here gives a shit about frescoes.'

She could've made her excuses and scarpered, but I just remember her response: 'We could both go.'

Our ten-day Grand Tour gifted us a delicious itinerary of Pisa's off-kilter tower, the air-brushed touristy perfection of San Gimignano,

Siena's square – home to the famous horse race the Palio – and finally, eventually, wonderfully, the main event, Florence. To drive into Florence is to contemplate therapy. It's fraught, and a bit like dodgems, only without the deliberate collisions, but with collisions all the same. Approaching the centre, we circumnavigated an enormous roundabout the size of a small principality, a perilous expedition with cars jockeying for space, beeping their way into gaps, lane markings a mere suggestion. Italy is a religious country and, as I discovered, praying is a driving necessity.

We'd arrived in Italy with just our accommodation in Lucca pre-booked, but armed with a *Rough Guide*, a phrasebook and a Nokia from the dark ages we'd arranged a series of sleeps en route. In Florence, we stayed in a backstreet hotel a short walk from the cathedral of Santa Maria del Fiore, one of the spectacles of the city. Closer still was the Basilica di San Lorenzo, resting place of the Medici, ruling dynasty of the Middle Ages and patrons of the Renaissance. From the window of our room, we could see its dome bulging above the terracotta rooftops, our chests thrumming to its bells. And that, of course, is the problem with Florence, if it could be described as such: there's just too much to take in, bludgeoned as you are by sensory overload. We had two days of cramming in this wonderful city but could've spent a hundred and still left without seeing all that begs to be seen.

That first night, we ventured out to eat, finding a restaurant nearby. An overlapping man in a sweat-soaked white shirt was perched on a stool inside the door. Rousing himself, he flashed a weak smile and gestured towards a choice of tables. There'd been a queue for the restaurant next door.

We sat and looked at the menu. Two young women with American accents and expressions that didn't belie joy stood, leaving not even half-eaten meals, and exited. A waiter appeared, or at least a man dressed to impersonate one. With an interesting collection of facial scar tissue, I guessed he doubled as security. We were beginning to wish we'd queued next door.

He took our order and ducked into the kitchen. The remaining few diners departed, shaking their heads and muttering dark incantations. Anna and I thumbed through the Italian phrase book for food-related complaints, suspecting they might come in handy as the waiter returned and slapped two plates of food down. We lost our appetites as we stabbed at our meals, unsure as to whether they'd been assembled by anyone remotely purporting to be a chef or, a more serious consideration, with any regard for basic hygiene; the place was grubby.

'Let's go. I really don't like it here,' said Anna.

The dripping colossus by the door ran up our bill while the blank-faced waiter stood behind us. To no one's surprise, least of all the author of the bill, we were to be merrily overcharged. I wanted to leave but not at the expense of being fleeced. I knew enough Italian to count to a hundred, so grabbed a menu and added up the actual cost of the swill they'd presented to us. On being rumbled, he grunted and accepted my arithmetic. The next night we were careful to choose a busier place.

Florence is an open-air museum, with everything on show to be touched and marvelled at. Not behind Perspex, no ropes keeping you away, no 'don't touch' signs. Mid-afternoon, we were strolling along a connecting alley between the Ponte Vecchio and the Piazza della Signoria, one of those untrammelled backwaters busy with delivery vans dropping off at the rear of restaurants. Air-conditioning units filled the air with the expunged aroma of devoured lunches. Kitchen staff leant against walls having a restorative smoke. It was the back stairs, one of a hundred hidden arteries that kept the city functioning. I stopped by the entrance to a passageway for a rest – walking tours weren't my forte and the day had caught up with me.

I glanced around, and there above me, adorning the arch into the passage, was a faded, flaking fresco, portraying some celestial scene – angels, stars, all very heavenly. There it was, hiding, just off a service alley, decorating a passage that led to a dirty door studded with stacks of apartment buzzers. Wall art, perhaps from the time of the Medici.

It was in Tuscany that I began, tentatively – perhaps reluctantly – to view myself as a serious photographer, and not just someone who indulged in it as a hobby. I say reluctantly, as I was wary of allowing myself to imagine something too fantastical; the therapy of seven years earlier had taught me to dream, but some dreams were surely beyond my grasp.

The camera that hung round my neck now, though, felt more like an extension of me, as I began to appraise my finished prints as having merit, composed as they were with more care, being aware of what to include, but just as importantly what to leave out. Photography seemed to be getting easier, as I saw more opportunities – more compositions – which in the past would've been invisible.

In years gone by my camera had been an excuse on which to hang a day. It'd been incidental. Now, my camera was the backbone of those days, providing me with the motivation to explore. The photos I took in Tuscany were good. Or at least, they were good when compared with earlier efforts. But, were they good enough to dream big?

Chapter 24

When I met Anna, she worked as a reporter on the local paper, the *Western Telegraph*, a job she'd dreamt of doing since she was a child. My very own Lois Lane, I thought it insanely glamorous and exciting, all of that newshound stuff. So did she. I was proud to tell people what she did, basking in a reflected kudos, her stimulating career compensating for my dull job, just a little. I remember being awed when I accompanied her to work's Christmas parties, mingling with all of these bright people with a job to die for, all so sparky and engaging.

I graduated from the University of Glamorgan in Pontypridd with a degree in business studies, which promised a future career of bland disengagement. I had the certificate, proof of my academic rigour, but it brought little sense of satisfaction, and certainly little sense of excitement at what lay ahead. It'd seemed like a nice safe choice, a qualification that'd open up a gamut of uninspiring options. I wish I'd studied history. History engrossed me, made my heart sing. To have been a history teacher would've been quite something. But no, I opted for business studies and on graduating had to accept the consequences of my academic cowardice.

Soon after returning from Pontypridd, I got a job as an admin assistant with a facilities management company overseeing the maintenance of the army tank firing range at Castlemartin, near Pembroke; the bland disengagement began early. My duties consisted of inputting data onto an archaic computer system, answering the phone and doing menial administrative tasks for a team of surveyors, in between making tea. I felt overqualified and underwhelmed.

Shirley, one of the loveliest and most genuine people I ever met, ran the admin side of the office. We talked a lot and laughed a lot; it helped fill the days. Considerably brighter than her pay grade, she turned up each day to do a job that didn't in any way challenge her.

Once a month our comfortable billet was disrupted by an old raptor from head office who'd descend to check our administration procedures were compliant, to smell the paper trail and grill those who produced it. Flinty and joyless, she brought her own cup and saucer, as she deemed drinking from mugs to be uncivilised. When her car disappeared up the road at the end of the day Shirley and I would whoop with relief at having, yet again, foiled her quest for anomalies within a system that felt as if it were suffocating me with its tedium.

Colin was the chief surveyor, a man of unbending principle with an honest purity dripping from his pores. He charged around the office with Brunel-like gusto and the energy levels of two men half his age and could be volcanic if anyone was less than truthful or failed to own up to an error. This set him on regular collision courses with Terry, one of the surveyors, who'd readily resort to fabrication if it meant saving his own neck.

'You're a fucking liar,' was Colin's blistering riposte at Terry's verbal wriggling one day. I relished these occasional gladiatorial confrontations, if only to remind me that I was still alive.

Then there was Dave, easy going and amiable. He'd been doing the job forever and, with Colin nudging retirement, sensed his rightful inheritance. But he hadn't reckoned on Andrew, the cuckoo in the nest. Young and inexperienced, he arrived with the blessing of head office as Colin's heir apparent.

The office politics were more engaging than the job. Picking fluff out of my toenails would've been more engaging. It was the living death of Trecwn but without the excitement afforded by a proximity to high explosives; the office was a mile from the army base. A short-term contract, I was relieved when it came to an end.

Just when I thought I couldn't plumb the depths of career disillusionment any further, I successfully applied for a job in the

Benefits Agency; a Kafkaesque groundhog of triplicate paperwork, filing and brown envelopes, enlivened only by the occasional unsavoury claimant running amok in reception. As an admin assistant, yet again, I was on the bottom rung of a ladder I had little inclination to ascend.

I began to wonder whether I was hamstrung with that old sense of entitlement? The conviction that I was better than the job. That somehow I'd been short changed. Cheated. Certainly, when I left school with a brace of mediocre 'O' Levels, I'd got what I deserved – a junior storeman in Trecwn.

But now I had a degree. Surely that was worth more than another lowly admin job? Okay, maybe the degree didn't warrant some glittering career – of which, as already mentioned, there weren't many to be had in Pembrokeshire – but licking envelopes and filing bits of paper? Had I really studied for three years to end up doing that?

Time has dual speeds, depending on the circumstances. There's fast time, exciting time; the whizzing by of hours engrossed in some happy absorption or in great company. The sort of time that when the day ends you wonder where all of the hours went. Then there's slow time, dull time, bored- out-of-your-skull time. Like the time spent watching dust float above me in the Royal Infirmary after my accident. Dead time. Benefits Agency time was dead time too. Not much to do yet so much time in which to do it.

One afternoon, as I fought sleep in front of a computer screen, Carol from finance entered the large, open-plan office. My colleagues were busy processing benefit forms and inputting data. It was September 11th 2001.

'Well, there's a strange thing,' she said. 'Just listening to the news... on the radio. A plane's crashed into the World Trade Centre... in New York? You know, those two huge towers?'

Everyone stopped what they were doing and turned towards her.

'Anyone hurt? Aside from the pilot,' asked Christine.

'Don't know. That's all it said, really... a plane's hit one of the towers.' She picked up a stack of files and left the room.

'Be one of those small planes I suppose. Like a Cessna,' Roy said. It was duly agreed that it must've been a small plane that'd somehow gone off course and accidentally hit the tower.

Simon, though, with an analytical mind reluctant to accept such a blithe assumption, said, 'Yeah, but how could you accidentally hit something so big? You'd see it coming for miles.'

'Good point,' conceded Roy. 'Suicide, then?'

'Yeah. Sounds like it,' said Simon.

Suicide in a small plane it was, then. Everyone returned to their work while I slipped back to where I'd been before Carol appeared.

About twenty minutes passed and Carol shot back into the room and with great emphasis announced, 'You won't believe it. Another plane's hit the other tower.'

'What are the chances of that?' said Simon, our resident analyst. 'Did it say anything else?"

'Yeah,' she said. 'Apparently, they were both passenger planes. Could be a terrorist attack.'

Simon asked her to fetch the radio and we gathered round and listened to the ongoing coverage with a ratcheting sense of disbelief. The world changed that day, and not for the better.

We've all seen those films of eventual triumph over adversity, of the wrongly imprisoned – the character of Andy Dufresne in *The Shawshank Redemption* – when it's inconceivable that their fate couldn't get any worse. Well, for me it did get worse; the office closed and I was transferred to a contact centre.

I envisage a cruel perdition for the person who devised the concept of the contact centre. The idea is battery-hen simple and, I have to concede, cunningly efficient. Condition – or lobotomise if needs be – a group of people to clock in and sit for seven hours and twenty-four minutes at a desk with a headset on, answering a stream of calls from jobseekers. And when I say a stream of calls, I literally mean one after the other. A torrent really. To suck any spontaneity out of the exchanges, provide the battery-hens with a script. A script that I ignored.

Not surprisingly, morale was low and the rate of self-certified sickness amongst the staff was comparable to an outbreak of plague; nearly everyone went down at some point. When not at our desks, we congregated in the rest room, a large, soulless, rectangular space with padded benches against the walls. Staff would come in and sit on their own, often crying or shouting obscenities. It was like Bedlam Hospital, only without the interesting Georgian architecture.

The customers or clients or whatever trite Blairism we were expected to call the callers were a mixed bag. I doubt any of them wanted to be stood in a job centre in London speaking to a provincial voice about a low-paid job as a cleaner in an office block. In that respect there was a shared unhappiness: I despised the job I had while they despised the jobs they had to apply for if they wanted to keep their benefits. But for all of their sense of hopelessness, most were at least polite.

The Nigerians in particular were very cheerful. I spoke to a man from Lagos once, for about twenty minutes. Three minutes in, it was apparent he was unsuited to the job he was enquiring about. The rest of the time he told me about his family back home and how his relatives had clubbed together to get him to Britain, how he missed them terribly and hoped that once he'd made some money it'd be okay with them if he went back home. It got him down that it rained so much in London.

I had to wind the conversation up, as I was getting the look from Fiona, my line manager; we weren't a befriending service. He thanked me and said I'd been the kindest person he'd spoken to since he arrived. I was proud of myself that day. There were, of course, less polite customers. We had a script to deal with those too, trained as we were to ride the insults while mouthing bland platitudes and exhorting them to be nicer. It was another script that I ignored.

'David…'

I took my headset off.

'Can we have a listen back to how you dealt with that last customer? See how you think you handled it.'

Fiona was sweet, empathetic and I suspect hated being on that prison hulk as much as the rest of us. But like any overseer, she was expected to stamp on signs of rebellion. I followed her to her desk and listened; every call was recorded for 'training and monitoring purposes'.

'So, do you think that went as well as it could've?' she asked.

'Don't know. Suppose if he hadn't called me a fucking wanker perhaps the tone of the conversation would've been more constructive.'

'Fair enough,' she said. 'But maybe calling him a fucking wanker back didn't help?'

I felt for Fiona. She couldn't condone my descent to his level but there was a glint of admiration at my refusal to be cowed. She administered the lightest possible reprimand and I returned to my desk.

I set my stall out soon after arriving at the contact centre, my first job being in the admin section – where else! There was a particular line manager with a fearsome reputation. A stringy bundle of tightly permed energy, she ripped through the building like a typhoon, leaving a trail of quaking subordinates. Tales of her tongue-lashings were legion and she was in charge of admin, a huge room with multiple rows of desks and a wall of filing cabinets. One afternoon I was sitting motionless, staring out of the window, wishing I wasn't there, surrounded by a stack of paperwork waiting to be filed.

'David.' The voice was clipped, coming from the row behind me, where she sat.

I continued to stare out of the window.

'DAVID.'

Wearily, I spun round and as she motioned to speak, I interjected. 'We should get one thing clear from the start,' I said. 'Don't ever wake me up in the afternoon.'

It was meant as a joke, of course, but I remember the expression of a flunky sat by her side, a look that spoke of imminent evisceration.

But, aside from bemusement, nothing happened, and after that we got on like the proverbial house on fire.

Anna wanted a new challenge and so left the newspaper to become editor of news gathering at a soon-to-be-launched local radio station, Radio Pembrokeshire. I was proud of her, but terribly jealous; a bloody radio station – so rock 'n' roll. She was nervous leading up to her first broadcast on launch day, but pulled it off with admirable poise, after which she fell deeply into the job. As I walked one morning, with little urgency, across the car park towards the contact centre, one of my colleagues was listening to his car radio with the window down and I could hear Anna reading the news. I thought, do you know who that is? That's my girlfriend.

Like some needy groupie, I'd call in to see her at the station under the flimsiest of pretences, to immerse myself in her world, convinced that I too could work on radio. And when the call went out for a trainee DJ, I put some new batteries in a Dictaphone and recorded a demo tape. I mean, how hard could it be to talk between songs?

Escape from the contact centre seemed assured, certain as I was that what I'd recorded was radio gold. The tape got to the station boss – Anna made sure of it – along with other hopefuls. I asked Anna what he'd made of it, but I shouldn't have. Talking between songs, it seemed, wasn't as easy as I'd imagined.

Her hours at the station were brutal and the adrenalised excitement of those first few months became subsumed by exhaustion. I ran the house as best I could, ensuring there was a G&T poured ready when I heard her car pull up after what were often twelve-hour shifts, or more. Like Anna, the station enjoyed a honeymoon period in my affections too, before waning, the same songs coming round more often than a mini-cab in a small town.

So, whereas Anna – at least initially – galloped out of the door for the radio station in the morning with a freckly smile, to embrace whatever news events were thrown at her, I trudged to my car with that same feeling of dread that'd accompanied every job I'd ever had. Staring indignantly out of windows had been a recurring motif throughout my life.

At school, teachers' voices had faded like white noise as I gazed at the outside world, wondering whether all of that education stuff was necessary, and if it was, why was it so bloody boring. On the bus to technical college in Neyland, where I'd busied myself making lethal Chinese stars and emptying the Kit-kat machine, and later on the bus to Trecwn, I'd sit with my head against the glass, watching the landscape drift by, always yearning to be elsewhere, to do something exciting, embark on an adventure.

There had, of course, been the exhilarating sight, from the ward, of the fox among the trees at Rookwood, which'd motivated me. That'd been a good window. Sitting weeks later in that wheelchair on the lawn, prior to discharge, I told myself that I'd change my life. That fox – and the not inconsequential fact that my body moved – had made me believe. And yet there I was twenty years later, working in a contact centre near Pembroke Dock, nudging forty, looking disconsolately out of a window once again. I still didn't know the answer to the riddle of what it was that I wanted. What I did know was that I didn't want to be there.

Chapter 25

Sandra, an expat Londoner and holiday rep, had arranged the ceremony for eleven o'clock that Friday morning. Becoming fidgety, she glanced behind at the door, again.

'Don't worry, he'll be here soon,' she said, looking at her watch; it was ten past eleven.

Her cousin Giuseppe, co-opted as a witness, sat with an air of detached calm, his shorts, vest and flip flops an incongruous denial of the occasion. The door creaked open.

'Good, he's here,' sighed Sandra.

Positioning himself behind a large mahogany table, he turned to face us and with a warm smile announced, 'Good morning. My name is Alessandro and I am the Mayor of Amalfi.'

Anna and I had landed at Naples airport five days earlier. As anticipated, the lack of leg room on the three-hour flight had crucified my muscle tone. The plane came to a halt, and as the cabin began to empty, I pulled myself up using the headrest of the seat in front, eventually straightening to a standing position, and began stretching my legs, ready to disembark. Last off the plane, we made our way across the tarmac and into the terminal building, joining the back of the queue for passport control, with me doing half-squats all the while to try to loosen up.

Preoccupied as I was with my physical housekeeping, I couldn't help but notice a young man dropping back along the queue towards us and then behind. Perhaps he was having difficulty finding his passport, I thought. Anna and I reached the kiosk and presented ours. The uniformed man considered us with officious disdain, checked our passports and with an almost indiscernible tilt of the head nodded us through.

A policeman with a submachine gun and an Alsatian had been studying the queue as it filed by the kiosk. As we passed him, the dog tensed on its leash and darted for the young man behind us. Frantic grappling followed as other policemen pounced. Anna and I watched open-mouthed as they dragged the man away, face down with his arms pulled up behind his back, the dog snapping excitedly. They bundled him into a room and slammed the door. Walking hastily away in the direction of the luggage carousel, we heard one of the officers yelling from behind the door, 'OPEN. Open your mouth!' Whatever the young man had secreted in his mouth was going to be extracted, either there and then or hours later when nature had taken its course. If it was the start of a holiday, it wasn't going well.

We collected our luggage and made our way to arrivals, where we were to meet our chauffeur, who'd whisk us to Amalfi. Pietro could've passed for a Hollywood Mafia don with his shades, slicked-back hair and supreme air of confidence. With sinuous ease he scooped up our luggage and invited us to follow him to his Mercedes.

'My mamma lives in Amalfi. You'll love it,' he said as we surged onto the motorway.

Surely, only the cruel hand of fate had denied Pietro his rightful place in the Ferrari Formula One team. His exclusion hadn't dampened his will to keep trying for a place though. To our left we gazed, incredulous, at the blasted husk of Mount Vesuvius looming over Naples and its outlying urban spread. They'd built right up to the beast, as if poking it with a stick. The sign for Pompeii was a reminder of the dangers of poking too hard. To our right was the villa-dotted sprawl of the Bay of Naples, lit by the evening sun as it plunged west beyond the Med. A spewing monster on one side, and an aquamarine idyll on the other.

Pietro exited the motorway and began the climb into the Lattari Mountains, the spine of the Campanian peninsula. Anna and I marvelled at lemons the size of rugby balls as the road compressed into a collection of hairpin bends, each turn elevating the spectacular view of the volcano and its city. She gripped my hand as Pietro took corners with deft precision while half-turning in conversation to tell us about his bambinos, a driving tic for which neither of us felt much enthusiasm.

In a blackening dusk, we pulled up outside of our hotel. Pietro took our luggage in, shook our hands, jumped back in the car and hurtled off for supper with mamma. The hotel reception was near to the roadside at the top of a cliff, with the rooms in a separate villa at the bottom. A porter grabbed our luggage and cantered down multiple flights of dimly lit steps with the balance of a mountain goat.

He was soon out of sight as I descended, clinging on to Anna's hand, not wishing to crack my head on arrival. The pit of my stomach fell away as I realised that we may have made a mistake in booking such a precipitous place to stay. The owner followed us to our room.

'The steps. You don't like?' he said, perhaps concerned that the hotel's insurance policy might be called on to pay out to a plummeting guest.

'It's okay. I'll take my time. It'll be fine. Honestly,' I said.

He wasn't reassured, departing with a worried frown. It was late and we were tired so we decided to get some sleep and mull over the steps issue in the morning.

We woke to piercing daylight and an enveloping heat. I got out of bed and opened the balcony doors for some air.

'Jesus Christ, Anna. Look at this.'

The balcony jutted out over the sea, the surface of which glistened like a tray of diamonds as a small boat bobbed and a fisherman cast a net. What a welcome.

Breakfast in the restaurant, halfway back up the cliff, required a nervous scaling of those steep, shallow steps. I could see that there were indeed a lot of them, flight after flight. The owner was serving guests.

'*Buongiorno*. How are you?'

'Very good, thank you,' I replied. 'What an incredible view.'

'Yes, we are very lucky,' he said, gazing out to sea before turning to face me. 'I worry about the steps. You find them hard?'

I cupped my hand on his shoulder and smiled.

'Anna will help me. It'll be no problem.'

I hoped that I sounded relaxed, though inside I was anything but. With no handrail and just a low wall for support, it was going to be a challenge – nothing new there then. He nodded and went to get us a pot of coffee.

Sitting at a table, Anna leaned forward. 'Look, if the steps are worrying you, we could ask to be moved to another hotel. I think he'd be quite relieved actually.'

'No. We're here now and... well, it's just so beautiful,' I said, gesturing out to sea. 'Anyway, we could end up in a grotty dump. I'll be fine if I take my time.'

Anna knew that when I set my mind to a challenge, I was unlikely to relent, though I could happily have done without that particular one. It was daunting. With Puccini playing in the background and unable to take our eyes off the stunning view, we had coffee and croissants and contemplated our first day.

After breakfast, a hire car was delivered. We'd had a crash course on Italian roads, without the crash, the year before in Tuscany, but as we drove away from the hotel we sensed that the further south you went in Italy the hotter the motoring blood became. There appeared to be lots of drivers, of all ages, couriering freshly donated organs, as I had in my youth.

The Amalfi coast road presents intoxicating panoramas combined with the spectre of imminent death. On the seaward side the road abutted a low reinforced concrete wall over which you could plummet hundreds of metres, gifting ample time to contemplate your demise, and opposite was an unforgiving rock face hacked out of the mountain.

That first day I pootled nervously along the thin ribbon of shiny tarmac cut into the cliffs, nearly jumping out of my skin if I saw the front of a bus swinging round a corner and coming towards us – spatial awareness was a must. The locals didn't seem to have the time, or indeed the inclination, to pootle along, as we were overtaken regularly, once by a stooped octogenarian in a white vest driving an old Fiat. Flower-bedecked shrines on occasional corners, though, were a reminder of those who should perhaps have pootled.

Our days, then, were spent exploring the towns and villages of the Amalfi coast, but always we returned to our balcony to witness the horizon bleed out, with a bottle of local red and goats' cheese and olives from a scruffy little shop across the road. We drank and ate and read our holiday books as the sea washed over the rocks below. It was simple and beautiful, shared with a glorious woman with similar yearnings for an uncomplicated life.

As the days passed, I began to sense that old illusion of a return to physical normality being rekindled, as I became more confident of my ascent and descent of the steps, lunging less for the support of the low wall and holding Anna's hand more lightly. I graduated to going up and down unaided by either wall or hand and it made me happy. I felt good. I felt strong. I felt unstoppable.

But, of course, as with the first flush of the gym many years earlier, the tantalising prospect of completion was a fleeting euphoric deception. Yes, I was at a physical peak of sorts, but it wasn't, could never be, the start of a return to everyone else's normal. There'd always be limits, regardless of any punishing schedules. And yes, I could keep up a punishing schedule for a week or perhaps even ten days, but then I'd hit the wall. Run out of gas. On each of our holidays, though, I seemed to time my implosions for when I returned home.

As always, I caught the odd querying glance that'd bring me back down to earth; was it an accident, a stroke or maybe something congenital? The pity in the eyes was the killer, momentarily extinguishing the day's joy. But in seconds it'd be forgotten as at the core of my coping mechanism now was happiness. The physical loss was still painful if I cared to think of it, but the sum of my emotional parts was joyous, and so I didn't. My psychologist from '95 would've been heartened.

Sat on that balcony in the evenings, I couldn't quite believe my luck; I was with an incredible woman with the southern sun on my face, enjoying yet another adventure, and when it was over we'd return to our little cottage by the river. If I could just ditch the contact centre then all of my numbers would've come up. There seemed little prospect of that, mind.

The hotel's owner, who I guessed to be in his early forties, was a man of few words and even fewer expressions, traits he appeared to have inherited from his father. Enigmatic didn't come close. Anna and I reckoned they'd been resettled via a witness protection scheme, evading the vengeance of former criminal associates.

The father, who ran the restaurant, was as lithe as a gazelle, dancing effortlessly between tables while balancing platters of food on his shoulder. We gifted him the pseudonym Mr De Niro. The son, as it happened, was a dead-ringer for Jean Reno, the French actor adept at playing avenging angel roles. In their presence time seemed to slow, their rhythms a masterclass of effortless biomechanics. Reno's response when we clipped a kerb in the hire car and buckled a wheel rim was priceless. Anna and I were unsure as to whether it was still safe to drive. He thought it was fine.

'Are you sure?' I asked, unconvinced by his casual assurance.

'*Sicuro come la morte*,' he replied. 'Safe as death.'

We took the car to a garage he recommended halfway between Amalfi and mountain-top Ravello. While we waited, a mechanic removed the wheel, took the tyre off, grabbed a lump hammer and artfully beat the rim back into a near perfect shape. We drove in a more tentative fashion after that, impressed as we were by the mechanic's skill but aware that perhaps the wheel wasn't as reliable as when the car had come off the production line; we weren't quite convinced that it was as safe as death.

We continued our ascent to Ravello, high up in the clouds. After lunch in a cool restaurant, we wandered the narrow lanes that criss-crossed the village, inaccessible to the cars deposited in the car park at the entrance to Ravello. Goods and materials are moved around by donkeys with panniers. We passed one buckling donkey laden down with building blocks, no doubt wishing for an easier gig on a beach somewhere giving kids a ride.

We roamed and sweated and happened by chance upon the terrace of the Villa Rufolo, and were overwhelmed. Peering what seemed like miles down to the sea from its perch, I felt a sense of dizzying elation. This, I thought, was surely where God decamped while he laid out the world, making sure not to invest any other place on Earth with the same air of celestial perfection. I clung to the railings and wobbled.

Whereas Ravello was of the gods, Amalfi was sun-bleached and scuffed, the inhabitants less Chanel, more Primark. It's a faded town of bustle and energy, with dads and their kids – and sometimes the wife too – stacked on passing scooters. Squeezed into a ravine, there is no back door to Amalfi. You arrive by the coast road or boat. It is as if the town had poured down the mountainside and spread out along the shore, clinging to a shallow ledge.

The black and white marble façade of the Romanesque cathedral sits shoehorned amongst an irregular eruption of rooftops around a small square, the main street snaking back into the ravine, terminating a short walk from the sea at a dead end. From there I peered at narrow tracks winding up the steep inclines, sprouting houses that seemed to cling on for dear life. Amalfi, architecturally infused with Moorish influences, peppered with palms and under a baking sun, felt more North African than European.

Twelve twisting, hair-raising miles along the coast road is Positano, a place where the laws of physics have also been discarded. As with Amalfi, a slash in the cliffs gifted a ledge on which to establish a town by the shore. For Positano, though, the sandy strip didn't suffice, so they built on the mountains either side of the beach, houses and hotels clinging to near vertical rock. In a region bedevilled by earth tremors,

I wondered whether they might all just tumble into the sea one day.

We drove into a two-storey car park erected on a handkerchief of land in Positano's ravine's-width town centre. Italian civil engineering has perhaps had a bad press over the years, what with organised crime taking hefty cuts from bloated public contracts and the odd motorway bridge collapsing. Looking at the touchable crumbly concrete ceiling, I prayed that the spindly columns would support it long enough for us to pay and exit.

This tiny car park was a big employer; a swarm of young men, all coiffed and bronzed, darted around like pinballs, inviting customers to vacate their vehicles so they could shoehorn them into spaces designed for '50s cars. Payment was made to an older man sitting at a table near the entrance, from where he controlled the pinballs. It felt to me like familial testament to a culture resistant to that dead-eye protestant North European efficiency ethic, and it appealed to me.

It was early season May in Positano, so only madly busy – never visit in the summer. We did a bit of sightseeing and then Anna said, 'Fancy a coffee?'

We entered a busy café, spying two seats at a table in the corner.

'Quick, grab them,' I said.

Anna scurried over with me in her wake and we sat down.

'Shall we have cake too?' she suggested with a twinkle.

'That'd be very nice.'

Anna went to order and five minutes later returned with a rueful smile and shake of the head.

'What's so funny?' I asked.

'You wouldn't believe the system here.'

'System?'

'Yeah. See that little kiosk over by the entrance?'

I'd noticed a young woman sitting in it doing her nails on the way in.

'Went to the counter to order and was told to go to the kiosk. The menu's there. So, the girl in the kiosk takes my order then traipses over to the counter I've just come from.'

I was warming to the place more by the minute.

'Now, see the young man sat at the end of the counter nearest us?' she said, *sotto voce.*

'Yeah.'

'When it's ready he'll bring it over.'

'God, I love it,' I said.

In Britain, an officious bod with a clipboard, stopwatch and supercilious attitude would've streamlined the process and dumped a few out of a job. We sat and watched the operation with joy.

Alessandro, Mayor of Amalfi, straightened his tie and began the ceremony, a translator filtering his words into English. Sandra smiled, more with relief that we were underway than any genuine happiness for a couple she didn't know. Her cousin Giuseppe, press-ganged as a witness late on, alighted from his seat. If he'd felt underdressed – which I suspect was unlikely – he'd have been heartened by the mayor's cargo pants which gave the ceremony a refreshingly informal air, though they did clash with his badged blazer, shirt and tie.

And so, in the town hall of the ancient maritime republic of Amalfi, with a view of the sea through an open window, Anna and I were pronounced man and wife. The mayor hugged us as if we were long-lost relatives, Sandra said how wonderful we looked, wishing us a happy future, and Giuseppe nodded and slipped out. On 16th May 2003, we walked out into the sunny courtyard as Mr and Mrs Wilson, and kissed.

Chapter 26

Amalfi had been an idyllic glimpse of a sun-drenched life and the perfect antidote to the drudgery of the contact centre. My camera had accompanied us everywhere, an expression of who I was and what I wanted to be; a photographer proper, and not just a casual snapper. The dream had begun to acquire a solidity in my mind as the notion of it being an unattainable aspiration receded.

The landscapes of Italy had inspired me to what felt like a higher plane of compositional appreciation; I was seeing more possibilities through the viewfinder. Amalfi, though, had been a honeymoon, a state of bliss from which there had been no choice but to return. My job-seeking customers and headset awaited.

President George W. Bush and Prime Minister Tony Blair's 'War on Terror' roadshow – cobbled together after the 9/11 attack on the twin towers – rolled into Iraq in 2003, following a successful tour of Afghanistan, where the ruling Taliban – a bunch of fundamentalist zealots with a liking for chopping off hands and inflicting death by stoning for extramarital misdemeanours – had been ousted. Osama Bin Laden and his merry bunch of jihadis had found the Taliban to be welcoming hosts; from his base in Afghanistan, he'd masterminded the 9/11 attack. US retribution, then, had been the dish of the day, served fast and hot with an extra-large portion of ground-juddering violence.

Emboldened by the speed with which a ragtag of poorly equipped medievalists had been obliterated, Bush and Blair – assuming the guise of a tired Vaudeville act – were persuaded that Iraq should be next. After all, they were in the neighbourhood, so it kind of made sense to pop by; two birds, one stone and all that. Problematically, they needed a legitimate excuse for invasion if they were to secure UN backing. The fact that Saddam Hussein, the psychotic despot who ran Iraq as his personal fiefdom, was a thoroughly bad sort just wasn't reason enough. So, Saddam's enormous, and unverified, pile of weapons of mass destruction were cited. If he wasn't deposed, he'd kill us all, it was argued. Expert opinion said that there were no weapons of mass destruction, but that didn't deter George and Tony; especially Tony, who'd been in touch with God and been given the go-ahead for the 'crusade'.

The US and Britain versus Saddam was like Premier League champs Man City taking on a Sunday league side from Arbroath; it was a trouncing. A swift victory enabled the 'liberators' to dismantle the state apparatus that ran Iraq, leading to the breakdown of society, with resultant *Supermarket-Sweep* levels of looting, kidnappings and murders galore, and a car bomb round every corner. To no one's surprise, least of all the architects of the disaster, no weapons of mass destruction were found.

Tony subsequently relinquished the role of Prime Minister to become a peace envoy for the Middle East – akin to tasking an arsonist with rebuilding the house they've burnt down. Iraq, then, was an inglorious folly, driven by hubris, which killed an awful lot of people.

Like most photographers at the turn of the millennium, I used film, the digital revolution being in its embryo stage. By this time I'd made the decision to shoot just black and white, sensing a creative evolution in my photography. And to fire this evolution I acquired a serious piece of kit, as befitting my now serious aspirations: a Mamiya 645 – a medium-format camera with a waist-level viewfinder. If you're not a photographer, that'll mean nothing!

The Mamiya was a precision piece of yesteryear mechanical perfection, a camera that infused its user with a sense of artisan pretension. You really did look and feel the part. When not in the contact centre staring out of the window, I toured Pembrokeshire and beyond, immersing myself in landscape photography. Mounting the Mamiya on a tripod, I'd look down into the viewfinder, teasing out areas of light and shade, the building blocks of black and white images, and composing the scene with care. No more point and shoot.

On finishing a roll of film, I'd take it to a developer, the creative revealing of the image out of my control. Flicking through the photographs on collection, I'd groan at the machine-processed greyness of the prints, picking out an acceptable few and discarding the rest. The compositions showed promise, artistry perhaps, but the third-party printing was disheartening. Where was the punch and contrast of a Bill Brandt print? Where was the drama?

Handing a roll of film over to be developed and printed is like an artist sketching a rough in the field and then asking someone else to paint the soul into the picture. The vision in my mind's eye could never be realised. The solution would be to develop film and print the images myself, overseeing the entire process of crafting a photograph from opening the shutter to holding the finished print.

And so, in anticipation of building a darkroom at home, I enrolled in an evening class at the college in Haverfordwest, where I'd previously been a student, to learn how to develop film and reveal the magic of a photographic print. I was so excited at the prospect of gaining control over the whole process, aware that this was the missing piece of the jigsaw.

About a dozen students turned up that first night, all eager to get in the darkroom, switch the enlarger on and pour out those chemicals. I mingled and chatted and over the weeks they revealed themselves to be a warm and engaging bunch. In particular, I have fond memories of working in the darkroom alongside Kevin, a bearded bear of a man with a bottomless generosity of spirit. In Kevin's company I felt so positive. He laughed a lot. And so did I.

The lecturer, Ray, was in his sixties, a smiling and compact man, forever decked out in a pastel-coloured V-neck and sharply ironed slacks. Deeply committed to his photography, over the months he taught us in a quasi-religious fashion the techniques of developing and printing. With an accumulated wisdom stretching back decades, he'd wander round the darkroom, watching us with paternal interest as we enlarged, dodged, burned, fixed and washed the images materialising before our eyes. We were infused with the zeal of prospectors panning for gold, such was the buzz of the reveal.

I became hooked and took to rifling through my old negatives to see if I could breathe new life into them. It was electrifying to see that my efforts, when compared to the previous machine-produced duds, were more powerful and engaging. There was drama. There was soul. The same compositions that'd been butchered by automation now shone.

Ray brought his own work in too, partly I suspect to absorb a collective wonder but mostly to inspire us. There were a lot of monochrome images which were striking. As I learned about developing black and white film, the language of photography began to speak to me in a way colour never had. It was revelatory. Ray also happened to be a member of a camera club. With his soft Pembrokeshire burr, he said to me, 'You should come along. I think you'd like it.'

'We have a new member with us tonight… David,' announced Doug, the chairman, gesturing to where I was sitting. 'I trust I can rely on you to make him feel welcome.'

The club met in a cavernous neo-gothic church hall which reeked of what I came to embrace as that distinctive camera club smell – the cushioned seats and furnishings were cold to the touch, damp and musty. Even in summer, layering was the key to warding off a deathly chill. More deadly, though, were the competing members jockeying for supremacy, eyeing rivals' efforts with dark suspicion.

I'd watch these big beasts in their peacock splendour prowling about and realised that I'd quite like to emulate them. One night, the power failed and the place was plunged into darkness. When the lights came back on, I half expected one of the more politicking members to be lying face down with a knife in their back. It felt as if I'd stumbled into an Agatha Christie novel, and I loved it.

I remember with great affection, an older married couple who were a soothing balm to the static air of distrust. They circulated together, always smiling, with what seemed like an invisible thread connecting them, as if to venture too far from the other's orbit might deprive them of oxygen. I adored them and their generous company, imagining that to be like them when Anna and I were older would be a fine thing indeed.

The members embraced me, making me feel as if I'd found something, solved a puzzle in my life. One member in particular fired the dream of one day ditching my works' headset and becoming a professional photographer. His name was Alan. Stocky and proud, and resplendent in the club's unofficial uniform of pastel V-neck and slacks – what else? – he was acknowledged as the black and white supremo, with the ability to make light and shade dance within sublime tonal compositions. On the rare occasions when he brought work in, it was as if some ancient scripts of divine wisdom were being unfurled and that by loitering in their proximity some of the magic might rub off. I hung on his every word.

The members nurtured and encouraged me in my transition from casual snapper to a photographer with promise. I'd never put so much thought into the making of an image, endeavouring to capture light in such a way as to invest the resultant photograph with a transcendent majesty. But there was a large hulking elephant in the room: to gain full control of the development and printing of a negative meant building a darkroom. The college course was coming to an end and I'd have to commit to a major upheaval at home. Where the hell would I put a darkroom anyway? I hadn't really thought it through, and a tough decision was looming.

Then, one fateful club night the answer revealed itself like some shining prophecy. Ivan Wilson – no relation – ran a local camera shop, and he was invited along to give a demonstration of the latest digital cameras. There, right in front of me, was the solution to my elephantine problem: ditch the film camera and invest in cutting-edge digital. The processing would be done on a computer with no need to convert a spare room we didn't have into a darkroom I didn't want, and I'd avoid breathing in noxious chemicals to boot. A great weight had been lifted.

In the spring of 2004, Alan, the black and white supremo, collared me.

'You know it's the salon soon,' he said.

'Sorry?'

'The Welsh Photographic Federation's annual jamboree?'

I shook my head.

'Okay. Members from all the clubs round Wales – loads of them – enter images into this salon,' he said. 'It's a kind of best of the best, if you like. A big deal, I can tell you.'

'Sounds good. You entering?'

'Nah, not this year. But you should.'

'You're joking.'

He lowered his voice. 'Look, I've seen some of your monochrome stuff and it's good. Have a go. If nothing else, it'll be good experience.'

I hadn't heard that threadbare endorsement since the countdown to my driving test.

'Okay. Maybe,' I said.

'Never mind maybe. Do it.' He glanced around. 'Never know, you might ruffle a few feathers round here,' he said with a chuckle.

Anna and I returned home from the cinema, having been to watch *Starsky & Hutch*, starring Ben Stiller and Owen Wilson, a limp comedy spin-off of the hit seventies cop series. The original *Starsky & Hutch* was a programme I revered during my childhood. Paul Michael Glaser, who played the character of Dave Starsky, had a tanned complexion, dark curly hair and was the owner of a busy run. The early teens David Wilson had a tanned complexion, dark curly hair and was the owner of a busy run. The similarities, at least in my mind, were uncanny. I often became him – it helped me escape my woes at school, at least in my head.

Driving the milk float for John as he ran to place pints on doorsteps, I was Dave Starsky. Running to the tennis club to break my latest racquet, I was Dave Starsky. Taking pot shots with my mate Graham's air rifle from his bedroom at the drunks staggering out the pub opposite, I was – yes, you've guessed it – Dave Starsky. The film, then, seemed like a desecration of some of my happiest teen memories.

Anna opened the front door and went in while I emptied the mailbox. A brown A5 envelope was addressed to me. Inside was a copy of the 2004 Welsh Photographic Federation's glossy catalogue of category-winning photographs and typed lists of dozens upon dozens of commended entries. Everyone who'd entered the salon received a copy, affording the overwhelming majority of entrants the opportunity to rue their luck at being denied a category win, or even a paltry commendation, while losing out to members of rival clubs whose images were inferior to theirs; it was a gripe-fest of vendetta-like proportions.

Flicking carelessly through the catalogue, I glimpsed a black and white photograph of an oil refinery on the horizon with a farmhouse in the foreground. There were eight category winners in all and this photograph had won best image for 'Industry in Wales'. It looked like – very much like – a photograph I'd taken. Identical, in fact. And not only taken but had submitted to the salon. It couldn't be mine though, so I closed the catalogue and placed it on the kitchen table.

I grabbed two glasses and a bottle of wine then opened the catalogue again, just to make sure. I mean, how could it be my photograph? That would've been ridiculous. This time I noticed the photographer's name. It contained all of the letters of my name, laid out in the same order. Could there have been two David Wilsons that'd entered the salon? It was the only plausible explanation, as the alternative was just too mad. Then I saw the image title, 'Neighbour from Hell'. That was the title I'd given my entry. In the face of my reluctance to accept the incontrovertible evidence, I was, it seemed, a category winner in the 2004 Welsh Photographic Federation's salon of photography. I felt dizzy, sat down and shouted, 'Anna. Anna! Come here. Quick.'

She rushed into the kitchen. 'What? What is it?' she said, eyes darting around for the emergency.

With a stupefied smile usually attributed to the village offspring of cousins, I showed her the photograph.

She pondered a moment. 'That's yours, isn't it?'

'Yup.'

'And... you've won one of the... the categories?'

'Yup.'

If the actual Oscars had awarded me best leading man, I couldn't have been more elated. It was huge. Enormous. I poured myself a very large glass of Chianti and kept returning to the catalogue to ensure the image was still there and that it hadn't been some weird dream. I didn't sleep that night.

My next appearance at the camera club was met with a generous round of applause and a perceptible re-evaluation of my place in the pecking order. Suddenly, this new guy was someone to be reckoned with, a category winner in the Oscars of Welsh camera club photography. Not only that, but in his very first year as a member. I felt elevated to the status of peacock, more than happy to strut my stuff, inebriated with success. Alan came over and patted me on the back.

'Worth entering?' he asked, with a huge smile.

Anna wrote a press release for the local papers, announcing my arrival – in my opinion – as a serious photographer. Seeing my name in print alongside the image added to my conviction that something momentous was stirring. The dream that I was going to become a professional photographer was now, to my mind, pretty much guaranteed.

The refinery in question wasn't quite so ecstatic at my success. They contacted the Welsh Photographic Federation through their solicitors and threatened court action, asserting that the photograph and its caption were libellous. I thought it a little rich seeing as a huge explosion at the plant some years earlier had persuaded a majority of residents to abandon a nearby village, permanently.

I now sat in the contact centre a little less disconsolate, mentally digging a tunnel, determined that I'd escape and become a photographer taking black and white images of the Pembrokeshire landscape. It would be my job, my living. At least, that was the Hollywood version swimming around my head. As a business plan it presented as pure madness. For starters, who on earth made a living from taking monochrome photographs of the landscape? As far as I could determine, not many, if any.

More pertinent perhaps, how was it conceivable that a man approaching forty – a decrepit forty – where just remaining upright on uneven ground was a challenge, going to get out into that landscape to take photographs that could generate a living? Lots of nagging questions registered but I was buoyed by such fervency that any doubts were discarded. I'd spent my adult life doing what I thought other people would approve of, avoiding the helter-skelter of risk, and allowing myself to be constrained by what I perceived as insurmountable physical limitations. I now saw my chance to change all of that.

On days off, I stumbled my way across the countryside, driven on by the dream, and despite the odd tumble, for the most part in good humour. A body of work grew in tandem with a growing self-assurance. Then, out of nowhere, I got my big break locally.

Lynne Crompton, who ran the respected Oriel Q gallery in Narberth, not far from where we lived, gave me space to exhibit a dozen frames at an upcoming show. My very first exhibition. Okay, so the space was on the stairs leading up to the main gallery, but it was a start and it felt like things were happening.

On the opening night I was so proud I thought I might pass out as people came up to me to talk about my work and congratulate me. I'd entered into a sparky and creative world, surrounded by talented individuals, and I loved it. Best of all, when Anna and I were leaving at the end of the night, I could see red dots on some of my frames: they'd sold.

Prior to the exhibition, I decided to donate a percentage of any takings to Rookwood spinal injuries unit in Cardiff. It'd been twenty years since being discharged and the sense of a debt owed had never left me. The knowledge that my bed would've been, in all likelihood, occupied by one patient after another like some conveyor belt of despair, saddened me. I just hoped that whoever was its current occupant, they could make a life for themselves more quickly than I had.

I reached a point where I had a large enough body of work with which to approach galleries and other outlets to see if they'd be interested in selling my photographs; to see whether I could become a professional fine art landscape photographer and dump that bloody headset. A part of me had dreaded reaching that point, as it brought with it the prospect of rejection. The prospect of being confined to the contact centre for the rest of my working life.

You see, all those years ago, sitting drunk on a wall after last orders constructing fantastical narratives in my head was one thing. Having the bravery to follow through on a grand scheme, though; well, that was quite something else. After all, if you don't try, you can't fail; a guiding principle that'd stymied me all of my adult life. Well, at last I was trying.

Anna and I visited outlets in Pembrokeshire which research and word of mouth indicated were desirable spaces to sell my work. Like a pair of mystery shoppers, we sneakily appraised the galleries, the quality of work on display, and whenever possible chatted oh-so casually with the owner, giving no hint as to the motive for our over-inquisitiveness. Satisfied with our research, I contacted the galleries to request meetings, half-hoping they'd decline so that I didn't have to endure the humiliation of being turned down.

I recall the confusion of excitement and nervous immobility as I stood rooted outside of the Waterfront Gallery in Milford Haven, clutching my artist's folder containing a dozen mounted images, girding myself to make my first pitch. I glanced back at the car, convinced that I should just go home.

Convinced that I was foolish to imagine that I could aspire to something as incredible as being a photographer who earned their living by selling their work. Half an hour later, I stood on the same spot feeling as if I were on drugs. It'd been a yes. And over the coming weeks I had meetings with the remaining galleries on my list, each one saying yes. I supplied them with work and soon they requested more stock to replace sales. I was delirious.

As gallery sales grew, I dropped hours at work and the time came to cut free, walking out of the office for the last time. I looked back at the building with a pang of pity for the good people who'd been left behind to continue their sentences, but I'd come up with a plan and escaped. All of that gazing out of windows was over as I began a new phase in my life. Or maybe I was beginning my life, with Anna beside me.

Without Anna's support and encouragement, I would never have been brave enough – some people thought mad enough – to have made the leap. And believe me, it was an enormous leap. A chasm of a leap. Anna was convinced that I could do it, and so I did. It was confirmation – not that I needed it – that I'd married the most incredible person I'd ever had the great good fortune to meet.

Chapter 27

I studied him closely, mapping every peachy blemish, every fold of his plumpness, as I inhaled his newness, a milky purity. He was a wondrous collection of billions upon billions of cells which had come together to form a miraculous perfection. He curled and scrunched and straightened and twisted and glanced blindly around. He was Charlie and Charlie was us; our son. Anna was asleep, exhausted, and so I just kept staring and crying and dreaming how extraordinary our lives together would be.

Nothing can prepare you for the joy, and terror, of coming home from hospital with a baby. A brand-new human being. A helpless human being at that, reliant for all its needs on you, its shell-shocked parents. We carried him in from the car and looked at him. Then we looked at each other. And then looked at him again, as if all of this looking would somehow make sense of it all. It did, kind of. We were now three. And the littlest and most incapable of the three was in charge.

Anna and I had to learn a new language, the language of gurgles and cries. When he made a noise, we jumped. When he cried, we jumped more quickly. Deciphering this new addition was hit and miss. Was he warm enough? Was he too warm? Too warm was bad, dangerous. Suddenly, everything revolved around the body heat of a tiny person. Is that hunger? Does he need changing? For us, as with all first-time parents, it was confusing and not a little unnerving.

Reassurance arrived in the form of our mums, and a few days later Gill the health visitor. Here was someone who knew how these baby things worked; I had trouble programming a video recorder, so working out how Charlie ticked was mind-boggling.

Gill was an ebullient and opinionated godsend. If she'd ever been indoctrinated into the vocabulary of public sector blandness then she'd chucked it aside. She was delightful and irreverent and straight to the point. We knew where we stood and if we were doing something wrong, she let us know without ceremony. But best of all she assured us we were doing just fine. So long as he was healthy, not much could go wrong with these baby-things. Make sure he's not too hot or too cold, listen out for hungry, change when he poos. We discovered the panicked confusion of colic a little later. Gill had perhaps left that one off the list as a test.

It's a parent's gorgeous burden to love so unquestionably, in the knowledge that your child may not comprehend the depth of that love till they become parents themselves. I now knew what it was all about. I now knew how much Mum and Dad had loved me, continued to love me, and how crushed they'd been after my accident. I'd been so consumed with my own misery at the time, that I hadn't noticed theirs. They were just these two deflated people who orbited me. And now, when I looked at Charlie, which I did a lot, my past indifference to Mum and Dad's suffering shamed me. They'd deserved better.

There was a period in my life – if many years could be described as a period – when I could never have imagined the joy of 2005: married to an amazing woman, father to beautiful, pudgy Charlie and with my new job of work as a photographer, which felt neither like work nor a job, words I'd always associated with a wasted forty hours a week.

I'd been the employee from hell, resentful and bloody infuriating to deal with, never reconciled with what I felt to be my rightful inheritance in the world and the jobs I blundered into. It'd all seemed so unfair. Yet I should've been grateful. After all, it's not as if I'd left school with glowing results and gone on to shine at university, or indeed shine anywhere. No, I'd been a lazy entitled bastard.

But somehow I'd managed to manipulate the narrative so that at the age of forty I was earning a living from my hobby. My innings was still progressing, of late my strokes more cavalier, the elation of the odd boundary imbuing me with the hope of a comfortable fifty. I was in the groove and enjoying the game.

For our first family holiday, Anna, fifteen-month-old Charlie and I headed to Cornwall, the photographable terrain and coast having a familiarity that made me think I hadn't left home. Charlie aided me, unwittingly, in scaling heights of endurance too; pushing a buggy up hills with what could only be described as a well-padded and robust passenger sharpened my stamina no end.

It was rainy one day – it was rainy lots of days – and we decided to go for a drive, get out of our accommodation, and get some air. With a deliberate absence of plotting, we made our way north and descended into a coastal village. Something about the place bugged me: one or two familiar-looking buildings and a pub that seemed to invite reminiscence. I was driving and asked Anna where we were. She looked at the map, 'Er... I think it's Portreath?'

Portreath? The name was familiar but I couldn't figure out why. We parked by a walled harbour populated by a smattering of pleasure and fishing boats. The rain stopped, so we put Charlie in his buggy and went for a stroll. Anna popped into a shop to get some ice creams while I looked around, sensing a gradual dawning: the stunted lighthouse perched on the headland and the particular sweep of the bay began to fall like angled runes into remembered shapes and the answer to the puzzle. Portreath, 1979.

Dad had spied the Captain's Cabin in a small ad at the back of the *Daily Express*. With no pictures but with a description evoking a retreat fit for a seaman of rank, he'd booked it. Perhaps there was still a bit of salt water running through his veins from his Navy days. Confusion reigned on arrival in Portreath, though, when we drew up outside a 1930s bay-windowed bungalow.

'Don't look much like a cabin to me,' said Dad, peering from the driver's seat.

'It's lovely,' purred Mum, pleasantly surprised that it wasn't as expected. Mum was partial to a nice-looking bungalow.

The owner was to meet us with the key and we were early so we wandered up the path for a closer inspection.

'I really like this, Harry,' said Mum, looking through one of the windows.

'Aye,' replied Dad. Perplexed, he took a piece of paper from his pocket, on which he'd written the address. Glancing at the number on the door, he said, 'Well, it's the right place.'

It looked cosy and welcoming and the garden was huge. We were itching to get in. Just then, a man walked round the corner from the rear of the property.

'Mr Wilson?'

'Yep.'

'Hi. I'm Mike. Welcome to the Captain's Cabin.'

Dad shook his hand.

'Right then, let's get you settled in,' he said.

We edged towards the green-painted front door as Mike turned and walked back round the corner. We shrugged and followed. To the rear of the bungalow was a flat-roofed extension – about the size of a double garage. He opened a door and we followed him inside, where we were presented with what appeared to be a cramped bedsit.

'Right then, a quick tour,' he began, pointing airily. 'You've got your cooking facilities over there. Dining area and sofa – which doubles as one of the beds. Great fun for the boys!'

Mum and Dad glanced at one another, a creeping disappointment scouring their faces. Dad interjected. 'Hang on a minute. So, this is it? The Captain's Cabin?'

Mike's polished spiel faltered. 'Well, yeah, as described in the ad. Sleeps four, near the sea...'

'You're joking,' interrupted Dad. 'This is a bloody garage.'

'As I say, it was all accurately described in the ad.'

Dad's jaw dropped as Mum grabbed his arm and pulled him close, a cue to remain calm.

'If you need anything, we're in the bungalow. Just knock on the green door,' said Mike, retreating out of the cabin – sorry, I mean converted garage.

Mum and Dad were crushed but smiled as if we were the luckiest people in the world. Without excitement, we got our luggage in from the car and Mum rustled up supper in the kitchen corner of the room. There was a partitioned-off space with a double bed shoe-horned in – as if the room had been built around the bed – and a cramped bathroom with an interesting array of mould patterns on the wall. It was one-star Britain, three-star Soweto.

Dad was a kind but principled man with no qualms in resorting to working-class retribution if the situation demanded. I remember a neighbour of ours being manhandled off our property once when he came to complain about Andrew and me throwing stones at him. We assured Dad that he'd thrown the first stone, and, believing us, the man was ejected, very roughly.

There were a number of similar incidents during our childhood, with legitimate complainants given short shrift; Dad was blind to our misdemeanours. One time, whilst he dealt with an angry man on the doorstep – Andrew had been firing crab apples at a group of old people on the bowling green with my tennis racket – Andrew and I retired to the safety of the living room and stood by the window, laughing and flicking the Vs at the man as he retreated down the path in a crimson fury.

One memorable incident involving Andrew was the saga of the flying fish. In his early teens, he had a friend whose neighbour kept koi carp – goldfish to the uninitiated – in a garden pond. His friend's father also kept fish, of the exotic variety, in a huge tank in the lounge. Andrew and his friend took a fancy to the koi carp in the pond, as Andrew had a tank in his bedroom and reckoned they'd make an interesting addition. His friend gifted the ones he poached to his dad for his birthday. A day or two later, the pond-owner happened to be in his neighbour's lounge, where he noticed koi carp swimming amongst the exotic fish in the tank. Curious, he took a closer look.

'They're my fucking fish!' he exclaimed.

Andrew's friend told him he'd been rumbled and that he'd better return the fish that were in his bedroom before he too was found out. Andrew rushed over to his friend's house with the koi carp in a bucket. They peered over the fence at the pond in the centre of next-door's garden, convinced they'd be caught if they tried to put them back. Then, with a flash of inspiration, the solution came to Andrew. One at a time he lifted the koi carp from the bucket and tossed them high in the air, over the fence, and into the pond. With admirable accuracy, all were safely returned, though perhaps a little traumatised.

Back at the Captain's Cabin, Mum dissuaded Dad from going round to the bungalow to discuss our holiday accommodation. We settled in best we could and made sure to avoid Mike.

One aspect of the holiday was to be the cause of regular discord. Andrew and money, you see, were soon parted, as if holding onto it were a curse. His favoured location for divesting himself was an arcade a minute's run from the cabin. As the week progressed, Mum and Dad tired of his profligacy and refused pleas for further advances. I, on the other hand, was miserly and took inordinate pleasure in wafting my wad of fivers in his face.

The cabin, then, was pinched and damp, lacking the comforts you might associate with the rank of captain. But at least it propelled us out, whatever the weather – rain being the usual accompaniment. We went to Land's End to see the feted end of the land and the endless sea. Andrew, once again, was cash-strapped and stroppy, walking ten paces behind, a remonstration we ignored. An hour was more than sufficient to witness the termination of terra firma, as Andrew decided it was an opportune moment to ratchet up his grievance. He clambered over a low earth bank into a field and turned his back to the car.

'I'd better go and get him,' said Mum.

'Don't bother,' said Dad as he eased out of the parking spot.

Andrew half spun on hearing the tyres rumble over chippings. Dad pulled up adjacent to give him an opportunity to get in. Andrew turned his back squarely. A patient man, Dad's patience had evaporated, and he drove on.

'Harry, stop! You can't leave him behind,' pleaded Mum.

'Just watch me.'

I looked out of the back window to see Andrew sprinting after the car.

'He's running after us,' I said, laughing.

Mum glanced backwards over her shoulder. 'Harry, we can't leave him behind.'

Dad turned to her, smiling, and said, 'Just a bit further.'

He stopped at the exit to the car park. Andrew caught up and threw himself in, bank-robber style, before we set off again. From that day on, the Wilson vacation was imbued with a happier dynamic as the demands for financial assistance ceased.

Despite the disappointment on arrival and the unfavourable weather, it was a happy holiday. There were chip suppers strolling around the harbour and evenings in the pub opposite our shack with its jukebox and plentiful Cokes. We went to a 1930s flea-pit cinema in Helston to watch the dire *Superman II*. And not forgetting an hour of thin distraction at a model village and a wander around glorious St Ives. Mum and Dad's determination that we should enjoy ourselves, in spite of a host of weak distractions, made for a memorable time.

Nearly thirty years, then, had elapsed since Portreath, 1979, as I found myself intruding on a treasured timeline. It was as if I were in *Back to the Future*, treading in the footsteps of a life that'd been innocent as to what was coming. Standing with Charlie as we waited for Anna to emerge from the shop, I looked up the road and visualised Andrew and I running from the cabin down to the beachfront with the smell of candyfloss and seaweed in our nostrils. It was all so touchable.

Anna appeared with the ice creams and we headed to the harbour to eat them, Charlie after a fashion, then I suggested we head on to our next mystery port of call. I wanted to leave. I strapped Charlie into his car seat and the touch of him and the smell of him cheered me. Like Dad, I'd always believe the other person threw the first stone.

Chapter 28

Now, when I woke each morning, rather than groaning at the prospect of a day of stacked calls from the unemployed, a sense of liberation greeted me, knowing I had the freedom to roam the countryside with my camera. In fact, knowing I had the freedom to indulge in a host of pursuits that didn't involve putting on that damned headset. I breathed in the hours that stretched ahead with an almost intoxicated excitement.

I missed the people I'd worked with. They were conscientious and dedicated, traits that I'd lacked. As for those on the other end of the line, I felt sorry for them – or at least most of them. Some had been rude and even threatening – I'd given them short shrift, a response frowned upon by Fiona, my ever-patient line manager.

There'd been no sense of public service in me, consumed as I was with resentment at being there. It was conceited of me to imagine that I was the only one who felt the anger. Many of my colleagues hated the place too, but they managed to leave it behind in the car park when they started their shift. I entered the building angry and left even more so.

'You got everything?' asked Anna.

'Think so.'

I kissed her and Charlie and was out of the door for a day's photography. My working day. The dream. The Preseli Hills were my destination, an area of Pembrokeshire I had a vague remembrance of from my biking days and was eager to explore once again. Deep down, I knew that those hills were where the heart of my photography would lie.

The sun shone as I drove out of Llangwm, camera and tripod packed, sandwiches and a flask of coffee made, Ordnance Survey maps at hand and AC/DC cranked up. It felt glorious yet somehow fragile, as if it could be snatched away. I experienced tremors of anxiety, an awareness of the need to capture income-generating images, as that was how I now contributed to the bills. But for all of the niggling uncertainty, I felt in charge of the direction of my life. Whatever happened, I could not, would not, go back to that contact centre. Not that they'd have had me back anyway; they were probably glad to see the back of me.

As a child I'd never known the hills. Family days out for the Wilson clan meant the coast: Broad Haven or Newgale or Nolton Haven, a cluster of beaches finger-spread apart. At the age of seventeen the motorbike became my passport to the interior of my home patch, weaving along high-hedged lanes accompanied by the frenetic buzz of that tiny engine and bathed in the sweet aroma of ignited two-stroke fuel. The bike was always up for it: darting up unmapped bridleways, crossing shallow streams, pootling through woods and on occasion toppling off harmlessly. The bike took me to places that felt remote and lost before chancing upon a road that led back to the known. Back to Haverfordwest.

After the accident I made the occasional return to the hills in my car during the late '80s and into the '90s, driving hastily along those same roads, stopping at a view to snap with the camera and acquiring a library of forgettable images. The off-road biking had been replaced by a series of roadside pull-overs.

Looking into the landscape, I could see where I wanted to get to but convinced myself that I couldn't reach it, that my walking range extended only to the edge of the tarmac or an adjacent ribbon of grass. I'd yet to make the mental leap into imagining that I could take photographs for a living and so lacked the motivation to push myself and wander away from the car.

Gazing out into that landscape, though, something inside of me would come alive. Fantastical thoughts rifled through my head of an imagined life unlike the barren one I led at the time. Then I'd kill the thought stone dead. Dreams were dangerous. I distrusted dreams back then. Road trips and photography had been a part of my coping strategy, an excuse not to be stuck in the house eeking out the *Daily Express* or listening to a killed-off soap star attempting to resuscitate their career on *Pebble Mill at One*. The camera had provided an illusion of creativity while eating up days.

How times had changed. I now believed in my photography – courtesy of that category win in the 'Oscars' of the Welsh Photographic Federation. I studied the landscape like a map maker charting a newly discovered territory, noticing every fold, cluster of trees, stream, farm and cottage, sensing a growing confidence in my compositions and experiencing surges of euphoria when the elements fell into place. I was beginning to realise that I was good at something.

I drove through Mynachlog-ddu, a one-blink village in the Preseli Hills, and out onto the common, pulling off the road at the bottom of a hill. I put some sandwiches and a bottle of water in my camera bag, grabbed the tripod and began stumbling upwards, concerned about a fall but gradually flushing out the spasticity in my legs and acquiring a rhythmic pace, of sorts. I was going off-piste and leaving the tarmac behind.

It was early spring but warm as summer as I strode with a delicious burn in my thighs, stopping and turning occasionally to admire the view and catch a breath. Away from the wide thoroughfare the gorse was thick, the bright custard-yellow flowers filling the air with a heady scent. Looking up at the ridge that links the peaks of the Preseli Hills, I felt energised, though there was no prospect of me getting up to that ridge. Climbing an appreciable way up that little hill would have to do.

I pushed and pushed, the gradient steepening, until after ten minutes the tank was empty. With legs like jelly, I careered over to a large boulder placed there just for me during the last Ice Age, dropped down on the stone seat and took a swig of water. As my breathing regulated and I offloaded some of the lactic in my legs, I stood and surveyed my new office, open-plan and endless. Weeks after walking out of the contact centre, I punched the air.

With a fancy to carry on upwards, I glanced behind at the summit of the hill and realised it was impossible, but it didn't matter. To get where I was had been a test to determine whether I could put some distance between myself and the car; seeing the Matchbox black dot at the bottom of the hill, I realised I'd passed that test. I'd ventured into the landscape.

I took some photographs and inhaled the views. Inhaled my new life. The change of career had been a shock to some. Dad had been obliged, of course, to point out with wry northern understatement that I was mad to give up a secure job with a good pension. But, if it's what I wanted to do, he said to go for it. It'd been as good an endorsement as I could've hoped for. More important had been Anna's support, which'd been unequivocal. She much preferred the new Dave after a day's work, upbeat and positive compared to the miserable article that used to slump in from the contact centre.

'Have you seen this?' Anna said, pointing to a feature in a *Sunday Times* supplement. A celebrated interior designer was working on a new hotel in Laugharne, Carmarthenshire, not too far from where we lived. 'They've included her email,' she continued. 'Might be worth contacting her? Never know.'

A week later, Anna and I pulled up outside the soon-to-be-opened Hurst House Hotel, situated on the salt marshes near Laugharne, for a meeting with Juliet, the designer, who was helping to transform the tired three-storey gentry farmhouse into a luxury establishment.

'I'll go in, have the meeting and see what happens,' I said, feeling embarrassed at having the temerity to imagine I could get my foot in the door. It was a high-end development and I felt out of my depth, a fraud. This Juliet would rumble me for sure, I thought. Anna was nervous for a different reason: Juliet – as mentioned in the supplement – was the partner of the singer Billy Bragg, which was a big deal apparently, though it didn't have much resonance with me.

An hour later, I emerged with a commission to produce images for incorporation into Juliet's designs. The spectre of the contact centre slipped further away as I began to realise that this photography gig might be for keeps.

I spotted it on an Ordnance Survey map: Trinant – Welsh for three streams – a remote abandoned farm full of promise. I opened a gate by a busy road, drove through and shut it. Still new to this trespassing lark, I was a bit edgy, glancing around for anyone who might object to me being there.

To my left was a dense plantation of fir trees, impenetrable and uninviting, while to my right open fields stretched away to the sparsity of houses that comprises Rosebush village about a mile away. In front of me, parallel tracks roller-coasted down a steep incline of grass and jutting stone. Common sense told me it required a 4x4 – I was in a two-wheel drive Renault estate. I couldn't park and walk down, as it was too steep and uneven for me to physically negotiate, but I knew that down there somewhere, waiting for me, was a great photograph.

Buoyed with a newfound sense of derring-do, I told myself that I just needed to be bold – I'd drive down. The stones embedded in the tracks made by previous vehicles – tractors and Land Rovers – were sizeable, and puncturing a tyre was a possibility. So, in first gear I approached the descent off centre with the passenger-side tyres on the grassy middle hump of the track and the driver's side on the outer grass verge. I tiptoed down the incline, my foot brushing the brake to stop the car running away, bringing it to a halt regularly to kill any impetus. The hundred-metre descent took an age, but I was down on a flat track and could see the prize ahead of me. The gamble had paid off.

Trinant was everything I'd hoped for. Situated in peaty grassland and surrounded by an amphitheatre of low hills, the small double-fronted farmhouse had fallen into dereliction, the roof caving in on one side. There were no window frames or front door, just empty black rectangles. A large corrugated iron shed extended out from one side of the house and corrugated pens to the front were suggestive of a former sheep farm. Sitting in the car, I was suddenly gripped by a disinclination to get any closer. In a film, Trinant would be an encounter with a ruddy-faced man with a malicious smile and a shovel! But I'd pushed my luck to get there, playing off-road Russian roulette, so I got some backbone and got out.

Opening the gate up by the road there hadn't been a wisp of wind, but down there the corrugated sheets rattled and creaked a dark lament in Trinant's own private breeze. It was creepy. I grabbed my gear and walked towards the house, braced for an apparition at one of the glassless windows; the guy with the shovel perhaps.

I stopped and looked back at the car. Car or house, I thought. After a momentary internal debate, I continued towards the house, approached the doorway and looked in. There was no one there. Of course, there was no one there; it'd been abandoned for years. Having exorcised that bit of silliness, I put some distance between myself and the building and began framing images and clicking the shutter. For all its Hammer Horror credentials, it was photographic perfection.

It began to rain and I returned to the car, frustrated. I didn't want it to be rained off, not after the risk I'd taken to get there, so decided to wait. Watching the water bead and roll down the windscreen, wipers on intermittent, I ate a sandwich and imposed my own backstory on the farm, visualising a bright past: children cantering out of the front door, swishing through the long grasses, playing hide-and-seek; mum strolling down to the stream to fill a pail; men corralling sheep. A hive of activity. A working farm. Finishing a lukewarm coffee and a Bourbon, the rain eased then stopped, so I hopped out and walked around again, eyeing-up, squinting, looking for that distillation of elements that shouted 'photograph'.

The weather indulged me as I circumnavigated the house and bagged all of the angles I desired. Just as I finished, Trinant's breeze blew a few spots in my face and I bolted for the car. I sat and listened to the increasing tempo of the pitter patter on the windscreen with a sense of elation. The gamble had paid off. Time for home.

I drove back along the flat section of track to the bottom of the incline and suddenly felt rather vulnerable, and stupid. The ascent had impossible written all over it. It was steep. Very steep. And with the rain that'd fallen, very wet. I selected first gear, let the clutch out slowly and tickled the throttle, allowing the torque of the diesel engine to carry me up. Retracing the flattened grass of my descent, I'd gone a matter of metres when the tyres lost grip and the wheels began to spin. I applied more power and span to a standstill then dropped back down to the flat stretch of track with a sense of panic.

A minor bout of punching the steering wheel and swearing loudly cleared my head enough so that I could reappraise the situation. The only option, it seemed, were the established parallel tracks, pitted with those large stones. It was a daunting prospect, but at least their jaggedness would provide grip.

I let the clutch out and began to climb at a mule's pace, bumping and jarring over the stones, conscious that an edge could puncture a tyre but beginning to sense an escape; there's always a way! About halfway up the slope I was thinking of supper with Anna and Charlie when the wheels began to spin on the wet stones and the car came to a halt. I dipped the clutch and pulled the handbrake up. Shit. I was in trouble.

I took a breath, then eased the clutch out as gently as I could while releasing the handbrake. The wheels spun. I tried again. Same result. I was stuck. I contemplated leaving the car and walking up to the main road, but it was a fanciful notion; with my balance I wouldn't have made it.

It was beginning to get dark. I looked at my phone. No signal. What the hell had possessed me? I hadn't even told anyone I was going there. I sat looking up that steep track as if strapped into a space shuttle, ready for take-off. There was only one thing for it: attack at speed.

I eased the car down to the flat section of track, again, and reversed far enough for a good run-up. Accelerating hard, I was into second by the time I hit the slope. The tyres bit into the stony surface and the car juddered and shook as it began to claw its way up. I had momentum and began to feel victorious as I passed halfway, seeing the gate up by the road. I was getting out.

Then the tyres began to lose traction. I knew that if it came to a halt I was stuffed and so floored it. With fresh impetus the Renault bolted, up and up and up till with its very last breath it pulled itself to the top and safety. I slumped in the seat and shouted a celebratory expletive, relieved as hell and thankful for my deliverance. I got out and checked the tyres, which were intact. Never again, I promised myself. Got some damned good photos, though.

In the coming months, the more photographs I took that had what could be considered artistic merit, and were being stocked in an increasing number of galleries, the more confidence I gained; that self-fulfilling prophecy of a conviction in my ability to produce images that people wished to have. It was intoxicating.

Yet, on occasion, it was difficult to shake the nagging reproach that I was some kind of fraud. I mean, if I could pull off this photography lark, then anyone could, surely. Couldn't they? After all, there'd never been even an inkling that I possessed any talent aside from providing drunken mirth on lads' nights out with streams of cutting ripostes, usually at other peoples' expense; verbally dismantling some poor bastard wasn't a foundation on which to build a happy life, but it was the only thing I was good at. The only thing that gifted me self-esteem. The more they laughed, the more I performed.

Nick would say – jokingly, but perhaps with some prescience – 'You know your problem, Dai? You're bitter.' And we'd all laugh and I'd shoot him down with some clever retort and another round would be ordered. Now though, I had, it seemed, a talent that I could be proud of. Over a year had elapsed since I'd escaped from the contact centre, and with each passing month the prospect of the dream dissolving became ever more remote. Photography, it seemed, was for keeps, each day being like winning the lottery, only without the money.

'Just walk round that corner and make your way over there,' he said, pointing. 'Then set your camera up and start photographing.'

Carwyn Jones was the director, cameraman and all-round genius in charge of producing a programme for BBC Wales, on his own. Annoyingly talented and affecting a self-deprecating humour bordering on the dark end of the spectrum, he seemed to get by on the occasional cigarette and atomic levels of nervous energy.

And there we were, filming on a summer's morning on the foreshore at Port Lion, an inlet of the Cleddau Estuary, right next door to Llangwm. I can't remember how this golden opportunity landed in my lap, but I do remember the sense of astonishment that it was happening to me.

I went around the corner as directed and awaited his call as Llangwm's resident gaggle of geese flew overhead.

'Okay. Go,' he shouted.

I set off for the choreographed square metre. There'd been a time, not that long before, when walking in front of strangers, an audience, had caused all manner of psychological hang-ups; walking across the stage in front of hundreds of people to accept my degree in Pontypridd had been a stumbling nightmare. Yet there I was, strolling in front of a camera for the later delectation of many thousands of viewers. I strode round the corner with that old mantra running through my head – pick your feet up – and reached the designated spot, planting the tripod and setting the camera on top. I screwed the filter holder onto the lens and plugged in the cable release with deliberate, artisanal care. As Carwyn filmed, I looked into the middle distance, eye-acting the scene, and falling into the performance. I loved it.

Having shot the photography bit, I spoke to camera about my journey from failed stunt motorcyclist to the unlikely photographer I'd become. Sitting there by the river with the sun gaining strength, an early mist burning off and the scent of seaweed in my nostrils, I felt invincible.

The programme aired weeks later. I was excited, and nervous, at how I'd present physically; no one wants to see their imperfections in glorious technicolour. Like most people of my generation, I'd grown up with a near reverence for the output of that box of sound and vision in the corner of the lounge. Television was religion and seeing myself on it was a surreal experience.

After the programme it seemed that wherever I went there were pats on the back and congratulations, which was heartening and encouraging. Best of all, though, people were beginning to acknowledge me as that photographer bloke, which felt special. Better than that angry shouty bloke from the contact centre.

And it got better.

'What do you see as the finished product?'

Peter Gill, managing director of Cardiff-based publisher Graffeg, looked impassive, awaiting my response.

'Well. I suppose a hardback book with... I dunno... fifty... black and white images of Pembrokeshire, with... maybe, er... a caption accompanying each image?' I replied, with all the conviction of a salesman trying to flog a Sinclair C5.

The problem was, I couldn't believe that I was in this man's office making a pitch for a book to be published of my work. And after the garbage I'd just spouted I doubted very much he'd be inclined to proceed. On the Richter scale of visual cues, Peter registered a barely discernible tremor, the ultimate poker face. I had a sinking feeling. After all, who on earth would place their faith in such a jabbering fool? He considered what I'd so ineloquently said, glanced again at the photographs I'd brought with me and said softly, 'Okay, let's do it.'

Inside I erupted, while outwardly affecting an attitude of relaxed indifference, as if it'd been a foregone conclusion. We agreed on a format, the content and an approximate publication date. And that was it. I had my first book in the pipeline.

I floated out of his office to my car and sat in the driver's seat paralysed with joy while staring at the building I'd just left. A book with my name on it; how the hell did that happen? As the minutes passed, the joy receded as doubts began to creep in. What if I couldn't bag the photographs I needed? What if Peter had second thoughts? He was bound to. What if, what if, what if. And, the most terrifying 'what if' of all: what if the whole fraudulent edifice came crashing down and I had to get a proper job?

I mean, ditching a civil service job to become a landscape photographer had been mad. To secure a commission to produce imagery for a high-end hotel in Laugharne then making a film for the BBC had magnified that madness ten-fold. And now, a publisher had agreed to produce a book of my work, having been subjected to the direst of pitches. Was it all some sick practical joke? Was someone going to jump out at any moment and say, 'Sorry, Dave, back to the contact centre for you, pal.'

Shell-shocked and conflicted, I drove home down the M4, a journey that'd been a recurrent motif in my life, in yet another guise: soon-to-be-published author. Probably. It certainly beat my last retreat from the city as a failed law student, incubating an imminent breakdown. All I had to do was get out and photograph the shortfall of images to reach the agreed fifty and write the copy. No pressure, then.

I embarked on numerous mini-expeditions across the county in search of images for the book, often pushing myself to the point of physical collapse. But of all of the trials of stamina, it was Barafundle Bay that came closest to breaking me.

One mid-February morning before sun up, I parked at Stackpole Quay and set off on the half-mile trek over the headland to one of the most beguiling beaches in Wales. I felt taut and energised and as ready for the challenge as it was possible to be. Leaving the car park, I ascended a flight of earthen steps which opened out onto elevated views along the coast in both directions. Strolling with a rare vigour, I surged onward, my feet catching the odd raised sod and bracing myself for a tumble that never came.

I arrived at the summit of the steep path that leads down to the beach and lay down on a low earth bank, racked with intense leg burn, my lungs rasping. To anyone else the walk would've been a mere warm-up to an onward hike of miles, but to me that half-mile was a marathon effort. But I'd done it. I was there.

Once recovered, I set my tripod and camera up. Looking through the viewfinder, my heart raced at the sweep of the bay and the headland opposite, with the stone arch in the foreground, a feature synonymous with Barafundle.

To trek to a wondrous location to witness the sun rise is special and as I awaited its arrival, I thought back to that morning in Avebury twenty years earlier when I'd lent against a stone as the sun lasered across the fields. And now, as I looked east over the sea, I saw that it was coming again. Gradually, the beach and headland lit up and I started clicking the shutter release, imagining the view fixing itself onto the camera's sensor. I didn't see another soul, and it was as if the show were just for me.

Now for the return. I'd blown a gasket getting there and doubted whether I had enough in the tank to get back. Every bit of me ached and throbbed. I needed a strategy, a distraction to take my mind off the tiredness in my legs, and so decided to count my steps, both to preoccupy and motivate me.

Off I set – one, two, three, four – and on it went, hitting the tens, fifties, hundreds. At a thousand steps and a dozen semi-trips, I dropped down onto a raised bank by the side of the path. I was empty, my limbs refusing to countenance another step. Lying on the dewy grass facing the sun, eyes closed, my world became an orangey hue, with black-dot floaters darting around like pond life. I began to uncoil to the sound of waves surging against the cliffs away over the edge. Spent but happy, I drifted off.

'You alright?'

Startled, I half opened my eyes against the glare of the sun to make out the silhouette of a man standing over me.

'Everything okay?' he pressed.

'Yeah, just resting.'

'Okay. If you're sure.'

'Yeah, honestly. I'm fine. Thanks.'

My thwarted Good Samaritan continued on his way as I sensed a replenishing. Grabbing a fence post, I pulled myself up and continued – one, two, three, four. I reached the car and headed home to bed.

Carwyn from the BBC came calling again, our first collaboration having been well received. He was producing a series called *My Secret Wales*, searching for those obscure gems that loiter off the beaten track, and I knew exactly where to take him.

Glyn Griffiths had lived in his cottage at Treleddyd Fawr, near St Davids, all his life. I'd discovered it by chance a couple of years before, when Anna got a book from the library about unique Welsh buildings in which Glyn's cottage featured. I remember the first time I walked up the grass track leading to the low house, hunkered down out of the fierce storms that rip off the Irish Sea and across St Davids Head.

The stunted door and teeny windows were splodged with a sky-blue gloss, the whitewashed walls were a weathered grey and the limed grout on the bowing roof looked in need of repair. It was old and tired and I loved it, as well as being rather surprised that the curators of St Fagans – the Welsh Folk Museum near Cardiff (an open-air zoo for endangered buildings of historical value) – hadn't whisked it away to be rebuilt stone by stone.

I knocked on the door and braced myself. A bolt slapped back and the door edged open. A small, whiskery man with gale-cracked features, dressed in a tatty, dog-toothed jacket and even tattier V-neck, emerged, squinting into the daylight.

'Oh, hello. Sorry to bother you...'

He turned his ear to me. 'Speak up. Can't hear you,' he said.

'Sorry to bother you,' I repeated, 'I'm a photographer and I was wondering if I could photograph your beautiful cottage, please.'

It was January and biting cold, with a keen wind whipping up from Whitesands Bay, as he invited me in. He was, I soon discovered, almost blind, yet there I was, sitting chatting to him in his house, an old-fashioned trust in the goodness of strangers.

As the conversation progressed, it was apparent that he saw himself as the protector of a piece of built heritage, a vernacular style that, though once a common sight, had disappeared across the county. This cottage was it, a last survivor, and he was determined it'd continue in its original state after his days.

'I've left it to the National Trust, see. An important building, boy,' he said, with a resolution that stirred me. He appeared to be in his eighties, though when asked he dodged specifics.

He sat by the *simne fawr* – big chimney – its fire long extinguished, the space now occupied by a defunct telly and a scattering of plastic bags. The sole source of warmth was an electric fan heater, acting like a lit match in a walk-in freezer. With my North Face jacket zipped up, he peeled an apple, oblivious to the morgue-like chill while describing the Heath Robinson safety measures he incorporated when repairing the roof in the summer months.

'I bring a rope up with me, see, and ties one end round my ankle. Other round the chimney. Then I grout and patch. Those winds are a bugger. Do a lot of damage.'

The length of rope was calculated so that if he fell from the roof, he wouldn't hit the ground. I squirmed at what the jolt would've done to his hip joint though. I asked if I could photograph him, a request he was only too willing to grant. He then invited me to explore the house. I peered with warm curiosity at the handmade planked doors, blacksmith-beaten hinges and latches, the many-layered wallpaper draped loosely like full-length paper curtains over the rough stone walls and a settle that had witnessed thousands of conversations.

After that first visit, I called whenever I was in the area, conscious that Glyn was indeed the last of a dying breed, a throwback to a self-sufficient generation that desired not much more than hearty social interaction, a regular meal and the affirmation of the outdoors to feel fulfilled. I liked calling on him.

When Carwyn and I turned up to film, Glyn was canny enough to negotiate a fee before committing – the place didn't run itself, after all. The interview I did with him by the *simne fawr* is very special to me. He spoke of his early life, his parents farming the land and his determination to preserve the building for the nation.

Months later, I heard he was in hospital. In the interior gloom, with his failing eyesight, he'd fallen and hit his head against a cupboard. One of the pros of being hospitalised was a bath; when I visited him on the ward, he looked pristine, with the decades scrubbed off.

While in hospital, public health took the opportunity to enter the cottage and evict his housemates; a colony of rats had burrowed under the stone walls, emerging inside out of the earth floor in a sort of reverse Great Escape.

Against cosseting social-service advice, Glyn was determined to go home on discharge, but it was short-lived. Within a year, he left Treleddyd Fawr for the last time and moved into a residential home near Fishguard. I visited him, and he was warm, fed and happy. He had friends, and the staff adored him. He died in 2013, aged eighty something. The house now belongs to the National Trust.

I reached the agreed fifty photographs and settled down to write the introduction and extended captions to go alongside the images. That boy on the motorbike could never have had any comprehension of the odyssey I'd been on. I'd explored every corner of my home patch, driving along myriad Pembrokeshire lanes and coast roads. Trawling my thoughts, I put into words my motivation, the emotional response to the compositions, and the sheer joy of roaming the landscape. The sheer joy of freedom.

Describing the patient, yet glorious, waiting for the light, I began to feel like I was writing my very own self-help manual. A manifesto of rebirth, this book would be an expression of who I was and how far I'd come. How satisfying it would be, I mused, to have a foreword written to the book by an independent voice, a person who could validate my efforts.

One day, I went to Narberth to restock The Golden Sheaf gallery. It was and still is one of my very favourite outlets, brimming with spirit-lifting laughter. I always leave feeling brighter, especially when a strong coffee is brought out.

'Guess who bought one of your framed photos the other day?' said a lady that worked there.

'Dunno.'

'That Jamie Owen from BBC Wales. The newsreader?'

'Who'd have thought it,' I said casually, while inwardly feeling rather chuffed.

Jamie Owen had been an anchor on the regional news for years. As one of the most recognisable faces in Wales, he spoke confidingly to the nation each night, as if sitting in our living rooms relaying events face-to-face. And to top it all, he was a Pembrokeshire boy. The perfect candidate. I came home, wrote an unctuous letter inviting him to write a foreword and posted it off to the BBC in Cardiff, convinced I'd never hear from him.

Two days later, the phone rang. It was him. He professed to have been delighted to receive my request and that it'd be a pleasure to write the foreword. The beautiful piece he wrote betrayed a shared love of Pembrokeshire and its landscape, and with his endorsement the book was wrapped up and ready for publication.

Chapter 29

In January of 2009 we were blessed with the arrival of Harry, and all those core-quaking emotions with which we'd greeted Charlie came flooding back. I was overwhelmed studying newborn Harry just as I'd been with his brother, and again, I cried with disbelief.

Considering ourselves, now, to be seasoned parents, we brought him home from hospital without the trepidation that'd accompanied Charlie's maiden journey; we were old hands at spotting the nuanced cries to action stations. It also heralded the return of the ebullient Gill, as we won again in the health visitor stakes. She knew we could ride the bike so her visits were relaxed as she went about her weighing and measuring of Harry over the weeks, plotting his growth in the little red book of his development. She drank tea and made us laugh, making us think we were doing just fine. And though, again, she left colic off the wary list, we knew it'd make an appearance and were ready with the dropper of orange-flavoured wind dispenser. The buggy pushing was easier too; Harry was more a winger compared to Charlie the prop forward. There was a sense of completion to our lives which Anna and I could never have imagined in our craziest dreams as our little house accommodated the Wilson four.

Anna and I went to register Harry's birth. The registrar conducted the formalities with cheerful efficiency and after we'd signed the documentation, she turned to me.

'Mr Wilson, do you mind if I ask you a question?'

'Course not.'

'Where is Trinant?' she asked. 'I bought a print of it from a gallery for my mum. She was born there.'

She wanted to take her mum back, to see it perhaps for the last time. After my – eventually successful – attempt at getting back up the stony track I advised going in a 4x4. The encounter with the registrar was affirmation of the love that I felt for my work, a connection with those stories out there in the landscape. I left the registry office with visions of her young mum running through the grasses that surround Trinant just as I'd imagined when I was there.

I'd photographed another abandoned farm not far from Trinant. At an exhibition of my work a couple of years before a lady who knew the farm studied the image and then told me about how the farmer's daughter had gone to live in Japan in the 1980s, an unusual path for someone from the Preseli Hills. It'd been just her and her father on the farm. A year or so after she left, he too left one day and never came back. Nobody knew where he went. He just went. Once again it gave the photograph I took of the farm and the landscape it sat in that vital human element. The story.

The book launch for *Pembrokeshire* was held at the Kooywood art gallery in Cardiff. I arrived early and was looking at some paintings when Jamie Owen strolled in and so I went over to introduce myself, a little nervous at being in the presence of regional televisual royalty!

'Hi, Jamie. I'm David. Thanks for coming.'

He shook my hand.

'Lovely to meet you,' he said. 'And thank you so much for inviting me along. It's a real honour.'

An honour? It was a good start. The event was well attended, with many of the guests vying for his attention, which he dished out generously; I realised I'd be playing second fiddle. In between taps on his shoulder and gentle tugs of his arm, we managed to quaff a few reds and talk of home and the powerful draw it still exerted on him even after all his travels and work assignments throughout Britain and the world.

'I go back whenever I can. Helps me unwind,' he said.

He was of Pembrokeshire and it'd never leave him. Rhian, the gallery owner, called for everyone's attention and handed the floor over to Jamie who made a short speech about the book and how it dovetailed with his own innate sense of Pembrokeshire. We then took questions and talked of our favoured featured locations, indulging in a tourist-board sell of the county.

'So, what's next?' he asked, bringing the talky bit to a close.

'Next? Must be joking. I need a rest – camera's going on eBay tomorrow!' I replied.

It got a laugh, but a bit of me meant it, as if the achievement of the book was enough in itself. I could call myself an author and that felt good. But a bigger part of me craved more books; three, four, a shelfful. And having mused about the possibility, I couldn't unthink it. It began to nag at me.

It was a memorable night and the beginning of a friendship, which many years later was to coalesce around something that, looking back, was perhaps inevitable.

Publishing my first book, then, opened a benign Pandora's Box, and I couldn't simply close the lid. I felt compelled to come up with another idea, embark on another adventure. I was realising the dream, finally, of that hopeful boy sitting in the wheelchair on the grass at Rookwood hospital a quarter of a century earlier. *Pembrokeshire* was also selling well and my confidence was high. Perhaps, I thought, for the next book I could push the bounds, stretch myself, both photographically and physically. So, after much deliberation I decided on a daunting and grand project: a book of Wales. No half measures, then.

I put the idea to my publisher, Graffeg, sketching out some vague notions of what such a book would encompass, and much to my surprise they gave me the go-ahead after yet another woefully thin pitch. I signed the contract and set about getting on with it before they changed their mind. Logistically it would be a far vaster enterprise than *Pembrokeshire,* which had, after all, been a manageable wander around my back yard. I was unsure of my ability to sustain what would be a punishing project but I'd set myself up for it so had to crack on. I was bloody terrified.

It was 2010 and the New Labour project burnt itself out after a thirteen-year run with the eviction of Gordon Brown from Downing Street and the installation of David Cameron. Though Cameron was of a different political persuasion to Tony Blair (who'd passed the prime ministerial baton onto the hapless Brown) they were cut from the same slick PR cloth, and prone to the fatal indulgence of all deluded leaders – hubris. Blair had invaded Iraq and Cameron eventually gambled on Europe and lost.

Snowdonia had been calling for the five years since I'd become a photographer, a delayed rendezvous with mountains proper. From books and online research, I gleaned a self-evident truth: it was inhospitable terrain for a person with limited mobility. For a person who fell, often. Compared to the undulating bumps of Pembrokeshire, Snowdonia is an angular land of giants, the mountainous crucible of many of the foundation myths of a nation. And it'd be bloody hard to get about that rock-strewn landscape safely. As Anna and I drove up the coast road skirting Cardigan Bay, I was anxious, afraid of being defeated by that terrain. This new career of mine was an anomalous and occasionally frustrating endeavour; a landscape photographer denied access to much of the landscape. In moments of doubt, I felt like I was feeding off scraps while the physically able brigade ventured off for the feast with their loaded rucksacks and chunky hiking boots. Bastards!

We booked into a guest house in Llanberis, the perfect base for exploring. The next morning, after a monumental breakfast, I fully took in that brutal landscape of lorry-sized boulders and cloud-blanketed summits, a film-set-perfect vista around every bend. I found it overpowering and formidable. Too much to take in. There's a condition known as Stendhalism, which can best be described as a sense of visual and emotional overload experienced by visitors to overwhelmingly beautiful locations. The nineteenth-century French writer Stendhal had become unhinged on a tour of Florence and, having been there myself, I have an inkling of how he felt. That first morning in the mountains my head swam and my heart raced as I was gripped by a sense of panic. What on earth do you photograph when everything screams out to be photographed?

We pored over an OS map and decided to head for the Ogwen Valley, which scours its way down to Caernarfon and the sea from under the steely gaze of Tryfan, one of the highest peaks in Snowdonia. At the very top of the valley, in the armpit of Tryfan, we stumbled across Blaen y Nant, a tiny whitewashed farmhouse, seemingly hewn from the rock and nestling between waterfalls. I had to photograph it.

We approached the front door and knocked.

'Oh, hi. Sorry to bother you,' I said. 'Would you mind if I took some photographs around the farm?'

'Don't see why not. Help yourself,' came the welcome reply from Gwyn Thomas, a bright man in his sixties for whom English, I soon deduced, was a second division language. 'Be careful, mind. Very uneven.'

Anna and I set out to roam the parts of the farm that allowed for my unsteadiness, basking in a romantic setting straight out of a Richard Wilson painting of the eighteenth century. It was the edge of wildness, stone-hard and hostile, so not a good place to fall. Fortuitously, as a photographer I have no yearning to scale mountain peaks or trudge across empty wilderness, all of which are inaccessible to me anyway. Certainly, I'm in awe of such natural vastness, the bigness of it, but my photography is about storytelling and intimacy and the human imprint on the landscape. And for that I require farmhouses, receding roads, dry-stone walls, a line of washing flapping in a breeze in the shadow of a mountain.

When we got back to the yard, Gwyn invited us in for a cuppa. We sat at the kitchen table within the comforting orbit of his hissing Aga as he told us of his upbringing on a farm a bit further down the valley and how he'd arrived at Blaen y Nant. He spoke with a near religious certainty of the farm he'd painstakingly transformed back to an organic concern, enticing a return of bird and wildlife species that'd deserted the land decades ago. Then there were the winters.

'Terrible snows when I was a boy,' he said. 'Was my job to keep the shovel in the house... to dig our way out. One morning, Dad called up the stairs. "Gwyn, where's the shovel?" I'd only gone and left it in the shed. Out the bedroom window I went. Dug my way back in. Didn't make that mistake again, I can tell you.'

He pushed a plate of fruitcake towards us as he reminisced about his dad.

'Worked down Penrhyn quarry,' he said, gesturing to the bottom of the valley, 'down by Bethesda. In the sheds splitting slate. Hundreds a day. And he ran the farm! Never stopped. Splitting those bloody slates, though... did for his lungs in the end. The dust, see.'

He sat there proud and taut, seeming to want for little aside from his farm and the mountains and we could've listened to him for hours. Gwyn lived in an incredible location, but within a landscape that could be harsh and which required a single-mindedness to get by. A physical, and mental, resilience. He was no hermit, though, but rather a gregarious man with plenty going on down in Bethesda and beyond. He gave a rueful smile and said that when he got old and felt the time approaching, he'd somehow make it up Tryfan with the dog and just lie down and wait. He certainly didn't strike me as a man who'd ever wasted a moment gazing out of a window wondering how to improve his lot.

Lifted by Gwyn's humble philosophy, the next day we headed for Cwmorthin, near Blaenau Ffestiniog. Parking in a dusty clearing in the village of Tanygrisiau, I saw up close the mountains clothed in millions of pieces of slate slag, the discarded remnants of a once great industry, and which seemed just a hair trigger from avalanche. Sitting on the tailgate of the car, I put my hiking boots on and looked at the initial incline strewn with large stones. Anna saw my unease.

'Sure you want to do it?' she asked.

I was as unsure as I'd ever been, but said, 'Yep, let's go,' with sufficient enthusiasm to hoodwink her.

I used the tripod to steady and propel myself up the slope, eyes glued to the floor, picking my way between stones, wary of turning an ankle. It was early April and T-shirt warm as Anna strode beside me. Once my walking-gait had limbered up, I began to embrace the challenge of the ascent, with the occasional half-stumble but avoiding a fall. After ten minutes with the odd breather, the path evened out onto a wide track that led onwards to our destination. An endorphin burn drove my legs, my lungs sucking in fuel.

'Dave. Slow down,' cautioned Anna. 'You can't keep this up.'

I felt as alive as I ever had as we strode and strode with the odd stop, eventually reaching a lake. And what a reward: Cwmorthin, an abandoned slate mine, secreted away in a mountain valley. Sinewy men once disappeared into tunnels in the half-dark to blast out slabs of slate to be split in the sheds above ground. A smattering of roofless buildings, themselves constructed of slate, fringed the lake abutting the mountains. In its heyday men lived in barracks, rising early to enter the mountain. Now, it was so still and peaceful, with birdsong the only sound. We found a patch of mossy grass at the water's edge and lay down in the sun, staring up at the sky and listening to the birds. It was strange to imagine it'd ever been anything but idyllic. Lying on that mossy bank beside the woman with my name on, and her aside the man who belonged to her, felt perfect and I could've lain there for hours. We were indissoluble. As one.

There'd been snow in Pembrokeshire. It was an event. As ever though, it was a light dusting destined to thaw all too quickly, with just enough time to roll a slushy snowman. The Brecon Beacons, on the other hand, had been gifted huge snow, the kind that encourages the sledgers out – and the photographers. The Beacons was another area of Wales I'd yet to explore and so I hit the A40, stopping at Llandeilo halfway to capture some oak trees in the snow at Dinefwr Park. Trudging across the white landscape, I photographed the stark, leafless shapes, becoming cold and leaking energy, before returning to the car. Sipping a coffee with the heater on full blast, I decided to carry on to the Beacons in spite of wet socks, making a mental note to invest in a pair of water-tight boots. Perhaps jeans hadn't been a wise choice either – ankle soaked by now – but I was thankful for the long-johns which Anna had insisted on; I really was remiss when it came to dressing for the outdoors.

The Brecon Beacons differ to Snowdonia where the mountains look like – well, mountains really. Snowdon – or Yr Wyddfa as it's now known – and the rest of the gang rise from a wide, rocky base to a pencil-sharp peak. The grass-covered Beacons, though, look more like a pack of wolfhounds stretched out having a kip; high and long and sinuous. But, as with Snowdonia, there's still a sense of overwhelming compositional choice; that film-set-perfect headache. I probed lanes and tracks in the car but the snow away from the tarmac was deep and the land inaccessible, at least to me. I did see a man wading through a field up to his thighs, the furious look on his face suggesting he'd made the wrong decision. Even with a regression to the restrictive roadside photography of old, though, I bagged some pleasing photographs of an epic landscape.

By late afternoon, with a few hours of the Beacons under my belt, I drove into Talybont-on-Usk as the light was dimming. Logic dictated that I rejoin the A40 a mile away and begin the journey home on well-gritted roads but the Beacons were all shiny and new to me and I didn't want to let go. I consulted the map and plotted what appeared to be an achievable minor detour – well, okay, not that minor perhaps – with the proposed route taking me past the Talybont Reservoir and over a mountain pass to the Pontsticill Reservoir. It wasn't a great distance and on reaching the Pontsticill I could drop the few miles down to Merthyr Tydfil and join the Heads of the Valleys dual carriageway west. There was a mountain pass to traverse but there was no harm in having a prod and, if the going got tough, I could always turn round. As I headed towards the pass, I noticed that the road was blanket-white and tread-free, overlooked by the gritters and it seemed other vehicles too. Not for the first time in my life an arrogant faith drove me on, drowning out the nagging voice that questioned the wisdom of my route. I knew I was taking a risk but was convinced that all would be fine. He who dares, and all that.

I arrived at the foot of the pass which would take me over the mountain to the Pontsticill Reservoir. The snow was deeper and still there was no evidence of other vehicles having been that way. Like a First World War general blithely sending men over the top, I knew that I was embarking on an ill-advised course of action, but I'd committed to it so had to continue. Anyway, it was just a bit of snow: first gear and crawl up. No problem. I could always turn back. Too many people had lost any sense of adventure, I thought. I mean, would Scott have reached the South Pole if he'd been required to fill out a risk assessment? Actually, that wasn't the best analogy, as we all know what happened on his return journey. Anyway, nothing was going to stop my attempt. Not even common sense.

To the right of the narrow mountain road was a snow-covered grass verge which gave way to a steep drop through woods to a stream. To my left, the edge of the road dropped into a deep drainage gulley which abutted a near-vertical forested slope that stretched up out of sight. I set off. The first couple of hundred metres were plain sailing as the tyres crunched over virgin snow. Then the road steepened and very soon the wheels span to a standstill. I applied the brakes and to my gut-wrenching terror the car began to slide backwards.

There was no barrier to prevent the car from sliding across the grass verge and down the steep slope to my right, which would've resulted in serious consequences amongst the trees or worse in the swollen stream at the bottom. Instinctively I turned the steering wheel hard left, hoping, praying, that the rear of the car would slew towards the drainage gulley instead. At worst I'd drop the back wheels into it but at least it'd stop the slide. The back end veered left – as hoped – and as the car began to slew sideways the edges of the tyres dug into the snow, momentum was shed and I came to a halt across the road's width with the front of the car pointing a little uphill.

I got out and edged my way gingerly towards the boot, not wanting to slip and fall. In the fading light I could see that the rear wheels were inches from the gulley but hadn't dropped in. Phew. Assessing the situation, aside from my good fortune at still being on the road, I appeared to be in an unrecoverable position. There wasn't enough room to attempt a three-point turn to face downhill, as the width of the road was little more than the length of the car.

Abandon the car and walk to get help, I thought. It wasn't so much an option as a fantasy really. With the physical abilities of an undamaged person, I could've made my way down the snowy pass to the valley and trudged the mile back to the last house I'd passed. It was getting dark and the temperature was plummeting but it would've been feasible. Embarrassing but feasible. But that course of action wasn't available. That mile could just as well have been a hundred. A thousand. Getting down to the valley alone would've required a miraculous incident-free descent; my impaired muscle function and compromised balance weren't a good mix on slippery surfaces. Once fallen, I couldn't have got back to my feet. And I would've fallen, guaranteed. Phone for help? A look at my mobile confirmed the worst: no reception. Panic and a sense of world-beating stupidity engulfed me. I was as trapped as if I'd been in the wilderness of Canada.

In the blackening twilight I looked down the hill. The steeper part on which I was stranded gave way to a more gradual gradient within about fifty or so metres. Further down, out of sight, and I'd be in the valley, back to safety. How to get there though? I dragged a foot through the snow. It was dry and powdery and with ease I managed to expose ice-free tarmac. That tarmac could be the key, I thought. The car was sideways across the road but facing slightly uphill. If I could just manoeuvre it so that it was pointing directly upwards again, then maybe I could drop down to the more manageable gradient and then the valley. Considering how the car had slid merrily of its own accord into its current position it was straw-clutching of epic proportions but I couldn't walk out and I couldn't phone for help. No one would be coming that way, not if they had any sense. I was stranded.

It was then that it began to snow heavily, big feathery flakes like volcanic ash coating everything. I thought of Anna and the boys and wanted to cry but knew that I couldn't. I had to focus, remain calm, make the right decision. Not that there was a raft of decisions for me to choose from. No one knew I was in that area as I'd given just a vague geographic idea of where I was going, and the Beacons are vast. With fresh snow and nightfall coming I was running out of time to implement any plan of escape. Mind, calling whatever it was that I hadn't quite formulated at that point a plan was perhaps imbuing my hunch about the tarmac with undeserved merit. The truth was, I was facing a night in the car and it was beginning to get cold. Very cold.

Tarmac or bust then. I started the engine and put it into gear. I turned the front wheels uphill and brushed the accelerator. The tyres bit momentarily then span. Bugger. Gently wouldn't do it. So, I floored the throttle, the wheels spun madly and with the engine howling like a banshee, I felt it; the tyres gaining traction. The tyres kissing tarmac.

I continued the heavy throttling, ripping away snow and gripping tarmac, slowly turning upwards. There was a claggy stench of overheating and I feared the engine was about to blow, but as if beginning to emerge from a nightmare, I found myself facing directly up the hill. The first part of the plan had been accomplished. All I had to do now was hold my nerve and drop down, avoiding a slide or, worse, going over the edge to my right. At that moment God came into my life as I prayed like hell for salvation, muttering the shallow devotions of someone in a fix, and how I'd be far more attentive to the big man if he got me out of there. It was shameless canvassing, but it felt good. In neutral, I took my foot off the brake and the car began to drop back. I let it roll a few metres then gently pressed the brake pedal. The temptation was to let it roll further before braking, to get out more quickly. But I couldn't allow the car to gain speed. I repeated the stop-start process dozens of times and reached the less steep section of the pass.

It was only now after this initial success that I acknowledged how dark it was. Not town dark but cloak black. The road snaked downwards behind me but I couldn't see it in the mirrors. So, selecting reverse gear, I kept the clutch depressed, and used the white reversing light as the dimmest of illumination. I could just about see the shadowy outline of the drainage gulley to my left in the wing mirror and used it as a guide as to where I should be on the road. I studied that gulley as if my life depended on it and after what seemed an eternity, I reached the safety of the valley. I'd escaped. I got out of the car, shaking with disbelief at how reckless I'd been, and slammed a fist into the roof in anger. Never again. First the escape from Trinant, and now the inestimably more insane gamble of attempting to scale a mountain pass in deepening snow in a two-wheel drive car. My blind faith in 'things turning out okay' had been smashed. A month later I drove out of the Volvo garage in Swansea in a four-wheel-drive estate. I'd learnt my lesson – for the time being.

Making the Wales book was revealing as, after all the years that'd passed since my accident, I bagged feats of endurance I hadn't imagined possible. The days were punishing, having to function within the confines, and intense frustrations, of a compromised body. I make no bones about it, but dragging my carcass around is tough. The withered muscles, balance issues that often felt like a precarious ground-level high-wire act and a lack of stamina had to be factored into every outing. On bad days even getting out of my chair and fetching a coffee from the kitchen sparks an anguished internal debate as to the feasibility of getting to the damned kettle. But on the good days I travelled and took photographs and did well.

Back at the turn of the millennium my physical world had become less adventurous, as I shunned challenges. And each challenge I turned down compounded an ever-decreasing willingness to take on subsequent challenges; a vicious circle of narrowing horizons. In the immediate years before becoming a photographer then, I'd shrunk psychologically and become a less brave person.

My state of mind, and fitness, weren't helped by a string of office jobs, which by their nature are deskbound and sedentary. I wouldn't have admitted it at the time, but I'd given up. I didn't go to the gym anymore, and so the strength and resilience I'd slogged to acquire had, to an extent, gone. Why did I stop going to the gym? Simple – I'd hit the ceiling of potential recovery of the pre-accident me and felt there was no more to extract. I lost the motivation. I became lazy. There were hopeful interludes after my gym days when I experienced a physical renaissance of sorts, such as tackling those flights of steps at our honeymoon hotel in Amalfi. I returned from Italy feeling that maybe I could turn things around but soon lapsed. As the noughties progressed those purple patches seemed to belong to another lifetime. I became a less capable person. And, repeating the most damning indictment of all, a less brave person.

Leaving the contact centre to become a landscape photographer meant changing my mindset and taking on challenges that were surely impossible, such as the trek to Barafundle. Even as I'd walked up the steps out of the carpark and onto the headland that led to the beach, I thought about turning around and going home. But I didn't. I kept putting one foot in front of the other and got here. It was a defining trek that helped to bolster my physical confidence.

But whereas Barafundle had been a single marathon effort, the Wales book turned out to be a regular triathlon of pain. One day trip of many summed it up. At seven in the morning, I set off for the Cambrian Mountains in north-east Ceredigion for the first location on an expansive, and wildly optimistic, shot list that'd devour over two hundred miles in the day. Overoptimism had become my default which I suppose was better than pessimism. Certainly, my newfound enthusiasm was at odds with the negative outlook that'd once dogged me. Finding something you're good at helps I suppose.

My itinerary took me from the Cambrian Mountains over the border into Powys and down the Elan Valley, fanning out in all directions and covering huge swathes of territory as if taking part in a meticulous manhunt. It was a grand tour of a day with numerous mini-treks to capture images. I should, perhaps, clarify what a mini-trek could entail – as little as metres from the car, or if the location demanded, upwards of hundreds. Lots of short strolls, the cumulative effect being a gradual depletion of my reserves as the day progressed. The alternative to mini-treks was a single long trek to one location, à la Barafundle. Walk there, return to the car and go home, usually to bed.

Anyway, this particular day ended at around eight in the evening in Rhayader in mid-Wales, having exited the Elan Valley. Time for home. The two-hour drive quickly became torture as the quiet troubled hints my body had been making since late afternoon became desperate screams; I didn't just hit the wall but went through it with all the bricks landing on top of me. When I got home Anna helped me out of the car and supported me into the house and upstairs to bed. I ache all of the time regardless but that night the aching morphed into something akin to pain; everything hurt, even my face. I slept through to late afternoon the next day and spent the day after that slumped flu-like in my chair, drinking coffee and napping. Like someone with the hangover from hell questioning their drinking habits, I wondered whether it was worth it. Once recovered though, I downloaded the photographs and was reminded of why I'd put myself through it.

Wales is a small country, most of which lends itself to day-long excursions. Or, as I discovered, day-long triathlons. For the furthermost regions of the country – Snowdonia especially – I stayed in B&Bs. A sense of anticipation accompanied huge breakfasts as I fuelled up for hard yet fulfilling days. I loved the day trips from home too, packing sufficient food to get me through to late afternoon, when an exhaustion of supplies would excuse a takeaway on the way home, the gratuitous pleasure of empty carbs at the end of a tough day. Heading home via Carmarthen a certain well-known fried chicken emporium would be patronised, but my favourite day's end was chips in the car by Aberaeron yacht club watching the sun fall into the sea, while looking forward to getting home to Anna and the boys.

As for the planning of the book, there was no rationale as to what to include or indeed exclude. Wales is a photogenic country, which is at once a godsend and a headache, and I omitted locations that some people invest with huge affection. So, as with my first book, *Pembrokeshire*, and indeed all the photographs I've ever taken, it was to be a selection of bits of Wales that appealed to me. It would be my story of my country. My indulgence, if you like.

Whether arriving at a location that I'd researched or just happened upon by chance, I was never anything but awed and excited, scanning the terrain for compositions and snapping away in my head before I'd even got the camera out. If it were an abandoned farm – a favoured discovery – I'd be a little anxious; what if someone appeared and asked what the hell I was doing there. There'd be an initial urgency, at least till I'd bagged some insurance shots, so that if I lost the light or those threatening clouds overhead burst, I'd have something to show for my efforts. Then I could relax and enjoy my surroundings. Enjoy the freedom. Photograph at my leisure. Perhaps break off and have lunch. Make it an event.

As the months slipped by and the project progressed, I sensed a crescendo building, an anticipation of completion. A certainty that I'd actually publish a book of photographs of Wales. What'd seemed impossible at the start had become probable and then definite. Driving around a country gave me a lot of time to think, mostly of my boys and Anna, but also of a hotchpotch of plans and schemes, hopes and aspirations, and, of course, reminiscences. Always reminiscences! I'd become a sentimental old-ish fool as I thought of all the good times, and occasionally the bad. I recalled holidays with the lads way back when, aghast that perhaps a quarter of a century had passed when it seemed so recent. So touchable. Gramps had made a point of telling me when I was in my early teens that life sped up as you got older. I'd laughed at him, but he wasn't wrong.

There was also a gorgeous disbelief that driving around this land taking photographs was my job. I'd been a photographer for seven years and still it felt special. Still it felt like a privilege. That I was lucky. I thought of the meetings in decades gone by with well-meaning Jobcentre advisors who, having ticked the disability box – a label that made me retch with anger – would suggest jobs suitable to their perception of my limitations. They were dedicated and kind people but they had no idea how demeaned I felt, how bloody pigeonholed. Worse than that, I bought into their view of what was suitable for me, acquiescing in a string of work placements and office jobs and the tedium of lost days. I allowed myself to be persuaded that that was my lot; a denial of the possibility of dreams. As I drove around Wales taking photographs though, I thought to myself – smugly, if I'm honest – 'If only they could see me now.' I felt victorious.

There were incidents, of course, some of which literally stopped me in my tracks. One morning I parked at the foot of Dryslwyn Castle, perched on a hill overlooking the Tywi Valley in Carmarthenshire, to be greeted by hard frost and a rising mist. Perfect. In the three-quarter light just before dawn I began the climb up well-laid paths and clusters of steps. I remember the numbing cold of gripping the handrail with un-gloved hands. There's something about the purity of a cold morning that seems to recalibrate the mind, clearing out the mental clutter, a reminder that life is a gift in spite of any petty concerns. And a reminder that a pair of gloves might be a good idea – inappropriate attire, or lack of it, continued to be a theme.

Feeling buoyed, I leant into the hill and strode with purpose. It's only a couple of hundred metres to the top but the gradual rate of incline soon began to sap me. Maybe it was the sense of anticipation of nearing the summit or, more likely, the exhaustion of the ascent, but on the last few steps I caught a tired foot and fell. Going down, I threw my camera bag onto a patch of grass to save it while at the same time assessing my landing spot – falls are always slow-motion affairs. My arms aren't strong enough to break a fall so my head helped out, connecting with a step. A few seconds were lost as I struggled to remain conscious, but somehow, I stayed with it and rolled over onto my back, clutching the side of my head which hurt like hell. After some furious swearing, I regained enough composure to figure out how to get back to my feet. A wooden fingerpost was close by so I shuffled along the step and pulled myself up on it. Satisfied that I was unhurt enough I carried on up to the castle in time for sunrise. Just another comedy tumble in a catalogue of falls.

Having completed the photography, who to badger for that much coveted foreword? After some deliberation my literary-stalking sights fell on Griff Rhys Jones. He had a house in north Pembrokeshire and was evidently fond of the outdoors, what with all those roaming travelogues and a propensity for clambering up mountains. He'd recently rediscovered his Welshness too, so a book of Wales might appeal to him. I'd been a fan of *Not the Nine O'clock News* in the early '80s and who could forget his portrayal of the thuggish and imbecilic Constable Savage? After leaving Neyland Technical College in 1982, jobless, my friend Martin and I were virtually penniless so we chipped in half each for a twin cassette recording of the series. One cassette apiece, which we swapped regularly.

I approached Griff through a mutual acquaintance and was overjoyed when he agreed to write it. Like Jamie Owen before him, he truly got it and understood my motivation. Also, like Jamie, he wrote a beautifully evocative piece. He invited me up to his place in Pembrokeshire so that I could take a photograph of him to go with the foreword, and he made a pot of fresh coffee, was warm and welcoming, and asked lots of questions about my travels. PC Savage, it seemed, was a decent sort.

In the summer of 2012, we holidayed in Brittany and on the way to the ferry I called into my publisher's office in Cardiff to pick up an advance copy of *Wales: A Photographer's Journey*. It was big and heavy and I was proud. Once settled into our accommodation in France I got the book out and studied it forensically for any heart-stopping typos and to ensure the photographs had been printed well. Satisfied, I settled down to enjoy it, feeling like I was thumbing through a pictorial record of some grand expedition by an intrepid explorer. When I'd finished, I slumped back in the chair happy and began musing about what to do for the next book.

Chapter 30

I was cold. Core-trembling, hand-shaking, teeth-chattering cold. I juddered and shook and just couldn't get warm. And then there was the intense ache, a blunt, vice-like compression throughout my body, in every muscle and joint. I put the central heating on and took two paracetamol but still couldn't get warm. I put another fleece on. Still cold. I put my North Face jacket on and zipped it up. Still shaking. Flu? Seemed like the most obvious candidate.

I sat huddled in my chair, with arms crossed and hands shoved into my armpits, trying to stifle the tremors. I looked at the clock. Half four. Shit. I had to collect Anna from work. Somehow, I got to my feet and shuffled to the door. At least the Volvo's furnace-like heating and electrically stoked seat would warm me up. I drove the six miles into Haverfordwest in a sauna and waited outside Anna's office. She came out and got in the car.

'Jesus, you look terrible. What's wrong?'

'Dunno. Just really cold. And aching like hell.'

'You really do look awful. Terrible,' she said, with particular emphasis.

'Yeah, okay, I get the picture.'

'Sorry. Taken paracetamol?'

'Yup.'

'Temperature?'

'Not yet.'

'I better drive,' she said.

'It's okay. We'll be home in ten minutes.'

'I really think I should.'

'I'll drive,' I snapped.

We got home and I took my temperature, which was considerably north of thirty-eight. A fever.

'Just go to bed. Sleep it off,' said Anna. 'Could be flu?'

'Yeah, think so.'

I'd experienced similar symptoms in the past, though not as severe, recognising the feeling, if not the intensity; those day trips for the Wales book sprang to mind when I'd come in from the car and collapse onto the nearest padded surface. The shaking was novel though. But a good night's sleep would sort it. Always had in the past. So, racked with an all-over ache and mired in a fuzzy delirium, I dived into a deep sleep.

I clawed myself awake the next afternoon, a Saturday, feeling as if I'd been run over. Not satisfied with mowing me down, for good measure the driver had reversed over me too. And during the night someone, possibly the inconsiderate driver, had scored my throat with razor blades. Attempting to swallow even a sip of water was excruciating. The beacons of mild concern from the previous night had ratcheted up, as even the act of breathing seemed to require a conscious effort to draw in air as if my chest were constricted by a steel band. Instinct told me to stay put but a determination to explore any possibility of respite from the terrible aching forced me downstairs. If I get up, I'll surely feel better, I thought. A strong coffee, shower and get changed would help too. Grabbing the stair-rail, I descended to the lounge and fell into my armchair. Anna came in from the kitchen.

'God, Dave, you look even worse. I'll get some paracetamol.'

After ten minutes the dense ache in my body had become painful and it hurt to sit in the chair so Anna helped me back to bed and the relief of lying down. I began to register the first inklings that maybe I hadn't experienced these particular symptoms before after all. But so long as I was able to wake up, surely whatever it was couldn't be serious. Anna wasn't so convinced.

'I'm phoning that out-of-hours line... speak to a doctor,' she stated, with a look of worried confusion.

'No. Leave it. It's flu. No point bothering people,' I replied, barely able to project my voice.

I waved Anna away, as I didn't have the strength to discuss it. The uncontrollable shaking of Friday afternoon had made a number of appearances since and it was back again. She left the room as I shook myself into a sleep that I couldn't climb out of. I was, it seemed, getting deeper and deeper.

On Sunday afternoon I came around, just about, to discover a blotchy crimson rash covering my body. The painter Jackson Pollock would've been rather impressed; it was a unique composition that spoke of inner angst and a desperate scream for help.

'Right, that's it, I'm phoning for help,' said Anna.

I didn't argue, limply running up the white flag. Anna told the out-of-hours service of my ongoing fever which was impervious to paracetamol. She told them of my sore throat and difficulty in swallowing water let alone food. She told them of the pain I was in; I questioned whether flu could cause a person to welcome death, such was the discomfort permeating every square inch of my body. She told them that I couldn't physically get out of bed and that I was finding it difficult to stay awake. Finally, she described the rash; red, angry and covering my whole body. The call ended.

'They said it sounds like flu. Plenty of bed rest and fluids?'

So, it seemed that I did indeed have flu. Lashing the pain and increasing delirium to a diagnosis made me feel safer, as I could make sense of what was going on. Flu it was, then. I certainly knew that I'd never had flu before as I'd never felt so desperately ill. I'd heard how awful flu was, but could it really be that awful? But it'd pass. The listlessness and pain were a concern but my adult life had been punctuated with incidences of physical implosion, paying the price for having pushed a little too hard. Not acknowledging my limitations. I hated the notion that I had to take it easier than others so drove myself all the harder, especially since becoming a photographer. So, grudgingly, I accepted that I'd be bed-bound for a few days before rising once again from the ashes. I went back to sleep effortlessly, as if I'd been switched off.

By Monday I woke, if only to check I was still alive. The criminal justice system used to inflict a punishment known as being 'pressed to death.' A felon would be chained to the floor of a dungeon and large flat stones placed on their chest, one after the other, till the life was literally pressed from them. I was beginning to appreciate what that punishment felt like as my breathing had become very laboured and the notion of death heartily embraced. It would've been a relief.

I'd been in bed since Friday evening – 'plenty of bedrest' as instructed – but it didn't make sense that my symptoms were becoming more severe. How many days would it take to turn the corner? You hear people who say they're ill and feel like death while putting clothes in the washing machine or making supper for the kids. They're doing stuff while apparently feeling like death. The difference was, not only did I feel like death but I was beginning to see it in the room with me. I began to feel as if I might actually be slipping away. There was certainly no chance of me rustling-up fish finger sandwiches for the boys or cleaning the bathroom, that's for sure.

By Tuesday Anna decided to enact the nuclear option.

'I'm calling your doctor out,' she said.

'No. I'll be fine. It's flu.'

With every sentence, I felt as if I were haemorrhaging life. It was painful to talk.

'I don't like this. Something's not right,' pleaded Anna.

Flu was getting a bit scary.

Later that morning, I half-stirred, sensing someone in the room. It was Dr Cooke, my GP. I'd been at sea for days, treading water, convinced that a passing ship would rescue me, and at last, HMS *Cooke* had pulled alongside. All I had to do was keep him there, but if I looked as bad as I felt, that wouldn't be a problem.

Something deep down signalled that I was in grave danger. Call it intuition, a hunch, whatever, but surely flu couldn't be that bad. Put simply, I couldn't imagine it humanly possible to feel any more ill without dying. He examined me – noting the rash – took my temperature, which was very high, blood pressure – very low – and recorded some other indicators.

'You're really ill, mate. I'm calling an ambulance,' he said.

The ambulance arrived and I was carried downstairs strapped to a stretcher. In my flaky state I noticed that Mum and Dad were there but more surprisingly Andrew, my brother.

'Alright, Dai. You'll be fine now. Don't worry,' he said.

As the manager of a busy builders' merchants, Andrew making calls to the sick during work hours was unheard of. Presented with the wake-like gathering, it suddenly struck me that I was indeed close to a permanent blackout.

As I was being loaded into the ambulance, I remember Jo, our neighbour, coming out and asking if everything was okay. Leaking consciousness, I cringed, as the flip side of my premonition of death was that I found all of the attention embarrassing, like I was wasting valuable public resources – calling my doctor out, summoning an ambulance. All of that for flu. How ridiculous. Anna and a paramedic got into the ambulance with me and moments later it glided, as if on a cushion of air, away from the house. Anna held my hand and smiled. Whatever I had – flu or some other ramification of a medical evil – it'd be diagnosed and treated and I'd be home for Harry's fourth birthday three days later.

Wheeled into A&E, I lay in the vicinity of a series of conversations between medical staff that I couldn't hear but which involved occasional earnest glances in my direction. One of the huddle – a junior doctor – peeled away and came to take blood. She poked and prodded, apologising profusely, as she struggled to find a vein. I now willed whatever it was to be life-threatening, if only to warrant all of the fuss being lavished on me. After repeated attempts, she drew blood, after which I was transferred to the intensive care unit with Anna walking beside the trolley. It, whatever 'it' was, was serious.

A doctor came to stitch intravenous channels into the veins of my neck. I was being prepared for something, a something that

I was oblivious to. But at least things were happening, the downside of which, of course, was the sense of urgency around me which intimated that the something was serious. Deadly perhaps.

'What are you doing?' I asked, as curiosity overcame the urge to sleep.

'Just preparatory. Don't worry.'

'What's wrong with me?' I demanded.

Feigning deafness, she continued with her needlework.

'What's wrong?'

Delivered in a tone she couldn't ignore, she said, 'The doctor in charge of your care will be along soon to explain everything.'

She finished her embroidery and beat a retreat. Like some finely choreographed stage act, no sooner had she gone than another doctor appeared.

'Hi, David. My name's Doctor Green,' he said with a matter-of-fact charm. 'First of all, I just want you to know you're in the best place possible...' Best place for what? 'The tests are inconclusive at the moment...' he continued, '...but we're trying everything we can to determine what's wrong.'

In the absence of a nailed-down diagnosis, flu, it seemed, was still *Top of the Pops*. I was beginning to feel, though, that flu's grip on the top spot was under threat. But by what?

I was being pumped with mysterious liquids via a drip and, as Dr Green had said, 'you're in the best place possible'. Being in hospital and hooked up didn't equate to feeling better though. Everything still hurt like hell, as if I were being fed through a mangle. But, now that they're getting drugs into me, I'll be fine, I thought. After all, drugs are good. Perhaps Harry's birthday in a few days would be a squeeze but surely a week, max, of being medically rescued would suffice. Expensive machines were disassembling samples of my blood at that very moment and it was only a matter of time before *voilà*, the answer to the riddle of my symptoms would present itself. No need to panic.

I spent a sleepless night with Anna curled up beside me on an upholstered armchair trying to find a comfortable position. She too enjoyed little success. Looking around in my wakefulness, I was struck by how bright and noisy the ward's night was. Umpteen machines connected to patients by tubes and wires, pinging and beeping a cacophony of electronic disruption that made sleep impossible. The reassurance of technology. There appeared to be as many staff as patients, milling about tending to people who were either asleep or more likely unconscious, plunged deep into a personal medical crisis from which they might never emerge. I was surrounded by the barely living dead. And, incredible as it seemed, my situation was deemed worthy of the intensive care administered on that ward. For the patients around me this place was the last chance saloon, the edge of darkness. There was just one other room, down in the basement, that was more unwelcome, and it had lots of refrigerated capacity.

The next morning, which felt like a seamless extension of the night, Anna, bleary eyed, was advised to nip home and collect some essentials for me. It seemed that my stay was going to be longer than I'd hoped. She wanted to see the boys too, who were at her parents', to tell them I was ill and in hospital and to reassure them there was nothing to worry about. Mum and Dad picked up the baton, coming in to sit by my bed, a ritual they'd endured nearly thirty years earlier in Cardiff after my motorbike accident. They took it in turns to hold my hand and tell me everything would be fine, again, as they'd done in Cardiff.

As the minutes ticked by though, their positive words were subsumed by a marked deterioration in my condition. They watched with helpless horror as I began to drift in and out of consciousness, sucking in frantic gulps of air, my arms jerking involuntarily as if attached to strings that some bastard was mischievously yanking. Emitting animal-like grunts, I became increasingly distressed as I fought what felt like suffocation. Dr Green came to my bed.

'Right, David, your breathing's becoming a worry. Oxygen levels in your blood are very low. So we're putting you on a ventilator. Putting you into an induced coma.'

Through the fog of an oxygen-starved brain, I computed what he'd said.

'When?' I whispered.

'We're getting a side room ready for you right now.'

He turned and walked away with the calm urgency of a man with no time to waste. That is, none of my time to waste.

Minutes later, my bed was wheeled into a side room. Events had overtaken Anna's mission to pack a bag and she hadn't returned. My aunty Jenny was there, though, with Mum and Dad sat by me. As with Andrew at the house I was bemused by Jenny's presence. The three of them engaged in a merry-go-round of unconvincing reassurances as they took it in turns to break down and cry, like some solemn relay. Unlike them, I hadn't been made aware that I was careering towards the big fridge downstairs.

A nurse and a doctor came into the room eager to get me ventilated, to oxygenate me before I went into cardiac arrest – again, I was unaware of this. But Anna hadn't returned and I needed her to be there as I sensed a potential finality in being put to sleep. Drunkenly, I pleaded with them to wait for her return. They acquiesced, but said, 'We can't wait much longer.'

Right on cue, Anna came rushing in. Through floods of tears, she hugged me, told me she loved me and said everything would be okay. Mum and Dad approached and did likewise. Jenny walked out, sobbing.

There was a scratch on the back of my hand and the room left me, followed by a sensation of something hard being shoved down my throat; the breathing tube attached to the ventilator.

Later that day, a nurse asked Anna to join her in a small office on the ward.

'The results are back and we now know what's wrong with David,' said the nurse.

'Flu?' asked Anna.

'No,' said the nurse. 'Have you heard of sepsis?'

Anna shrugged and said, 'Something to do with the blood?'

The nurse began to explain.

In January 2013, most peoples' appreciation of sepsis was just that – 'something to do with the blood'. Bad blood. Infected blood. Just blood really. In the intervening years, though, sepsis has gained a certain notoriety in the public conscience. On social media, it trends. There are X accounts and websites and charities all dedicated to getting the message out: sepsis kills and it kills very quickly. Some of us have become informed sepsis pundits, aware of its terrifying death toll, having read about Mrs Thomas or Mr Jones or whoever rocking up at A&E feeling like shit and being fobbed off with paracetamol, only to return home to die within hours.

These days the NHS is much more on it when it comes to sepsis. There are checklists and charts and all manner of prompts and tools for spotting it. Back then though, it was a stealthy killer, sneaking under the radar, often misdiagnosed, and scything tens of thousands a year. Sepsis, you see, can masquerade as a range of illnesses such as... oh yeah, flu. I was on the ventilator at this point but had I been given a choice between flu and sepsis, flu would've won hands down. Sepsis, as I was to discover, was the grimmest of bastards.

Now for the scientific bit. Sepsis is a systemic overreaction to an infection in the blood. White cells, the Red Cross of the blood, detect an unwelcome guest – in my case what transpired to be the streptococcal bacteria – and move in for the kill. But strep is a hardy bugger that can survive the best endeavours of the white assassins. So, frustrated at their lack of success, the white cells, programmed to cleanse, begin to run amok, searching out alternative targets and going on a killing spree, initiating a holocaust of the blood. Meanwhile, the red blood cells are minding their own business, carrying oxygen around the body, enabling major organs to function. Ambushed by the crazed white cells, a massacre of the reds ensues, and your body begins to shut down as organs are starved of oxygen. With frightening rapidity, complications double, then square, and finally cube as your body self-harms over the edge of a cliff. Systemic suicide.

As the nurse relayed the unvarnished truth of my situation, Anna glanced at a poster on the wall: overlayed on a graphic of angry looking blood cells was the message – SEPSIS KILLS. The nurse parroted the poster's stark message.

For the next two and a half weeks my world became a ventilated hell. As if sepsis hadn't been bad enough, I was now in septic shock, which represented an alarming decline – a bit like genocide being more serious than mass murder. My particular variant of septic shock, known also by its unsexy alias of toxic shock syndrome, was a complication known as DIC (Disseminated Intravascular Coagulation). If a name alone can intimate the gravity of an illness, then mine was a proper medical catastrophe. Certainly, it sounded more serious than flu. The calling card of DIC is the formation of blood clots throughout the body, particularly in the microscopic blood vessels known as capillaries; if a main artery is a motorway, a capillary is a narrow footpath off the beaten track. The clots prevent oxygenated blood getting to muscle tissue at the extremities – fingers, toes, hands and feet. Even the lips, around the mouth and the tip of the nose are at risk. The skin can develop a mottled, blotchy rash – the Jackson Pollock I'd acquired at home – before turning black. Black is bad. Black is gangrene. Gangrene means amputation. Upwards of fifty percent of people that develop DIC die. Of the survivors many emerge from a coma to find some if not all of their limbs removed and parts of their face cut away, or suffering permanent organ damage or, indeed, a combination of the two. Thankfully, I was ignorant of this as I drifted beneath the waves.

Anna, Mum and Dad – in fact, anyone with an emotive stake in my unlikely survival – became acutely aware of what having septic shock-induced DIC meant. Dad had been told, with compassion but without any pretence at rosy illusion, by Dr Green that, 'He's very seriously ill. Lots of people die from this.' Anna was advised that, if possible, she should be close to the hospital when not at my bedside. My parents lived a couple of hundred metres from the hospital – a perverse stroke of fortune – so she decamped there. When not on the ward at my side a phone call at any moment could urge her back if things threatened to turn terminal. What increments of terminal we were talking about is hard to fathom. For the first two weeks on the ventilator, it was a moot point as to whether I was ever not in the death zone. Every hour of every day the medical staff contrived to conjure up new ruses to stop me checking out. It was the desperate bailing of a sinking ship, engulfed in flames, with a well-stocked ammunition magazine ready to blow and a force twelve coming over the horizon; pressing concerns aplenty.

A witches' brew of medical complications coursed around my body, each with its own capacity to kill, treatment for one symptom exacerbating another. They pumped drugs in to kill the streptococcal infection, searching for that magic bullet that'd annihilate the source of all my woes. Lots of bullets were fired. There were drugs to keep my blood pressure up, or at least at a level that'd sustain major organ function. DIC had clotted up my capillaries and so I was pumped with anti-clotting agents to ward off the dread of blackened skin, the precursor to amputation. Thinning the clots to save my limbs meant my major arteries were bleeding out red water internally. Blood products were transfused to replenish the oxygen-carrying red blood cells that were being massacred by the psychotic whites. It was high-stakes medical poker, making finely nuanced bets on the alleviation of one symptom in the knowledge that it could go bust elsewhere. And then there were my kidneys; they'd packed up before I even got to hospital. Regular dialysis cleaned the impurities from my blood and in between sessions I bloated with sludgy waste, becoming the ward's Michelin man. As if that weren't enough to contend with, the medics awaited the certainty of pneumonia. It didn't disappoint, and when both lungs flooded, drains were surgically inserted into either side of my chest to draw off the fluid. If it'd been a game of critical illness Top Trumps, I'd have held all the cards.

Two days after being hooked up to the ventilator was Harry's fourth birthday. I didn't make it after all. Anna got up early at my parents' house, two hundred metres from my bed, and raced down to her parents', where Harry and Charlie were staying, to be there for when he woke. Surrounded by protective love and fragile smiles, he asked, 'Where's Daddy?'

It was the killer question, the one that tested Anna's bravery but demanded an answer.

'Don't worry, sweetheart, he'll be home soon. Just a bit unwell at the moment.' What else could she say?

He was four and innocent and yet, the tectonic plates, the foundation upon which his emotional security rested, had shifted out of alignment. He knew something wasn't right but didn't know what. So, he played, pushing his new tractor around the kitchen. Charlie would be eight in a couple of weeks; another birthday I wasn't going to make. His instinct was that much more attuned to the underlying sense of dread that surrounded him. Anna thought he should know the truth. He was told that I might die. At that point it seemed the odds-on outcome.

Anna kept a diary, to compartmentalise her trauma and to try to make sense of the nonsensical; an exorcism by writing. She'd arrive early on the ward each morning to talk with the nurse who would've been with me through the night. I was never left alone. Those chats could be fortifying, that yearning for even the tiniest morsel of positive news, and to be thankful that I was alive. Alive was a good start to the day. Occasionally, Anna would be asked to take a seat in the waiting room, a soulless antiseptic space, while they conducted some procedure. She'd look out of the window, the bottom half obscure, staring up at the sky, and pray; it was now her turn to invoke God's help. He'd come through for me on that snowy pass in the Brecon Beacons and maybe he had another get out of jail free card with my name on.

There was nothing else to cling to really. No silver lining besides me being technically, electronically, alive. Death was a regular visitor to the ward, igniting desperate grief in the waiting room and corridor, with families huddled together trying to come to terms. Once called back, Anna would spend the day – relaying with my parents – by my bed, jockeying for space amongst a host of machines, talking to me, holding my hand, reading and killing time to the end of the day, when another feat of survival on my part could be ticked off. And that was the pattern day after day, hoping that they wouldn't become part of a grieving huddle.

A week had passed as I sailed on oblivious, and a doctor entered the room with the ashen look of someone groaning under too many life-or-death demands, darting from one seriously ill patient to another. No respite for a medical mind having to make finely balanced decisions. He didn't notice Anna sat camouflaged amongst the monitors and drip stands, speaking only to the nurse and glancing at the charts.

Frowning, he said, 'I really don't want to lose him at this stage.'

All those days that Anna (and Mum and Dad) had sat there and it could still have been snatched away. Time didn't necessarily equate to healing.

One particular night was very fraught, and suggestive of an end. The staff were doing everything to keep me going but the waves were lapping the deck. I was going down. Fearing the worst, Anna huddled up in a corner, hoping like some stowaway that she wouldn't be noticed.

'Anna, it's half ten, my love. You really ought to go and get some rest,' said Donna, one of the gatekeepers trying to stop me from drifting to the other side.

'It's okay. I can stay here. Won't get in your way. Honest,' said Anna.

'Look, sweetheart, you're not far away. If anything happens, we'll call you back.'

Anna went back to my parents', convinced that that was it. She lay awake waiting for the call. And she waited and waited till she could wait no longer. At three in the morning, she rang the ward expecting to be told it was over. By six she was back, watching over me as I fought to stay.

I was sedated to keep me under but not so deep that I didn't tune in to voices in the room, which was a disconcerting intrusion into my melting world. Combined with the discordant beeping and pinging of the paraphernalia monitoring my vital signs it seemed that I was trapped in some psychotic Mad Hatter's Tea Party. Imagine your very worst nightmare, the one you woke from in a cold sweat, panting and clawing at the walls. The one that tapped into your deepest fears. Multiply that terror by ten, without being able to wake from it. Then keep it rolling like some unending matinee performance for two and a half weeks. I was being psychologically annihilated, and it was terrifying.

As a kid I loved to hold my breath to see how long I could stay underwater. Didn't we all? In the swimming pool, at the beach, the Sunday night bath. I was a little deep-sea diver pushing to the point where my lungs filled with concrete and I couldn't possibly last a second longer but going another ten before breaking the surface, gasping. Then the elation when I looked at my watch – 'Wow, seventy-three seconds.' I was half-boy, half-fish. One time in Tenerife with the lads I lay motionless on the bottom of the pool looking up at the shifting elongated shapes walking around the edge, the compression of airlessness finally forcing me to the surface. A man was primed at the poolside ready to dive in.

'Christ, thought you were bloody drowned,' he said, in an aggravated northern drawl.

'Ah. Good lungs, see,' I replied, laughing.

On the ventilator, I was plunged into that world repeatedly but not for a mere seventy-three seconds. Over and over, I drowned to blackout point and past, desperately clawing at but unable to break the surface. For some people, their phobia is snakes. Others squirm at the sight of spiders. Or heights. Or open spaces. Or Tony Blair's smile. The list is endless. My number one phobia is potholing. Can't even bear to watch it on the telly. But there I was, buried in a Tolkien nightmare of dark narrow passages, squeezing through rib-pressing gaps into caverns, and then it would come; the in-rush of water.

Or the roof would collapse, trapping me under tons of rock, crushing the breath from me. Day after day, this denial of air, on the cusp of death time and again. Drowned and crushed, the darkness kept coming at me, relentless.

I wanted – if I was even conscious of a want – to throw in the towel, as I was bludgeoned by a *blitzkrieg* of illnesses, each ailment enough to kill in its own right. Each ailment doing its damnedest to do me in. Then there was the cocktail drip of powerful drugs, which combined with the toxins of infection, conspired to poison me and destroy my internal equilibrium. Destroy my will to continue. I wanted an end to the pain and the drowning and being crushed. I wanted death. And just when I was ready to be taken, two voices would call in my head. Two boys. My boys. And I'd cling on once more, while inside I wept, waiting for the next onslaught, the next attempt to get me to give in. But each time the boys called me back. And they persevered, till after two and a half weeks I heard a soft voice, 'Dave. Dave. Everything's fine. You've been ill but you're okay now.'

It was Anna. I was being eased out of sedation. The strep was in retreat.

Chapter 31

I was back on the surface, and aside from the chatter of the machines it was library silent. Certainly, the other patients weren't making much noise. Medically I was better, in that I wasn't about to die, but I was still hostage to the possibility of complications. A lot could still go wrong.

All of my limbs were attached but at the time I had no idea of what a glorious reprieve that constituted. My kidneys had begun to filter blood and produce urine but dialysis was still necessary; I never imagined I could feel so euphoric at seeing a nurse hold up a bag of piss. My piss! I was now ventilated through a tracheostomy that'd been cut into my throat when I'd been under. Over a period of days, the oxygen tube was withdrawn for increasingly longer periods to encourage me to breathe for myself. My lungs rattled with residual fluid, the legacy of double pneumonia, so at regular intervals a nurse fed a thin plastic tube through the slit in my throat to hoover out the phlegmy soup. It was ticklish and irritating, causing me to convulse with fits of coughing.

A condition known as ventilator psychosis accompanied me back to life, like some mental plague. Two and a half weeks of being carpet-bombed with powerful drugs had broken me, my mind shattered into tiny pieces, unable to comprehend the magnitude of what I'd endured. Unable to make sense of it, I descended into a full-board, all-inclusive LSD-type trip from hell, a state of paranoid terror every bit as horrific as when I'd been under. Never having taken LSD by the way, I'm just surmising that my warped outlook might correspond with such a trip! Nothing made sense. Nothing was real or unreal. There was no logic, no rationale as to where I was or why I was there. Is that what dementia feels like?

Piecing together the dislocated and fragmentary evidence swirling about me, I concluded that I was on a French hospital ship sailing around the coast of Europe. This, by the way, was my deduction during my waking hours. I didn't question why I should be on such a vessel as that would've required logic. All I knew was that I was on this ship and I had no clue as to which port it'd pull into next. Glancing around, I was struck by, and indeed impressed with, the fluency with which the crew spoke English. And they were ever so helpful, wheeling me up on deck to sit in the sun, taking me to the onboard theatre to watch a film, administering bed baths, and the most selfless act of all, removing my bodily waste. It was quite some pampered cruise that I was on.

Darkly, though, there were covert whispers and placatory smiles as the crew planned heinous deeds. For at night, in the dimmed light, with potential witnesses absent, they set about culling the patients. They came to kill me, often, lunging at me moon-faced and gurning, as I looked frantically around emitting empty distressed voice bubbles – the tracheostomy silenced all attempts at audible speech. The most terrifying vision was of a particular crew member emerging from the dialysis machine by my bed. And all the while the machines and drip monitors beeped and pinged and the nocturnal ward became a dank cave, as the potholing nightmares returned. Then daylight would come and I'd be back on deck in the sunshine. It was confusing.

A week after emerging from sedation, Mum was sitting at my bedside one evening.

'I'll have to go now. Getting late,' she said.

I smiled through hooded eyes as she leant over to kiss me goodnight.

'Your Dad and me will pop over tomorrow afternoon.'

I mouthed a silent goodnight as she turned and walked away. How will she get home? I thought. We were at sea, after all, and even if she could get to shore, how would she know which bus to catch? She'd given up driving a couple of years before. At least the questioning of her possible route home was an improvement, though logic, evidently, was still elusive. Maybe we're in port, then. But which port? The questions stacked up and I had no answers. No answers that made any sense, that is. Then, as if a bank of fog had suddenly lifted from my brain, I experienced a moment of clarity. A moment of sanity. The unaligned cogs in my head synched and clicked into place and I realised that she must be walking home. And if she was walking, she couldn't have far to go – 'Your Dad and me will pop over tomorrow afternoon.' The riddle was solved. I was in Withybush General Hospital in Haverfordwest, and not on some bloody mad French hospital ship. Why I was in Withybush, though, was still a mystery, but at least the dementia was easing. And best of all, no nurses came to kill me that night.

A shower was suggested. Well, maybe not so much suggested as demanded. After four weeks of festering in my own juices, not being able to get away from a smell because you are the smell is demoralising. In a rerun of Rookwood thirty years before, I laid on a padded plastic trolley with warm rain cascading over a soaped-up me. It was beautiful and therapeutic and for the first time since the drama began I felt alive. I felt hopeful. As I was being pleasantly sponged, I became properly conscious of my surroundings for the first time since coming off the ventilator and was able to compute what'd happened to me, acknowledging a lingering mental trauma but also a realisation of how lucky I'd been.

I thought of those recurrent fights for survival on the ventilator, still lucid and scary, and my two saviours. The boys had got me through it. Simple as that. Without them I'd have allowed myself to die. I wondered whether there was a scientific formulation that determines whether a person survives solely due to medical intervention or through sheer bloody-mindedness. An unwillingness to die. Or, is it a combination? One thing I knew was that I'd fought like hell to stay even though it would've been easier to give in.

After the shower, the tracheostomy was removed from my throat and the silence was broken. As if by the flick of a switch I could speak again, croakily at first. There were lots of questions as I attempted to piece together the certainties of what'd happened. And, I could now issue instructions to the good fortune of all of those that came within my orbit, which mostly involved turning the telly over, helping to shift my position in bed, and pulling the covers over me when I was cold – the air-conditioning on the ward was a bit Soviet, with inexplicable arctic blasts liable at any moment. I wondered how many patients had survived their medical travails only to die of exposure.

I was allowed my first drink of water; with the hole in my windpipe still not sealed there was no knowing where the water might go! But there were no leakages. I was also encouraged to eat. My stomach had shrunk due to the absence of solids over the previous month and I had no appetite. I didn't want food, especially anything savoury, as it made me feel sick. But I did crave fruit, and when asleep, I now dreamt of cold crushed pineapple forked from a tin. From potholing nightmares to splendid visions of eating tinned fruit. An improvement of sorts. But whereas I had a craving for crushed pineapple, the thing that I became addicted to – and I mean full-blown heroin dependent – was fizzy drinks. I'd dispatch Anna to the hospital shop each day, returning with bottles of Fanta, Lucozade, Coke, and all manner of pancreas killers. Suitably sugared-up, I'd lay there buzzing before the comedown and my next fix.

With the return of logic though, came a terrifying reckoning; I was so emaciated and weak. The slightest constriction of bed sheets around my legs trapped me into positions that I couldn't adjust out of. When I lifted my arms into the air they flopped back down onto my chest. I couldn't even conjure up the strength to depress the buttons on the TV remote. I was weighed, which in itself felt like a surreal embarrassment, suspended in a canvas sack from a set of overhead scales like a baby. I'd lost two and a half stone and I hadn't been carrying any extra when I'd been admitted. Most of that loss of mass was muscle, or at least what'd passed for muscle. I kept thinking of Rookwood, the similarities uncanny, and realised I'd have to rebuild, again.

A physiotherapist called David – the name alone reeked of competence! – appeared with a robust frame on casters to help me stand. He and a colleague pulled me upright onto the side of the bed and fitted me into a harness attached to the frame. There was a control pad connected to an electric motor which was to lift the harness and me into a standing position.

'We'll set the dial quite low to start with,' said David. 'See if you can stand without too much help.'

It was dispiriting, as after a number of failed attempts it became apparent that I required every watt of power to get to my feet. I stood for a few seconds before collapsing into the support of the harness. It was the moment when reality bit and the gravity of what lay ahead slammed into me. When a football team is relegated from the Premier League to the Championship, it has bright expectations of a return to the top flight the season after, as the gulf between the two leagues is bridgeable. Well, I'd been dumped from my version of the Premier League to pub team Sunday League obscurity on the northernmost tip of Scotland. I was as far from my top level as it was possible to be.

The psychological accumulation of the illness and the ventilator had broken me, and added to that now was the physical destruction so amply demonstrated by my inability to even stand. I fell into a dark place, despairing of what I'd done to deserve, in my opinion, the duffest hand ever dealt. Why me? Again. I felt angry and sorry for myself, a combination of emotions ill-suited to the challenge I faced. The resolve, the dogged spirit that'd sustained me for decades' left me. I'd had enough. I stopped talking, even to Anna. Life had got to me. *My life had got to me.*

After a couple of days of self-absorbed silence, Wolfgang, a nurse on the ward – affectionately known as Wolfie – pulled up a chair. With a faint German accent, he said with quiet authority, 'You're angry. And why wouldn't you be? You've been through a hell of a time.'

Wolfie was good, bloody good, even though he'd tried to kill me during those long, paranoid nights. Since my return to sanity,

I'd watched him glide between patients with a doctorly air, as if in possession of every vital medical contingency. But I wasn't in the mood for a pep talk.

'Been through enough shit, and now this...' I said, wafting a weak hand over what was left of my body. 'Don't give a fuck anymore.'

I would've rolled sulkily away but I didn't have the strength to roll. He leant forward.

'Look, your family still has you,' he said, glancing at the photo of Anna and the boys Blutacked to the bedside cabinet. 'You have to do whatever it takes even if it's just for them. And maybe, just maybe, for those in here who didn't make it.'

I glared at the ceiling but Wolfie's deliberate eyes sought me out and reeled me in. I couldn't escape that gaze.

'What's the point?' I said, 'There'll only be something else waiting to get me.'

'Maybe,' he said. 'And maybe I'll walk out after my shift and be run over. Who knows? But just think of those who would've liked another chance.'

People had died on that unit during my tenure and I suddenly felt ashamed. I glanced at the photo. Anna and my boys. Anna and my saviours.

'Okay. I'll try,' I said, with weak conviction.

'Good. There were times when we didn't think you'd pull through. Lots of times.'

He gave my arm a gentle squeeze, smiled and walked off. He had critically ill people to tend to and I wasn't one of them anymore.

Anna came in that afternoon with the perfect tonic: Charlie and Harry, come to rescue me once again. It was the first time they'd seen me since before I was ill. Seeing them lifted me, as I ditched the last remnants of self-pity. I had to fight, even if it was just to show them that you never give up. And, unlike Rookwood, I knew that this time it was just a case of regaining mass and strength. I had a fight on my hands but I could do it. I had to do it. The boys seemed oblivious, both to my recent ordeal and the multiple cases of potentially fatal illness lying all around.

'When you coming home, daddy?' asked Harry airily, as if I'd been kicking my heels back and playing the old soldier for a month.

'Oh, couple of weeks perhaps. Won't be long,' I replied, apologetically. He shrugged and started flicking switches on one of the nearby machines; not attached to anyone by the way.

'Harry, don't touch,' said Anna.

Charlie was in his rugby kit, having come straight from a match.

'So, did you win?' I asked.

'Yeah,' he said quietly, without meeting my eye. The sight of me was unnerving: the weight loss, the waxy, pallid skin tone. I looked as you'd imagine someone might look having been as ill as it's possible to be without dying. There was also a large, encrusted scar on my chin. It was an ugliness I'd yet to see, an angry weld of a gash. On the ventilator I'd been determined, it seemed, to yank the oxygen tube from my throat, so it'd been taped to my chin with industrial intent. A nurse removed the wodge of tape hastily and tore the skin. With blood the viscosity of red wine it just poured and poured. After much soaking up with wadding, I was left with what looked like a large desiccated slug stuck to my chin.

Each day I moved more, ate more and began to sit in a chair by the side of the bed for short periods. The tubed medical intrusions into my body had been removed and the incisions stitched up. The only remaining support was the catheter that drained my bladder. At last, I was deemed stable enough to be transferred to a general ward. Unlikely as it may have seemed when I entered the unit, I'd avoided the big fridge in the basement. During my stay, others hadn't been so lucky; seeing curtains pulled around a bed and porters arriving with a coffin-sized metal box on a trolley is dispiriting. The staff who gathered to see me off had cared for me and saved me, and now they had others to save.

Chapter 32

I was moved to a six-bed bay on a general medical ward occupied by coughing geriatrics, a nuisance who was forever alighting from bed and threatening to discharge himself and Ralph, an old-timer who'd been in the bed beside me in intensive care. Ralph would often stop by my bed on his way to the bathroom to enquire with warm concern how I was, always signing off with a hearty, 'We're survivors, boy,' and a watery wink. A loud man, resplendent in brushed cotton paisley pyjamas, he pontificated from a bedside chair to all and sundry on a multitude of subjects for which he deemed himself expert, and that's not forgetting his many charitable endeavours. But for all of his pomposity, he helped make the time pass, was kind to me, and I liked him. And as with Rookwood, time was the enemy. Time to ponder the annihilation of the physical me. Time to contemplate the long journey that lay ahead, again.

The staff-to-patient ratio was as diluted as a weak G&T, relegated as I was from five-star attendance to my every need in intensive care to scrambling for attention amidst a melee of what I deemed to be the other patients' petty demands. The nuisance in particular in the bed next to me soaked up an inordinate amount of the nurses' time with his threats to abscond. If I'd had the strength, I'd have throttled him. I felt fragile and invisible, as if I'd been pushed into a siding and forgotten.

The physiotherapy department decreed that I should be sat in a chair often, to awaken a midriff – my core – that'd collapsed into a wobbly mush. To get in the chair, though, was no easy feat. I was rolled onto my side and a canvas sheet spread out behind me, then rolled the other way and the remainder of the sheet flattened out.

A tracked winch was manoeuvred above and a hook lowered. The four corners of the canvas sheet had reinforced straps which were placed over the hook. I was then hoisted up and transported over to the chair. This was often done to a gawping audience of patients and sometimes their visitors. It was degrading, being hauled and deposited like some inanimate carcass. With no core strength and still afflicted by a residual sludge of powerful drugs and the toxins of illness, I became exhausted in minutes, slumping forwards and pleading with staff to be hoisted back.

'Not yet, sweetie. Another ten minutes will do you good.'

I could never work out whether it was tough love or just a case of shunting me down the order of play. The nurses were on a treadmill of medical housework, rushing from one task to another: changing a sheet; administering tablets; emptying a bedpan; the morning wash cycle. Oh, and rounding up that annoying twat in the bed next to me. I'd seen it all before, of course, and acknowledged the need to remain calm, but when the act of sitting in a chair is beyond your physical capabilities it's difficult to be stoic when a return to bed is being kicked down the road.

I'd been sucked into the ordeal of sepsis lacking the capacity of the average middle-aged male to withstand such an onslaught, sweeping through me as it did like a tornado in a trailer park. Since becoming a photographer, it'd been a struggle to accommodate my daily aspirations, dogged as I was by the compromised resilience of someone always on the cusp of physical implosion. I hated having to ease the pace when I sensed a meltdown on the cards. Having to listen to my body. I was in the wrong job, of course, and just about every outing into the landscape was a trial.

Then again, the strep bacteria's an evil bugger, capable of taking down a Mike Tyson. Undoubtedly though, had a Tyson come out the other end, he'd be walking around the ward, or likely be back home in his condo contemplating his next facial tattoo. He'd have lost muscle bulk but he'd have had plenty of bulk to spare. Not me though.

I was stripped to the bone and a baby once again, being fed, dressed, washed, hoisted in and out of bed and having my arse wiped. There was no dignity.

Once a day, a physio appeared to initiate some rudimentary exercises. Sitting and lolling in a chair, I rolled a small football along a table and back for five minutes. Core strengthening apparently. And that was it; a paltry pebble-a-day towards that Chesil Beach of recovery. Rookwood, by contrast, had been so intense from the moment the traction had been unscrewed from my head. This, though, was threadbare treatment limited by an absence of equipment and a lack of time; no sooner would the physio arrive than they'd be gone – taking their ball with them.

A few days of being becalmed on a non-specialist ward began to eat away at me. I was becoming desperate and angry. I was beginning to give up. It was then that I heard of a possible solution. A nurse let slip that the stroke ward had its own dedicated team of physiotherapists and a gym on the actual ward. It was the only ward in the hospital with those facilities, the holy grail of potential recovery. If I remained where I was with its five minutes a day of ball rolling, I feared I'd become another Tom, the old guy who'd been institutionalised in Rookwood. It was an irrational fear, but it spurred a determination to get onto that stroke ward.

One night I rolled, with great effort, onto my side to go to sleep. Being able to roll was an improvement. I wasn't tired. How could I be? I'd done nothing all day aside from sit in a chair and stew with anger and lie on the bed and stew with anger, in between being encouraged to eat meals I didn't want and having to remind myself to be nice to visitors. My mind, then, whirred with a telephone book full of anxieties and fears till somehow I slipped beneath the waves.

Immediately – or at least it felt immediate – I was woken by faint voices. In the half-light of the six-bed bay I made out a gathering around the bed in the opposite corner by the window which'd been empty when I went to sleep. A man was being tended to by a nurse, half sat up with pillows stuffed behind his back. A doctor was speaking to a woman and a younger man stood by the bed. Then, with no intimation of concern, the doctor and nurse departed. The woman leant forward and kissed the patient and I heard the young man say, 'Sure you're okay now, Dad?' Dad nodded in the affirmative and the woman – presumably his wife – said they'd be back in the morning and they were gone too. A late admission, I thought, and went back to sleep.

I was woken, a while later, by a commotion and urgent voices. The curtains were drawn around the newcomer's bed. There were animated silhouettes and clipped instructions. I went cold at the realisation of what I was witnessing: a medical emergency. A doctor rushed past with a piece of equipment on a trolley and slipped behind the curtain. I thought of the man's wife and son by the bed earlier and willed the situation to end well. The activity behind the curtain was now frantic as I kept hoping. Then, as if suddenly in the eye of a storm, there was silence and stillness. A voice asked what time it was and the light was turned off above the bed. The staff filed out from behind the curtain and departed. I went back to sleep.

Breakfast was being served as Ralph regaled a patient with an anecdote concerning a personal commendation from a VIP, or some such tale. The curtains were still drawn around the bed in the corner. I was being fed a passable full English when two nurses swept into the bay and drew the curtains around all of our beds. The curtain material wasn't exactly blankety as I saw two figures walk past my bed on either end of a trolley in the direction of the night-time emergency. A couple of minutes passed and the figures left with the trolley and our curtains were pulled back, including the ones around the corner bed. It was empty and neatly made up as if no one had ever been there. I asked the nurse feeding me where the man was. She shook her head solemnly. Two porters had taken him, just like the others that'd been taken from around me over the previous month.

On my fifth day in medical limbo, with Anna sitting beside me, a nurse stopped by and said, 'Time to pack up, you're moving.' Anna grabbed my few possessions and my bed was pushed to the stroke ward.

I'd begged to be transferred and was excited at the prospect of being in the right place, as being there would get me home more quickly. Arriving on the ward, the first thing that hit me was the din. Shouting, crying, howling – every vocal shade of hell. I was gripped with sickening panic, instantly regretting my determined lobbying to be moved. This is a mistake, I thought. I was fragile and the distress in those voices was overwhelming. Pushed into a bay of six beds, I was transferred onto the middle left-hand bed. The racket in the bay was more immediate and intense. And frightening. I dared not look at any of the patients. I'd arrived in Bedlam.

'Welcome, David. Bit noisy at the moment but you'll get used to it,' said a nurse, no doubt seeing the shock on my face. 'If you need anything, just press the buzzer.' She flashed a weak smile, perhaps concerned for my sanity at having requested such a billet, and went. I asked Anna to pull the curtains around, desperate to keep out the madness.

'What the fuck have I done?'

Anna held my hand.

'Honey, I feel so sorry for you. I didn't think it'd be like this,' she said.

The same nurse popped her head through the curtains. 'Supper trolley's here. Would you like anything?'

I was too distraught to answer.

'Maybe not tonight, thank you,' said Anna.

I closed my eyes and put my hands to my ears to try to shut out the ward. Anna lay beside me and hugged me and told me all would be fine, that I needed to be where I was to get fit and that I'd soon be home with the boys. In less fraught circumstances that reassurance may have worked. But I hadn't fully shaken the ventilator psychosis – that recurrent sense of terror – and so lacked the robustness in my head to cope. Like a soldier in the trenches of World War One, I hunkered down to survive the bombardment of my shattered senses. Of my shredded nerves.

About half an hour had passed and I was determined to return to the old coughing men and Ralph on the other ward when the noise began to ease. And it was then that I heard a beautiful sound, a voice as welcome as birdsong at dawn. It came from behind the curtain to my right. A soft lowland Scots accent with a lilting cadence that drew me up and made me smile.

'Aye, the meeting's in the main office. I'll pick you up. Be no problem.'

Who was that voice? I wondered.

'Car's just round the corner,' he continued. 'I'll just grab my keys.'

I was both curious and transfixed. Then, another voice that'd dominated proceedings since my arrival barged in. It was Essex and it was angry and it came from the other end of the bay.

'Nurse. NURSE.'

Whoever he was, his volume control was broken as I sensed my anxiety levels rising again, but thankfully the musical Scot piped up.

'Aye, the car's just round the corner. I'll get it now.'

From the same direction came a kind but authoritative voice, 'Bobby. Bobby... no, sweetheart, don't get out of bed.'

'Just getting my keys.'

'Come on now, Bobby. Back into bed, there's a sweetheart,' she said. Bobby, then, was a patient, and I could've listened to him forever. A warm hug amongst chaos.

Then, 'NURSE.' Mr Angry was back.

The vocal competition was heating up, and I was beginning to detect some entertainment value. I felt calmer and less afraid than on my arrival and although I hadn't seen these people yet, I somehow sensed that I was getting to know them and perhaps like them. All I had to do was face them.

'Anna, can you open the curtains, please.'

'You sure?'

'Yeah, can't hide forever.'

She drew them back and I glanced around at a bay of broken and damaged individuals. A harmless, befuddled and bloody loud bunch too.

'NURSE.'

I looked to my left. The Essex harangue was sat in a wheelchair by the window. Late sixties, in stripey pyjamas, with an incandescent face. He'd shouted himself crimson, and his name was Phil. He barked and growled and complained about anything and everything, each remonstration accompanied by the banging of a clenched right fist on the window sill. He was a trembling mass of anger, and nothing, not anyone, could placate him. And he was totally paralysed down his left side, the stroke's favoured blight, so why shouldn't he have been nuclear?

And to my right was the man I knew to be Bobby. Bobby with the sweetest, most golden voice. He was still wittering on about an imaginary set of car keys, but who was I to deny him his escape? He looked at me, smiling. It wasn't a smile for me in particular; he just smiled all of the time. And beneath that sixty-odd years of living I saw a face that in its prime must have been a stunner. Bobby had been a dashing man. But now Bobby had dementia and just to rub it in he'd suffered a stroke. But that voice, those radiant eyes and that smile were joyous.

The vocal tableaux of the daylight hours flared up during the night too; Bobby didn't call off the search for his car keys just because we were trying to sleep. He'd alight from bed and be persuaded back ever so sweetly by the night staff. He had wanderlust but also a propensity for falling; the stroke had weakened his legs. So, Bobby acquired bumps and bruises but it didn't stop him. Essex Phil was less wakeful but startling as hell when he did fire up. Being wrenched from a shallow sleep by a sharp 'NURSE!' was unsettling. With the intermittent cacophony and lighting levels you could read a newspaper by, sleep was a longed-for dream.

The next morning, as the staff did their rounds of washing and dressing before breakfast, I was shot through. Empty. I had the deepest sympathy for those around me but sleep deprivation, it seemed, was going to be the dominant theme during my stay.

'Bobby, back into bed, my love.'

It started early. The staff almost audibly breathed a collective sigh of relief when Lyn, Bobby's wife, would turn up mid-morning, every day. She'd sit by the bed chatting to him, feeding him, reading the paper, preventing his escapes and freeing up members of staff who didn't have to worry about shepherding him back to bed.

To my immediate left was Roger. In his younger days he'd been a submarine captain, one of that hardy breed living beneath the surface for weeks on end. Roger was now permanently submerged, a stroke rendering him semi-conscious. He'd stir when he was turned to prevent bedsores but I never felt that he was ever truly awake, not in the conventional sense; he groaned but never spoke, at least not in a language that I understood. His wife was another selfless and loving bed-sitter. A gentle lady, she sat all day tending to him while knitting. On occasion he'd surface and formulate sounds that she somehow managed to decipher.

'A drink, is it, dear? Okay, I'll just get one.'

Opposite and to my right was Vince. A sinewy, shrew-like man with a nut-brown complexion, he too had wanderlust. He spent hours sitting in a chair mumbling into a toy mobile that buzzed and made shrill ringing noises. Then he'd be gone, bolting for the corridor. He never got far. One day he fell in the bay, sustaining a gash to his forehead which had to be bandaged. Like the occupants of Colditz, Bobby and Vince's failed escapes only seemed to embolden them.

And so, as I glanced around, these were my new disconnected fellow travellers. Their plight certainly made you reappraise your salt usage, visits to the chippy and all the other excesses that may have brought them to that. But who knows, even the most disciplined and ascetic of lives may not be a guarantee against such a fate. Studying and listening to them, it was difficult to contemplate they'd once been complex, functioning beings, full of hopes and dreams. Now they had to be cared for and guarded, and protected from themselves. Like Jack Nicholson's character in *One Flew Over The Cuckoo's Nest*, I was the lone possessor of those vital cognitive elements that gifts us a whole life.

'Hi, David. I'm Tim, one of the physios. Ready for the gym?'

He and an assistant pulled me up onto the side of the bed, swivelled me into a wheelchair and whisked me down the corridor to the gym. I was excited. Progress, at last. In that first session they worked on my sitting unaided on the edge of a large, blue, square, padded bench. Nearly thirty years on from my previous rebuilding I was having to start again and the familiarity of my surroundings and what lay ahead wasn't lost on me. I felt like Sisyphus, the mythological Greek king destined to push a bloody boulder uphill for eternity. But at least I was conversant with the narrative for the coming weeks; gut-wrenching graft and determination would be in order. I sat on the edge of the bench and Tim applied tiny pushes to see if he could topple me. The more I resisted the harder he pushed. There could only be one outcome. I fell over.

'Don't worry. Won't be long till we get that core sorted. Everything else will follow. Trust me,' he said.

I was returned to the bay. Just the act of sitting and resisting tiny nudges had been enough to exhaust me. I slept through to supper.

When I woke, Bobby had car fever while Lyn, his wife, read a paper. Vince was on a long call to nobody. Essex Phil was angry, not necessarily about anything in particular. Captain Roger was grumbling, eyes flickering, while his wife knitted a row. I wouldn't enjoy much, if any, sleep that night but I was beginning to feel privileged to be amongst these people. They didn't ask for what they'd been dealt, neither the victims nor their watchers, but they were getting on with it. Well, perhaps Bobby and the other boys didn't have any notion that they were getting on with anything but they were. Each time they started up, I felt like breaking something but I'd be out of there in weeks. They possibly wouldn't ever leave and if they did it wouldn't be to resume their previous lives.

As predicted, that night those damned car keys were still elusive and angry Phil was very angry. More upsetting though was a brittle elderly voice in the ladies' bay next door calling for her mother, who could never come. The next morning the cumulative denial of sleep had taken its toll. I was as knackered as I'd ever been, aching with exhaustion. The arrival of breakfast just about gave me a reason to stir. My stomach was expanding as I became more enthusiastic about eating. I had to put that lost weight back on and load-up with protein and so started each day with the kitchen's signature dish, a full English, with a nurse forking it in as if chucking coal into a steam locomotive.

Phil started up.

'I want a FRIED TOMATO!' he shouted, a repeat of his request from the previous morning. The left-hand side of his body was a corpse, yet all he wanted, all he craved in the whole wide world, was a fried tomato with his bacon and eggs. The nurse who'd delivered his breakfast became embroiled in the thankless diplomatic minefield of explaining to Phil that his request wasn't possible. It appeared that fried tomatoes weren't on the menu.

'I just want a FRIED TOMATO!' he shouted, chucking a bedpan with his good arm. Thankfully it was empty, but they weren't always.

And so, it went on each morning like some bellowing groundhog.

'You're going to stand today,' said Tim with absolute assurance. 'Don't worry about falling. We'll catch you.'

I'd known Tim just a few days but trusted him as if I'd known him for years. I knew he'd catch me, if he had to. I sat on the edge of the bench, felt for that core – as I'd done all those years earlier in Rookwood – leant forward and drove up with all of my strength, which wasn't much. My backside lifted off the bench, I pushed up to a skiing position then plopped back down. Tim adjusted the hydraulics, raising the bench a little.

'You'll get it this time. Easy,' he said.

I went through my pre-lift-off routine again and I was up. Unsteady, swaying, on the verge of collapse, but up. I could stand unaided.

After the gym I slept, an inadequate catch up for the night-time shenanigans. It was never going to replace what I'd lost as I began to sense the prospect of home slipping further away which upset me. I confided in a nurse that although I had the greatest sympathy for the other patients, I needed sleep if I was to get to the point of discharge, which I yearned for so much. Home with Anna and my boys was where I wanted to be.

My special pleading paid off and I was moved to a four-bed bay reserved for stroke patients newly admitted to the ward, where they could be stabilised before being transferred to a bigger bay like the raucous six-bedder I'd left behind. Only one bed was occupied, the lack of check-ins a welcome state of affairs.

'Strictly speaking you shouldn't be in here...' said the sister, '...but it's okay for now. You'll have to move if we get busy though.'

She'd bestowed the most wondrous gift upon me: peace. It felt like I'd arrived at a retreat.

A man, perhaps ten years older than me, was in the bed opposite, his head propped up with pillows. He glanced at me. I nodded and smiled. Without acknowledgement he shifted his gaze out of the window. Suddenly the quiet hush felt fragile, as if I'd intruded on a private grief, for himself. There was an angered detachment that I remembered all too well from Rookwood. The anger of the lost you. I fumbled for my book and read.

Supper was a very palatable chicken casserole and chips which I was able to eat without help, having regained sufficient strength to cut up and fork food to my mouth. There were to be none of the Rookwood corned-beef crime scenes of old, as the kitchen churned out a decent impersonation of good pub grub. A nurse was trying to feed the man opposite.

'Look, you've got to keep your strength up, lovey. Can't go starving yourself,' she said.

No matter how many times she put the fork to his mouth, he turned his head away. I lost my appetite.

During the evening, I snatched the odd furtive glimpse of him. Behind that blank exterior was the most dreadful sadness. And that sadness settled on me like a radioactive cloud. I felt so sorry for him but I just wanted to get away, half-convincing myself that maybe I did crave the frenzy of the other bay after all.

The next morning, he was moved to one of those bigger bays. I was ashamed of my relief at his going but I was alone and it was beautiful. Alone to plot my way out. Alone to rue my luck. Alone to thank my lucky stars for having survived; I was very conflicted. Spinal injuries often have a destructive finality to them, something I'd known since I was eighteen. Allied to that misfortune, I now knew what an ill-advised combination spinal injuries and septic shock syndrome were. And to cap it all, I'd been reintroduced to what strokes can do. Nan had been gifted, by God or whatever, a stunning recovery from her first stroke. It really was a proper verifiable miracle. A Lourdes moment, if you like. Little did she or any of us know that it'd been a dry run for the second stroke. Such a cruel twist; bounced back from the first, only to be rendered completely incapable by the second. And now I was witnessing the catastrophe of strokes all over again.

To have the physical you snatched away is to experience a sense of injustice every bit as visceral, I'd imagine, as that of the wrongly imprisoned. Worse actually, because at least they can appeal, whereas there's no way back for the spinally injured and irredeemably stroked. What's lost is lost. And never mind what coping mechanisms you devise, there's always anger. There's always, 'Why me?' If you're lucky, it can be mitigated, almost erased, by other aspects of your life which are truly golden; in my case, Anna, my boys and my photography.

With a blanket over my legs Anna wheeled me to the lift and outside. Sitting by the main entrance in the sunshine, a suitable distance from the fag-gang pariahs, I sucked in fresh air. To feel those warm rays on my face and a breeze in my nostrils was incredible. From the direction of the car-park I spotted two camera club members from my past walking towards me. I hadn't seen them for years.

'Hi, how are you?' I said brightly, looking up from the wheelchair.

They considered me for a moment and passed on by.

'Who were they?' asked Anna, aghast at their lack of engagement.

'Oh, just people who used to know me,' I said, deflated. 'I'd like to go back in now.'

Was I so changed as to be unrecognisable? I'd lost a lot of weight but I was still me, surely. The same me, just gaunt and deathly pale. The same me, but in a wheelchair. But there was something I hadn't factored into my puzzlement. In the lift I caught myself in a mirror for the first time since becoming ill and there it was, the fat ugly weld across my chin. Sure, I'd felt it but that first sight hit me like a freight train. A bloody mirror had done for me yet again just like in Rookwood when I'd seen my ravaged body after the bike accident. In that instant in the lift, I plummeted. How much more could I take? Certainly, my survival from sepsis – sorry, septic shock syndrome – had been near miraculous and should've sufficed yet the sight of that hideous scar pulled the rug.

Back on the ward Anna read a book and stayed off my radar. I lay on the bed and stewed and fell asleep. I'd become rather adept in the previous weeks at stewing, with each perceived setback sapping just a little more of my resolve. I came round for supper, though, recalibrated. During pretty much my entire adult life I've had to snap out of any disposition towards self-pity. Once it gets a grip you're stuffed as I discovered after my law degree debacle and subsequent bout of depression all those years earlier. I couldn't allow a cosmetic by-product of having had my life saved eat away at me.

'It's a duelling scar,' I pronounced.

'Sorry?' said Anna, breaking off from her book.

'It's a duelling scar. From now on I'll imagine some heroic duel.'

I shook my head and smiled. 'With all I've been through I can't let this...' I said, pointing to my chin, '...get to me. I'm lucky to be alive... and with all my bloody limbs attached.'

And, just like that, the scar became a memento.

Sunshine arrived in the bay in the guise of Michael, a loser in the stroke lottery but bright as a button, mentally astute and chatty as hell. Actually, when I say loser, he was one of the luckier losers. His left arm and leg had been weakened but there was movement, and as each day passed those blighted muscles and that clobbered brain woke up a little more, spurred on by his determination. God, he was so positive it was like sharing with a faith healer. He laughed and talked and joked all through the day, his anecdotes lifting my spirits.

'Lived in France for ten years,' he said. 'Down in the Dordogne. Loved it. The lifestyle. People. Everything. Would've lived out my days there, no problem.'

'Why didn't you?'

'Ah, well, she missed the family, see. So we came back.'

His expression suggested that perhaps he hadn't missed his family quite as much. He'd hunted with neighbours, shooting and gutting wild boar, unearthed truffles and cut down trees in his own wood, spending the autumn chopping logs for winter. I envied him. And I could see a glint in his eye that hinted at life's journey still having much to offer. Perhaps even a return.

One night after lights out we were joined by another arrival as the curtains were drawn around the bed next to me. There was a one-way settling-in conversation, before the nurse said, 'Okay, John, comfortable now, sweetheart?'

John didn't respond. The curtains were pulled back, the nurse turned the light out, and I rolled over and went to sleep. Sleep. When you rediscover its glory, having been denied it, you feel like you're in possession of the most priceless thing in the world.

At least, I was in possession of it until being woken in the early hours. It was John. In the half-light, I could see him thrashing around. His right arm was under the sheets, clawing at something halfway down the bed. He was angry, and unable to put into words whatever it was that was bugging him.

Repeatedly, he yanked his arm out before plunging it back under the sheet. Then it hit me; the stench. I called for a nurse.

'What's wrong, John?' she asked as she lifted the sheets. 'Oh. Don't worry, sweetie, soon sort that out.'

I mouth-breathed, waiting for her to return with a colleague. They pulled the curtains and went to work, speaking reassuringly as they changed the sheets and washed him. The curtains were then opened again and, seeing me awake, one of the nurses came over.

'Sorry about that,' she said.

'Don't worry. Is he okay?'

'Yeah, just got a bit upset. All sorted now.'

She was about to walk away when she did a double-take.

'Oh. Really sorry,' she said, pointing at my sheet which had a number of fudgy flecks on it. 'I'll change it.'

John was a farmer, or at least he had been; a strong and physical man. And now, there he was, hacked down, unable to speak, lost in a world of broiling anger. Each night there was a repeat performance, though I was unaffected as I insisted on the curtain between us being drawn as a barrier from telly-off time.

After a few days John departed for the big bay as sweet William arrived, garrulous and rotund, straight out of a Dickens novel. With impeccable manners, boundless optimism and rosy cheeks he was our very own Mr Micawber. And best of all, he didn't chuck bodily waste around at night. Michael, William and I forged a triumvirate of uplifting chatter as I considered myself fortunate to be sharing with people who possessed all their cognitive capacity, exuding incredible positivity in tackling their respective blights. Both were in their seventies with curls of gossamer white hair, topped by bald crowns. I was happy for them to take me under their wings, listening to their stories and their wisdom, a Private Pike to their Corporal Jones and Private Godfrey in a stroke ward production of *Dad's Army*. During the day William hid his anxiety behind that smile, but there were night terrors, often frantic in his sleep and calling out. And so, I became his wingman, summoning help during the long nights. He was always very apologetic the next morning. But with just one remaining empty bed I was moving closer to the door and a return to the big bay.

As it'd been in Rookwood all those years earlier, each day in the gym felt as if new peaks were conquered. I progressed to walking between a set of parallel bars, initially in a harness suspended from the ceiling which ran along a track in case I fell. I soon dispensed with it, plotting lengths of the bars with Tim close behind, a five-metre stroll, gripping tightly. Two, three, four lengths and more followed in the ensuing days, my strength and muscle memory returning. The physios didn't work weekends so a nurse was entrusted with wheeling me down to the gym so that I could walk the bars. Finally, I tackled the *pièce de résistance*, a version of Rookwood's wheeled walking frame of old, the one that I imagined had been bequeathed by Brunel, such was its robust engineering. I'd come full circle.

Walks from the gym back to my bed became exits from the ward and along the corridors as I ticked off ever longer plods. I was surely strong enough to go home, I thought, as I dreamt of discharge, the day when I could restart my life. The staff counselled patience on my part, which wasn't easy; I just wanted to get out of there.

On the afternoon of 16th March 2013, Michael, William and I gathered around the telly to watch Wales play rugby against England at the Millennium Stadium. Wales trounced the old enemy 30-3 and the bay erupted. We almost jumped out of our seats in celebration. Almost. A nurse or two would pop in on the pretence of checking on us and stand glued to the telly, whooping along. I was puzzled as to why the three of us had been left in splendid isolation in a bay reserved for admissions. After all, myself, Michael and William were stable. In fact, they were both going great guns. So was I. Perhaps though, just perhaps, it was due to our good fortune in being able to chat, laugh and joke. Mentally, we were on top of our game. It seemed, at least to me, that we'd been corralled in a little bubble of normality.

No sooner had I been told, 'Good news, you're going home Monday,' than a plague of diarrhoea and vomiting swept the ward, with patients and staff going down like ninepins. I awaited its grim embrace as the boys in the bay became excruciatingly afflicted. A dose would certainly have postponed my discharge so I implemented unilateral quarantine measures, such as pulling the curtain permanently between myself and William, handwashing religiously, and even using the ether-based wash on cutlery before eating. Poor William apologised profusely from the other side of the curtain one lunchtime as he was lifted off the commode just feet away from my half-eaten chips and beef stew. It remained half-eaten. But somehow, call it divine providence if you like, my constitution managed to rebuff the seemingly inevitable. After nine weeks in hospital, I departed for home.

Chapter 33

I was home, a joyous closure to my ordeal which'd seemed unlikely during the first weeks of illness. As with 1984 – not the dystopian novel by George Orwell but my own bleak version – and coming home from Rookwood there was a sense of reprieve as I could've, perhaps should've, died. But, much like the boys when we first brought them home from hospital, I was incapable and utterly reliant on Anna. It'd been dispiriting being discharged in a wheelchair, as in 1984 I walked out of Rookwood, albeit leaning on Dad, but this time the trek to the car was beyond me, providing one of those crystallising moments that were to define so much of my life in the coming weeks and months. 'It'll be a year before you get back to normal,' a doctor had said. My progress since leaving intensive care, though, had been a cause for hope and so I blithely dismissed what I saw as an overly-pessimistic prediction. Give me a month and I'll be back to my version of normal, thank you very much. Anna wasn't so convinced, being more inclined to believe the doctor, and took a year's unpaid leave from her job.

For all of my stubborn, perhaps ignorant, bravado, it was year zero, just like all of those years ago in Cardiff in the aftermath of the bike crash. I had to be rebuilt and the only person capable of doing that was me, with help from those around me, of course. And for someone as determinedly independent as I was, the frustration of reliance was to boil over on occasion. I hated asking for help to get into the shower or out of a chair or to have my socks put on amongst a host of other minor indignities; that prickliness of a reluctant acknowledgement of physical inferiority that I'd railed against since 1984.

An array of aids for the infirm, installed prior to my return – a glut of ugly plastic handrails were particularly revolting – included a lightweight, four-wheeled walking frame with handgrips and a brake; a pimped-up Zimmer. The stability of the frame reduced the risk of falls in the house and it had a padded bench which'd come in handy for snatching breathers when I progressed to walking outdoors. I'd stooped, it seemed, to filching OAPs' hand-me-downs. Manoeuvring it around the house took some getting used to, clattering into doorframes and scraping furniture. The boys thought it highly entertaining, of course. It often went missing and I'd hear them careering around in another room, which cheered me, even taking into account the inconvenience of waiting for them to finish with it.

For thirty years I'd refused to acknowledge that amongst my peers and wider society I was viewed as disabled. That label didn't apply to me and woe betide anyone who might suggest otherwise. Certainly, I knew that I was damaged, walked a bit comically perhaps, but at no time did I think it warranted the category of disability. For starters, it's such a demeaning tag to apply to a person; to disable something is to render it of no use. Kaputt. So, at worst I saw myself as being less able than your average person but most definitely set apart from those with what I perceived as having genuine physically restrictive issues. Definitely set apart from '*the* disabled'.

Indeed, on good days when I strode with vigour, I imagined that I presented as someone who'd suffered a serious leg break, for example, and was left with a slight limp. Heroic rather than pitiful. There were bad days, of course, when my muscles and joints felt like they'd been bound tightly with bandages, and when the placing of one unguidable foot in front of the other was a lottery. Would I even make it to my destination without falling? Why is that bloody woman gawping at me? But whatever day I was having – good or bad – when I saw someone walking with great difficulty (quite likely on a par with myself) or maybe in a wheelchair, I'd think 'poor bastard' and pity them as being a disabled person. But it didn't apply to me.

I remember at Rookwood a bunch of us being taken out for a drink at a golf club in an adapted minibus. A kind of 'easing back into society' exercise, even though I hate golf. A huddle of us in wheelchairs enjoyed a pint by a huge window looking out at the eighteenth and the setting sun. Normality away from the ward, or as near as. For an hour we could forget what we were sitting in as we became our old us, as if the previous six months hadn't happened. One of the guys had been alone by the bar since we arrived so fearless Pete wheeled himself over to encourage him to join us. Pete returned, saying that the offer had been declined, as the guy didn't want to be seen with 'a bunch of fucking cripples'. He didn't, it seemed, consider himself to be one of us, or more likely didn't want to admit to it, though deep down he'd have known it only too well. Ditto me in the ensuing decades. Now, though, after sepsis, I felt like, and moved like, one of the 'poor bastards'.

Due to the risk of falling, I was never alone, my guards ever present, as if being suicide-watched. I needed help with just about everything. Decisions such as to sit in my armchair – a favoured occupation of old – required forward planning; the placement of a book, the newspaper, telly controls and a coffee within easy reach. I felt that I had to commit to a lengthy period in the armchair, as to get out of it required help and I was loath to ask for it, as I didn't want to be a burden. I began to adopt an apologetic tone for putting those around me out, even though they assured me it was no problem. Another coffee whilst sitting in the armchair? I had to call for someone, that someone invariably being Anna. Having drunk the coffee, biology would filter it to the other end and, again, I'd have to call for help to get out of the chair so that I could go to the toilet. I encouraged Anna to go outdoors into the sunshine with the boys as much as possible and so my parents or Anna's mum, Caroline, would stand guard. I felt a newfound sympathy with full-time carers.

Mealtimes were a dogged exercise in cramming in protein to fuel my exercise regime. I ate so many eggs we considered getting chickens and I complemented my apprenticeship of binge eating with heaps of protein powder. Pushing the wheeled frame around the house, going up and down the stairs and standing from a sitting position without help was as much as I achieved in that first couple of weeks. Gradually, though, I added more stresses and demands on my body as I felt my strength return.

A few months of photography business required attention: emails, backed-up print orders and a mountain of admin. Anna had done a fantastic job at letting people know what'd happened, but I had to catch up.

'I'm going to do some work,' I announced.

'Okay,' said Anna, 'but don't overdo it.'

'Don't worry, I'll be fine,' I said.

Like Mum and Dad all those years earlier when I came home from Rookwood, she chaperoned me upstairs to my office. I got comfortable at the computer and with a surge of brio began.

'Come and get me in an hour,' I said.

I felt as if I were back in the groove and all was fine. Ten minutes later I was exhausted, slumped over the keyboard, breathing heavily. It perfectly encapsulated the challenge that lay ahead, as a bit of typing had knackered me.

My first foray out into the street was equally deflating, if not more so. The aim had been to walk using the wheeled chariot to the end of our terraced row and back, not even a hundred metres. It was a tortoise-paced stumbling shuffle, stopping dead still when cars came along, excruciatingly conscious of how pitiful I looked and not wishing to fall in full view of the cars' occupants, or worse into the car. At that moment it hit me just how long the road back to my version of normality would be. That month I'd anticipated was disappearing fast.

I began to make coffee, a concession prized from Anna, who sanctioned all of my reclaimed independence. She was understandably anxious that I shouldn't hurt myself, as every physical action came with a risk, especially of losing my balance and falling. Getting a mug from the cupboard, a spoon from the drawer, fetching milk from the fridge, putting water in to boil; all had the potential for me to end up on the floor, not to mention being scalded. I concentrated on each element of the task as if climbing a rock face without ropes. Once I'd made a coffee, Anna carried it to wherever I wished to drink it.

One morning, mug in hand, I looked out to the garden from the kitchen. The sun was shining, birds were singing and the patio looked so inviting.

Harry saw my yearning.

'Want to go in the garden, Daddy?'

He looked up at me, four years old, so knowing and wanting to help.

'Sorry, Harry. Can't. Mummy will have to help me out.'

He smiled. 'I can help you,' he said, offering his hand.

I turned away and welled up as Anna came into the kitchen, took my coffee out to the patio then helped me over the threshold to step down to the level of the outside path. All planned, nothing spontaneous, life was slow, as if a handbrake were partially, or not so partially, on.

I managed to dump the chariot, buoyed that I'd discarded a symbol of reliance. The boys were sad to see it go though. I was more mobile but still terribly unsteady, ever braced for that fall which played out in my head. I lunged at furniture to catch stumbles, eyeing sharp edges and wincing at the thought of what they could inflict. Everywhere I saw deadly landing strips. For my ever-longer walks outdoors I acquired a pair of hiking poles, imagining myself as Sir Ranulph Fiennes trekking across the Arctic to excuse the necessity.

Anna found a set of moulded dumbbells in the back of a cupboard and I pumped them while viewing run-down houses going to auction in *Homes Under the Hammer*, part of my morning junk-viewing schedule. *Heir Hunters* was another favourite, the premise being somewhat thin: a team of private investigators hunting benefactors to estates left without a valid will – a race against the clock before the state nabbed the lot. The manufactured joy on the beneficiaries' faces when told of an inheritance by dint of a reclusive second cousin they'd not seen in years or even knew existed.

'And you say he lived nearby? Such a shame.'

Then came the souring of that moneyed smile when informed they'd be sharing the dosh with twenty other distant cousins. TV gold.

It was a glorious May day and I fancied a coffee – yes, I know, another coffee – out in the morning sun with my book. Ann had popped to the shop but I had it all sorted. With the book clamped under my left arm and the mug in the same hand I stepped carefully out of the kitchen, placing my left foot down onto the outside path, all the while holding the doorframe with my right hand. A doddle. The moment I let go of the frame my left knee buckled and I found myself face down on the path with blood trickling from a gash on my nose. On hearing me hit the concrete and the mug smash, a neighbour rushed round just as Anna was returning from the shop. They got me off the floor and into the car for a visit to A&E for stitches to the bridge of my nose and a bandage to a graze on my forehead. In addition to the large scar on my chin, my face began to resemble a Jack-the-Ripper practice slash.

That month to recover had come and gone, and my version of normal wasn't back. Okay then, it'll be two months, I thought. Even as I thought it, I knew it wasn't possible. It would indeed be months. Many months. That realisation was like a punch in the guts as I began to despair at the gruelling journey that lay ahead. For a few days the distant growling of the black dogs could be heard. Twenty years on from therapy, they were coming back to get me. And so I destroyed them before they could get their teeth into me.

The reason for my mental robustness was my family, the ultimate motivation to plough on. I was determined that I wouldn't let Anna down, who was pouring all her energies into my quest for a return to the old Dave. And then there were my boys, who didn't want to see their old man moping about feeling sorry for himself. It was going to take longer than I'd hoped, but I would recover, eventually.

Harry was four years old, attending school half-days, and was home for lunch. Sitting at the dining table with the sun streaming through the window, listening rapt to an account of his morning while not taking my eyes off him, was heaven. I said little, stroked his arm a lot and ate. Charlie would come bounding in like some dyspraxic rhino at four o'clock and proceed to crash around the house with a half-eaten sandwich lodged in his hungry mouth. I'd ask him about his school day, an enquiry he'd wilfully misconstrue as he told me of playground skirmishes, the inadequately sized dinners, and how he'd perfected the ruse of being first in the queue for food, wolfing it down and joining the back of another year group for seconds. 'It's easy. The dinner ladies never look at you,' he said. The wonder of home made me float: Harry's little voice reading a bedtime book; watching Charlie whittle a stick with a penknife *a la Just William*; the craftiness with which they accidentally squirted too much ketchup on their meals; seeing them come in dripping with mud from wading in the river. Normal service was resumed and I felt blessed to be able to witness it, those tiny pleasures infusing me with lottery-winning ecstasy.

It was around this time that I began to notice stories in the papers about sepsis and how avoidable the genocidal death toll was. Whether the illness was suddenly in vogue and newsworthy or I just simply hadn't noticed these pieces before I couldn't say. I just remember getting very emotional when I acknowledged how lucky I'd been. Reading about an illness that could have, perhaps should have, killed you, when your kids are rampaging around the house filling it with exuberance is sobering. But I was alive, and each day I managed to do something that I hadn't been able to do the day before.

At the end of May, Anna and I went to Brecon to stay in a B&B. I drove, the first time I'd been behind the wheel of a car since coming out of hospital. The next day I was to do a talk about my latest book, *Wales: A Photographer's Journey*, at the Hay literary festival just up the road. We had a large, airy room with clunky floorboards in an old house in the centre of town with views out to a walled garden, and it was lovely.

I saw the invitation to speak at the book festival as my reward for eight years of photographing the landscapes of Wales. From winning that category at the 2004 Welsh Photographic Salon – with the image of a refinery and the allegedly libellous title of 'Neighbour from Hell' – to appearing at one of the biggest celebrations of books in the world. It felt mad. The walk from the car to the marquee with Anna supporting one arm and the other clutching a hiking pole was daunting as we threaded our way against a tide of people exiting a talk. Helped onto the stage, I sat next to Carolyn Hitt, journalist and author, who was to interview me about the book.

'Excited?' she asked.

'God, yeah. This is crazy, Carolyn.'

When we were given the green light to start, the venue was packed, or so it seemed from where I was sitting. Carolyn lauded the book and asked lots of prescient questions; she'd done her research. I was a little overawed and hesitant to begin with but gradually gained confidence, perhaps sensing that I had the audience with me, while wrestling with that old recurring insecurity bubbling away just beneath the surface. A feeling that I was a fraud. Me at a book festival? Who the hell was I kidding? They'll rumble me soon enough, I thought, but kept talking.

You see, in the summer of 1976, I sat the eleven-plus, that fag-end of Empire litmus test by which the state determined academic promise – and a place at grammar school – from irredeemable mediocrity. I failed it and was shunted off to secondary school. At the end of the first term, though, there was promise of a renaissance when I placed third in a class table of overall attainment pinned to the wall; success or failure as public spectacle – I don't recall the name of the poor sod at the bottom. I was very proud. Doing well at school was also profitable; a lovely lady called Kath who worked with Mum in Oliver's shoe shop in Haverfordwest was so impressed when I popped in after school that she gave me fifty pence – a princely sum in 1976. That was the high point, though, as I soon deduced that being seen as moderately bright made me a bigger target for verbal and physical digs, so I endeavoured to dumb myself down. It didn't stop the digs, of course, but the pattern was set. Like a method actor taking on a challenging role, I dumbed myself down very convincingly. An ingrained laziness helped too.

Combined with the apathetic teaching, I bombed school, leaving at sixteen with three scraped 'O' levels and not a clue what I wanted to do. No plan. No desire. I was as empty a vessel as any educational psychologist could wish to study; an intriguing thesis of nothingness. With no job I drifted to technical college for a year to study an engineering course I had no interest in before landing a job in RNAD Trecwn, where I moved bombs around and slept. Oh, and I bought a motorbike, which didn't end well.

I'd spent my adult life with no reason to believe that I was good at anything aside from being a sarcastic, wise-cracking clown. The go-to funny guy. Making people laugh was intoxicating but not a talent on which to build a future. Maybe, though, sitting on that stage at the age of forty-eight, it was time to reset my mental compass. Perhaps I did deserve to be there. Perhaps it was time to believe in myself as being something other than talentless.

After the talk, I did a signing session in the bookshop, with Ruby Wax signing her new book on the table adjacent to me. Her queue was considerably longer than mine, but I didn't care. As I scrawled my signature on the last book in the queue, I felt like curling up in a ball, as the physical effort of the day had crushed me, but I was determined that we should enjoy our complimentary lunch and collect the crate of wine in lieu of payment; I could live with that kind of remuneration. Anna dragged me back to the car, where I slumped in the passenger seat for the hundred miles home, spent but happy. The year 2013 was shaping up to be momentous, for both good and bad.

A week after Hay, Anna supported me into the leisure centre, having been enrolled on a public health fitness programme by my doctor. This wasn't the sticky gym of my youth in the school sports hall but an all-new complex in which everything worked, the rickety multi-gym from decades earlier supplanted by various machines specific to certain muscle groups. For two months my fellow masochists on the programme were an aged assortment of recovering stroke patients, rosy-cheeked slaves to high blood pressure and a scattering of new joints and heart valves. We congregated in a geriatric offshoot of the main gym, leaving the dedicated meatheads to pump the serious iron, and huffed and puffed ourselves in the right direction to a soundtrack of fatalistic bonhomie.

'Bloody hell, Bob, slow down. You'll have another bloody coronary the way you're going,' was one memorable wheezing refrain.

In their ill-fitting supermarket tracksuits they pushed and pulled in stooped slow motion like a bunch of tortoises who'd left their shells at home, old people determined to get older. Once I'd completed the course, I was free to enrol in the main gym, where the real action lay. That's when my recovery took off, going two, three times a week for months, initially conscious of my laboured gait and stiff, mechanical torso but increasingly with a fluidity borne of building muscle, stamina and core strength. With each passing week that twelve-month prediction of a return to normality shrank to meet me till after about nine months from falling ill I felt fitter and stronger than I'd been before catching the strep bug, crossing the imaginary finishing line months earlier than I was supposed to. I felt great. Unlike previously though, I wasn't about to be seduced by that old delusion of a return to physical normality. I'd remain incomplete, but more complete than I'd been for many years.

One of the high points of that summer of 2013 – and there were many – was a visit from my friend David and his wife Karon. Nudging fifty, I felt it time to stop referring to him by his nickname of Mucky. Just didn't feel right. He was grown-up David now, but thankfully still in possession of Mucky's giggling sense of humour. Almost thirty years earlier he'd left Haverfordwest to make a life for himself and, subsequently, his family in England. And it'd been ten years since I'd last seen him, which was unfortunate; to have seen him more would've been a joy. The afternoon passed in a whirl of mutual ribbing and warm conversation, each of us attuned to and in sync, with our respective wry view of life. I'd missed him. Sat in the garden, watching him laugh, I was reminded of his friendship of old, amongst many others, when I came home from Rookwood in 1984 after the bike crash. He'd called often to take me out in his Morris Marina Coupe – British racing green, of course – oblivious to my recent trauma and driving as if competing in a time trial around the coast roads before stopping for an ice cream. Those memories were now far enough in the past to be filed under 'N' for nostalgia.

In September I felt strong enough to stand and watch Charlie play rugby at the start of the under-nines season, my first spectate since January, a week before becoming ill. There was a round-robin tournament in Whitland, the ground choked with parents and kids darting here and there. I was insistent that I'd do it solo, without Anna's supportive hand or the hiking poles, even though it terrified me. Nothing like a bit of fear to concentrate the mind.

Witnessing all that youthful on-field energy haphazardly unleashed had never failed to lift my spirits. Tactically, rather than adhering to the structures inherent in the game of rugby, the Llangwm boys were more inclined to hunt the ball like a pack of hounds, converging in a frenzy on the oval-shaped object as if it were a joint of meat. This tactic inevitably gifted the opposition acres of space out wide when they came into possession of the ball, which was a lot of the time. Although Harry was only four years of age, he evidently viewed his omission from the starting fifteen as an oversight and duly trotted onto the pitch regularly to join in – Anna eventually decided he needed a long walk, in the opposite direction. Charlie played his allotted games with unfocused gusto before firing down a brace of hotdogs, and as we departed the ground for home, I was able to tick off another feat of normality.

The morning TV schedule was dropped, an occupational crutch I no longer needed. No more vermin-infested flats going to auction and clutches of second cousins twice removed sharing a paltry inheritance. I'd recently returned to the landscape and my next book. Before becoming ill I'd formulated an idea for a book of Welsh buildings. It was broad-brush and lacking detail, but over the summer months the basic proposition began to take shape: a journey through Welsh history as represented by a selection of buildings and sites of national importance. I co-opted two architectural historians to research and write the copy while I gambolled about the country, another adventure masquerading as work.

In the turned-down heat of an October day Anna and I ventured off for the first shoot: Soar y Mynydd chapel, which sits in the grasslands of the Cambrian Mountains just within the border of Ceredigion. It's miles from anywhere and that anywhere is miles from anywhere else, the isolation beautiful and precious. The door to the chapel was unlocked, so in we went. A faint whiff of beeswax lingered on pews worn pale by generations of worshippers. It was austere and simple. Combining photography with my addiction for history, I was already clamouring for the other locations on the shot list.

Anna accompanied me often after that, partly to help lug equipment, partly because she enjoyed our days out. We hatched plans, dreamt up schemes and, as the days drew to a close, drove home to bask in the glow of our boys once again.

When I look back on that year, in a perverse way I see it as a blessing that I endured what I did. I emerged from sepsis a different person than the one who'd woken on New Year's Day, embracing life even more, knowing that I'd very nearly lost it.

I'd considered myself immune to illness, indestructible, always pushing in the belief that nothing could touch me. I just kept going at it, driving myself on and on, with the occasional physical meltdown seen as the price I had to pay. Always that need to prove myself, to portray a person no different from anyone else. Sepsis, though, was a wake-up call, the lesson being to listen to my inner self. I had to go at the pace of *my* body, not someone else's.

There was more to it than that though, as I came out of it a calmer person. A seam of residual anger over the spinal injury had stayed with me even after the therapy all those years earlier in '95, surfacing on occasion when I was exhausted and stressed. I'd snap. That's not to say that I'd been an angry person per se, but there was something within me that could erupt when I hit the wall. Learning moderation in my physical exertions, I triggered that latent anger much less often and, when it did erupt, it barely registered on any Richter scale – more a strong breeze than the previous tornado.

I don't recall any mention of 'in sickness and in health' during our wedding vows in Amalfi, but what I do know is that without Anna's unflinching support and encouragement during this year I'd have wavered. The boys' voices in my head may've stopped me checking out when I was on the ventilator, but after that it was Anna who was instrumental in getting me back to my version of normal. She was extraordinary.

Chapter 34

I took a moment to register the odour of kept-warm food, a lingering miasma in the corridor. The supper wagon, then, had done its rounds, disgorging its lank chips and corned beef, over-boiled veg and hydrogenated tomato soup. Driving up the speed-humped access road, I hadn't quite believed I was back. The stench of murdered cabbage, though, confirmed it. Thirty years had passed and nothing seemed to have changed, at least not from a culinary point of view. The senses were additionally assaulted by an array of cleaning agents and stale urine in the slops room, all topped off with a faint whiff of despair, a fragrance I once knew only too well. I never imagined that I would ever return to Rookwood. I certainly never wished to. But there I was, searching out my friend Jeff, who was a patient.

Even at the tender age of eighteen, in another life, I'd been struck by how make-do it'd all felt, an establishment seeking to convey a sense of specialism despite its worn-out fabric and ad hoc bolting on of flat-roofed extensions. And all these years later this was still the best Wales had to offer the spinally unfortunate.

Anna and I found Jeff on a ward in a part of the maze I'd not previously known. He was as bright as I knew he'd be, considering. Statistically, he was marked down as a toppled-off roof repair, not as numerous as failed stunt motorcyclists but still with an impressive tally of victims over the decades.

I hadn't spoken to Jeff since the rugby tournament in Whitland months earlier, just prior to his fall. He'd welled up with joy that day at my survival from sepsis. And now it was my turn to well up, though not perhaps with the same sense of joy, on seeing him in a wheelchair. We chatted and laughed and shook our heads in rueful agreement on a raft of current affairs like a pair of village elders leaning on a farm gate as I helped him out with a surfeit of chocolate he'd accumulated. The other patients nodded warmly when I caught their eye and the staff were busy, of course, beetling about with their endless tasks. Everyone was resolved to be cheery, affecting a Blitz spirit in spite of the inadequacies of the place. Jeff was now, as I'd once been, one of the convoy being wheeled across the car park through the weather to the archaic gym, when there was a physio available to do the pushing, that is; the patients had complained of a lack of treatment.

To suffer a spinal injury is a deeply traumatic experience and in many cases the loss of function has a gut-wrenching permanence. So, when the physical injury stabilises and you alight at last from bed after perhaps months of horizontal frustration, there's a gnawing desperation to discover what there is to reclaim from the wreckage. To find out where your limits lie, while not wishing to terminate at the point of a new normal but hoping for a return to your old normal. Jeff and his ward-mates so wanted to see where that line was. To then perceive a rationing of physio was crushing.

The time came to depart and Anna and I said our goodbyes and exited the ward. It was then that I sensed a yearning to retrace thirty-year-old steps.

'Hang on a minute,' I said, getting my bearings. 'If we head up this way it'll take us past the... yeah, past the canteen.'

Sure enough, just round the curve of a corridor there it was, doors locked.

'God, I remember coming down here with Dan and Pete for lunch. The food was hot here. Better than the half-cold crap on the ward,' I said, brushing my hand over the door, as if that would somehow conjure up more memories. 'Huh, I remember, to get my legs working they took the foot plates off my wheelchair. Used my legs to pull myself along.'

'Quite a climb back to the top,' said Anna, pointing up the corridor. 'Is that the way you came?'

'Yeah. Poor Dan, struggled like hell on the way back.'

'Well, must've been hard for all of you.'

'Yeah, but Dan only had one good arm, see.'

I explained that his legs and his right arm didn't work. Anna looked aghast.

'He'd pull himself up using the handrail on the wall,' I said, nodding to it.

'Couldn't the staff have helped?'

'No, they wouldn't. Their attitude was, "Do it yourself." And Dan wouldn't have let them anyway. Too bloody proud.'

Chips and identifiable corned beef – not the pink sludge from the wagon on the ward – and then the return slog.

We walked up to the main atrium, from where a number of corridors sprouted like the spokes of a wheel. I contemplated making my way to the ward I'd been on but decided against it, realising I'd stepped into a timeline I had no wish to explore any further. That boy I was looking for no longer existed; I'd polished him off in therapy in '95. It was time to go. I left feeling sad both at Jeff's felling but more so by the shame of Rookwood's continued existence. Surely we can do better than this, I thought.

Earlier that day, before seeing Jeff, Anna and I had visited Castell Coch, that fairy-tale confection of an imagined medieval stronghold just north of Cardiff. It was to feature in the book of Welsh buildings that I was working on. Concocted by the 3rd Marquess of Bute on the back of coal, I found it a difficult place to photograph, not through any lack of suitable material but due to my instinctive dislike of what all of that obscene wealth had produced. I struggled to admire the exquisite wall paintings edged in gold leaf and the opulent fittings that decorated this palace of excess, a late nineteenth-century chav fest. The marquess decamped there when the whim took him, entertaining plutocrats and politicians while beneath them the moles burrowed to generate his wealth. It was one of my least favourite locations on the shot list.

There were more engaging locations in the book. The story of the disappeared village of Capel Celyn in the Tryweryn valley in north Wales was poignant. The village and its fields and farms and woods were submerged to provide Liverpool with drinking water. Families and neighbours who'd lived and worked side by side for generations were dispersed to the wind, rootless, their homes demolished and a dam wall built. The abomination of the London-based decree fired a resurgent sense of nationalism amongst the Welsh. Headstones were removed from the chapel's graveyard before it disappeared beneath the lapping waters and transplanted in the vicinity of a squalid little modernist pile by the edge of the reservoir. It only serves as a searing reminder of loss and powerlessness.

In 2014 we went on holiday to Normandy. Charlie was nine and enamoured of soldiering and armies and war. It was the seventieth anniversary of the D-Day landings and he was to have a disproportionate say in our itinerary. We stayed in a converted barn south of Caen belonging to John and Suzanne, who'd filled it with an eclectic mix of French countryside finds, and it was idiosyncratic and lovely. They lived in an adjacent house, having escaped the south-east of England, leaving behind over-work, vanishing green space and choking traffic. Their new rustic life sang to them, punctuated by John's occasional bit of building work in the neighbourhood, content for the most part to tend their vegetables, feed the chickens and quaff the odd red.

'You miss Kent, then,' I said, in jest.

'Yeah, like a bloody hole in the head,' replied John.

They'd found their little bit of utopia and ambled about with a faint beatific smile. I was envious.

Excursions revolved around the D-Day landing beaches, museums of war materiel and the boys running through sand dunes with stick guns. One fine day we decamped to what'd been designated as Omaha Beach, scene of the bloodiest landing. The endless sands shrank away in both directions, with clustered dots of people as far as the eye could see. Charlie set to positioning his toy soldiers and tanks to replicate the Americans' landing on 6th June 1944, Harry dug holes and chased a ball in the breeze and Anna and I slumped in deckchairs. At one point I opened my eyes and acknowledged a macabre unreality; families frolicking and playing on sands that'd once been soaked in blood. Somehow it just didn't seem right, especially witnessing Charlie's little tableau, replete with exploding sound effects.

'Don't know about you, but I'm a bit uneasy. Knowing what happened,' I said to Anna. It was the sunbathers that got me, lying motionless like corpses.

'Yeah, know what you mean.'

We packed up, got the boys an ice cream and departed for a tour of a reinforced concrete gun battery on a headland a few miles away instead.

There was a sense of sombre duty, wandering around battle sites and thinking of all of those killed or wounded. As the week wore on, though, we paid our respects less, veering from yet another martial remembrance and seeking out lighter pleasures. As for me, I was just happy to be on holiday with my family, as there'd been a time in the near past when that'd seemed an unlikely gift.

Children often express themselves through drawing – I certainly did and our two were no different. Charlie tended towards battle scenes while Harry preferred a good old disaster. Sailing back to Plymouth he sprawled himself out on the floor of the passenger lounge with an A4 pad and pencils and began his latest masterpiece. Oblivious to passengers stepping around him and lost for a good hour in his drawing, we awaited the reveal. Suddenly, he sprang to his feet, pad in hand, and we took in a detailed work that drew on his then fascination with the sinking of the *Titanic*. The angle of the upturned stern as it slid towards the icy waters was spot on and the passengers falling from the upper decks into the ocean was something to behold. Feeling proud, and perhaps mischievous, he strolled around the well-populated lounge showing it to all and sundry. There were polite and indulgent smiles while others looked a little unsettled.

I continued compiling the images for the buildings book and over the horizon once again came Carwyn with the irresistible offer of a short film about the project for *Wales Today*, the regional daily news programme. I met him at Llanerchaeron, the Victorian model farm run by the National Trust near Aberaeron, which was to feature in the book. As with our previous collaborations, Carwyn was a one-man band; just him and an admirable ability to lug around huge volumes of equipment. Mo Farah would've been impressed by his stamina levels. As he filmed, I wheeled out what he alluded to as my trademark meaningful glances into the middle distance while hobbling around at his direction. By early afternoon we were on the meandering back roads heading for Soar y Mynydd in the Cambrian Mountains to continue filming. It was lovely to be back at the little chapel on the prairie that Anna and I had visited a year before.

Filming, as I'd come to appreciate, is a dislocated process, with more time spent in breaks from filming than being filmed. For some, the hanging around inactivity must be frustrating. Carwyn's breaks, though, were filled with conversation and laughter, his black humour chiming with mine. Indeed, we hit it off too well, as there came a point in the dying of the afternoon where we realised the need to get more focused; to stop gabbing and crack on. Come four o'clock the November daylight leeched out just as we finished. Dropping down in our cars to Llandovery, he turned left for Cardiff and I right for the west. I was beginning to feel like Carwyn's muse! Actually, I liked being Carwyn's muse. The piece that'd taken a pleasurable day to bag was aired and was beautifully shot and narrated, as always.

For my fiftieth in 2015, a milestone any betting man may've been reluctant to put a wager on, we went to Italy. It'd been twelve years since Anna and I had got married in Amalfi and we wanted to show the boys the country. We flew to Pisa, picked up a hire car and drove an hour down the coast to a Eurocamp – a bit like Butlin's but with pine trees and sun – imagining it an ideal base from which to explore Tuscany, which Anna and I had toured back in 2002, a year before our marriage. Our static caravan was cramped and budget-end functional but it didn't matter as we weren't anticipating being in it much. Anna and I realised that compromise would be the key to a harmonious holiday and so the boys had the freedom to explore the park till early afternoon when we'd bundle them in the car and venture off to a cultural must-see.

It was mid-May and the sprawling unheated open-air pool had an Arctic nip. We mostly swam alone, as the other campers seemed to think better of it. And when in the pool, boy did we swim, or simply thrash around frantically in the hope of retaining sufficient body heat to continue to function. Harry would emerge from the water with blueish lips and lie on the sun-warmed terracotta tiles tightly wrapped in his Spiderman towel. Once revived, he'd jump back in.

Volterra was suggested to the boys for our first outing, talking up its vampire credentials, courtesy of a recent Hollywood film, and thinking it wise to avoid any mention of Renaissance architecture or frescoes. We arrived as the sun was dipping and parked by one of the city gates that puncture the circuit of walls. Much to our relief, the boys embraced it, asking questions, peering down dark alleyways and imagining murderous deeds and chasing one another around the square in the blackening night with sticks-cum-swords. Supper in a cosy backstreet trattoria concluded the perfect maiden excursion.

Having got away with Volterra, we tried San Gimignano on them. Playing on Charlie's fascination with all things military, I drew his attention to the many towers, regaling him with a potted history of the warring medieval city-states, with Harry aping his older brother's enthusiasm. We shared a pizza the size of a dustbin lid on the main square while watching a colourful parade of flag-waving citizens in mock Renaissance costume banging drums and discharging replica firearms. It was noisy and smoky and they loved it.

The day before our holiday's end we caught a train to the main event, Florence, stepping off at the station into fan-oven heat. It's a euphoric city, a city that overpowers at every turn. For Anna and I, thirteen years before it'd been a place to see and touch and marvel. And now we'd returned with our boys. We crammed in a hectic five-hour itinerary: standing on the Ponte Vecchio and gazing into the emerald waters of the Arno while fending off a succession of aggressive street hawkers pushing their wares in what felt like a reverse mugging; a stroll past the Uffizi gallery – which Anna and I had viewed on our previous tour – but declining to queue for half a day; a second-mortgage funded ice cream in the magnificent public square, the Piazza della Signoria, as the boys sniggered at the nude statue of David by Michaelangelo; and finally the outsized splendour of the cathedral of Santa Maria del Fiore, before a laboured trudge back to the station. The air-conditioned train was a relief as I slumped into a seat with a dehydrated thud in the back of my head. That old obsession with bladder control could be quite punishing.

For all of the heightened joy of the holiday, something just wasn't right. I felt physically flat and leaden the whole ten days. Everything, every single action, was a panting, aching effort. I attributed it to broken sleep – there were nightly shoot-outs in the adjacent fields, a traditional lamping for rabbits with fusillades from midnight till dawn. It was the season, apparently. Anna and the boys slept majestically while I lay awake flinching, contemplating whether I should acquire a gun of my own and head out there myself; not to shoot rabbits though.

The flight home was as torturous and cramped as the outbound flight had been, the difference being that I boarded it shot through. Landing in Bristol, a packed transfer bus waited on the runway while I stretched legs that'd turned to stone just enough to get down the steps, and haul my carcass across the tarmac to climb aboard. The boys were wonderfully brave, walking beside me in solidarity when they could easily have put some distance between themselves and the embarrassing wreck. Entering the terminal building I stumbled and fell into a slight lady in front of me. She lurched forward and grabbed a handrail, her backward glance bristling with anger. I apologised but she wasn't placated, shaking her head with such a look of disgust, probably assuming I was drunk. I'd seen many reactions in people's eyes over the decades – pity, embarrassment, ridicule even. But drunk had the most power to hurt, especially as I was with my boys.

Passport control was woefully understaffed as it took an hour to bustle our way through, corralled like away fans at a football match. Dragging my feet towards the luggage carousel, I sensed my will to carry on leaving me. I swigged a bottle of water, took deep breaths and fought to remain upright as we grabbed our cases and wheeled them towards arrivals. I was visualising the hotel room just a twenty-minute drive away and the relief of bed when Harry's six-year-old appreciation of basic driving etiquette undid me; he beetled past with his wheeled case and cut across my path. Down I went, thudding hard on the tiled floor. Thankfully, we weren't quite within sight of the arrivals lounge so at least my demise was private. Dazed, I glanced up to see an officious-looking middle-aged lady in a hi-viz speaking into a walkie-talkie. 'A passenger's collapsed. Might need to summon an ambulance,' she said frantically. I cut in and suggested in a forthright manner that it'd be more beneficial if she, Anna and Charlie helped me to my feet. Once up, she began to fill in an incident report and ask irksome questions, so I limped off through arrivals and out to the car. I hugged Harry and told him it wasn't his fault, which was a lie, but that's what parents do, and headed for the hotel, convinced that I was in the grip of something.

The next morning, we partook of the ritual of the Premier Inn breakfast, a curate's egg of an experience. As a bed for the night to break a journey, the Inn can't be beaten; guaranteed to be comfortable, quiet and clean. Breakfast, though, is a queasy reminder of Britain's obesity epidemic, as the knowing and as-yet oblivious Type Twos waddle back and forth restocking groaning plates. I ate looking down. Sufficiently fed, we grabbed our bags, jumped in the car and headed home, that beckoning journey that ends with the reward of opening your very own front door.

I imagined, hoped, prayed even, that home and a few lie-ins would reenergise me. It didn't. I couldn't offload the deadness and after a few days it arrived: an uncontrollable shaking. Surely not, I thought. My temperature had rocketed, but I was cold. Or was I? I was certainly aware of an infection, lying in bed with a plastic urine bottle in place to catch the searing drips. A water infection from not drinking enough water on holiday? Oh, the irony of it. The sepsis ordeal of two years earlier was raw enough to set off alarm bells and Anna was resolute and determined.

'Okay, this isn't good. You're off to A&E,' she said with a stridency with which I dared not argue. I didn't want to argue. There'd be no phoning a hotline for a stab-in-the-dark diagnosis this time.

We pulled up outside the entrance to A&E. I couldn't walk in so Anna fetched a wheelchair. That shadow was falling over me again. I knew it. I knew the feeling. Anna went to the reception desk and said, 'I think my husband's got sepsis. He's had it before. He needs to see a doctor quickly.' Through the shaking, I felt proud of her determination to get me the attention I needed.

The waiting room was empty except for two padded women in their early twenties, sitting together, decked out in bobbly pastel-coloured shell suits. Whatever ailed these ladies it didn't prevent them scrolling on their phones, only breaking off to watch me shake and judder. I really was putting on quite a show. A nurse emerged from the treatment area and called my name. The shell suits rolled their eyes and huffed then resumed their scrolling. Anna wheeled me into the treatment area.

'So, what have we got here?' said a young and sturdy Dr Jones, with a rumbustious presence that suggested previous med school rugby. He immediately made me feel that I was in safe hands, even though I was convulsing and juddering and found it difficult to speak. Anna gave him a potted resume of my previous sepsis episode and the concern that perhaps I was heading the same way. He took my temperature and blood pressure, both of which brought a grimace.

'I'll just take some blood,' he said, seemingly with a presumptive sense of where the diagnosis was heading.

With practised fluency he drew some in a flash and disappeared.

There was a ratcheting unease at what could be coming down the line. In fact, what I knew to be coming down the line. Anna was clutching my hand, nervously turning to check for Dr Jones' return.

'I don't. Think. I can. Fight it. This. Time,' I said, blurting out the words in between convulsions.

Anna hugged me and we cried as if I were about to be taken out and shot for a crime I hadn't committed. It wasn't so much the prospect of an end that bothered me, as I'd felt death's clammy grip and knew how easy it'd be to let go. And I knew that I would let go. Not even the boys calling in my head would've stopped me. Not this time. I cried at the unfairness of it. I cried because I was angry that at the age of fifty I was being chivvied towards the big fridge by some nasty, squalid illness. I mean, we all have to check out sometime to make room for the next lot. That's a given. But sepsis? Christ, no. To have died in the motorbike accident would've been tragic but memorable. To have died when I was either a passenger in a speeding car or driving like a prick myself would've been reckless and memorable. Memorable for all the wrong reasons, but memorable all the same. To die from dodgy piss, though, would be pitiable and instantly forgettable. Ignominious even.

Dr Jones returned.

'Analysing your bloods right now. Had a quick read of your notes. Lucky to be here! Temperature's high. Blood pressure's not great and then there's the rigors,' he said with a demonstrative sweep of his hand over my juddering body. Rigors are a medical term for uncontrollable shaking, the body's attempt to cool its core temperature. You shake like you're on top of Everest in a pair of Speedos but you're actually overheating.

'I'll just see how those bloods are doing,' he said.

Like some medical Pimpernel, he vanished again. I didn't like it when he disappeared, as if him being there would somehow make a difference in itself. So, I shook and cried and stared at the ceiling. After what seemed an age, he bounded back into the room.

'The bloods are showing uro-sepsis... a urine infection that's got into your blood. So, I'm going to knock this on the head before it gets out of hand.' From behind his back, he produced a syringe containing what he assured me was the largest permissible dose of the most powerful antibiotic in the hospital.

'This should sort it,' he said.

Sledgehammers and nuts sprang to mind but I was reassured by the triggering of the nuclear option. As I lay there, I wondered whether I'd been entered into some macabre competition – survive, let's say, three variants of sepsis and win an all-inclusive holiday to the Maldives! First streptococcal and now dodgy piss. What, I wondered, would the third manifestation be? There was bound to be a third blight somewhere down the line. I was becoming resigned to what seemed like a susceptibility to serious illness.

Within half an hour of the injection I'd stopped shaking, my temperature was down and my blood pressure began to climb, a little. Action Man had saved the day, or me to be more precise.

'Right, time to ship you on,' he said.

'Thank you so much. Really don't know what to say,' I blurted with relief.

'Don't worry, all in a day's work,' he said, laughing, having just put that creeping shadow to the sword. How many people presenting with symptoms of sepsis would still have been alive if they'd been seen by a Dr Jones?

Anna accompanied me on the short push to the High Dependency Unit, secreted behind A&E. I was safe. I wasn't going to die. Not this time anyway. I suggested she go home. There was nothing to worry about. Well, not much. She left.

During the night I lost count of the times I grabbed a disposable container to pee into. And with just a few frantic seconds between the urge and the delivery, timing was crucial. Losing control of my bladder meant no sleep. My mind was racing too much to sleep anyway. I felt wired. And, I figured that if I were awake at least I'd have a head start on alerting the staff if I detected a downward spiral. Every couple of hours a doctor came to check for any indicators that might cause concern. I'd stare at them anxiously, praying for a continued reprieve from escalation, looking for that satisfied nod or thin smile.

I lay in that side room in the half-light staring through a large window into the corridor, the occasional nurse or doctor striding past, inducted once again into the constancy of the hospital machine which never switches off. After the strep episode two years earlier, I'd consoled myself, prematurely it seemed, that I'd had my allotted go at that sepsis lark and it'd never darken my door again.

The next morning, stabilised, I was transferred to a single-bed side room on a ward. I'd been in this room once before. Five years earlier, my friends and I had gathered around that very same bed to say goodbye to Anthony, one of the boys. The proverbial human dynamo, he fizzed and crackled with energy, brimming with ideas and schemes and as often as not, a hefty dose of mischief. One of the sweetest and most generous-spirited people I ever knew, he possessed an edgy unpredictability which could manifest itself in outrageously entertaining behaviour. Or, on occasion, outrageously scary behaviour. One Saturday night, having had our fill of what Haverfordwest had to offer (not that much), he insisted on taking a bunch of us for a spin in his newly acquired BMW. We imagined a few showy laps around town but found ourselves instead on the A40 to Fishguard – sixteen miles of rapid road along which Anthony drove very rapidly. It was the most disturbing car journey of my life, even when set against many diabolical journeys over the years, some with me at the wheel.

As we'd stood around his bed – now my bed – with just a day or so of life left, he roused himself from within the deepest, darkest recess, opened his eyes and flashed that golden smile, wanting us to feel good. Wanting to cheer us as he'd done so often. Generous to the end.

I was in hospital for a week, each day regaining more control of my bladder and dispensing with the jitters. Uro-sepsis, it seemed, didn't possess the same sting as the strep of two years previous, which'd put me in for nine weeks. On discharge, though, I still felt raw, as if I'd been flushed out with an industrial cleaner. Very weak. Very deflated too. It'd got to me. It'd got me down. A wheelchair from the ward was suggested, but I insisted on walking out to the car, clinging to a handrail all the way to the hospital entrance. It very nearly proved to be a case of pride before a fall. And I had a new mantra to accompany 'pick your feet up' – 'drink more'.

Gripped with resigned fatalism, I mused in a surprisingly cheery way over what to choose as my funeral songs. Well, after staring into the abyss yet again, I thought it apt that I should consider the logistics of my bowing out. Having skirted the dark side a few times, the sting of death was, it seemed, losing its potential to unnerve me. Not that I was embracing the thought of it, mind. Anyway, to get the tears rolling at the crem it could only be INXS's 'Never Tear Us Apart'. It was played at the funeral of Michael Hutchence, INXS's lead singer, after his misguided shenanigans in a Sydney hotel. To sing at your own funeral – now there's something. Anyway, to accompany me behind the curtain and the awaiting hellfire, it'd have to be 'Fisherman's Blues' by the Waterboys, a heartening shanty with a touch of jaunty fiddle thrown in to put a smile on the mourners faces as they emerge into the sunshine – I'd ruled out any chance of it raining on my parade. There'd be no religious tosh to mar the ceremony so maybe they could slot in 'Islands in the Stream' too, by Dolly and Kenny. Just a shame I wouldn't be able to enjoy it. There but not there.

Months after being discharged, I was reading the local paper and noticed the proceedings of a coroner's court. I wouldn't ordinarily have read such a piece but something drew me to it. It was a tragic tale of a lady around my age who'd contracted uro-sepsis and died. Not just made her ill but took her life. As I read it, I could feel my blood run cold. Not a Third Division pretender to Premier League strep after all. No, uro-sepsis was a killer too.

After a second helping of sepsis, I was reminded that I needed to be attuned to changes in my body, to recognise the warning signals that could spell trouble. Avoiding behaviour such as not drinking on hot Tuscan days was top of the list. Not that I anticipated having to drink often on hot Tuscan days, more's the pity. I'd made a similar covenant with myself two years earlier after the streptococcus nearly did for me, but as time passed I'd become blasé, considering a repeat evermore unlikely the further I got from the original nightmare. Twice bitten was enough though. I didn't fancy a third variant, even if it meant missing out on a chance of the Maldives!

Chapter 35

There was a new television crime drama set in Ceredigion, west Wales. It came in two linguistic flavours: first up, the Welsh-language *Y Gwyll* and later the English *Hinterland* – the same scenes shot twice in two languages. It was strong, with gripping storylines and sweeping cinematic direction. And yes, it was grim, with its unrelenting diet of murder. Ceredigion, it seemed, was a dangerous place. Watching, and reading, the subtitled 'foreign' language production – the Haverfordwest of my youth wasn't a natural stomping ground for our native tongue – made me feel a touch cosmopolitan.

The only other subtitled television series I'd stuck with was the German U-boat drama *Das Boot* in the mid-80s. A few years before that, me and my mates used to hurtle into town on our bikes on a Friday night to catch subtitled French art – okay, soft porn – films in The Palace Cinema, the titles alone promising plenty of illicit action. Inevitably, they were a series of carnal disappointments, both to us and the dozen or so solitary hunched men scattered about the cinema. There was to be no nudity in the bare landscapes of Ceredigion though. Too cold I expect.

That landscape was brooding, reflective perhaps of the terrible secrets buried within it. Scoured by the weather blasting in from the Irish Sea, this was a land where the people and buildings skulked down out of the winds and sideways rain. A landscape drained of colour, with its bleached hues and mere hints of life, the peeling paint and rust of farm buildings and dilapidated cottages the only vivid cues. A murderous land, then, and a place of dark deeds. And I loved it. It was new and daring and the landscape was the star, at least for me.

At the beginning of the second series in late 2015 – following a ping-pong of mutual appreciation on social media – Ed Talfan, one of the show's producers, asked if I'd be interested in making a book to celebrate not just the programme but Ceredigion itself. Once again, as on many occasions over the years, I had to pinch myself, replying very quickly in the affirmative. And so, in early 2016 I set off into the landscape of Ceredigion while Ed and his co-producer Ed Thomas began filming the third and final series.

While filming, the cast and crew decamped for long stretches to Borth, a tired seaside town near Ceredigion's northerly border with Gwynedd. Borth has the feel of a forgotten frontier settlement, a place on the edge, a bit Wild West, if you like – but in a nice way! One long street wide, it sits between the broiling Irish Sea and an expanse of boggy grassland. You don't go to Borth to go anywhere else; it is the destination. And, unlike, say, Llandudno – which I'd photographed for an earlier book – on the North Wales coast, with its creaky parade of the elderly along the oh-so-neat prom, killing time before dying, there are no pretensions to grandeur in Borth. With the sea nibbling away, one day the town will be gone, a folklore memory, off to join the other drowned coastal settlements around Cardigan Bay swallowed up over thousands of years. And hunched behind the town like some sleeping giants are the Cambrian Mountains, a series of rolling grassy uplands with a prairie-like vastness. This was my kind of country.

Thirty years had elapsed since that day when I'd driven up the coast road to Aberystwyth and turned inland with the haste of someone couriering a freshly donated organ for transplant. It'd been one of those coping days during the bad years. Days of distraction that stopped me thinking of all the negative stuff in my head. Stopped me thinking of how empty my life was. How scared my life was. But something happened to me that day. The hills had seemed to whisper some incantation as I'd brunched on ham sandwiches and a Mars Bar by a disused lead mine in Cwmystwyth. I remember looking at the hills and imagining myself as a photographer. As if it were an actual possibility. As if I belonged out in the landscape, visualising a life that might offer more than just eating up days sitting in my parents' lounge staring at patterned wallpaper. That day marked the beginning of a belief – tentative at first – that eventually led to the fulfilment of a dream. A dream of being a photographer.

And now I was back at that disused mine as I had a book of Ceredigion to do. This time, though, I'd driven at a socially acceptable speed; age diminishes the reckless streak, thankfully. Age, and an accumulation of fixed penalty fines in the late nineties for various driving offences; it'd been prudent to slow down to keep my licence and I never sped up again.

Standing on the same spot, nothing had changed except for the disappearance of some of the mine buildings. The crest of the hill line, the river Ystwyth running towards the sea, were all remembered shapes. I thought of that young man, with his artless mullet, hooped earrings and groin-splicing shorts, straight out of a Wham! video. His beloved red Ford Escort XR3i parked by the roadside as he ate brunch, with little idea of where he was going that day or indeed any day after that for a long time. Rudderless.

That previous life had been lit by the occasional bright moment but the litany of emotions that dominated were anger, fear and a touch of paranoia. Actually, more than a touch; a bloody big wedge. There was Tenerife with the lads, of course, the Avebury adventure, Silverstone, college, even girls – never enough girls though. Shiny nuggets that made me believe in the possibilities if only I could be brave. They were castles in the air that crumbled all too easily, corrupted as I was with a burning resentment of loss. The loss of the physical me. Eventually, that enfeebled person was killed off in therapy. Good riddance, too. Out of the ashes rose a bloody determined me. And that was the me that stood there that sunny morning in March 2016 gazing at my new place of work, the landscape of Ceredigion.

I was fifty-one now though, not twenty-two. What's it matter? You're only as old as you feel. Perhaps. But I felt old. Very old. At fifty-one my physical abilities were leaching away in spite of my efforts, like a bungalow perched on a crumbling cliff with the garden ever shortening. Time running out. After that first sepsis crisis in 2013 I came back with such thunder. God, I felt good, as if I could take on anything. Reborn and bristling with energy. That second bout of sepsis, though, robbed me of something, something physical, something in my core which, never mind how hard I tried, I just couldn't get back. The same regime of walking and the gym that'd brought me back after the first illness failed to reignite me. My physical world had shrunk and there seemed to be nothing I could do about it. And when I stood there looking down the valley into the river Ystwyth I sensed that I was in a battle against that inner cliff. A battle to do things and go places before I couldn't. But, here's the thing, it didn't matter. And it didn't matter because I had so much to be joyful for: my boys, Anna, my work, my life. Definitely my life. So, in the words of Churchill, I endeavoured to 'keep buggering on'.

The most unnerving experience in the making of this latest book was a visit to the Teifi Pools, an innocuous-sounding location suggestive of a fishing trip with your favourite uncle – fans of *Gavin & Stacey* may put another spin on such a trip! At the heart of *Hinterland* was darkness, each episode stained with fresh murder, with the three series built around the scaffolding of an ongoing cold case. Venturing into the Pools in the Cambrian Mountains, I felt that I got closer to the essence of the programme than anywhere else on my travels. It's a haunting prospect as you drive along a twisting slither of tarmac, weaving between a series of domed, grass-covered hillocks, getting deeper and deeper into this other world, passing them one by one, the still pools like huge puddles, their surfaces an impenetrable black mirror.

I walked down to the edge of one of the pools, about the size of a small lake, convinced I was being watched. I've been to many isolated locations over the years and have often felt as if someone else is there. Watching. Perhaps the nature of the programme from which this latest project spawned heightened my edginess. And it got worse; peering into the watery depths I imagined a hand breaking the surface and making a grab, so I took a few steps back. Wandering away from the water I followed a dip between the grassy mounds and became disoriented as if in a maze, the usual beacons of the land absent – no trees or buildings to navigate by. And all the while I anticipated an encounter with a ruddy-faced villain with a shovel; it really is the perfect location to dispose of a problem, and *Hinterland* had a lot of shovel carriers.

It's the not being able to run that spooks me, you see. Running away, after all, is a useful get-out when confronted by snarly dogs or a herd of excitable cattle – or, indeed, someone with a shovel. When I could run – before the bike smash – I was prone to the same dark imaginings. One of the underground bomb storage magazines in Trecwn was said to be haunted by a worker killed during its construction in the 1930s. Years after the tragedy, a storeman ran out of the tunnel leading from that particular magazine in a white panic. Working alone, he'd felt a tap on his shoulder. He turned, and there was no one there. The magazine wasn't frequented much after that. There were a lot of easily spooked types in Trecwn, me included.

Tuscany and the uro-sepsis episode of 2015 had sounded the death knell for my exhaustive wanderings abroad, that hunger for a packed itinerary that'd defined holidays for Anna and I from that first jaunt together when we landed in Bilbao nearly twenty years earlier. I'd pushed hard to see all that I could, surpassing the usual confines of my limited range, returning from each holiday burnt out while at the same time feeling as if I'd gone up a notch physically.

The prerequisite for holidays after uro-sepsis though was a comfortable billet from which Anna and the boys could roam far and wide if the fancy took them but where I could relax and conserve myself or join them if I was up to it. And so, in 2016, we fell upon a little piece of secluded perfection in the southern Loire region of France. Guy and Colette's honey-stoned gite with exclusive use of a pool seemed to belong in a higher price bracket; we couldn't quite believe it was all ours for two weeks. It was jet-set luxury compared to the static caravan of Tuscany the previous year. Guy and Colette lived in a fortified manor house in the grounds, padding about discreetly, always on hand yet never intrusive.

I fell into my new regime not too begrudgingly; reading in the shade, swimming with Anna and the boys, dozing on a sun lounger and, crucially, drinking lots of water! In moments of reflection, I found it difficult to believe I was the same person who'd set such a ferocious pace in northern Spain and Provence and Tuscany the first time round and, of course, Amalfi, where we got married. They'd been manic holidays, out after breakfast for the day or driving long stretches to our next accommodation. I suppose as people age they lose bits of who they once were, it's just that it was happening to me a lot sooner than I'd have liked.

One morning, before the sun had risen to blistering, Anna and the boys set off to go kayaking on a river. They were very excited as I waved them off wishing them a great adventure. I hadn't kayaked – or canoed in old money – since I was a teenager. There was a science teacher at school called Goggy John – I doubt he was christened Goggy, but that's how he was known. Anyway, during the summer he hired out small rowing boats and canoes on the river Cleddau running through the centre of Haverfordwest. My mate Paul – witness to my tennis racquet shames – and I canoed upstream one day, ignoring Goggy's instruction to remain within his sight, and found ourselves paddling through a tangled wooded area, as if in the Louisiana swamps – all submerged tree roots and death-green water, but no alligators, thankfully. Our allotted hire period expired as we explored bits of the Cleddau that were a mystery. It was very exciting. On our eventual return, Goggy left us in no doubt that disappearing, and grossly exceeding the stipulated hire period, had been a mistake. There was to be no more canoeing.

With half a day to kill before their return from kayaking, I made a coffee and sat under a parasol with my book. The air was fresh, the scent of flowers and shrubs perfuming the garden before the later suffocation of a ratcheting heat. As I read, I tuned into the sound of the rippling pool; cool, Moorish and comforting. Other sounds seeped in and so I put the book down, sensing there was more enjoyment to be had in listening to the clacking of insects, watching bees careering drunkenly from flower to flower and pigeons cooing in an adjacent wood.

I made another coffee accompanied by bread and apricot jam, little rituals to eat up time. Returning to my book, I sipped the coffee and ate the bread and jam. Feeling energised, I decided on a stroll around the gardens before it got too hot. And down by the shade of the plum trees I encountered Guy.

'Bonjour, Guy. D'accord?'

Anna, who speaks French, had coached me a few stock phrases and my confident opening gambit must've intimated fluency, as Guy reciprocated with quite a flourish. Aside from an authentic pronunciation, I had little else.

'Je ne… comprends… pas,' I replied, shrugging my shoulders. 'Mon Français… très petit.'

In other words, I hadn't a clue what he was saying. He laughed generously and patted me on the back. His English was even thinner, so the conversation became physical, with sweeping gestures at the sun and theatrical wiping of brows. We soon ran out of things to mime and carried on our separate ways.

I put off checking my business emails till late morning so that there might be something to reply to. Something to do. I made another coffee and switched on the tablet. A dog-whistle sequence of pings brought reassurance and a string of tasks that'd take time: a print order from a lady in London (I sent her an email saying it'd be delayed); a query from my publisher about the ongoing *Hinterland* project; and some other inconsequential stuff. But, stuff to do. X (Twitter), Facebook and Instagram served up the usual high-carb nibbles; an instant boost from the recognition of others followed by a sense of emptiness and the questionable allocation of time to something so trifling.

Poring over my limited options – a swim was out of the question, as I needed help to get out of the pool – I decided to wander over to an outbuilding that'd been converted into a games room by the artisanal Guy. Evidence of his handy-crafting was everywhere, particularly in the gite that'd been restored from a collapsed wreck. He was annoyingly gifted. I shot some pool without enthusiasm as the midday heat persuaded a quorum of flies to join me, so I went back to the cottage, continued with my book, made some lunch and fell asleep on the sofa. I woke on hearing the rumble of tyres over chippings. They were back. In minutes we were all in the pool and everything felt right again.

I had a first meeting with Ed Talfan, one of the producers of *Hinterland*, in a cafe on Aberystwyth seafront to discuss the book's progress. Unshowy and personable, he dressed like a man who had no wish to spend precious time in the morning musing over what to wear; I too was in a checked shirt, hiking boots and shapeless jeans.

'I want a book that celebrates Ceredigion...' he said, '...rather than just *Hinterland*.'

It was apparent we shared a vision which didn't involve knocking out a Christmas annual of the programme. Chatting over coffee, I sensed that I didn't have his undivided attention; they were filming down the road outside the old Victorian police station and he had to get back.

'I tell you what'd be good,' he said as he was heading for the door. 'Come on set. Out in the wilds. Get some shots of the cast and crew.'

We agreed it was a good idea and he was gone. I finished my coffee and walked back along the seafront to the car on the hottest day of the year, hugging the shady side of the road. Consulting a map, I decided to head for Ynyslas boatyard a few miles up the coast to take some photos for the book. The yard had featured in the last episode of the second series and seemed like a promising location.

The boatyard sits behind the dunes of Ynyslas beach aside the Dyfi estuary in an expanse of reclaimed bog. I parked in the middle of the yard and stepped from the air-conditioned sanctuary of the car. Immediately, it felt as if a heavy rucksack had been loaded onto me, with the air viscous and still like setting concrete. I waded towards the boats, routinely checking how far I was from the car, conscious of putting too much distance between me and the air-conditioning.

A decayed wooden hull caught my eye and I went over for a closer look. Peppered with holes, with its sea-going days behind it, the texture of the weathered wood hinted at the stories it could tell. As I composed some shots, I noticed that my breathing was becoming laboured. Looking around, I spotted a rusted hulk in the far corner of the yard which had a pleasing sinuous shape. I considered whether it might be wiser to get back to the car, as I could feel myself overheating, but no, I had to photograph it. So I panted my way over, and as I approached the boat the yard began to spin like a fairground ride starting up. I turned for the car, which was perhaps forty metres away, and began to drag my feet across the black slate chippings, eyes fixed on the Volvo, warped in a heat haze as if in the Serengeti. Almost within touching distance of the car, my legs buckled and I went down on my knees and elbows, somehow preventing the camera from hitting the ground.

I rolled onto my back and looked over to the car, lying on what felt like a half-cooled griddle; black chippings on the hottest day of the year and a light cotton shirt weren't an ideal combination. Without the tripod, or anything to pull myself up on, I was unable to get off the floor. But I had to get to that car, as I was being slow cooked. Rolling back onto my stomach, I pushed up on my hands and knees, crawled the few metres to the car, reached up, opened the door, pulled myself up onto the driver's seat and clambered in. Shaking, I started the engine, put the air-conditioning on Arctic and began to guzzle a bottle of water. In minutes my core began to cool, my breathing regulated and I stopped shaking. I was reminded of several such meltdowns over the decades, which made it all the more idiotic that I'd allowed it to happen yet again.

My autonomic system – part of the triumvirate of nerves along with the motor and sensory functions – was to blame. And my stupidity. The autonomic system is the quiet housekeeper of the body, a diligent worker ant dealing with waste management, setting the internal thermostat, ensuring enough pressure in the pipes to keep the major organs functioning and overseeing a whole host of unconscious microadjustments which get us efficiently through the day. My nervous system was compromised after the bike accident, undermined by a plague of impairment. Nothing worked in quite the same way as it had and that included functions under the remit of the autonomic system. Extremes of hot or cold in particular cause me to malfunction.

I'd been foolish to step away from the car in an open, airless space, carpeted with black chippings under a baking sun. My palms had certainly paid the price as I'd crawled along the floor to the car. Mine has been a photographic career peppered with examples of foolish or at least unwise behaviour, mostly getting away scot-free, with the attempt at traversing a snowy mountain pass in a two-wheel-drive car being a particularly ridiculous caper. There've been other escapades which I won't regurgitate. But then, just walking over uneven ground invites a tumble. Over the years I've gone down countless times, clambering back to my feet intact, if you discount cuts and bruises. If I were risk-assessed, no doubt I'd be advised to get an office job. Had one of those. Didn't like it. So, I accept that when I go out, I may encounter a mishap. Operating on that premise, the least I could do, though, would be to avoid courting disaster by indulging in a course of action that was odds-on to be detrimental. Ynyslas boatyard was a lesson learnt, for the time being.

Devil's Bridge, twelve miles inland from Aberystwyth, hid the macabre secret of the *Hinterland* story, the chilling kernel from which the three series sprang. Standing on the bridge by the hotel – which doubled as a children's home in the programme – Anna and I peered down at the waterfall cascading one hundred metres to the bottom of a narrow ravine, a geological sword slash hacked into the Cambrian Mountains. Down there was where we were headed as we entered an admissions cabin just off the road.

'Good morning. Welcome to Devil's Bridge Falls,' said a jolly lady, resplendent in a logoed fleece. 'Have you come a long way?'

I was apprehensive and not in the mood for small talk, so turned away to look out of a window. Anna enquired after two tickets and I turned back.

'How long does it take to walk down and back up?' I asked.

'Depends really. Some do it in, say, forty-five minutes. If you're taking photos,' she continued, pointing to my camera, 'you'll take longer, I suppose. Couple of hours maybe. Like I say, it depends.'

On photographic shoots I liked to know the terrain in advance, to determine the feasibility of my conquering it. I didn't like surprises.

'And how many steps are there?' I continued.

I knew there were a lot but craved specifics, something that I could quantify. Something that I could persuade myself was doable. Or not. I hadn't researched the falls thoroughly enough and was annoyed at my lack of preparation.

'To get to the iron bridge at the bottom and back up the other side is about seven hundred steps,' she said.

I scrambled to compute what she'd said. Did she say seven hundred? Not seventy?

'Sorry, did you say seven hundred?'

'Yes. That's right. Seven hundred,' she replied.

I took a sharp intake of breath and felt faint. Faint and stupid. Faint and defeated, already. We walked out of the door to the head of the path.

'Seven hundred fucking steps. I can't do that.'

Anna smiled. It was a fragile smile.

'Let's set off and see what it's like. If it's too difficult, we'll just call it a day,' she said.

I turned away, muttering darkly.

'Come on, honey, you can do it,' she continued. 'And like I say, if it's too much we'll turn back. Maybe go somewhere else.'

Beneath her casual assurance was a nervousness. It was beyond me, but she couldn't say, 'Yep, you're right. Seven hundred steps is fucking ridiculous.'

I was angry at my lack of planning, but then again, if I'd researched more thoroughly we wouldn't have been there. Even before the shock of 'seven hundred steps' I'd prepared myself for a huge day, one which'd demand a Herculean effort. Physically, I didn't equate to the challenge. I knew it and I wanted to turn around and go home but it would've been too damaging to the brittle edifice that masquerades as my self-confidence to give up. I was trapped and had no choice but to probe, to see what was possible.

'Look, we're here,' I said, 'I have to see, even though there's no fucking chance.'

'Brilliant,' said Anna.

The initial walk took us gently down through woodland bathed in warm sunshine. I kept my eyes glued to the path, alert to erupting bedrock and trip-wire tree roots, stopping occasionally to lift my head and peer around for potential photographs. On the move, Anna was my eyes, suggesting a stop if she spied a possibility. The path began to steepen and single steps bunched into three or four. We emerged from under the tree canopy, coming face to face with the immensity of the waterfall hurtling down to meet us before dropping away. The sound of that biblical mass of plunging water seemed to enervate me.

'Okay?' asked Anna.

'Yep, let's keep going.'

The concentration required to gauge every stride and place my foot onto a surface that wouldn't turn an ankle was exhausting. It was head down like a pit pony, one foot and then the other.

We arrived at a covered viewing platform. I sat down, drank some water and munched on an energy bar while Anna scoured the vicinity for possible images. I photographed the waterfall plummeting amongst the trees with the hotel perched way up at the top, then took a few detail shots close by and tried to ignite a spark within me. Tried to persuade myself it was worth carrying on. We'd descended a long way from the road but when I looked down at how much further there was to go, I faltered.

'I'm knackered and we're nowhere near the bottom,' I said.

'Do you want to go back?'

'I don't know.'

I hadn't quite dredged up my most sepulchral tone of voice – which, trust me, has a real deathliness to it – and my body language hadn't yet reached white flag territory. But I was pretty damned close on both counts.

'No. We'll go a bit further,' I said.

The path steepened as the steps bunched into flights of fives, sixes and more. Some flights had handrails, some didn't; the tripod and Anna got me down. As we got deeper into the ravine the steps were cut from bedrock. Hacking steps from rock is laborious, necessitating the common-sense design of shallow treads and big drops. I was experiencing a loss of control as I placed a boot down towards the next step, only for my load-lowering knee to give way under the strain of easing that descending foot so far down. The risks were escalating as I stopped for another breather.

'I'll have a look round the corner. See if I can see the bottom,' said Anna. I poured a coffee and took a Bourbon biscuit from my camera bag. She returned a minute later, looking crestfallen.

'What is it?' I asked.

'You're not going to like it.'

It was Jacob's Ladder. Reassuring biblical connotations? Nope. Jacob's Ladder is one hundred continuous steps. A cliff-face of steps – handrails included, mind. I looked down and swayed, a sickening vertigo welling up.

'You've got to be fucking joking.'

Anna shrugged her shoulders and said, 'You don't have to do it. We can go back.'

It wasn't so much a suggestion as a plea. I looked away from the steps, partly to avoid the urge to throw up. We had, it seemed, gone as far as we could. The only option was to go back. But I couldn't just turn and walk away immediately. I had to take time to properly assess the challenge, conclude its impossibility, and then turn.

'Give me a minute,' I said, stepping back from the precipice.

Before me was a physical trial and, perhaps even more so, a mental challenge the scale of which I'd never encountered in my life. And I mean my whole time of living. It was colossal.

'We've come so fucking far,' I said. 'Now this. Just not fair.'

I handed my camera to Anna so that I couldn't chuck it down the steps.

Minutes passed by and I was still there. Still mulling it over, as if the act of mulling would somehow lessen the challenge. But the more I looked at the steps, the less daunting they became, as I began to convince myself of the feasibility of a descent. Two stark options ricocheted around my head: summon every last bit of bloody-minded determination to continue or throw my arms up in surrender and go home, broken. And that's what kept me there; the knowledge that to retreat would break me. I mean, I'm terrified of anything higher than a stepladder, never mind Jacob's fucking Ladder. I was as trapped by circumstance as I'd been up by the admissions cabin. More so really, as I'd invested huge physical and mental reserves to get to where I was.

I studied the handrails either side of the four-foot-wide steps. If I clung to them as if my life depended on it – and it would – then at least I couldn't fall, except in my head. I had to try.

'Okay, we're going for it,' I said, without conviction.

Anna's jaw dropped. Her inclination was to turn back but she couldn't now that I'd committed.

'Great. Just take your time. You can do it.'

That one sentence summed her up; resolute, even when contemplating the ridiculous. I grabbed the handrails, arms wing-spread apart, and placed a foot down to the next step while not daring to look further than that step. I knew instantly it wouldn't work. The handrails were set too close to the level of the steps – a good gripping height for children or seven hiking dwarves but not for a six-footer. With my arms outstretched like an albatross in flight, and having to stoop at knee level, the descent had head-over-heels potential.

'There must be another way,' I said.

I turned my feet through ninety degrees to the right so that I faced one of the handrails. I grabbed the rail with my right hand at shoulder height, my left hand gripping the same rail at waist height. I felt stable and secure. Best of all, I was looking at a rock face a couple of feet away and not down the steps. Looking down, after all, made me nauseous. Crab-like, I placed my left foot sideways down to the next step, followed by my right, while loosening my grip and sliding my hands down the handrail.

'Yeah, this is okay. I can do it.'

Perhaps it was foolish to come up with novel biomechanical solutions on such a precarious flight of steps, but I'd found the answer and began my descent, slowly and methodically. On occasion people came down the steps and I stopped and waited for them to pass behind. Pleasantries were exchanged but I resisted the temptation to turn and face them, remaining glued to that rock face. It took half an hour to complete the descent. When I looked up at what I'd conquered I felt euphoric, like an Everest climb, only in reverse.

At last, we reached the arched iron bridge at the bottom of the ravine which would take us over the frothing river Rheidol. I'd completed the most treacherous bit of the trek – the downward bit. What'd possessed me to take on such a challenge? Or, more pertinently, why had I been so reckless? Of course, it was that old need to prove myself, to not be stamped with the crushing label of disability. Incongruous as it may've been, I was a landscape photographer. It was what I did. Yet, on days like the one I was embroiled in, I did wonder about my sanity.

Standing on the iron bridge, I looked around at the natural wonder of that other world. Deep in a subterranean fissure with a foam-specked torrent surging past, Wales became the Amazon. Thick with humidity, I studied fronded and tropical-looking species that seemed to belong in the Eden Project in Cornwall, and through a kaleidoscope of trees, rock, water and spume I spied a patch of brightness as if at the end of a long tunnel; the sky was still up there.

We stepped off the bridge to begin the climb, which was less scary; I wouldn't be plummeting down rock-cut steps if I fell. It was more physically punishing, though, as many of the steps were at knee level and higher, more like ledges, and I couldn't raise a leg high enough to place my foot on them. The solution was to sit on the step I needed to get up to and pull my knees up and swivel my hips so that my legs were deposited on that target step. I then scrambled onto my knees, grabbed a handrail or clung onto Anna and hauled myself to my feet. It was laborious but laced with that sense of victory over yet another obstacle; there's always a way. We detoured along paths to get close to the falls, which weren't exactly the Reichenbach from Sherlock Holmes but impressive all the same. The thrum and roar of the water colliding with rock was brutal and elemental. There was a musicality to it, a thunderous overture to the wildness of the Cambrian Mountains.

We continued our climb till the rock-cut steps ended and we strode into sparse woodland, the earth path drawing us up towards the late-afternoon sun. Six hours after departing the admissions cabin on the other side of the ravine I stumbled out onto the road like a survivor of a plane crash emerging from the jungle and collapsed onto a bench. The Barafundle trek of years before had been knocked off its pedestal, as a new personal best of physical endurance was set. I sat, panting, bathed in self-congratulation and sweat while Anna fetched the car, pulled up and helped me in.

On the journey home the euphoria ebbed as my body realised what it'd been tricked into. Every bit of me let go. The next day I remained in bed like some Victorian invalid, a deep thudding ache welling up from within. I rose the day after, still numb but knowing that I'd achieved something momentous. Something that hinted, perhaps, at a reversal of my recent physical decline.

I was directed to meet the *Hinterland* crew at Syfydrin Lake in Ceredigion. Anna and I set off from home early; besides the filming location, I'd factored in other places to photograph for the book. We reached Aberystwyth and headed inland, as I'd done many times, turning onto ever-narrower roads then tracks before arriving at the lake in the wilds of the Cambrian Mountains where they were shooting scenes for the very last episode, tying up the loose ends after three compelling series. It was July on the coast but November in the mountains, bone-cold and with intermittent curtains of heavy drizzle. The crew had heaved their equipment across boggy grassland to set up on top of a low hill under a waterproof gazebo, open on three sides to the elements and overlooking the lake.

In a break in filming, Anna and I trudged up to the gazebo. Ed Thomas, co-producer, greeted us. 'Welcome to a typical summer's day in the Cambrian Mountains,' he said, laughing, encased in waterproofs. He introduced us to Richard Harrington, who played the lead character of DCI Mathias and was stood huddled against the weather, waiting for the next scene.

'Ed says you're doing a book?' he said, as a bead of rainwater dripped from the tip of his nose.

Like myself, Richard was blessed, or perhaps cursed, with a countenance that didn't invite conversation but once struck up he proved to be bright and inquisitive. It felt strange to be looking into those doleful eyes, gateway to his character Mathias' dark backstory. If there were ever a BAFTA for eye-acting he'd have it in the bag. He was surprisingly upbeat considering he'd been immersed in three years of murder in a less than hospitable landscape and those eyes lit up as he spoke dreamily of the holiday in hot climes that awaited him once the last episode was wrapped up.

The drizzle returned, and every member of the cast and crew not in a vehicle down the hill crowded under the gazebo. Richard continued to grill Anna and I, perhaps finding it difficult to shed an investigative persona he'd lived in for so long. As we spoke, I noticed three mountain-bikers on a muddy track about a hundred metres away. They stopped and peered towards us.

'They must be mad,' piped up a member of the crew sheltering under the gazebo.

'Perhaps,' I said, 'but think about it. They're in the absolute middle of absolutely nowhere and they see a bunch of people crowded under a small gazebo on top of a hill in the rain?'

The rain eased and everyone bolted to their positions to get some filming done before the next curtain swept in. I moved about searching out compositions, all the while staying out of their camera shot. With a trickle running down my back, I was cold and wet yet feeling privileged to be photographing the people behind this iconic programme. Having got what I wanted, we departed, leaving a bedraggled outfit on a hill in deepest Ceredigion.

Chapter 36

I met Jamie Owen at his farmhouse in the Preseli Hills. Since the launch party for my first book, *Pembrokeshire*, seven years earlier, at which he'd spoken of his love for the county, we'd washed up together on occasion, mostly being interviewed by him on his Radio Wales programme about my various book projects. At that launch, I sensed that our paths would cross and coalesce around a book at an indeterminate point in the future. He, it transpired, had felt the same. Well, we'd arrived at that point.

The Gwaun Valley in north Pembrokeshire is out of kilter with the outside world. The blame lies with Pope Gregory XIII – an uncommon refrain – who centuries ago decreed that Christianity should adopt his shiny new Gregorian calendar; maybe he'd had a load printed for Christmas. The people of the Gwaun, though, declined and stuck with the old Julian calendar. And so, on 13th January 2017, Jamie and I ventured into the midst of this private community near Fishguard to document their celebration of New Year or, as they refer to it, *Hen Galan* – Welsh for 'old new year'.

The two-roomed Victorian-built school, perennially threatened with closure and with its roll call of two dozen pupils aged between three and eleven, welcomed us. Subsuming village schools into one large holding pen a bus ride away might make sense on paper but witnessing the bond between the kids in the Gwaun did make you wonder whether our decision-makers have got it wrong. As we chatted with the head, herself a former pupil, the children drifted back into the playground from their morning exactions. The tradition is, they herald in the New Year by singing at people's doors, whereupon they get paid royally in coin or sweets. Returning like little robbers, their rucksacks bulged and their faces beamed.

Further along the valley floor the Dyffryn Arms had been run by Bessie Davies's family forever. In an increasingly homogenous world uniqueness is a rare commodity, but this place had it in spades. No music. No menu. No bar, in the traditional sense. Just one square room, sparsely furnished and seemingly set-dressed for a Thomas Hardy adaptation. To attract service, you press a buzzer by a hatch, whereupon an obscured glass panel slides back to reveal Bessie, a wizened apparition and conversationally economical. You order a pint, she slips on her dipping glove, grabs a jug and submerges it into a barrel. The frothy brew is then allowed to settle before she pours. It's Dickensian hospitality dispensed with Victorian warmth; like it or lump it.

Bessie, in her eighties, emerged from behind the hatch and sat by the fire, eyeing us warily. She'd been told to expect us but the community is mindful of gawpers, being proud of its traditions and loath to perform for outsiders. To her it's a pub, not an attraction. Jamie's opening questions were tentative but Bessie appeared to warm to him and she began to speak freely of her childhood in the valley and *Hen Galan*, the New Year celebration. I sat at an adjacent table bagging furtive snaps of the old lady; she wasn't enamoured of the lens. Then, three teenagers shuffled into the bar and began to sing for the customers. Bessie fished her purse from her cardigan and rewarded them. For many who descend into this wooded groove in the Preseli Hills, their arrival is a mistake, the result of a wrong turn. But what a pleasant mistake to make. One of my most treasured books is Laurie Lee's *Cider with Rosie*, a lament to a world long gone, full of nuggety recollections of a backwater childhood. In some ways the Gwaun Valley reminded me of Lee's book. It's a place determined to cling on to the good bits of its past while embracing modernity, on its own terms.

Our final stop was Penlanwynt Farm, high above the tree-line, exposed to the scything winds of the uplands, and with views straddling miles. Bonni and Vivian farm there with the help of their grandson, Llŷr. We dipped our heads through the front door of the farmhouse, an Airfix scale down from the usual abode. Bonni is the keeper of stories, inheritor of an oral tradition, a mobile hard drive of Gwaun history and anecdotes. While Jamie chatted with her and scribbled notes, Vivian sat quietly in the corner, coming in on Bonni's cue when instructed. Llŷr, ox-strong and deep, listened intently.

A faint singing could be heard from outside the front door. The children had arrived; their last call after a profitable day of belting out songs fuelled by excess sugar. Bonni opened the door with quiet ceremony and invited them through to the kitchen, where the table groaned under a weight of sandwiches and cakes. One little girl was keen to show Jamie her takings for the day while Bonni and Vivian decanted beakers of squash. Everyone was happy.

Our wanderings in the Gwaun conformed perfectly with a shared preconception of what our book would be. I began the year-long journey confident that Jamie's writing would complement my images and he felt the same sense of ease about my photography. There were to be no creative tensions. It just worked.

We weren't embarking on a Louis Theroux-type exposé, searching out some prurient underbelly; anyway, crystal meth dens and drive-by shootings haven't taken off in Pembrokeshire, yet. There was, though, on occasion, a sense that we were witnessing the winter of a tradition. That perhaps in a generation some of what we saw and experienced may no longer exist. However, we were determined to avoid elegiac obituaries. The book was to be an affirming celebration of people, communities and working practices within the county, communicating a sense of place and belonging. It was our homage to the land we call home, a love letter to Pembrokeshire. Rural, and perhaps romanticised, our gentle travelogues during those twelve months were some of the most enjoyable of my photographic career.

For Jamie and I, our respective Pembrokeshire childhoods had the river in common. He and his brothers had a small boat with an erratic outboard engine in which they explored the upper reaches of the Cleddau Estuary, enacting some imaginary West-Walian sequel to *Swallows and Amazons*. My best estate-friend Aled and I had cycled the lanes hugging the river, ambling through unkempt woods down to the shore at Little Milford and Boulston, and wading through the mudflats at low tide. Since moving to Llangwm I've been horrified at tales of those drowned after becoming stuck in the mud – time and tide await no man. Famished, Aled and I would search out the shade of a tree and tuck into our packed lunches, mine being warm Princes chicken or beef paste sandwiches and a melted Wagon Wheel, washed down with weak orange squash – again, warm. As for the Preseli Hills, Jamie discovered them on picnics with his family as a child and during driving lessons with his grandfather while the motorbike at seventeen had been my passport to the area. Calling at his farmhouse that day, I recalled riding my motorbike along the thread of tarmac that wound around the hill past the place back in 1983 on one of my semi-lost afternoons, not wishing to see a sign that pointed me back to Haverfordwest.

I lay awake waiting for the radio alarm. I'd been waiting a long time. My legs had twitched and jumped and thrashed about all night, nerves crackling away, oblivious to the huge day that lay ahead. It was as if some malicious scientist had attached electrodes to my limbs and had been twiddling the control dial. On cue, Radio 4's *Today* programme burst in. Anna gave me a gentle nudge and bound from under the duvet.

'I can't do it, Anna.'

'What do you mean?'

'Haven't slept a wink. Twitched all bloody night.'

There was a pause.

'I'll put some coffee on. Don't have to leave for an hour so just lie there and relax. It'll be fine.'

Anna's was the voice of reassurance, the rock I lashed myself to when the going got tough. And the going doesn't get much tougher than a lost night, my impaired muscles greedy for their eight hours of sleep and more if I'm to function to the best of my abilities. Or even to just function. I lay there empty, convinced the day was dead already. Then I heard Charlie's voice. He'd been looking forward to it, even foregoing the opportunity to hang around with his mates. I felt honoured – he was only twelve after all. The thought of denying him encouraged me to get up, to see whether I could manoeuvre around the house well enough to contemplate committing. I made my way to the kitchen using book shelves and furniture to steady myself and sat down at the table.

'You're up. Great. Coffee's ready. Scrambled eggs on toast?' asked Anna.

'That'll be lovely. Thank you.'

Anna was canny in gauging my mood, picking her time to broach what might or might not be feasible. She waited till I'd finished eating and had sunk the coffee.

'So, we going?'

I looked up wearily from the table. 'Think so.'

'Great. Don't worry, I'll do all the driving,' she said.

To love and to be loved is the most incredible gift. Love, to me, is oxygen. Love is the intuitive recognition of the needs of the one you love. Love is two halves of a perfect whole. Without it we wither. I am a blessed man.

And so, loaded up with scrambled eggs and coffee, and with Harry dropped off with Anna's mum, the three of us hit the road for the Hay Literary Festival; the *Hinterland: Ceredigion Landscapes* talk was scheduled for that evening, but first there was a radio interview with BBC Wales in the early afternoon about the programme and the book, along with *Hinterland's* co-producer Ed Thomas.

The festival's annual irruption in a field in Hay-on-Wye is impressive. I imagine the ceremonial pressing of a button and, *voilà*, the tented village rises up from beneath the grass. I levered myself from the car, limbs cramped and uncooperative, and clung to Anna as

I threw my legs forward in an ungainly lunge and onto the site with Charlie following. I was as empty as it was possible to be and my heart sank at the exertion required for many hours to come. If I'd been at home, I'd have been in bed. Yet it felt good to be back amongst the marquees of all shapes and sizes, connected by covered walkways in case the weather turned a bit British. It's a world of books and eager readers and authors' talks and going for a coffee to talk about the talk you've just attended.

We got to the BBC Radio Wales tent, with Ed Thomas arriving just after us, and were ushered backstage to await our introduction.

'I'll take the seat nearest, if you don't mind,' I said to him, pointing on stage.

The thought of tiptoeing over cables to reach the farthest chair was alarming as it'd be a struggle to walk once released from Anna's hidden hand. Ed could see I was struggling.

'I can hold your hand going on if you like,' he said.

It was terribly kind of him, but I declined, as I didn't wish to expose an ex-rugby player to scurrilous gossip about his leanings, but mainly I was too bloody proud to be seen to need help. The show's presenter, Eleri Sion, introduced us and 'pick your feet up' had never felt so pertinent.

A thickish audience peppered the venue and the interview went well, though I had to focus like mad as my brain fought to process the questions through a sleep-deprived fuzziness. As Ed and I walked off stage we came face to face with the next guest – Brian May of Queen. Ed nodded warmly and continued on. I stopped.

'Mr May, lovely to meet you,' I said, holding out a presumptive hand. He shook it.

'Just... just so love your music.'

With an accommodating glimmer of a smile, he brushed past to take his place on stage. Unbeknown to Brian, we went back a long way.

It was 1983. The bus coughed and laboured up the hill, the clanging diesel engine ever fraught as the gradient steepened, while all around me the old men indulged in hushed conversation, as if part of some secret society. The journey home from Trecwn was another reminder in a day full of reminders that my life was going down the pan. I hated the place and I hated the docile acceptance of those around me. Most of all, I hated myself for not having an alternative plan, being complicit in my own misery. It was all very well despising that busload of time-servers but I was fast becoming one.

I remembered a Princes paste sandwich that I had left over and delved into my lunch box. Eating it would devour a few miles, get me closer to home. As I nibbled and rued my life, a man I only ever knew as Tommo, owner of a phlegmy growl, lit up across the aisle adjacent to me. Tommo was a purveyor of the Senior Service cigarette, on a par with the Woodbine, the heavy brigades of lung kippering. The fug drifted over and I put the sandwich back in the box. At that moment, when all seemed hopeless, came salvation; the opening chords of *Bohemian Rhapsody* struck up on the radio and I felt a surge of happiness, immersed in a private world away from Trecwn. I slumped back against the dusty headrest, closed my eyes and dreamt of lives that weren't mine. The bus clattered on and the grumbling of the old men receded as the cigarette smoke thickened, but I didn't care, as I had Queen.

'Bloody hell, Bryn, what's this crap?' came a voice from behind. 'Turn it off, man.' Bryn, the driver, hunched and apologetic, turned the radio off. The old men didn't like Queen.

After the radio interview, Anna, Charlie, Ed and I headed to the green room, an area set aside for authors and their entourages to relax. I fell onto a sofa, aching and dizzy with exhaustion. It was an important day, but I just wanted to crawl out to the car and go home. Anna got me a couple of strong coffees, which failed to ignite me. An injection of adrenaline straight to the heart may've had more success. I felt beyond resuscitation and slumped, falling half-asleep, the hubbub of a roomful of chosen ones ebbing.

When I woke, Anna, Charlie and Ed were gone and the earlier

coffees had percolated to the other end. I needed the toilet but had little confidence that I could get to it, wherever it was. Panicked, I looked to the entrance hoping for their return, in need of a supporting arm that didn't appear to be coming. I couldn't wait. I spotted a Portaloo outside, in a fenced-off grassy area populated by offshoots of the green room, sitting around tables drinking in the sun. I calculated the challenge; ten metres to the door, down a shallow ramp, across the grass slaloming between tables and into the bog. Not a hope, I thought. I looked back to the entrance. Still no sign of them. My bladder had now cranked up to red alert. It was either risk a fall or soak myself where I was sat; I'll bet Hobson was never presented with such a shit choice.

I attempted to stand from the low sofa but fell back down. I tried again. Same result. There was a stirring of judgemental looks amongst the literati; 'A drunk amongst us, perchance?' And, as with the obligatory bomb at the end of a James Bond movie, my bladder was about to blow. Third time lucky? I was up. I had to be. Now for the catwalk to the door. I swayed, staggered and stumbled, cursing under my breath, grabbing the door frame on exit. Down the ramp and between the tables I went, steadying myself on unobliging shoulders and up the steps to the toilet. I shut the cubicle door and stifled the yearning to scream.

Emerging from the Portaloo I was greeted with sour glances from those whose shoulders had recently come in handy as I dragged my feet back up the ramp. On entering the green room, I tripped on the thin, ruffled events carpet and a security guardian angel grabbed my arm, stopping a certain fall.

'Thanks,' I said begrudgingly.

He smiled. 'It's okay, buddy. I'm like that when I've had a few.'

He flashed a conspiratorial wink, like it was fine to be hammered.

'I'm not drunk,' I replied. 'Just a bad walking day.'

He apologised and offered to fetch a wheelchair. I didn't know what to be more offended by, the presumption of drunkenness or the offer of the chair.

'I'll be fine,' I snapped, and returned to the sofa exposed to a host of sly glances. I wanted to shout, 'I'm not drunk, you bastards!', but instead just shrank into the seat, wishing to become as invisible as possible.

A little time after, Anna, Charlie and Ed returned.

'Everything okay, honey?' asked Anna.

'Yeah, fine, thanks.'

She couldn't do anything about my dire approval rating amongst the green room gang so there was no point in reprising my public shame.

Ed Talfan – the other *Hinterland* producer – appeared late afternoon along with arts correspondent and writer Jon Gower, who'd be hosting our event. The cast was complete. A young lady from the venue came to round us up. The Eds walked on ahead with Jon and Charlie while I repeated the lunging stagger of earlier, clinging to Anna. From backstage I could see the auditorium filling and it hit me that in a few moments I'd be walking out. I became anxious, not so much at the impending performance as the prospect of getting to my seat intact. At least the anxiety helped to disperse some of the cloudiness in my head, allowing me to focus on what was imminent. On the signal we filed out and took our seats. I'd already bagsied the closest one.

Jon hosted the talk with urbane confidence and incisive observation, bringing the house down with his wit and warmth. My abiding memory of the event was laughter, both on stage and in the audience; we had them on side. At the end, with the crowd applauding, there I was, sitting with the producers of an internationally acclaimed crime drama, pinching myself for the umpteenth time since leaving the contact centre. After the book signing, we returned to the green room for a well-earned glass or two of red before leaving.

A full moon accompanied us as we skirted the Brecon Beacons along the A40, a silvery light teasing out mighty Pen y Fan. We drove the twisty road to Llandovery, where we'd booked a room for the night, breaking our journey in time-honoured fashion at a former coaching inn. Metres from the door, I fell. Finally. I was too exhausted to be angry. Anna and Charlie got me up, I felt the bits that hurt to ensure it was nothing serious, we signed in and retired to bed. I slept beautifully, despite the absence of skin on my elbows.

Ed Thomas and I hawked the book at subsequent festivals and events during the summer months, talking to appreciative crowds and rounding off with a signing and a quenching beer. My proudest appearance was at my home gig, the Llangwm Literary Festival. Michael Pugh – lawyer, Russophile and international man of mystery – had inaugurated the festival the year before. Unlike Hay, there was no requirement for a helipad – yet – but this little village on the banks of an estuary in West Wales pulled off a big-town event.

Pembrokeshire doesn't possess wilderness in the Siberian sense but standing outside Gernos Fach farmhouse in the Preseli Hills you feel the need to reassess that truism. Gernos is remote. Spin round and signs of human imprint are nowhere to be seen; just the ripples of the uplands. Lyn and Gwyndaf live there. They always have. They always will; two brothers farming in the footsteps of their parents. Jamie and I approached the front door and knocked. Lyn answered.

'Come in,' he said, beckoning us along the hallway and into the kitchen.

The first thing I noticed was the heat: sweltering. Gwyndaf was perched on a settle by a hissing Rayburn, plump and smiley. They offered the leather armchair to Jamie, who produced his notepad and pen. After a cup of tea and some cake I set the camera for the dim light and began to shoot as Jamie interviewed.

The boys are north of sixty, Gwyndaf appreciably so. But they're still farm-fit, with forearms like a calf's thigh and the stamina of marathon runners from decades of lifting and heaving. And yet, for all their beast-like heft, they're two of the gentlest people you could ever meet, their conversation wrapped in a temperate cadence which, in tandem with the tropical warmth, was hypnotic. They live by the seasons, out in all of the weather, their sunny outlook testament perhaps to the trendy notion of green therapy. Gathering flocks in the hills can be contemplative work. Work that can't be rushed. With sheep there's no ticking clock, just perfectly honed actions leading to a desired goal.

They spoke of their parents arriving at Gernos in the forties after the war, the snows of their childhood, fetching water from a well in the yard and the hand-to-mouth lot of the upland farmer. It was mesmerising. Private people, they'd welcomed us in and opened up. Jamie and I departed feeling like we'd stumbled upon some great secret, as if that little farm provided the template for an inner contentment. I'm sure the boys would argue otherwise when they're out in gales repairing fences or rounding up escaped sheep. But to have had the opportunity to meet them and to listen to the story of their life on the hill was a joy.

Months after visiting Gernos Fach, Anna's mum, Caroline, rang one lunchtime.

'If you put S4C on, *Cefn Gwlad* is in the Preselis. Might be interesting?' she said.

Cefn Gwlad, which translates as countryside, enjoys exalted status in Welsh-language broadcasting. The premise is simple: a stout farmer, Dai Jones, roams the countryside visiting other farms; a busman's holiday with lots of tea and cake thrown in. The programme announcer heralded it as a classic episode from the year 2000 – a repeat, in other words. Dai's first visit – with cuppa and cake – was to a farm overlooking the Gwaun Valley that I'd passed many times over the years. Doing the geography in my head, I worked out that somewhere over the hill was Gernos Fach. And having said his goodbyes, that's where he headed, the opening shot of the farmhouse dwarfed in that landscape, familiar and heartening.

It was a delight to meet Lyn and Gwyndaf's late parents, Ianto and Cymraes. The production values were traditional and perhaps a little chauvinist: we had Ianto leaning on his staff in a top field, chatting with Dai about farming issues, and Cymraes stood on a stool in the yard cleaning windows, with Dai's conversation centred on domestic concerns and her new hairdo. But there they were, two humble farmers talking of their life in the hills. And who should come bounding down the field and through the gate into the yard but the boys themselves, Lyn and Gwyndaf, a touch more sprightly and less weather-beaten but with that same outdoors smile. I recorded the programme and will treasure it forever.

Compiling the photography for this latest book with Jamie presented some novel challenges, getting on and off boats being the most fraught. The Tenby Harbour manoeuvre, in particular, was memorable, more so for my two unwitting accomplices. I descended the wide stone steps of the harbour's breakwater – minus handrails – with Anna and Jamie either side clutching a hand to steady me. Once adjacent to the boat I traversed through ninety degrees and strode across the gap between bobbing boat and land. My heart leapt and I was elated, whereas they looked less than relaxed. I repeated the feat, in reverse, on reaching the breakwater on Caldey Island, just off the south Pembrokeshire coast, aware of the return lunges that awaited. We were visiting the island to record the life of its monastic community for a chapter in the book. That day, poor Anna and Jamie were like the nervy parents of an errant risk-hungry child.

Another episode when I trusted that 'things would turn out okay' was when I edged down a stepped cliff face to St Govan's Chapel, hidden in a cleft of rock, again on the south coast of Pembrokeshire. The early Christian hermit who allegedly built it single-handedly must've been tenacious. Jamie's face on our adventures was often a picture as he deduced my physical parameters, only for me to indulge in a gambit. I lost count of the times he asked, 'Are you sure about this?' He squirmed often, which gave me a perverse sense of pleasure.

Two consecutive days at the Pembrokeshire County Show, the second largest agricultural show in Wales, held on Withybush Aerodrome on the edge of Haverfordwest, comprised another chapter. On the first day, I got around with the aid of hiking poles, a dependency that was fast becoming the norm, as I covered a lot of ground – for me anyway. The next morning, though, I was spent, with the contemplation of another day on my feet beyond me. Jamie's niece Jemma worked in the show's main office and he'd taken the precaution of reserving a mobility scooter, just in case. When he'd informed me of his ever so considerate forward planning a week earlier, I bristled with indignation. No bloody way I'm resorting to that, I thought. Anyway, on that second morning, Jemma showed me the rudimentary controls and off I zipped, consoling myself that at least it'd be fun – what else could I do? I felt as much on show as the livestock in the rings.

Mobility scooters have become a common sight and when used by an OAP or someone with evident physical difficulties are viewed as a beneficial mode of transport. When the occupant weighs the same as an adult brown bear, though, we tend to question the user's self-discipline. I, being youngish and slim, presented a dilemma. What category did I occupy? Some people, judging by their expressions, looked rather sceptical.

The boys, though, thought the scooter hilarious as I swerved between strolling groups on the wide thoroughfares at a death-defying ten miles per hour, the two of them running alongside me like secret service agents protecting the president.

It was painful to concede that without the scooter I wouldn't have reached all of the dispersed photographs that were essential to the visual story of the show. I still had my pride, mind, shooting off the main drag if I saw someone I knew heading my way.

The acknowledgement during this year of my physical world contracting was more acute than ever. I'd felt it the previous year during the making of the *Hinterland* book, the Devil's Bridge trek feeling increasingly like some last epic hurrah; a final personal best. When out photographing now, or just going for a walk, the hiking poles were a constant companion. And yes, there was a quiet sadness at the loss of the person I was. I'd fought for decades to retain the physical abilities I possessed but my hold on them was weakening;

that crumbling cliff was snatching more and more of the garden. In fact, it felt like it'd reached the bloody patio by the back door.

Nevertheless, I'd produced my fifth book. Six, if you include *The Starlings and Other Stories*, an anthology by a group of crime writers, each story inspired by a photograph I'd taken. When *Starlings* came out in 2015, I wasn't sure what to think, having my work form the basis for tales of murder and other dark deeds. But then, so many locations I've visited over the years have had shallow grave written all over them. So why not? How many more landscape books or travelogues were there in me though, I wondered.

During the making of *A Year in Pembrokeshire* with Jamie there was an evolution in my work. A change of direction. A very welcome change of direction too. There were landscape images, of course, but most of the photographs were of human activity and interaction; I'd developed a documentary style. I'd captured people. Unlike landscape photography, where the sitter just sits and sits, the human subject is forever moving – if you miss the moment, you can't rewind. Interpretation is everything, and I loved it.

There was an irony in that at the point of my most obvious physical limitations I'd found the confidence to approach people and photograph them, the self-consciousness of old gone. Perhaps with age comes an ebbing of that preening pride of youth as you grow into and accept your imperfections. And at the end of the project with Jamie I realised that my enjoyment in the people had outweighed my enjoyment of the landscape.

Jamie and I had begun our book as friendly acquaintances sharing a deep affection for the landscape and culture of Pembrokeshire. Like a couple of rural reactionaries chewing the fat, and sharing a mild contempt for aspects of the modern world, it often felt as if we'd been born a hundred years too late. And on our wanderings, the laughter had thickened and our weak exertions were made more bearable by the odd leisurely lunch. By the book's conclusion, we'd become firm friends.

Chapter 37

Lance and Andy were sweeping the fields of Essex, once again, in search of ancient artefacts, undeterred by their perpetual unearthing of drinks-can ringpulls and bits of ephemeral scrap. The third series of *Detectorists* hit our screens in late 2017. For what became a hugely popular programme, the pitch for the original series may've seemed a bit thin – a bunch of oddballs turning over sods of grass looking for treasure. But, oh, the uncomplicated joy of it: the two central characters – and best friends – content in their lack of ambition and basking in one another's company while tramping the open fields with their beloved metal detectors. Set within a quintessential England of bosky hedges, wild meadows and insects suspended on a summer breeze, the immediacy of Lance and Andy's horizons and their attachment to place sang to me. Forever searching, forever hoping for that dream find, but really the detecting and the companionship were enough in themselves.

I felt an affinity with Lance and Andy, as I too indulged my hobby, my photographic passion, not with any illusions of enrichment but because it made me happy. I woke each day to a feeling of fulfilment. Of being fortunate. In my childhood I'd dug for treasure too. Aled, from a few doors down, and I, mole-holed the local ruined priory, convinced there was a gold chalice or jewelled cross to be trowelled up. Without the aid of a metal detector, the likelihood of success was remote. Another favoured location for our Indiana Jones aspirations was the foot of the castle walls in Haverfordwest. Our hope that bygone sentries tramping the ramparts had been unusually neglectful with their possessions revealed itself to be misplaced. There were no coins or swords or helmets to be unearthed. The high point had been digging up a rust-encrusted chain link. Just the one link.

Nostalgia is a country bathed in sunshine and returned to more often as the years tick by. It's certainly a symptom of my own late-middle age that I trawl through the motion picture library in my head, playing all of those hit Cine 8 memories of my youth while censoring out the turkeys – of which there are many. Maybe it's having boys of my own and seeing them live their carefree lives that sparks my own reminiscences. Like many parents, I feel obliged to lecture them on avoiding my mistakes. There could, if I wished to bore them, be a lot of lectures, but I avoid the temptation. My most common refrain is, 'Don't ever get a motorbike.' I needn't worry, though, as they're evidently horrified at the idea, noticing daily how bad an advert I am for biking.

Driving through Haverfordwest, I stopped by the bakery where I worked part-time from the age of fourteen. Not sure why I stopped, as I'd never done so before and I'd passed it enough times. It was closed and boarded up. A sad building. In yesteryear summers there'd be a queue out of the door, with families on their way home from the beach keen to get their bread and cakes and ice creams, all the while swatting away the wasps, the air thicker than a Heathrow holding pattern. I'd be out the back sweeping the floors and washing huge metal trays alone, the bakers long gone. It felt like my own fiefdom. One of my jobs was to chuck unsold food and rubbish into a horse box in the yard to be taken to landfill. During wasp season I'd get a couple of cans of Raid from the storeroom and walk fearlessly into the trailer with both aerosols blasting before retreating to watch them drop like flies – or wasps! One time they seemed to cotton on to the source of their sudden woeful mortality rate and swarmed after me.

During the school holidays I'd go out on the vans delivering, usually with Brian, the owners' son. I liked Brian, another adult male after John on the milk round who took me under his wing and was kind and funny. But whereas John had prided himself on his boxing fitness, Brian would've been disinclined to climb into a ring. Martyr to a host of underlying health issues, Brian's athletic days – if indeed there'd ever been any – were well behind him in what were only his twenties. With a van full of sweet-smelling cakes and bread and a squadron of lucky wasps who'd managed to hitch a ride, we ambled around the back roads delivering to out-of-the-way villages and clusters of remote local authority cul-de-sacs – bored-housewife land. Pulling away from a delivery one day, the back doors flew open. Brian slammed on the brakes and we jumped out. The road was a strewn massacre of cream horns, apple turnovers, chocolate eclairs and other confections. He looked around.

'Quick, chuck them in this tray before someone comes.'

We collected up the few dozen casualties and drove to a lay by where we set about reconstructive surgery. A rudimentary triage system weeded out those beyond help which were thrown in a hedge. Finally, with the road grit removed, we carried on our round and sold out.

There was a man who'd enter through the back door of the bakehouse, appearing like a sudden apparition. He didn't work there but had the green light to help himself to bread and cakes; the owners were generous people. He took an interest in me, which I found flattering. Overly attentive, he laughed at my feeble jokes and indulged my immature conversation. He asked if I had a girlfriend, to which the answer was no.

'What, good-looking boy like you? Can't believe that,' he said, as he cupped my shoulder gently and squeezed. 'Tell you who you look like,' he said. 'That Starsky off the cop show.'

I inflated. That was it. He was my mate.

One night, he said, 'I've got a photo of you at home.'

'How? I mean, where was it taken?'

He wasn't a relative or a family friend. In fact, he didn't even know Mum and Dad.

He just laughed and said, 'I'll bring it in.'

A week later, he ghosted in as I was sweeping the floors.

'Got that photo of you.'

'Oh. Okay.'

I stood waiting for him to produce it.

'Come out the back. I'll show you.'

He walked off. I followed, intrigued, out to the yard.

'Let's see it then,' I said.

He glanced around then took it from an inside pocket, handing it to me confidentially. Peering at it in the half-dark, I barely made out a jumble of vague shapes, so I turned and angled it towards an outside wall light. All the while he was studying me, while keeping an eye on the door out to the yard. The image duly revealed itself and I felt a sudden coldness and panic.

'Told you I had a photo of you,' he said, grinning.

I staggered back a few paces and tried to get away, but my legs wouldn't work. I was rooted. At that moment, a lady who worked in the shop emerged out of the back door, a pack of fags in her hand. He snatched the photo from me and, quick as a gunslinger, slid it back inside his jacket. She glared at him then turned to me.

'Everything okay, lovey?' she asked.

Before I could answer, he said, 'Everything's fine. Just having a laugh, weren't we?'

It was evident from the look on her face that she knew him, or should I say knew of him.

'I wasn't talking to you,' she barked. Turning back to me, she asked again, 'Everything okay?'

'Yeah, just having a laugh,' I said.

My legs returned and I hurried back inside. He got in his car and left.

Around that time at school, we'd been corralled into the nurse's room to watch a sex education film. It was all very coded and Victorian, a crude cartoon alluding to certain reproductive processes and narrated by a plummy home-counties type straight out of a Second-World-War public information film. Without any specificity of technique or concise biological explanation, the sex act remained a mystery to me on leaving the room. But that one photo shown to me in the yard had filled in all of the gaps in my patchy mental jigsaw of sex. It was explicit, showing what slotted where and in close-up detail. One thing was certain, though, it wasn't me in the photo.

I prayed that he'd never appear again, all the while knowing he would; if nothing else, he was brazen. I was fourteen, naïve and unconfident, but I knew his game and prepared myself, scripting in my head what I'd say. A week later, I sensed his arrival and turned to face him before he could pat me on the shoulder.

'That photo thing,' he said. 'Just a laugh. Just pulling your leg, I was.'

He stood close up to me with his old cracked face and wet, faggy breath. I took a few steps back.

'Just keep away from me,' I said.

He shrugged his shoulders.

'What's the problem? Just a laugh,' he said, yet again, as if repeating the lie would make it so.

'I'm warning you. Just keep away.'

His face hardened.

'Huh, thought you were grown up. If you can't take a joke, that's your problem.'

I was angry at the accusation I was being overly sensitive to a supposed laddish bit of fun.

'If you think it's such a laugh, I'll show it to everyone else,' I said, looking towards the shop where the ladies were serving customers.

'Okay, have it your way,' he snapped. He turned on his heels and went. There were to be no more sudden apparitions. He knew the two nights I worked and stayed away.

There were other part-time jobs during my teens. Aunty Jenny – Mum's sister – was married to Jacky, a log man. Cousin John – the tanning king of the Tenerife fortnights of old – was their son. On irregular Saturdays I worked with Jacky and John on the local estates, filling huge baskets with logs and trudging mule-like to deposit them in people's sheds. There was a technique to emptying the baskets which I never perfected and by the end of the day the back of my head would be lumpy and sore, clattered by the edgy logs as I tipped them over my shoulder. Jacky had a devil-may-care attitude that manifested itself in reckless feats, his tree surgery in particular being quite a spectacle. Simian-like, he'd clamber up, holding a chainsaw on tick-over in one hand. Then, high up in the canopy, with no safety harness, he'd hop between branches amputating great boughs that fell to the ground. John and I watched, partly in awe and partly with a sense of dread, making sure to have clocked the nearest phone box just in case an ambulance was needed. Then there was the saw bench in the woods, a wrought-iron dining table with a toothed saw protruding out of a slit in the middle like some malevolent half-moon. With no guard or kill switch, it was a finely judged dance with death as he shoved huge and cumbersome elephants' feet of wood into the blurred teeth, sizing them down into logs.

Bumping down the muddy track out of the woods, the aged BMC lorry creaking under the strain, we'd stop for chips in Letterston. To improve fuel efficiency – and environmentally way ahead of his time – Jacky would switch the engine off for the gradual two-mile descent into Wolfscastle. Sitting on the engine cowling in the cab eating my chips, I imagined us gliding silently through the air behind enemy lines, oblivious – in the absence of engine power – to the lack of a functioning brake servo and the casual overloading; a potentially deadly combination.

Jacky's aversion to health and safety caught up with him. Having gouged swathes of his body with chainsaws over the years the saw bench exacted its own pound of flesh. One winter's day, working alone, it snatched a thumb. Unperturbed by the sight of his digit lying on the bench, he somehow fashioned a rollie, lit it, picked the thumb up and drove to hospital with his good hand. It was reattached, but those hungry teeth had robbed him of half an inch of bone, so it was a bit stumpy. Twelve months later, almost to the day, the bench took the other thumb. His hitchhiking days were over. John found the thumb a few days later frosted to the bench and threw it in a hedge. He began to have doubts about following in the family business and became a policeman.

The most arduous work of all though was picking potatoes. It was gulag hard. During the summer I often accompanied Mum for a day on my knees in the dust-dry earth with a baking sun on my back. Mum was an accomplished picker, notching up ninety bags in a day. I'd kill myself to twenty bags, with Mum annexing more and more of my tiny allotted strip as the hours passed and my whinging increased. At the end of the day, dehydrated and sunburnt, I'd mutter 'never again', then the farmer would dole out my earnings and after a few days' rest I'd be at it once more.

The part-time jobs compensated for the disillusionment of school, gifting me self-esteem and, more importantly, cash. The money came in handy for replacement tennis racquets and a Raleigh ten-speed Tour de France bicycle, courtesy of Mum's Grattan catalogue, of course. But it was another catalogue purchase that's lived longest in my affections: a two-piece suit. You might think that a neatly tailored fifteen-year-old could be deemed a bit Jehovah's Witness, but, you see, in 1980 I bought my very first vinyl LP, *The Specials* by The Specials. An unimaginative title perhaps, but what a rousing clarion call to the disaffected youth of a nation; Thatcher's Britain ignited much adolescent angst.

Swales music shop in Haverfordwest was the place to be seen. Browsing the rows of densely racked album covers, I endeavoured to strike an insouciant pose which probably hinted more at constipation. All around me the provincial punks and old-world Teds bristled past one another as I queued for a soundproof kiosk for a listen before committing. In ska music and the two-tone scene, I found a tribe, an identity. I discovered my youth.

Crew-cutted, and with a Fred Perry shirt, white braces and that suit, I imagined myself as Haverfordwest's answer to Terry Hall, The Specials' front man. The suit itself was a deft piece of nylon tailoring, its sleight of hand shimmering greenie brown or brownie green depending on which way I turned. The ensemble was complemented by a pair of cheap brogues from Stead & Simpson's shoe shop. With each stride the soles squeaked as if I were stepping on an endless trail of mice.

I'd rock up at the Market Hall disco along with my fellow two-toners. There was Paul, my long-suffering tennis partner, and Mark, who was a disciple of Madness. The Market Hall generated the kind of atmosphere you might expect from a cavernous rectangular space that only hours earlier had been full of stallholders hawking fruit and veg. The dance floor was vast, a football pitch of worn-out parquet. In a lager and blackcurrant frenzy we danced madly, wildly, eyeing girls out of our league and, as the evening progressed, settling on those deemed winnable and receptive to our beery chat-up lines. After a few jars of courage, the placid punks and tidily dressed Teds from Swales that afternoon would kick off, with chairs flying when it got really tasty. Your public stock was in the ascendant if you could finish the night off with a slow dance and a fumbling smooch. In my suit I felt quite the catch. Heady on a five-pint fill I strolled home a mannish boy, free from academic mediocrity and imagining only bright horizons, a dreamer of dreams.

In less than two years' time I was working in Trecwn and riding a motorbike, badly.

Chapter 38

A Year in Pembrokeshire, made with Jamie, was published in the summer of 2018, the latest book to emerge from a series of journeys over a period of a decade around Wales; an ad hoc collection masquerading as a job of work! I still couldn't quite believe my luck.

I was proud of all of my books, but this one seemed to reveal, at long last, what'd inspired those motorcycle safaris of long ago, distilling within its pages all that'd been unknown to me, yet hinted at, during those days in the saddle. I remember the pleasant confusion of thirty years earlier, riding around and over those hills. It'd been an alien environment – I only discovered the area when I got the bike – yet at the same time there'd been a comforting familiarity. A feeling that in some way I belonged there even though I'd never been there. A feeling that those hills and its people would collide with my future, somehow. With *A Year in Pembrokeshire*, then, there was a sense of arrival, the book I'd been in search of.

The call of the outdoors had always been there, even if I hadn't quite realised it. Going to work on the Trecwn bus on dark winter's mornings, with my head against the window, peering out at the silhouetted hills, dreaming of escape. Witnessing the grandeur of the sun rising in the spring months as I trudged through the gates of the open prison to clock on. It was all out there waiting for me. And best of all, lying hidden in the long grass at the top of the valley, overalls stripped to the waist, basking in the summer heat when I should've been underground loading bombs onto a train or sweeping out a magazine or painting yellow hazard markings or scything undergrowth by a tunnel entrance. There was always something to avoid.

'Where've you been?' my line manager would ask limply, as if obliged to, as I plucked an excuse from the tombola of lies that spun in my head, knowing they were too lazy or indifferent to check.

On evenings or at weekends, when not supping in the pub with the boys, I'd often be pootling along the high-hedged lanes, darting up sudden bridleways, exploring another world in the hills. An exciting and expansive world away from the smallness of estate life in Haverfordwest. When you live in a town your horizon is the end of the street. Up in the Preseli Hills, the horizons were endless. I have the bike to thank for that, before it tried to kill me.

The floor manager introduced me to Naga and Ben. They flashed a warm smile and shook my hand then motioned for me to sit on the sofa. As Naga was distracted by a voice in her earpiece, Ben said, 'Just going to the weather and straight after we'll begin. You okay with that?'

'Yeah. Looking forward to it.'

And I was.

'Nice book by the way,' he said.

'Thanks. It was a really enjoyable project.'

BBC Breakfast is a national institution. Since my escape from the contact centre, indulging the freedoms of self-employment, it's been a regular accompaniment to my mornings. Watching it over the years I'd imagined numerous camera operators, sound people, and a host of minions scampering around off-camera ensuring it all ran seamlessly, while delivering up sacrificial guests for the presenters.

Earlier, after a stint in make-up, Anna and I had been led across a vast open-plan office skirting a rectangular balcony which overlooked an atrium on the ground floor below. It was fire-drill empty except for a cluster of three sitting at computers in the very far corner where we were headed. I looked around for any hint as to where the studio was but all I could see was floor to ceiling glass and Salford beyond.

I was invited to sit, ready to be called. Maybe the studio was in another part of the building, I thought, and got a bit panicked at the prospect of having to rush up or down a floor; I'm not good at rushing. Then out of a door in front of me, which I'd assumed was a storeroom, a man emerged with headphones on.

'Hi, David, I'm...' I can't remember his name, '...the floor manager. You're on soon, if you'd like to follow me.'

He turned to Anna. 'You can come in as well if you like?'

We followed him into the storeroom, a windowless, dimly lit space about the size of a WHSmith at a regional airport. My attention was drawn to a bright area at the far end of the room and as we approached, I realised that two people, Naga and Ben, were sitting on a red sofa; *the* red sofa. It was the studio. Not some store room but the actual studio. Where was the glamour? Where was the busy scrum of people? Besides the presenters, there were only two others. Had they all nipped out for a fag? I turned to the floor manager.

'It's not at all as I imagined. So quiet.'

'It's all done from out there,' he said, pointing through the wall to the outside office from where we'd come.

Naga and Ben, it seemed, were the public face of an illusion, the front-of-house cogs in an efficient, low-glamour machine. It's we, the viewers, who invest it with an aura. The reality, for them, is spending hours in a brightly lit corner of a dark, air-conditioned box taking instructions down an earpiece while processing one guest after another, an endless cycle of current affairs and human-interest stories. Like pit ponies, they must've yearned for the end of their shift and daylight.

The beauty of that ordinariness, though, is that you relax and chat freely, not imagining for one moment you're being watched and dissected by viewers. The five minutes flew by and Anna and I emerged from all of that glass and steel into the sunshine and walked back to the hotel for breakfast. The interview about *A Year in Pembrokeshire* was a pinnacle, another summit if you like. I felt momentarily important.

I still remember the joyous implosion on receiving the advance copy of my first book *Pembrokeshire* all those years ago, and nothing's changed. I still collapse inside; go all mushy. I hold the new book in my hands, knowing it's about to go into bookshops to be picked up, flicked through and even bought. People, unknown to me – strangers – will buy a copy of my book. Hopefully, many people. Millions would be nice, but many will have to do. I've never taken for granted my continued good fortune, remembering that angry person in the contact centre. But, as with the publication of my previous books, that nagging question wasn't long in the offing – what next?

France issued its annual summons and we happily obeyed. After the wonder of Guy and Colette's honey-stoned gite in 2016, we'd discovered an even greater piece of perfection the year after. And so, we returned to that perfect place, south-east of Tour in the Loire Valley, in 2018. Into my third holiday of adjusted expectations, I did little aside from read, swim, doze on a sun-lounger and graze on endless baguettes, feeling my body uncoil a little more with each passing day. The occasional lunch or supper in the café in the village was pretty much the extent of my wanderings, content as I was to stroll around the spacious garden in the bludgeoning heat, seeking out shady spots, ever mindful of my compromised autonomic system and its propensity for overheating like some old banger, and cooling off in the pool when the fancy took me. One afternoon, lying on a recliner, I watched the boys wrestle and half-drown one another as my parents had once watched Andrew and me. As a parent, the notion of that generational cycle is never far away as I thought of my own childhood holidays and one in particular.

In 1977, the Wilsons jetted off to the Costa Brava, our first holiday that wasn't a week in Bradford visiting a string of dull and unenthusiastic relations of Dad's in the rain. We flew into Barcelona and were bussed two hours up the coast to Lloret de Mar. Dad had pored over stacks of brochures and booked us into the Hotel Don Juan, with its three glowing stars, in the centre of town.

The bus pulled up outside the hotel. It was dark and we were exhausted but I still remember the taste and smell of a warm Med night and the sound of insects clacking in the bushes. The holiday rep called our names, we grabbed our luggage and walked into the marble-decked reception feeling we'd gone up a notch.

'You stay here, Margaret. I'll book us in,' said Dad, proud of what his brochure browsing had bestowed upon us.

Mum, Andrew and I stood hunched over our suitcases aching for bed. Then, sharp discord began to float over from the reception desk. We turned. Dad was pointing at a small man in a dark suit, his voice raised. The small man, presumably the manager, gesticulated back in a manner which intimated a weak grasp of English, particularly the Yorkshire variant. The holiday rep was making placatory hand gestures to no avail. It all appeared beyond even the auspices of the UN to sort out. Dad stormed over.

'They've bloody double-booked us.'

Mum was confused. 'Sorry? Double-booked?'

'Yes, double-bloody-booked. Someone else is in our room.'

The rep came over.

'I'm so sorry about this, Mr Wilson. It's never happened before...' We later learnt it had, often. 'I'll ring round and get you another hotel,' she said, as if that would somehow defuse Dad. It didn't.

We walked through silent streets with our luggage to the emergency accommodation, which resembled a bail hostel; low-rise and grubby, with bars over the ground-floor windows. A chorus of mangy dogs trotted over from some adjacent scrub land as we approached the entrance, their growling speeding us into reception. Mum was quietly angry, Dad audibly so. Andrew and I thought it all rather exciting. Fun even.

The next morning, after a broken night's sleep, we realised that the hotel's long-term residents, the bed bugs, had feasted royally on us. Mum and Dad's anger escalated in tandem as Andrew and I found it less funny than we had the night before. Dad went off to find the rep, returning an hour later.

'Right, we're off. She's got us a hotel. Let's get out of this bloody dump.'

The Imperial Park Hotel on the edge of town was a trailblazer in the relentless expansion of what'd once been a tight-knit fishing village huddled around the shore. Behind the hotel was a large walled cemetery giving way to arid grassland and distant hills, a scene straight out of a spaghetti Western. Being 1977, I expect the hotel presented as a glorious utopia in the doctored brochure. It wasn't an all-inclusive holiday, though, and one of the things not included was any expectation of sleep. Our room was on the first floor next to a marble stairwell, the cavernous space echoing into the early hours with guests' feet click-clacking to bed, accompanied by loud, beery chatter. Sleep deprivation, then, that wouldn't have been out of place in a Mossad interrogation manual was compounded by starvation rations; we spent a lot of the holiday trekking a mile into town to eat at a hot-dog van. Nights were whiled away in a Scottish-themed pub with a resident organist, which cheered Dad, while a tartan-clad ginger barman insisted on hugging Andrew and me frequently while plying us with chocolate milk. We soon learnt to avoid the resort beach, packed like some makeshift refugee holding pen. Staff at the hotel directed us instead to a secluded sandy cove a short walk through a scented pine forest, a dreamy piece of old Spain.

With no organised excursions, we made our own entertainment, which was a challenge, seeing as the range of amenities that might be deemed desirable for a large resort hadn't kept pace with the town's rapid spread; there was nothing to do. One afternoon, out of desperation, we spent a languid hour in the cemetery behind the hotel marvelling at the ornate catholic extravagance in death, captivated by tiny photographs of the occupants inlaid into the tombs. It was only two years since Franco's passing and perhaps some of them had been shot for supporting the wrong side.

As a memento of our holiday Andrew and I had our photograph taken holding a chimpanzee – not in the cemetery, I might add. The poor creature looked pitiful in a stained, multi-coloured knitted jumper.

I had a track record with primates. There's another photograph of me aged three in a pushchair, with a tiny monkey like some shrunken old man sitting on my lap and Mum and Dad standing proudly either side of me. My reliance on wheeled transport at that age has often been explained by Mum, usually to an audience. 'Didn't walk or say a word till he was gone three,' she'd say, not minded to spare my blushes. 'We were on a bus once and this woman leant forward and said, "Aw, poor thing. What's wrong with him?" Took him to the doctors. Did some tests. Just lazy apparently.'

So I was, it seems, diagnosed as lazy, a condition that lingered through school and into the workplace.

Back in France, with Anna and our boys, my one arena of physical prowess, where I could morph into Competitive Dad, was table tennis by the poolside as the years rolled back to those sherry-fuelled tournaments in the kitchen at The Nest. Adopting the same strategy – my only strategy, as it happens – I positioned myself centrally, stretching albatross-like to parry wide attacks, feet rooted as if in concrete. The boys soon realised the value of the drop shot. As my sole avenue of sporting eminence, I gave no quarter, driving home every opportunity and euphoric in victory. Annoying in victory.

Our Olympian pursuits were supplemented by water rugby, an invention of Harry's. Anna and me against the boys. Played across the width of the shallow end, our game plan consisted of me sweeping the try line like a trawler taking on water, while Anna sallied forth to try and steal the ball. Harry would draw her in and toss the ball to Charlie, who'd surge like a battlecruiser straight at me. It was a daunting sight. With forlorn resignation I'd topple at his flailing torso, he'd batter me aside with ease and place the ball down behind the line. After being sunk a number of times I'd suggest another game of table tennis.

There is regret at not being able to play sport or indulge in strenuous activity with the boys. To chuck a rugby ball around up the park. To kayak upriver and pitch camp for the night. Ride bikes. Walk up a mountain. The list is endless. And so, I compensate. Find alternatives. I talk to them. I talk to them a lot. Whether they appreciate my chattiness is a moot point, but I do it all the same. We talk and we laugh. Or at least I laugh. I'm fortunate that self-employment allows me to see them perhaps more than most dads see their kids. I'm often around when they leave for school and on their return. Again, I can't comment on how lucky they feel, but I love it.

As a child I often felt that Dad was rationed. He worked twelve-hour shifts in the refinery – two days then two nights on, and four days off. On his rest days he often seemed lagged, as if his body clock was out of sync with the wall clock. He dozed a lot in the chair. He spent three decades doing a job which knackered him but not once did I ever hear him complain, about anything, ever. He just got on with it. When he retired, he suddenly sprang to life as he flushed nearly thirty years of shift work from his system. It was nice.

On New Year's Day 2019 Anna and I indulged in our ritual resolutions, she with more enthusiasm than me. She determined to continue with a book she'd been writing, a timeless story that I'm convinced will be a hit when published. It's clever and it's beautiful, much like the author. There were mentions of cutting this or that from her diet, fine tunings to a lifestyle that was already healthy. And lots more walking, as her occasional runs were giving her achy knees.

'So, what about you?' she enquired.

I puffed out my cheeks. 'Not sure. I'll give it some thought.'

It was my standard cop out when loath to commit. Each January we made resolutions, Anna keeping hers, or at least endeavouring to, while I allowed mine to ebb quietly, if I made any at all.

But this time I did give it some thought and the next day announced, 'I'm going to do that project of Llangwm I've been banging on about for years.' Every January I'd commit to the idea, only for February to creep up on me, then March, and it was too late to start. Not this year, though. Buoyed by the documentary photography in my latest book, I now had the confidence to capture people that'd perhaps been absent in previous years. We invited the boys to join us at the kitchen table and began writing up a list of people, celebrations and events that would fill a year and tell the story of an incredible place. The day after, I began photographing *The Village*.

Chapter 39

It was a steel-grey February morning as Anna and I pulled up outside of Gernos Fach farmhouse in the Preseli Hills, just over a year since Jamie and I had visited Lyn and Gwyndaf there as part of the *A Year in Pembrokeshire* book. I got out of the car, stretched some of the resistance from my leg muscles and took a deep breath. I was back where I felt most at ease with the world, the same feeling I'd experienced all those years ago on that first day of photographing in the hills after ditching the contact centre headset. This was where I went for inspiration and to reset the mental compass.

A milky sun flashed between pneumatic clouds that raced over the landscape, the sky faster than I'd ever known. Winter had begun to release its grip back home, but up in the hills I was glad to have layered up as I flapped my arms against my ribs to get the blood up.

'Fancy a coffee? Warm you up,' said Anna.

'No, ta.'

With a dicky bladder, diuretics before a trek were ill-advised. Plus, I was feeling anxious so tossing caffeine into the mix was unwise. In the distance I saw a car snaking along the track towards the farm.

'This could be them,' I said, pointing.

I was apprehensive of what the day might hold but I'd committed to it and there was no turning back. The car pulled up next to ours and Carwyn Jones emerged.

'Carwyn, great to see you,' I said.

'Good morning. What a fantastic location,' he replied, spinning round on his heels.

'Yeah. Thought you'd approve.'

He'd sold me the pitch for a new television series he'd devised for

ITV Wales called *Welsh Lives*. He didn't, of course, have to sell it too hard. It was to be our fourth collaboration and we were to do some filming not far from the farmhouse. Adeola, the programme's narrator and interviewer, got out of the passenger side and he introduced us. There was a rash of handshakes and hugs as another car bumped towards the farm; James, the cameraman and drone pilot. The anticipation was building. My anxiety was building. Carwyn repeated the introductory niceties with James then they began grabbing loaded rucksacks and holdalls from the car boot while peering like augurs at the clouds and gauging how many layers were necessary. They too opted for the multiple approach as Adeola wandered off for a look around.

I heard a faint asthmatic bark and turned to see Lyn and Gwyndaf emerging from the house, preceded by their dog, the most benign creature you could ever meet, about as threatening as an irate lamb. I'd ventured onto many farms over the years ever wary of the ubiquitous farm dog with their rabid snarling and bared fangs, often anticipating the loss of a leg. But the Gernos hound was no killer. I introduced Lyn and Gwyndaf, which generated much appreciation of the idyllic location from Carwyn and comments of how it's always so much colder in the hills. Lyn and Gwyndaf, in V-necks and open-necked shirts, declared it to be mild, making us all feel rather less intrepid. Carwyn snatched a glance at his watch, no doubt wishing to get going, but the boys feast on new people, asking questions, jocular and hearty, the warmest of hosts.

As they chatted, I turned to look at our intended climb. Well, not so much a climb to them as a gentle incline. A climb to me though. I'd had a bad winter, with the physical fitness I'd banked during the previous summer and autumn having leached away during months of debilitating low pressure and a collapse in my mobility. My body had come to despise the bare season, functioning at tick-over or worse, like some half-comatose tortoise. Often on winter days I ache so much I don't even attempt to get out of my chair. Yes, I have a chair. It's my chair and I sit in it. A lot. Hibernation would be my preferred option or perhaps relocating to France for the benefit of year-round sunshine and to tap into that gallic indifference which I find so appealing, and which I replicate with ease – or so I've been told. Having not walked any distance in weeks, then, the prospect of the gentle hill daunted me.

'Right, David, we're ready if you are,' announced Carwyn, laden down like a mule. I glanced at the car, aware that it was my last chance to back out and go home whilst knowing that I couldn't.

'Yeah, no problem. Let's get going,' I said.

He took a branded foil wrap from his pocket, tore it open, and popped a rolled fig-like substance in his mouth as we parted from the boys and began our walk. In all of the past tens of hours we'd spent together it was the first time I'd seen him eat, as in put something in his mouth and chew. I'm convinced he'd have survived a punishing day on the Burma railway on that rolled fig. I on the other hand had loaded up on oats and protein before leaving home, my system reliant on overfuelling.

It struck me as I began to attempt to walk that just a few years before I'd have comfortably tackled the hill without hiking poles. In fact, I had once, about ten years earlier. But no more. The stability of the poles was crucial, as well as being a convenient means of pulling myself upwards. I'd regressed to being a four-year-old again with the stabilisers back on the bike.

My leg muscles were as supple as wood, with my stride shortened, like a pair of rusty garden shears that won't open fully. It'll be fine though, once I warm up, I thought. And, after a couple of determined minutes, I began to acquire some tempo, a metronomic rhythm of sorts. Settled, at last, into the short trek, I was anticipating the relief of reaching the top when I caught my foot on a raised clump of grass and fell. It didn't hurt – the distance to the ground going uphill is short – with the long grass and soft earth cushioning the impact. Carwyn dropped his load and rushed over, his expression one of panic: those risk assessments completed back at the office in Cardiff which perhaps hadn't been as thorough as they could've been; insurance implications; the logistics of summoning an ambulance with no mobile signal.

It was a bad start. For him.

'Jesus. You okay?' he said.

I looked up and burst out laughing. 'Carwyn, don't worry. I'm fine. If you and James can give me a hand up.'

They got me back to my feet, Carwyn fussing over me like an old hen, wondering whether the day was feasible or if we should just pack up there and then.

'You sure you're okay to carry on?' he pressed.

'Yeah. Let's crack on.'

For the remainder of the ascent, he walked by my side, surreptitiously glancing at my feet, no doubt praying I wouldn't stumble again, but ready to lunge in and grab me if I did. The premise of *Welsh Lives* was to highlight people who'd overcome difficulties or trauma in their lives, achieving their goals in spite of the odds. As much as I hated to admit it, I fulfilled the brief. There were to be no more falls, though, much to Carwyn's relief.

It was a couple of hundred metres to the summit of the hill with its uninterrupted views across the top of the Gwaun Valley to rock-strewn Carn Ingli and Newport on the coast. The wind was brisker, the chill factor searing my hands, so I plunged them into my pockets for some respite. I'm reluctant to wear gloves, as with my impaired manual dexterity – the Action Man hands of Rookwood – they interfere with the fine control necessary to adjust settings on the camera. It's hard enough scrolling menus and pressing tiny buttons with naked finger tips, never mind adding a thick layer of material into the mix. The payback is that once my hands are exposed to the cold it's not long before I lose functionality. They get numb, and so photographing can be a stop-start process as I regularly resuscitate my digits.

'Okay, this is a great spot,' said Carwyn, glancing around at the compositional possibilities. 'James is setting up the drone and, let's see...' His eyes fixed on a spot twenty to thirty metres away. 'Yeah, if you can make your way over there, and when I give you the signal, start taking photos. And plenty of those meaningful glances into the middle distance,' he added, smirking.

'Yeah, yeah, very funny,' I said.

Off I went, picking my way around gorse bushes and placing my feet with care, avoiding raised clumps or ankle-twisting dips. Anna walked beside me, primed to lend an arm if I stumbled. This was how I now explored the landscape, with Anna in close proximity. She didn't always stop me going down, as when I'd fallen on the way up the hill, but she was there all the same. There was a perverse sense of satisfaction in my gradual loss of stability, in that Anna now accompanied me on any outing that entailed walking away from the certainty of tarmac. And I liked her accompanying me. It felt good. Thirty years before, I'd lacked the motivation, and perhaps the bravery, to venture from the car into the landscape even though I could've, and now that I couldn't – safely, that is – I had Anna with me so that I could. My work was now a fully-fledged partnership. A partnership of understanding. A partnership of love.

I reached the spot, switched the camera on and shoved my hands in my pockets awaiting the go-ahead. I looked over to Carwyn and he gave me the thumbs up as I heard the whir of rotor-blades overhead. As the drone buzzed past, I felt a surge of excitement and began photographing. Occasional gusts of wind threatened to topple me but a quick planting of the poles, hanging by straps from my wrists, kept me upright. With the drone circumnavigating me it felt epic, standing on top of a hill, camera in hand, capturing the landscape. Standing stock still with that wind whipping round me though, I could feel my energy sapping as the drone kept sweeping past one way then the other. God, how much longer? I thought. It seemed to go on forever, the cold turning me to stone, and just when I was about to throw the towel in, Carwyn beat me to it.

'Great stuff. All done,' he shouted downwind.

I began moving about to get the blood pumping round my limbs, anxious about what might be demanded of me next. What little enthusiasm I'd had down by the car was waning, fast. After some deliberation, Carwyn suggested that Adeola and I stroll back down the hill in the direction of the farmhouse, talking about the landscape and my photography while he recorded the audio and James bagged some more drone footage. He fitted me with a mic and I set off beside Adeola.

Anna had to stay out of shot, so I descended alone, which was a concern – going down is more fraught than going up, and I'd already fallen going up. I wanted to walk with assurance and discard the poles, put on a performance if you like, but it wasn't to be. It could never be. Ever since the *Hinterland* book and the acknowledgement that I was in decline, there was a sense of having entered a third physical phase in my life; there was the perfect pre-accident me followed by the imperfectly recovered me, and now the post second bout sepsis me. I couldn't be doing with a fourth phase – a bloody wheelchair-bound me no doubt. Anyway, it was a struggle coming down the hill and I knew that whatever footage they got I'd appear decrepit. But at least we were heading in the direction of the car, which I felt was a positive.

I liked talking to Adeola. Her interviewing style was empathetic without being cloying, engaging but not intrusive. She smiled and laughed a lot. I trusted her too, and Carwyn, of course, confident there'd be no manufacturing of some syrupy prurience. Foremost in my thoughts was the conviction, perhaps delusional, that it'd be a programme about my work and not my physical limitations. It was important that I held on to that. In reality, it was to be a bit of both.

We reached the bottom of the hill without any mishaps and continued our conversation, filming in the vicinity of the outbuildings by the house. The wind was gaining strength and the earlier shafts of sunlight were just a memory; it was very cold. Overcautious layering had preserved me, just, but Adeola hadn't been quite so thorough. She was suffering and was visibly relieved when Carwyn said he was happy with what he'd got and we could depart. She stampeded for their car's heater while I gave the boys a knock and thanked them. I'd enjoyed my visits to Gernos Fach and had grown quite fond of them. And the dog, of course. Despite my reservations about what'd been expected of me, it'd been an enjoyable morning.

The five of us returned to Llangwm to shoot some footage by the river and record interviews at our house. Twelve gruelling but satisfying hours after Carwyn, Adeola and James had first appeared, we were done and they were gone.

Exhausted, I sat down and recapped the day. Seeing Carwyn again had been the joy it'd always been. He's one of the most upbeat and dynamic people I've ever known, and in his company I feel like anything is possible. And I needed his positivity to persuade me that the trek up the little hill was indeed possible. If I'd been meeting anyone but Carwyn, I think I may've faltered.

A month later we settled down to watch *Welsh Lives*, excited, if a little apprehensive on my part. Anna was anxious too, about which bits of her interview would be included, not quite remembering what she'd said. She'd been reticent about being filmed, only steeling herself against her natural disinclination for me. Charlie and Harry, on the other hand, evidently thought that the programme might provide great amusement, which I suppose was a positive.

With all of the filming that I've done with Carwyn over many years I've found it a challenge watching myself on screen and I was certain that this latest programme would be the biggest challenge yet. Indeed, it turned out to be a vision of a truth I still resisted, a portrait of someone who was damaged; more so than our last outing four years earlier. So, why do it? Why put myself through the turmoil of witnessing that truth on screen?

There are many reasons. I'm proud of what I've achieved and of the work that I produce. Not prideful, but proud. And why the hell shouldn't I be? After all, to do what I do is bloody hard, and getting harder. Sure, nobody forces me to do it, but I need that challenge. I need to feel capable. And I need that buzz from doing something that logic says is beyond me; outside of my physical abilities. Logic, though, is no match for the human spirit, and especially my stubbornness. And working with Carwyn has provided one of the many reminders of my good fortune in having carved out this rather unusual career for myself. After all, I still recall how soul destroying it was working in that contact centre. I can still taste the despair.

I also want my boys to see that the physical wreck they share a house with has achieved something from that wreckage. That you never give up. That you strain every sinew of your being to survive and, more importantly, thrive and be happy. And yes, there is a bit of me that wants to demonstrate to people who may've experienced physical misfortune and are in a dark place that you can make a life. That you can, if you're bloody-minded enough, exceed the limited expectations of you held by other people, however well-meaning they are. That you don't allow yourself to be pigeon-holed as that less able person. So, there are many reasons why I subject myself to being Carwyn's muse! And yes, a hint of vanity plays a part too.

Even now, in public, I'm wary of prying glances, shrinking inwards from the curiosity of strangers. People can stare or, in the case of the woman in Bristol airport that I clattered into, crush me with a withering look. I reached a reckoning with the actual physical loss many years ago but have never shaken that self-consciousness in the way that I move about. Walking past or towards shops or glass-fronted buildings I try not to look at my reflection, as I know I won't like what I see. There must be a hint of Tourette's in me, though, as I often steal a glance and wish to hell I hadn't. Television multiplies that reflection manyfold with innumerable angles of revelation. *Welsh Lives* then, was a bittersweet watch.

Making programmes with Carwyn has always felt like a private affair. It's mostly only ever been the two of us. And he's never let me down with his sympathetic filming and kind and generous narration. Yet, ridiculous as it sounds, it still comes as a surprise to me when it airs, as if it suddenly dawns on me that I'd actually been contributing to a television programme and not just spending a day with someone whose company I enjoy. And in this latest production my confidence in him was justified yet again. He'd laboured over hours of footage and woven together a beautiful piece of television. After all of our collaborations his talents still elude adequate summary; genius is the best I can come up with.

The interview I did with Adeola in our living room was emotional as I talked about those that I left behind in Rookwood all those years ago, seeing their faces in my head as I spoke. I often wonder what happened to them, how their lives unfolded. Forever young, they haven't aged in my recollections. But thinking of them and that hospital now is like visualising someone else's memories, as if it couldn't have been me in that ward. Nothing from that time is immediate and touchable any more, which in some ways saddens me, though the pain and despair, too, have lost their sting, which is a relief. With all the years that've passed, then, a sense of dislocation has set in. But always, for me, there's guilt at having got off lighter than the others. The same guilt that on the ward had made me reluctant to move too much when they were around. Dan with his one working arm and Pete with his anger will, along with all the others – apart from the magnificent walker, of course – have endured tougher lives than mine. We're perhaps talking increments of misfortune, shades of bad luck, but I did walk out of that damned place, just.

The drone footage lent the programme a cinematic feel, particularly in the hills, the place where I've felt more at peace than anywhere over the years. The Preseli Hills are – increasingly, as my body fails, were – my refuge, a place to exorcise the mental struggle of decades of a wearing physical loss. A loss that accelerates with each year. Seemingly, with each bloody month. I was told on leaving Rookwood that my body would gradually break down under the strain of coping with an irregular walking gait and the unremitting effort required to function with weakened and compromised muscles and a buggered nervous system. That's the price of irreparable damage. And on screen I could see that prognosis fulfilled in all its glory.

But, so what? That's my normality. My daily expectation. I have, after all, just fading memories of who I was before the accident. Certainly, if I choose to – which I don't – I can picture that boy the press-up king, who ran non-stop to Nan and Gramps' on Sundays after lunch, who pushed himself past meltdown to finish twenty-eighth in the school cross-country – out of well over a hundred, by the way – or that young man visually mapped by the cute girl on the rock on Tenby beach. The fact is – my joy is – I've somehow edged past my half century, thankful to be older than I ever imagined I'd be. Thankful to still be at the crease nicking those runs.

The final scenes were by the river not far from our house. I picked a path along the foreshore, stepping around bedrock and tripping stones, with Anna by my side. We stopped, Adeola joined us and we talked to camera. There was a searching question about what makes us tick, an angling for that sentimental conclusion and a coming-together of all of the themes that'd been explored during the programme. I spoke of my good fortune in having such an incredible family, while living in an extraordinary place and pursuing a career that just happened to be my hobby. Then the credits rolled on the very last line of my fifteen minutes of fame, as I said, 'I'm a lucky man.'

Epilogue

France 2019

'You coming in, daddy?'

That's me. Daddy. A dad. A father.

'Yeah. Give me a moment.'

My boys wanted me to join them in the pool and so my holiday read would have to wait – no competition, really. I put the book down, hauled myself up from the low seating, stretched out some of the muscular spasm in my legs and emerged from the shade of the veranda into the sun.

'Phew, it's pretty hot, boys,' I said, walking as quickly as I could (slowly) towards the pool, the soles of my feet resting a fraction longer than was desirable on the baking tiles.

'Do your special dive?' pleaded Harry.

Charlie beamed and nodded conspiratorially.

'Okay, if you insist.'

Describing my intended entry as a dive was generous. Unsteadily, I turned around and shuffled back towards the pool's edge till my heels felt the drop.

'Look, Charlie. He's about to do it.'

Stiff as a plank, I toppled backwards into the water like a felled telegraph pole, surfacing to intense laughter. It always got them. It cheered me that it always got them; an element of physical comedy that wasn't me walking.

'Do it again. Please.'

'Later, Harry. Promise,' I said.

Now that I was in, I just wanted to float on my back in the bath-warm water with the sun on my face.

'Is anyone hungry?' asked Anna.

We all agreed that we were. Grazing through the morning on baguette, jam and croissant, combined with oodles of swimming and fresh air, gifted a recurring semi-hunger. Anna headed to the house to rustle up lunch.

Charlie emerged from the pool and, availing himself of the longest possible run up, launched into the air curled up in a foetal position, displacing what seemed like half the pool on entry.

'Best bomb yet, Charlie,' yelled Harry as he took a breath in between deep-sea diving items from the bottom of the pool. I paddled on my back to the shallow end and sat watching them, thinking blessed thoughts. They were happy, which made me happy.

It was more relaxed than earlier in the morning, when a hornet scare caused a panicked retreat to the house. It was a big bugger, mind, like a thumb with wings. On first hearing it, I thought someone was buzzing us with a drone or strimming grass in the vicinity. Aggressive too, dive-bombing with its business end pointing down. After a similar incident the previous year, I'd advised the boys not to scream, wave their arms or splash, '...as it disturbs the air and makes them angry'. Sensible fatherly advice. But this one arrived angry and it was understandable when Charlie ran indoors flapping his arms after it landed on his head, with Harry close behind. It took a while to coax them back out.

Harry swam over, stood and lifted his goggles.

'Daddy...'

'Yeah...'

'If you could go back in time...' Where's this going? I thought. 'Would you get a motorbike again?'

There was no malice in the question. He'd thought it and so had to ask it. Adult sensibilities hadn't blighted him yet, thankfully. I was still taken aback, though.

'Well... err... I don't know. I suppose if I hadn't got it, I wouldn't have had an accident and so… well, I'd be a lot better at getting around. I'd be normal, I suppose. So… that'd be good.'

He smiled in agreement as Charlie waded over.

'So, you wouldn't get one?'

I took a moment.

'Well, to be honest, I don't know really.'

I could see that my indecision surprised him. He'd witnessed me fall enough times to know how much it hurt.

'I suppose, thinking about it…' I continued, '…if I hadn't got one, I wouldn't have had the accident but maybe lots of other things would've turned out differently too.'

'What do you mean?'

'Well, perhaps, for example, I'd be playing water rugby – properly, mind – right now in a pool in, say, Spain or Italy or wherever, with two completely different boys. And that'd be horrible.'

I was relieved to see his shock at that hypothetical outcome.

'So, you would still get one?' he pressed.

'Well, yeah, suppose I would. Even knowing what would happen, it'd have to be yeah. Otherwise, you might not be here asking me the question. Maybe it was all meant to be.'

He nodded sagely, spun and swam off as Charlie went to the house to help Anna carry lunch out.

As we sat in the shade eating, I took in each of them and acknowledged with wonder that they were mine and I was theirs; we all had each other. If, indeed, I hadn't got a bike, which'd set me on a course for the accident, my trajectory would've been different. My life would've unfolded on some parallel timeline and my story wouldn't have contained the beautiful reckoning I wake to every day: Anna and my boys. As the Doc said to Marty in *Back to the Future*, 'You don't mess with the past', or something like that. So yeah, for me, it'd have to be the bike, and the accident, every time.

David Wilson

David Wilson is among Wales's most established photographers, well known for his black and white images that uniquely evoke the character and atmosphere of the nation's landscapes. His work with Graffeg includes the photographic studies *Pembrokeshire* and *Wales: A Photographer's Journey, Hinterland: Ceredigion Landscapes* and *A Year in Pembrokeshire*, with broadcaster Jamie Owen.

David Wilson Books

A Year In Pembrokeshire

by Jamie Owen and David Wilson

Hardback, 200 x 200mm

192 pages, £20.00 ISBN: 9781912213658

Pembrokeshire

David Wilson

Hardback, 250 x 250mm

120 pages, £20.00 ISBN: 9781802580051

Wales: A Photographer's Journey

David Wilson

Hardback, 250 x 250mm

160 pages, £25.00 ISBN: 9781802580068

The Village

David Wilson

Hardback, 200 x 200mm

128 pages, £20.00 ISBN: 9781802580488

Peeling Paint and Rust

David Wilson

Hardback, 250 x 250mm

100 pages, £25.00 ISBN: 9781802585681

For a full list of Graffeg titles and to place an order, please visit our website: www.graffeg.com.